Judgment and Decision-Making

Judgment and Decision-Making

In the Lab and the World

Nancy S. Kim

BLOOMSBURY ACADEMIC
LONDON • NEW YORK • OXFORD • NEW DELHI • SYDNEY

BLOOMSBURY ACADEMIC
Bloomsbury Publishing Plc
50 Bedford Square, London, WC1B 3DP, UK
1385 Broadway, New York, NY 10018, USA
29 Earlsfort Terrace, Dublin 2, Ireland

BLOOMSBURY, BLOOMSBURY ACADEMIC and the Diana logo are trademarks of Bloomsbury
Publishing Plc

First published in Great Britain 2018 by Palgrave
Reprinted by Bloomsbury Academic 2022

A catalogue record for this book is available from the British Library.

A catalog record for this book is available from the Library of Congress.

ISBN: PB: 978-1-137-26955-3

To find out more about our authors and books visit www.bloomsbury.com and sign up for
our newsletters.

For H. K. and N. K. K.

Contents

List of Figures

Note to the Instructor

Thank you for considering this book for your course. This textbook is designed to be a versatile supplement to each instructor's vision for his or her own course, and is somewhat modular in nature. The chapters can be read in almost any order (with the exception of Chapters 7 and 8, which are best read sequentially) or partially or entirely left out at your discretion.

This textbook also aims to address two central challenges in finding the right text for your course in judgment and decision-making. A key challenge in teaching a lecture course is finding a text that does not already say everything you want to say in your lectures, yet provides a backdrop of information that is useful to both the instructor and students. A major challenge in teaching a discussion-based seminar is providing background knowledge that will enable everyone in the class to read journal articles while understanding their context and the theoretical and methodological issues at stake. This textbook aims to fill both of these roles by giving an overview of critical issues in judgment and decision-making and describing a range of papers and debates in the field, providing fundamental context for lectures or additional articles. I have suggested discussion topics and outside readings at the end of each chapter, and boxed exercises and supplementary information are also included within some of the chapters.

This text is centered around the philosophy that basic and applied research questions are not only complementary but also mutually essential and, indeed, can be so closely interwoven that the basic–applied distinction becomes something of a false dichotomy (Narayanamurti & Odumosu 2016). Many concrete examples are included, and applied research is given a prominent platform alongside seminal experimental work grounded in abstract cognition. Taken together, this approach was intended to enhance understanding of core principles and findings in judgment and decision-making, and to highlight how the study of judgment and decision-making can address not only fundamental problems in cognition but also practical issues of undeniable importance.

Preface

Research in judgment and decision-making often defies classification. It encompasses basic science and applied science, valuing both as truly worthy of pursuit, and often addressing both simultaneously. Judgment and decision-making research also refuses to be contained within any single traditional field or subfield, fusing insights, theories, and paradigms from psychology (e.g., social, clinical, cognitive, developmental, comparative, biological), behavioral economics, experimental philosophy, marketing, and the practice of medicine, criminology, and the law. It has been a privilege to pore over the original works reviewed for this book.

I am grateful to everyone at Palgrave who worked on publishing this book, especially senior commissioning editor Paul Stevens and assistant editor Cathy Scott, without whom it would not have come into being. Jamie Joseph first got me thinking about writing a book, and Luke Block and Stephanie Farano guided it to publication in the final stages. Isabel Berwick and Jenny Hindley kept me on track during the early stages of writing. Alex Connock created the compelling cover art, and marketing guru Helen Jackson did an amazing job of getting the word out. Palgrave senior production editor Amy Wheeler, Integra senior project manager Sangeetha Sangiamurthy, and copy-editor Christa Ramey masterfully engineered the final product. Thank you so much for your expertise and work on this book.

A number of colleagues and students provided constructive suggestions on various parts of this book or test-ran some of the topics covered in this book in discussion, and to this end I sincerely thank Edward Park, Erienne Weine, Uma Karmarkar, Susan Latiff, Mason Jenkins, Mallory Gothelf, Nhi Ngo, Molly Sands, Nicole Betz, Yian Xu, and Stacy Jankowski. Many anonymous colleagues provided valuable feedback on drafts of this manuscript, for which I am very grateful. Finally, I thank Nam, Haesook, and Daniel Kim, Ed, Sophie, and Claire Park, and Chung and Soonja Park for their support.

As a student, I was fortunate to work with research mentors Woo-kyoung Ahn, Frank Keil, and Stephen Kosslyn, and I am grateful for their example. The tone and approach of this book were inspired by my students at Northeastern University, who combine scientific curiosity and rigor with practical work experiences and a strong internal drive to create positive change in the world.

N. S. K.

Notes on the Author

Nancy S. Kim holds a B.A. with high honors in Psychology from Harvard University and an M.S., M.Phil., and Ph.D. in Psychology from Yale University (supported by a U.S. National Science Foundation Graduate Research Fellowship). She is currently Associate Professor with tenure and Director of Undergraduate Studies in the Department of Psychology at Northeastern University. Her research program asks how lay people, patients, clinical trainees, and practicing clinicians make health-related judgments and decisions. In particular, she is interested in understanding when and how clinicians making mental health diagnoses choose to go "off-manual," and whether and when these departures from prescribed diagnostic guidelines are systematic, predictable, and explainable by core cognitive theory. She teaches undergraduate and graduate courses on judgment and decision-making, cognitive psychology, and cognitive neuroscience.

Introduction 1

Learning Goals

By the end of this chapter, you will have:

- Reviewed some of the different kinds of research questions that are examined in the field of judgment and decision-making, and considered how the field may be pertinent to your own life in a variety of ways.
- Compared two of the major empirical approaches to studying and understanding everyday judgment and decision-making – the cognitive illusions approach and the fast-and-frugal approach.
- Considered arguments for and against whether dual-process models of reasoning can serve as an organizing framework for the field.
- Understood and compared three major types of decision-making models (i.e., descriptive, normative, and prescriptive), how each type of model has distinct but important goals, and how they relate to one another.
- Reviewed the structure and content of this textbook, which is centered around five major issues in judgment and decision-making: How we make judgments of likelihood; how we reason about the past and the future; how we decide to expend our resources of money, time, and opportunity; how we make sense of the world around us; and how we make decisions in the context of social groups and societies.

Key Terms

Personal decisions	Rule-based
Cognitive illusions	Type 1; Type 2
Affect	Descriptive models
Fast-and-frugal approach	Normative models
Computational capacity	Prescriptive models
Dual-process models	Uncertainty
System 1; System 2	Risk
Associative	

Understanding judgment and decision-making

Why study judgment and decision-making?

What causes people to pass away prematurely? Among the top causes of death in such countries as the U.K., the U.S., South Korea, and Germany are heart disease, lung cancer, and cerebrovascular disease (i.e., resulting in strokes; Heron 2016; Lim, Ha, & Song 2014; Statistisches Bundesamt 2017; U.K. Vital Statistics Outputs Branch 2015). By default, we think of these medical diseases as killers, as of course they are. Yet we can also start from these medical causes of death and work backwards to the many factors that, in combination, make each of them occur in the first place (Keeney 2008). Some of these factors cannot be helped, such as genetic factors (e.g., cancer runs in the family, suggesting a genetic predisposition) and environmental conditions outside our immediate personal control (e.g., living in an area in which air pollution is not well regulated; working in a factory or mine with poor air quality out of economic necessity). Such factors contribute significantly to all three of these types of disease.

Yet it has also long been known that our **personal decisions** – that is, making choices that *are* essentially under our own control – also play major roles in contributing to these causes of death. In particular, smoking, poorly regulated eating habits, and the failure to exercise regularly increase the likelihood of dying from these major categories of medical disease (Keeney 2008). Undoubtedly, there are always many individual cases in which no personal intervention could possibly have prevented disease. In many more cases, however, it is possible to *reduce the likelihood* of succumbing to disease by reducing or quitting smoking, eating nutritious foods while avoiding overeating, and doing regular cardiovascular exercise (Emmons, Linnan, Shadel, Marcus, & Abrams 1999). Germany's federal statistics office, for example, estimated that the choice to smoke might be said to have cost some German women about ten years of their lives (i.e., those dying of smoking-connected diseases in 2014 were on average 70.9 years of age, whereas those women dying of any cause in 2014 were on average 81.3 years of age; Statistisches Bundesamt 2017). Furthermore, German men are approximately twice as likely to die of smoking-connected diseases as German women (Statistisches Bundesamt 2017).

In the same vein, Keeney (2008), in a systematic analysis of the causes of death, concluded that the number one cause of premature death in the U.S. can be identified as personal decisions. This claim, though a bit contentious, certainly provides food for thought. For example, of those people who died of cancer or heart disease in the year 2000, Keeney's (2008) analyses suggested that 66% and 46% of these, respectively, could be traced back to personal decisions (e.g., to smoke, to eat poorly or too much, and to fail to exercise). Even if we acknowledge that in some specific cases these behaviors should not be classified as personal decisions per se (for example, poverty can directly prevent access to nutritious foods), for a number of people there may still be enough power remaining in personal choice to affect the time of death. That is, for quite a few people, premature death is not solely the result of a total crapshoot.

Figuring out how and why people make the decisions that they do is important not only from a public wellness perspective but also to us personally as we live our lives. How we each make decisions and what we each decide changes our lives for the better or for the worse. Not only do our decisions bring us to healthier lives versus untimely deaths, they also underlie what school we decide to attend, what career track to adopt, whether to pursue (or accept) a potential romantic partner, and what belief systems to adhere to and defend. In this book, you will consider both classic and modern research that has been conducted to better understand people's judgment and decision-making in many different applied (i.e., practical) and personal settings, as well as in laboratory settings.

In this text, the science of thinking, judging, and deciding is also approached from a broad range of research perspectives. Research in cognitive science, social psychology, cross-cultural psychology, development, neuroscience, and affective (experienced emotion) science contribute toward solving the complex puzzle of how we make judgments and decisions. Applied research in domains such as business, law, economics, and health sciences expand basic findings beyond the laboratory and ground our knowledge of decision processes in the complex context of the world and daily life. The goal of this text is to integrate these findings to emerge with a multi-faceted, multi-perspective understanding of the field.

The view that applied problems and basic science problems are fundamentally connected to one another and absolutely essential to each other is also reflected throughout this text. Many may be familiar with the idea of discovering basic phenomena in the laboratory, such as discovering an incredibly strong bias in people's reasoning and then testing whether and how it operates in daily life by carrying out applied research. But it is essential that applied research influence basic research as well (Wolfe 2016). Applied problems highlight what issues really matter to people as we live in the world. For example, how do people come to adopt ideologically extremist views? Why do lay people sometimes reject overwhelmingly clear scientific findings (e.g., supporting the truth of global warming)? Why do people in opposing political parties so often mutually find one another to be willfully ignorant, irrational, and unwilling to listen to reason? Exactly how do people succumb to biases when drawing inferences about past versus future events? One might value living in a free society, but does total freedom and infinite choice lead to the most happiness? Basic research can help answer such questions that were originally driven by practical concerns. At a broad level, the study of judgment and decision-making is also the study of how we live, how to improve how we live, and how to help others improve how they live (and whether we should).

Some seminal approaches to understanding judgment and decision-making

Judgment and decision-making perhaps first came into its own as a major field of study with the original work of Tversky and Kahneman (1974) and their colleagues. They approached the question of how people make judgments by identifying cognitive illusions, or systematic ways in which people make errors in subjective judgment (Pohl 2004). In studying cognitive illusions, Tversky and Kahneman (1974) drew an analogy to the study of visual perception, in which perceptual illusions are commonly used to infer how the visual system typically perceives. For example, an artist drawing on a flat canvas may seek to create the illusion of looking at a three-dimensional scene with a road that goes off into the distance. To do so, the artist may draw the two sides of the road so that they converge more and more closely together from the bottom of the canvas to the top. By studying how people perceive the painting, we can infer that converging lines may cue people to perceive depth even on a two-dimensional flat canvas. Analogously, Tversky and Kahneman (1974) sought to take cognitive illusions as evidence for how judgments and decisions are normally made. This line of work, launched by many groundbreaking studies by Kahneman, Tversky, and their colleagues, subsequently took on a life of its own in follow-up research across many different laboratories. As the illusions approach propagated across labs, the illusions metaphor became less prominent as researchers began to focus more and more on the judgment errors themselves. Yet the original intent of Tversky and Kahneman (1974) was to show where people occasionally go wrong under particular conditions that researchers manipulated precisely to illuminate how people are really making judgments.

For example, in choosing between two job offers, a person might feel more positively about one than about the other, and be strongly influenced by that affect (i.e., emotion) in making the choice (Slovic, Finucane, Peters, & MacGregor 2007). Under most everyday conditions, relying on simple cues such as basic positive affect will probably yield judgments that are perfectly acceptable. The point of the cognitive illusions literature is to pinpoint the times when using these simple cues will lead to mistaken judgments. A researcher might show that you can change people's judgments by manipulating them to feel more positive affect (e.g., by having them watch comedians telling jokes that are completely unrelated to the judgment they are about to make). The primary point of such research is not to show that one can manipulate people's judgments per se, but rather to infer that people are probably using affect much of the time to make judgments.

Gigerenzer and his colleagues sought to swing the pendulum back to emphasizing more directly and straightforwardly the ways in which people's reasoning is actually quite effective and their judgments very often sound. In their **fast-and-frugal approach** to judgment and decision-making, the emphasis is on how the use of mental shortcuts is adaptive – that is, how it leads to the best *balance* between minimizing the costs of cognitive processing and time and maximizing the accuracy of decisions (Gigerenzer, Todd, & the ABC Research Group 1999). Like Tversky, Kahneman, and their colleagues, Gigerenzer and his colleagues have identified a number of systematic shortcuts or rules by which people appear to make decisions. Gigerenzer et al.'s (1999) approach also emphasizes very explicitly how such shortcuts or rules allow people to get through very complex decisions with comparatively little mental effort.

Both approaches address the core question of how people manage to make complex decisions under conditions of uncertainty, with time limitations, and with our own cognitive limitations. Many of the decisions we make – about what to have for dinner, what courses to take in school, whether to pursue a potential romantic partner – do not have an identifiably correct answer at the time the decision is made. That is, exactly how things will turn out in the future cannot be known at the time the decision must be made, and we rarely have complete information about the present. Even a decision about what to have for dinner is time-limited; we have to make a decision by a certain time or nothing will be eaten. And we have cognitive limitations, or **computational capacity** – that is, there is a limited amount of information we can process at a time (Simon 1955). Identifying what kinds of mental shortcuts people take to make decisions helps to explain how we manage to get through the world in spite of all of these limitations.

Over the past several decades, these two approaches to judgment and decision-making research have uncovered a vast array of mental shortcuts and the conditions under which they do and do not appear (Gigerenzer 1996). This enormous flurry of research activities across many different labs has resulted in a perhaps somewhat unorganized proliferation of new, and sometimes overlapping, phenomena (occasionally, one can even find separate reports of essentially identical phenomena that different groups of researchers have unknowingly given different names). Although a single unifying theory making sense of all these results has been elusive, attempts have been made to at least identify a broad framework that helps to organize these findings.

Probably the most popular of these organizing frameworks at the moment is that of dual-process models (Kahneman 2011; Stanovich & West 2000).

Dual-process models

Dual-process models are a broad group of theories suggesting that judgments and decisions are generally carried out via two distinct kinds of mental processes. These two kinds of processes (most commonly referred to as *systems* of processing, and more recently as *types* of processing) can basically be described as follows. Broadly speaking, System 1 is traditionally meant to refer to fast, intuitive, parallel (i.e., simultaneous), automatic, emotion-driven, and/ or not always consciously accessible processing. System 2 is generally used to refer to cognitively taxing, deliberate, serial (i.e., sequential), controlled, reason-driven, and/or consciously accessible processes (Evans 2008; Sloman 1996; Stanovich & West 2000). For example, consider ageist stereotyping and prejudice. System 1 processing might be argued to underlie a person's implicit, automatic negative assumptions and lack of friendly feelings toward an unknown elderly person, whereas System 2 processing would attempt to override such negative automatic responses by consciously reasoning that it would be unfair to prejudge anyone. In the context of organizing the body of work on mental shortcuts, the general idea is that such judgments most typically fall under System 1 processing. We can, if we choose and given enough time, override such judgments by more controlled System 2 processing.

Among the first well-articulated arguments for two systems underlying reasoning was a proposal by Sloman (1996), in which he suggested that one system is associative in nature; that is, that reasoning in that system is based on similarity and statistical information. For example, using the associative system, we might quickly classify a given bird as a robin, because it is visually similar to our memories of other robins we have seen, and birds with this appearance are statistically quite likely to be a robin. He suggested that the other system is rule-based, relying on either logical rules, the rules of the social or natural world, or computer algorithms that minds might use to compute decisions or judgments. For example, using a rule-based system, we might classify a bird as a robin because it meets a six-point rule that one might argue defines a robin: (1) Bird, (2) Small, (3) Dark body, (4) Red breast, (5) Robin genes, (6) Alive or formerly alive. At the time, many researchers had been treating associative and rule-based systems as two different theories for how reasoning works. That is, they were trying to figure out whether people had associative systems, or whether they instead had rule-based systems. In contrast, Sloman (1996) argued that people have *both* associative and rule-based systems for reasoning, that these systems can operate simultaneously in the same person, and that although the rule-based system can generate the same judgment as the associative system, it does not necessarily do so.

Building upon ideas such as these, Stanovich and West (2000) conducted a comprehensive review of the dual-process models that had been proposed over the years (e.g., Evans 1984; Shiffrin & Schneider 1977; Sloman 1996). They noted some striking similarities across these various models, and proposed that all these models essentially referred to what seemed to be two systems of processing, one fast, intuitive, parallel, automatic, emotion-driven, and not always consciously accessible, and the other cognitively taxing, deliberate, serial, controlled, reason-driven, and consciously accessible. Stanovich and West (2000) were the first to apply the terms System 1 and System 2 to suggest that global distinctions could be made between these two clusters of processes.

The idea that much of reasoning, judgment, and decision-making involved *two* types of processes was extremely powerful in that it explained an enormous number of seemingly opposing research findings in a comprehensive and efficient way (Kahneman 2011). For example, researchers had long been embroiled in debates over whether reasoning is similarity-based *or* rule-based, whereas a dual-process framework of thought allowed for the possibility that it could be both. Many researchers adopted the dual-process framework to explain mental phenomena ranging from categorization to infant language acquisition to decision-making. One widely used questionnaire, the Cognitive Reflection Test (CRT), was designed to detect individual differences in the tendency to rely on System 1 versus System 2 processing in reasoning (Frederick 2005). It has already been administered so frequently that researchers began to have difficulty finding study participants online who had not already completed it, leading to the development of a second, alternative questionnaire designed to measure the same thing (Toplak, West, & Stanovich 2014).

Despite their relative popularity among researchers in recent years, dual-process models have also been critiqued by a small but respected minority for being relatively vague and poorly defined (e.g., Gigerenzer & Regier 1996; Keren & Schul 2009). Over the intervening years, some dual-process model advocates have responded constructively to such critiques by adopting an increasingly refined approach to dual-process models. First, upon more systematic and careful reflection, it now appears to be quite unlikely that there are actually two separate, general-purpose "systems" per se (Evans 2008; Osman 2004). Across the dual-process models that have been proposed so far, it has become apparent that the proposed attributes of each system do not always co-occur. For example, being fast, automatic, and unconscious does not always coincide with also processing associatively and in parallel (Evans 2008). Furthermore, it appears to be possible for both deliberate and intuitive processing to be based on rules (Kruglanski & Gigerenzer 2011).

For example, in predicting the winner of a tennis tournament, we might apply the rule "the more quickly I recognize the player's name, the more likely I think that player is to win" either deliberately, applying the rule as a purposeful strategy, or intuitively, perhaps without even being aware that we are doing so.

Evans (2008) proposed, however, that the dual-process framework is still viable, because there are a few common elements to each process that can still be found across the different dual-process theories. The existence of such common elements shows that the two sets of processes are fundamentally different (Evans 2008). In particular, one type of processing common to dual-process theories tends to be automatic, non-conscious and fast, and the other tends to be deliberate, conscious, and slow. He suggested that the first type of processing might be more accurately called Type 1 (i.e., instead of System 1) processing and the second Type 2, to acknowledge that they reflect kinds of processing rather than entire systems of processing per se. Furthermore, only Type 2 processing is tied to working memory (i.e., our limited-capacity conscious thought), and is therefore disrupted under cognitive load. That is, Type 2 processing cannot operate well when you are carrying out another task that also takes up working memory (Evans 2008).

More recently, Evans and Stanovich (2013) collaborated to even further refine and narrow the definition of dual-process models, describing Type 1 processing more generally as *intuitive* in nature and Type 2 processing as *reflective*. They identified attributes that, they proposed, always distinguish Type 1 from Type 2 processing. The first attribute is the working memory distinction previously noted by Evans (2008): Type 2 processing necessarily engages working memory, whereas Type 1 processing can be carried out without working memory. Second, they suggested that Type 1 processing includes automatic processing, as well as processing that is carried out by habit. In contrast, Type 2 processing is reflective and can be carried out in detachment from the present reality. That is, when we think abstractly, hypothetically, and/or about the future, this is carried out via Type 2 processing (Evans & Stanovich 2013). The additional attributes that have traditionally been linked to Type 1 and 2 processing (e.g., fast versus slow; associative versus rule-based; unconscious versus conscious; parallel versus serial) often coincide with the above defining attributes, but do not always do so (Evans & Stanovich 2013).

In addition, earlier models suggested that affect is part of System or Type 1 processing (e.g., Evans 2008; Haidt 2001). Evans and Stanovich (2013) refined this view to suggest that, in particular, *basic* affect (e.g., regarding simply whether one feels negative and positive emotion) is associated with Type 1 processing. The general idea is that people – perhaps often automatically, and not necessarily with conscious awareness – rely on such basic affect as a cue to judgment (Slovic et al. 2007). More complex forms of affect, such as the more detailed interpretations people make to explain their basic affect (e.g., whether it reflects guilt, anger, hostility, or embarrassment) may be more appropriately classified as Type 2 processing (see Evans & Stanovich 2013). Later on, we will return to the question of how affect may influence specific decision tasks.

In sum, dual-process models may currently be the closest thing the field has to an organizing framework for judgment and decision-making as a whole. It has been argued that dual-process theories are not theories in the traditional empirical sense (Keren 2013), in that they are supported by observations of many empirical studies rather than having been derived from targeted experiments explicitly designed to test between dual-process models and some alternative theory. Although this is largely true, there is still a highly useful role for dual-process models in that they capture systematic patterns among the many research findings in the field, by which new research findings can also be organized. From a historical perspective, dual-process models have also drawn researchers away from the old driving question of whether people use Type 1 OR Type 2 reasoning in general by acknowledging that everyone most likely deploys both types of reasoning. And finally, among researchers studying reasoning, judgment and decision-making, the notion of dual-process models holds a very forceful intuitive appeal. The general idea that our judgments and decisions can be affected by both gut feelings and rational thought is enormously compelling, and difficult to dismiss.

Major types of decision-making models

Finally, in judgment and decision-making research, a distinction is made between three kinds of models of decision-making, each of which serves a different practical purpose (Bell, Raiffa, & Tversky 1988). Descriptive models attempt to describe how people *actually* judge and decide, without necessarily saying what we do is good or bad. Dual-process models fall into this category, as they simply describe the data we have about (for example) how people frequently use shortcuts to make judgments but can deliberately override them under certain conditions. In fact, in this book, the vast majority of models are descriptive, but we will also consider some very important normative models.

Normative models reflect *optimal* or ideal decision-making. For example, a normative decision process should be logical, consistent with one's past decisions and preferences, and take all known relevant data into account. Normative models also reflect the decision-making processes that should get the person closest to achieving his or her own goals over the long run. For example, if a person hopes to achieve a long and healthy life, a normative model for making this happen might include doing everything that has been statistically shown to improve health and lengthen life (e.g., quit smoking; eat balanced meals in moderate quantities; exercise regularly).

Finally, prescriptive models recommend a particular way in which people ought to judge and decide; it may or may not be the normative way of making decisions, but it is thought to be an improvement over what people are currently doing. For example, to reduce the likelihood that food workers in a cafeteria will transfer microscopic pathogens from their hands to the food they prepare, the cafeteria manager may order a number of dispensers containing alcohol-based hand sanitizer to be installed in the food preparation area. Research shows that alcohol-based sanitizer helps remove pathogens from hands and reduce the spread of foodborne illnesses, although hand washing with soap and water is a more effective and thorough way to eliminate such pathogens (Foddai, Grant, & Dean 2016). However, suppose that in this particular cafeteria, the lone sink is in use for food preparation almost all the time. The cafeteria manager may reason that the cafeteria workers will be more likely to comply with new hand cleansing rules if it is not a hassle to do so. The manager decides to make it easy for them to access alcohol-based hand sanitizer, and puts up signs recommending that they use it.

In sum, prescriptive models may often reflect a compromise between normative and descriptive models (Bell et al. 1988). Normative models tell us what would be best (e.g., hand washing with soap), descriptive models tell us what people actually do (e.g., they frequently do not wash at all), and prescriptive models attempt to make a reasonable, realistic recommendation for action (e.g., provide and require the use of highly accessible hand sanitizers to at least substantially reduce the spread of foodborne pathogens). Prescriptive models outline practical ways in which we can put our knowledge of decision-making (i.e., what people actually do, along with what they ought to do) to use in daily life to make concrete improvements. All three types of models are useful, but for these different reasons.

The content of this book

This book contains both classic coverage of fundamental research in judgment and decision-making and modern basic research. It also integrates research perspectives across major subfields of work, especially social psychology and applied psychology (e.g., informing pressing issues in medicine, law, economics, marketing, environmental science, and personal life decisions), but also developmental psychology, cross-cultural psychology, cognitive neuroscience, and affective science. By drawing upon multiple areas of work, I hope to foster a more complete and multi-faceted view of judgment and decision-making processes, especially when embedded in the context of problems outside the laboratory. In addition, this book centers around five major problems in judgment and decision-making: How we judge the likelihoods of events; how we make judgments about the past and decisions regarding the future; how we choose to expend our resources of time, money, and opportunity; how we make sense of the world we live in and how this sense-making affects our judgments; and how we make judgments as members of social groups.

Part I: Making Likelihood Judgments

How likely is it that one will get married within ten years? How likely is it that the dictatorial regime of a particular country will be overthrown in one's lifetime? In **Chapter 2 (Availability and Representativeness)**, we begin by asking how people judge the likelihoods of events such as these under conditions of uncertainty. **Uncertainty** is present when a numerical, probability-based prediction cannot really be made because the events in question are relatively unique and past events are not relevant enough to provide appropriate data for calculating probabilities (Knight 1921). For example, it is not really possible to calculate probabilities regarding who will be prime minister of Canada 25 years from now; not enough relevant information is yet available. In Chapter 2, we'll first consider experimental evidence for some of the mental shortcuts that we take to answer such questions quickly and with only an incomplete set of relevant information. In addition to considering seminal studies on this topic, we will evaluate alternative theories of how we judge the likelihoods of events. We will also trace how the use of mental shortcuts has been argued to unfold over development. Finally, we'll consider some of the potential health-related, interpersonal and social consequences of making such likelihood judgments in life.

In addition, does initial information play an important role in making our likelihood judgments? In **Chapter 3 (Anchoring and Primacy Effects in Judgment)**, we'll consider both seminal and modern research on how the *initial* information you receive may disproportionately influence your judgments of what kinds of personalities people are likely to have, and of how likely events are to occur. We will also explore the question of how initial information influences doctors' medical diagnostic judgments and drives sales and marketing tactics. Finally, we'll examine specific strategies that might help us avoid giving disproportionate weight to initial information in our judgments.

Part II: Judgments of the Past and the Future

At any given moment in time, the future holds great uncertainty and enormous complexity, as there are an infinite number of possible things that could still happen. In contrast, at that same moment in time, the past is fixed and relatively (at least compared to the future) simple. Yet we often find it quite difficult to separate our past thinking from how we are thinking at present. **Chapter 4 (Hindsight Bias)** is dedicated to understanding how well we are able to recreate our state of knowledge from a given moment in time, after it has moved into the past. There is robust evidence for a hindsight bias, such that we mistakenly think our state of knowledge was more certain and that we were better at predicting the future than was actually the case. We will discuss different accounts of what mental processes underlie hindsight bias, including motivation, memory, and causal reasoning; consider a number of closely related reasoning biases; and examine the hindsight bias over development and across cultures.

On a daily basis, we also make judgments about how much risk is involved in a particular course of action, assessing the potential costs and benefits of that action, and deciding whether taking the action is worth risking the potential costs. Some have argued that risk may be differentiated from uncertainty in that risk refers to judging the likelihood of events for which past relevant numerical data are available (Knight 1921). That is, such data can allow us to estimate the probability that the action could give rise to those potential costs and benefits. For example, deciding to skip this year's influenza vaccine, going snowboarding, driving a car, and drinking sugary sodas all carry with them some amount of risk to our personal well-being, which we know to be the case because of past records and large-scale epidemiological studies tracking the frequency of adverse outcomes. In **Chapter 5 (Risk Perception)**, we review how people weigh risks against benefits and whether or not the conclusions we draw tend to be reasonable. We review normative methods of risk assessment that could potentially help us to improve our own judgments in our personal lives.

In **Chapter 6 (Prediction)**, we go on to consider how we make predictions about individual people (e.g., their future performance; their behaviors) and specific events (e.g., tomorrow's weather; which players will win at Wimbledon next year). Would you rather have a physician or a computerized decision support system identify the most likely medical diagnosis for your condition? Would you rather have the new players on your favorite sports team selected by professional scouts or by a sophisticated algorithm operating over a statistical database? We will review evidence suggesting that most people prefer professional intuition, but that statistical methods may tend to do better at making accurate predictions. In this chapter, we'll also discuss people's systematic biases when trying to predict everything from how they will feel about a possible job promotion in the future to tomorrow's weather. We will apply such research to the practice of medicine, focusing in particular on the difficulties of end-of-life decision-making (e.g., trying to predict how we will want our own end-of-life medical care to be handled when the time comes).

Part III: Decisions about Resources

The resources we each have at our disposal – including but not limited to money, time, and opportunity – and what influences how we choose to allocate them are the focus of the third part of this text. In Chapter 7 (Choice and Mental Accounting), we begin by considering the problem of choice (e.g., which product to purchase; which way to spend our time) in the context of research on the mind and brain. We'll evaluate how particular characteristics of a given choice problem ultimately influence the decision that one makes. We will ask whether there can ever be complete freedom of choice, given that even the environment itself constrains and influences the choices most likely to be made. We'll also consider the knotty problem of whether manipulating the environment to guide people toward healthier choices is a praiseworthy prescriptive model, or whether doing so would be an unethical violation of people's freedom of choice. In the second part of the chapter, we will shift our focus to lay people's mental accounting – how we mentally track and classify our personal resources. We will compare descriptive models of mental accounting to rational, arguably normative economic theories, and consider what the differences between them might mean for developing ways to improve people's money management.

Across Chapter 8 (Expected Utility Theory) and Chapter 9 (Framing Effects and Prospect Theory), we will go on to consider major, general-purpose models of choice. Three of these models have been argued by at least some researchers to be normative models (i.e., expected value theory, expected utility theory, and multi-attribute utility theory) of choice, although expected utility theory has often been assumed to be a descriptive model. In addition, we cover prominent descriptive models (i.e., one-reason decision-making, robust satisficing, and prospect theory). Because prospect theory has been influential across a number of disciplines, including but not limited to psychology, behavioral economics, and finance, the majority of Chapter 8 is spent on detailing its claims and reviewing and evaluating the experiments that have tested them.

Part IV: Making Sense of the World

To more fully understand how we make judgments and decisions, we will consider how we organize and store our past learning and knowledge in memory, and how this organization influences our judgments. In Chapter 10 (Schemas and Framework Theories), we start with fundamental research detailing core domains of knowledge in infancy and childhood. We cover classic cognitive theories of schemas, scripts, and broader frameworks in which we mentally store and organize our knowledge. We then consider how framework theories inform our understanding of such complex judgments as jury decision-making and clinical reasoning.

In **Chapter 11** (Judging Covariation, Contingency, and Cause), we'll then review the rich and varied literature on causal reasoning from social, cognitive, and comparative (non-human animal) psychology. How did your teenage neighbor perform so well in school despite having a rather difficult home life? How do you think gene therapies for cancer work? Should a police officer be convicted of a crime for shooting a suspect who was unarmed at the time? What factors led to a military coup attempt? It has been argued that much of human reasoning is actually causal reasoning, in which we to try to figure out – from whatever evidence and prior knowledge is available to us – why or how something came about. We'll consider how people use very simple causal cues and statistical information to infer cause and effect, and how people distinguish between different kinds of causality – for example, how we decide who *caused* a tragedy versus *allowed* or *enabled* it to happen.

Figuring out how the world works sometimes also involves coming up with hypotheses to explain what we observe, and seeking out information to test those hypotheses further. We are often taught to revere the scientific method of investigation as the normative approach to testing hypotheses. In **Chapter 12** (Hypothesis Testing and Confirmation Bias), we'll go back to the origins and philosophy underlying the scientific method and critically consider their logic. Although modern science seems to generally value a disconfirmatory approach, in which we seek evidence against hypotheses, some have argued that under certain conditions a confirmatory approach is actually preferable. There are also times when scientists themselves adopt a confirmatory approach without appearing to realize it, and we will discuss what this means for science and how we interpret evidence. We'll then consider how judgment and decision-making research on hypothesis testing helps us better understand reasoning errors in the world. For example, it helps explain why people make critical errors in interpreting legal evidence in criminal trials and how medical experts come to make misdiagnoses.

In addition, people can come to form and maintain beliefs without any evidence at all, and how this process unfolds is the focus of **Chapter 13** (Belief). We will first consider the genesis of superstitious, magical, and paranormal beliefs – by definition, beliefs for which there is no concrete evidence, but which people can hold nonetheless. We will also consider in depth the rise and maintenance of conspiracy theories. Finally, we'll consider research in memory and executive control, which may help explain how misinformation continues to affect people's judgments even after they have realized that the information is false, and how beliefs are formed in the first place.

Part V: Judgment and Decision-Making in Society

In the final chapter of this book, **Chapter 14** (Moral Judgment and Cooperation), we discuss how people make moral judgments and consider how people engage in cooperative behavior in functioning societies. The role of morality in forming personal identity and the development of morality across the lifespan and across genders, cultures, socioeconomic levels, and age will be considered in depth. We'll discuss the role of affect in our moral judgments, as evidenced by research in cognitive neuroscience and psychology, and we'll examine how people choose between acting for their own good versus for the good of a group to which they belong.

Summary

In the field of judgment and decision-making, basic and applied science are intricately interwoven and interdependent. The study of how we make judgments and decisions is also the study of improving and optimizing our health, wealth, relationships, use of time, and personal well-being. In this book, we will consider descriptive, normative, and prescriptive models for decision-making as they pertain to everything from mundane, everyday decisions to ones that affect the entire courses of our lives, and from individual decisions to those made by groups, companies, and nations.

Suggestions for further reading

Evans, J. S. B., & Stanovich, K. E. (2013). Dual-process theories of higher cognition: Advancing the debate. *Perspectives on Psychological Science, 8*(3), 223–241.

Kahneman, D. (2011). *Thinking, fast and slow*. London, UK: Macmillan.

PART I

Making Likelihood Judgments

Availability and Representativeness 2

Learning Goals

By the end of this chapter, you will have:

- Considered the general problem of how people judge the likelihood of an event under conditions of uncertainty.
- Considered evidence for how people may take mental shortcuts such as the availability heuristic, representativeness heuristic, and other related heuristics to make likelihood judgments.
- Critically evaluated alternative ways of making sense of this evidence.
- Asked whether research on the availability heuristic can provide insight into understanding health-related reasoning.
- Evaluated whether, and how, the use of the availability heuristic changes over the developmental lifespan.
- Assessed the relationship between research on the representativeness heuristic and research on stereotyping in social judgment.
- Considered the role of the representativeness heuristic in shaping and influencing the study of human behavior itself.

Key Terms

Heuristic	Regressed-frequencies hypothesis
Availability heuristic	Representativeness heuristic
Availability	Representativeness
Accessibility	Prototype
Set-size judgment	Law of small numbers
Relative frequency-of-occurrence judgment	Law of large numbers
	Base rates
Availability-by-number hypothesis	Conjunction rule
Availability-by-speed hypothesis	Conjunction fallacy
Letter-class hypothesis	WEIRD

In the third installment of the popular fictional children's book series *Lemony Snicket's A Series of Unfortunate Events*, Handler (2000) writes of a trio of orphaned siblings who have just been appointed a new guardian, Aunt Josephine Antwhistle. The children learn that their new guardian has numerous deep-seated fears: She fears doorknobs, because it is possible that they could shatter and that a small piece could get into her eye. She fears her refrigerator, because it could conceivably smash her if it happened to fall on her one day. She fears doormats, because any one of these could become deadly if she tripped over it and fell, potentially snapping her neck in the process. Although these fears might initially strike one as being rather odd, consider that the kinds of judgments she is making mirror ones that we, too, make on an everyday basis. In each case, the character is making an intuitive judgment about the probabilities or frequencies of events in the world. Of course, most people probably wouldn't come up with the same probabilities: We believe this character to have overestimated these probabilities, given that we ourselves might judge the same events to be extremely improbable.

In this chapter and the next, we will work toward understanding how people make such judgments – judgments of how likely an event is to occur or how likely a fact is to be true. An important goal of research in this area has been to discover exactly what kinds of information we use to make such judgments, especially under conditions of uncertainty, where the event in question is unique enough that it can be difficult to draw upon existing data to calculate a probability (see Chapter 1). For example, if we don't have an accessible, numerical database of how frequently in the world doorknobs have previously shattered such that a piece got into someone's eye, then we have to base judgments of its likelihood on other information, presumably information to which we have mental access.

Tversky and Kahneman (1973, 1974) first suggested that we often tend to rely upon **heuristics**, or quick-and-easy rules of thumb that we use to make judgments under conditions of uncertainty. (We will also consider an alternative definition of heuristics in Chapter 3.) Applying heuristics can be much more efficient than carrying out numerical calculations of probability, especially, again, when data about the past are not accessible or relevant. Two important questions asked by Tversky and Kahneman (1973, 1974) in these early investigations were (1) exactly what these heuristics might be and (2) under what circumstances people use them. Under the organizing framework of dual-process models (Chapter 1), we can classify the heuristics we review in this chapter and the next (i.e., availability heuristic, representativeness heuristic, and the anchoring-and-adjustment heuristic) under Type 1 reasoning. That is, using heuristics is deeply intuitive. Furthermore, we may be able to override the influence of heuristics under some conditions by applying Type 2 reasoning. Because documenting how and when these heuristics are used drove the field of judgment and decision-making research for many years, we take some time in this chapter and the next to review and consider them closely.

The availability heuristic

In 1973, Tversky and Kahneman published a seminal paper entitled *Availability: A heuristic for judging frequency and probability*. They loosely defined the **availability heuristic** as follows: "A person is said to employ the availability heuristic whenever [that person] estimates frequency or probability by the ease with which instances or associations could be brought to mind" (Tversky & Kahneman 1973, p. 208). Suppose we are trying to judge how likely an event is to occur, or how likely a statement is to be true. Say that first we check how easy it is to call examples of that event or statement to mind. We might do this by trying to remember some examples and seeing how quickly they come to mind, or we might simply see how many examples we are able to call to mind. Then, we make an inferential leap – we *infer* that the easier it is to call examples to mind (or the more examples we can call to mind), the more likely the event or statement is to occur or to be true. For example, our complete inability to retrieve any real-life instances of a *doorknob shattering such that a piece got into someone's eye* leads us to infer that this is probably an extremely rare event.

To take another example, suppose you're introduced to a new person at work and you aren't sure yet whether the person is a new co-worker or a new boss. If you just recently watched an intensely compelling movie all about the working relationship between an entry-level worker and a new boss, then you may, just at this particular moment, think the new person at work is *more likely* to be a new boss than you would have if you watched that movie a long time ago. That is, the memory of the movie, newly stored and therefore highly accessible, influences your judgment of the likelihood of a superficially related case. Let's consider a third example. Suppose that, in a two-week span, two different friends both told you that their parents had decided to divorce. Your estimate of the current divorce rate might be higher now than it would have been a month ago, simply because you now have very recent examples of divorces in memory that can easily be called to mind.

The availability heuristic is, interestingly, something of a misnomer. In the memory literature, the term **availability** has traditionally been used to refer to memory traces existing in the mind, whereas **accessibility** refers to how easily one can retrieve these memory traces to conscious awareness (MacLeod & Campbell 1992; Tulving & Pearlstone 1966). Accordingly, some have argued that the cognitive process underlying the availability heuristic is the *accessibility* of exemplars (i.e., how easily we can call examples to mind). The idea, again, is that we then use our intuitions about accessibility to infer likelihood in the world.

The availability heuristic appears to distort people's judgments even when they have received all the information needed to be completely accurate (Tversky & Kahneman 1973). In one of their seminal studies, Tversky and Kahneman (1973) created two lists with names of entertainers and two lists with names of public figures. For each pair of lists, one list contained 19 names of very famous women during that time period (e.g., Elizabeth Taylor) and 20 names of somewhat famous men (e.g., William Fulbright). The other list in each pair contained 19 names of very famous men (e.g., Richard Nixon) and 20 names of somewhat famous women (e.g., Lana Turner). American participants listened to each list read aloud via a pre-recorded message and then completed one of two tasks. Some participants completed a recall task, in which they tried to remember all the names that had been read. The rest completed a set-size judgment task, in which they reported whether there were more women or more men on each list. In general, a set-size judgment task involves estimating how many individuals belong to a group or category (Maley, Hunt, & Parr 2000). Most of those completing the recall task remembered more famous than non-famous names; in addition, more famous than non-famous names were recalled on average (Tversky & Kahneman 1973). Similarly, most of those completing the frequency judgment task estimated that the gender of the more famous names on each list had occurred most frequently (Tversky & Kahneman 1973). Tversky and Kahneman (1973) argued, given these data, that people's frequency judgments appear to be based on the ease or frequency with which they could call names to mind.

Similar findings were unearthed in another seminal study in which Tversky and Kahneman (1973) showed American university students five consonants (K, L, N, R, and V), one at a time. As each letter (e.g., K) was presented, people were asked to judge whether that letter appeared more often in the English language as the first letter of a word or as the third letter of a word (among words at least 3 letters long). This type of task is generally known as a relative frequency-of-occurrence judgment, in which your job is to estimate how often an event or item occurs relative to another event or item (Maley et al. 2000). Tversky and Kahneman (1973) hypothesized that people would make this likelihood judgment using the availability heuristic. That is, they hypothesized that people would judge the frequency of each case by gauging how easily they could think of words that began with a particular letter (e.g., K) as opposed to how easily they could think of words that contained that letter in the third position. Among their study participants, 69% thought that the first position was more likely for at least three of the five consonants; only 31% of participants thought that the third position was more likely for at least three of the five. This difference was strongly statistically significant. Of course, only the latter group was correct; Tversky and Kahneman (1973) deliberately selected all five of these consonants because they actually appear as the third letter more often than as the first.

Numerous follow-up studies have provided additional evidence for the availability heuristic across a variety of different kinds of judgment. Judgments of the self – including predictions about the likelihood of different types of events in one's own future – are one example of judgments strongly influenced by the availability heuristic. MacLeod and Campbell (1992) suggested that if the availability heuristic does exist, then we can expect that any manipulation that alters the ease with which a set of exemplars are retrieved from memory will change people's likelihood judgments (e.g., likelihood judgments of future events). They put this hypothesis to the test in a sample of undergraduate students in Australia. Because it had previously been established that inducing a positive or negative mood makes it easier for people to retrieve positive or negative memories, respectively (e.g., Bower 1981), the hypothesis could be tested using a mood manipulation. After taking a baseline of people's current mood, MacLeod and Campbell (1992) used a standard mood manipulation to induce either a happy or unhappy mood. Specifically, they asked those people to read either 16 positive statements about their lives (e.g., that they had people who cared about them) or 16 negative statements (e.g., that they had no hope of ever being successful) and to use these statements to help create their mood. People's before-and-after ratings of mood confirmed that the mood manipulation was successful in changing mood in the intended direction.

With the mood manipulation in place, the main hypothesis could then be tested. To do so, people were then asked to carry out two main tasks. In the first main task, they were presented with specific types of happy events (e.g., receiving a nice compliment) and specific types of unhappy events (e.g., having a heated argument), one by one. As each was presented, people pressed a button as soon as they remembered a precise instance of that type of event in their own lives (e.g., for the event type "receiving a nice compliment," the person might recall receiving a highly enthusiastic written assessment on a term paper and press the button as soon as that recollection came to mind). In the second main task, people saw the same events again and were asked to predict the likelihood of each of those specific types of happy and unhappy events happening to them again in the next six months. The important test of the availability heuristic was whether the amount of time it took people to recall a happy or unhappy event correlated negatively with their predictions of how likely that type of event was to occur again in the future. This was what they found; in fact, the two were negatively correlated for every single one of the individual event types they tested. That is, the more accessible the memory (as indicated by a *shorter* response time), the more likely they thought the event was to occur in the near future – a direct demonstration of the availability heuristic in a likelihood judgment about one's own future life.

Schwarz, Bless, Strack, Klumpp, Rittenauer-Schatka, and Simons (1991) further suggested that the availability heuristic not only influences likelihood judgments but also people's assessments of their own personalities. They randomly assigned university students in Germany to one of four tasks. Some students were asked to think of and describe 12 situations in which they had felt at ease and acted assertively; others were asked to do the same for only 6 such situations. Another set of students was asked to describe 12 situations in which they had felt insecure and acted unassertively; the last set was asked to do the same for 6 such situations. (The researchers had discovered ahead of time that people found it very difficult to generate 12 of either type of situation, and quite easy to generate 6.) Then, they were asked to rate their own assertiveness versus unassertiveness and feelings of ease versus insecurity. The results showed that people who described 6 situations of assertiveness rated themselves as more assertive than did people who described 12 such situations, and people who described 6 situations of unassertiveness rated

Box 2.1: Exercise: The World's Population by Continent

Without looking online, fill in your best estimates of what percentage of the world population currently lives on each continent: Africa (_____%), North America (_____%), Latin America (including Central America and South America) and the Caribbean (_____%), Asia (_____%), Europe (_____%), Oceania (_____%).

Then, do a web search for the phrase "global population by continent" (e.g., www.statista.com/statistics/237584/distribution-of-the-world-population-by-continent/ or www.un.org/en/sections/issues-depth/population/). Compare your estimates to the percentages listed.

What aspects of the actual population distribution, if any, do you find to be surprising? What breakdown did you expect, and what factors do you think might have influenced your expectations?

themselves as less assertive than did those who described 12 such situations (Schwarz et al. 1991). More generally, the researchers found that both the content of their recollections and their accessibility influenced people's judgments about themselves.

The availability heuristic: Alternative views

Evidence for the availability heuristic has been heavily cited across many fields of study, and has generally been very widely accepted (Sedlmeier, Hertwig, & Gigerenzer 1998). Even so, there have been some critical analyses of the work; though less well known, they offer some intriguing alternative ways of considering the phenomena originally documented by Tversky and Kahneman (1973). Lopes and Oden (1991), for example, offered an alternative interpretation of the results of Tversky and Kahneman's (1973) seminal study in which people thought a consonant was more likely to appear in the first than the third position of a word. In particular, Lopes and Oden (1991) argued that the (K, L, N, R, and V) sample of consonants used in that study was atypical. They pointed out that of the 20 consonants in the English alphabet, no more than 8 (including K, L, N, R, and V), or 40%, appear more often in the language as the third letter of a word than as the first letter. Perhaps participants in Tversky and Kahneman's (1973) study, not realizing that the sample of consonants they had received was non-representative of the population of consonants in the language, assumed that the sample of consonants they received was most likely to appear more often as the first letter of a word than as the third (Lopes & Oden 1991). Although such an assumption would have been made in error, it is not the same as having one's judgments influenced by availability per se.

A prominent follow-up critique, building on the work of Lopes and Oden (1991), was offered by Sedlmeier et al. (1998), who proposed to test between four hypotheses for how people judge the frequencies of words. They argued that Tversky and Kahneman's (1973) description of the availability heuristic could suggest either one of two hypotheses: An **availability-by-number hypothesis**, in which we gauge how many examples we are able to recall before making a frequency judgment, or an **availability-by-speed hypothesis**, in which we gauge how easily and/or quickly we are able to recall examples.

In contrast, in their own **letter-class hypothesis**, Sedlmeier et al. (1998) suggested that people might judge how likely a letter is to appear in the first versus a subsequent position in a word based on the fact that it is much more common in the German and English languages for consonants in general to take the first position in a word than for a vowel to take the first position. This particular fact does not directly pertain to Tversky and Kahneman's

(1973) original results, because they used only consonants in that study, but it is certainly possible that the letter-class hypothesis might describe how people make judgments about the likelihood of words more generally.

Finally, it has been well documented that people generally tend to underestimate the probability of high-frequency occurrences and overestimate that of low-frequency occurrences, although they are pretty accurate at rank-ordering different occurrences by frequency (Greene 1984; Varey, Mellers, & Birnbaum 1990). That is, even though people's estimates of both high- and low-frequency occurrences tend to regress to the mean, people still know that the high-frequency occurrences are more frequent than the low-frequency occurrences. On the basis of this finding, Sedlmeier et al. (1998) developed their own second hypothesis, the **regressed-frequencies hypothesis**. Specifically, they suggested that people do keep track of the frequencies of where letters occur in words – for example, while reading – and that their memories of those frequencies tend to regress to the mean.

In a set of experiments with German university students, Sedlmeier et al. (1998) first mapped out the specific numerical predictions of these four hypotheses. Because the availability-by-number hypothesis is that we base frequency judgments on how many examples we are able to recall, they ran a pre-experiment to find out how many examples of words students were able to recall with a particular letter in the first (or second) position. If frequency judgments are made according to this hypothesis, then students' frequency judgments should correlate with the number of words recalled, such that more words recalled should predict higher frequency judgments. Similarly, because the availability-by-speed hypothesis is that we base frequency judgments on how quickly we are able to recall examples, they measured how quickly students could come up with a word with a particular letter in the first (or second) position. If the availability-by-speed hypothesis is correct, then their response times should correlate with frequency judgments. To be more specific, shorter response times should predict higher frequency judgments if this hypothesis is correct.

Sedlmeier et al. (1998) obtained predictions for their own two hypotheses in the same way. Again, the letter-class hypothesis was that people take into account whether the letter in the first position is a consonant or a vowel when inferring whether it is more likely to fall in the first versus second position. As it happens, about 27% of vowels that fall in either the first or second position of a word appear in the first position and 73% in the second position in the German language. In contrast, about 72% of consonants in the first two positions of a word appear in the first position and 28% in the second in German (Sedlmeier et al. 1998). After making the assumption of 70% regression to the mean, the predictions for the letter-class hypothesis were that there was a 57% chance the letter is in the first position if the letter is a consonant, and a 43% chance it is in the first position if the letter is a vowel.

Finally, again, the regressed-frequencies hypothesis was that people track the frequencies of letters in the different positions in a word, and that their perceptions of these frequencies tend to regress to the mean. Thus, Sedlmeier et al. (1998) estimated predictions for this hypothesis by taking the actual frequency of each letter in the first and second positions of German words and assuming 70% regression to the mean.

After calculating what numerical patterns of results would be predicted by each of the four hypotheses, Sedlmeier et al. (1998) presented people with one letter at a time and asked them to judge whether that letter appears more frequently in the first or second position of words (choice task). People's judgments aligned with the predictions of the two availability hypotheses about 50% of the time, whereas they aligned with the letter-class hypothesis about 70% of the time, and with the regressed-frequencies hypothesis nearly 80% of the time. Sedlmeier et al. (1998) argued that people's actual decisions on the choice tasks thereby mapped moderately more closely to the predictions of the regressed-frequencies hypothesis than to the other three hypotheses. As an interesting aside, although this hypothesis predicted the data better than did the other three, none of the four hypotheses consistently mapped particularly well to the data across all the *individual letters* for which people made likelihood judgments. It is important to keep in mind that even if any one of these accounts is supported by the data, it is unlikely to be the sole factor influencing judgments. In addition, note that the classic set-size and frequency-of-occurrence tasks may not necessarily be highly relevant to judgments made in daily life. More work embedded in the context of decision-making as it unfolds in different practical domains is necessary to consider alongside the above research.

The availability heuristic in health-related decision-making

The impact of the availability heuristic has been argued to appear in likelihood judgments made by both health professionals and patients. Health care is a particularly useful domain for studying heuristics because it provides a complex, important arena in which one can determine the advisability of applying a heuristic by comparing clinicians' frequency judgments to the correct answers (i.e., documented base rates). A critical review of the availability heuristic's impact in medical decision-making showed that evidence supporting the heuristic was found in 100% of studies observing decision-making in actual decision scenarios (Blumenthal-Barby & Kreiger 2015). As an easy rule of thumb for judging probability, the availability heuristic can allow health professionals to make faster judgments, but these judgments may not always be ideal. In an illustrative example, Dawson and Arkes (1987) described the case of a physician who spent several days feeling unwell and experiencing pain in his own abdomen. The physician was diagnosed with appendicitis and, after undergoing surgery and recovery, felt much better. After the physician returned to medical practice, however, many patients who came in complaining of abdominal pain were promptly diagnosed with appendicitis and referred for surgery. Apparently losing sight of the fact that many people with abdominal pain probably do not need surgery (they might instead, for example, need to eat fewer gas-producing foods), the physician seems to have been strongly influenced by the highly accessible memory of firsthand experience when judging the likelihood of appendicitis and need for surgery for his patients.

Empirical work in the medical field has been consistent with the availability heuristic in diagnosis, though the overall story is a little more complex. Mamede et al. (2010), for example, conducted an experiment to assess whether first- and second-year internal medicine residents in Germany relied on the availability heuristic even for cases in which using the heuristic reduced their diagnostic accuracy. First, residents were asked to evaluate the accuracy of diagnoses that had already been made for six patient cases. Then, they were asked to consider eight additional cases, and were asked to diagnose these cases themselves. None of the correct diagnoses for these eight additional cases were the same as those seen in the six initial cases. Critically, however, four of the eight additional cases had characteristics overlapping with those seen in some of the initial cases. For example, some residents saw a case diagnosed as inflammatory bowel disease among the initial six cases, and then among the eight additional cases, they were asked to diagnose a case describing celiac disease. Both inflammatory bowel disease and celiac disease share a small subset of symptoms, including diarrhea and unintentional weight loss, although many other symptoms can be used to distinguish between the two. The important question for Mamede et al. (2010) was whether residents would be less likely to correctly diagnose their four cases with overlapping characteristics than the other four cases, which did not contain symptoms overlapping with the six cases seen at the start of the study.

Interestingly, Mamede et al. (2010) found that second-year internal medicine residents seem to rely on the availability heuristic, showing a tendency to misdiagnose cases with overlapping similarities to those they had seen before. First-year residents did not demonstrate this tendency. Mamede et al. (2010) did not find this to be particularly surprising, suggesting that reliance on intuitive, as opposed to more methodical and analytical, reasoning increases with expertise in medicine, and speculating that there might be an even greater reliance on the availability heuristic in physicians with more experience. Future research in this area will be needed to uncover whether this is in fact the case. Furthermore, additional research is needed to assess whether any alternative models are better able to account for these data than the availability heuristic.

The availability heuristic over the lifespan

Developmental findings are consistent with the notion that using the availability heuristic to make likelihood or frequency judgments begins relatively early in life. In a study of 7- and 10-year-old children, Davies and White (1994) examined whether the famousness of names affected people's set-size judgments, as in Tversky and Kahneman's (1973) seminal study. To make accommodations for the children's likely knowledge base, Davies and White (1994) gathered the names of cartoon characters (human and animal) depicted in television shows and in newspapers. They first carried out a pilot test, in which they asked a separate group of children to rate these cartoon character names regarding whether they had heard of them before. These pilot data allowed them to determine how famous the names were to this age group. They created two short lists out of an initial collection of 143 names; one list contained nine famous human character names and ten less famous animal ones, and the other contained nine famous animal character names and ten less famous human ones. Children in both age groups were shown one of these lists and were then asked to recall as many names from that list as they could. Again, the logic was that the famous names should be more highly accessible from memory than the less famous names. Finally, the same children were asked to judge whether there were more human or animal names in the list they saw.

The results suggested that the availability heuristic influenced this final judgment in both groups of children (Davies & White 1994). Specifically, children erroneously judged the first list to contain more human than animal names and the second list to contain more animal than human names, even though the opposite was in fact the case. The heuristic appeared to have an even more powerful influence on the judgments of 7-year-olds than on those of 10-year-olds, but Davies and White (1994) pointed out that this may simply have been because the 7-year-olds actually happened to remember more famous names than did the 10-year-olds (which, in fact, they did). That is, the strength of the availability heuristic in their study can be explained solely by the accessibility of names, and wasn't necessarily affected by the difference in age between the two groups of children.

Although the availability heuristic itself appears early in the lifespan, the exact informational content that is most accessible may, of course, differ on average across generations or age groups. For example, Chou and Edge (2012) asked whether longer-term usage of Facebook among American college students influenced their judgments of how their friends' lives compared to their own. Of course, it has been well established that people put effort into presenting themselves in a positive light in general (Snyder 1974), but Facebook eliminates the many subtle non-verbal cues that characterize face-to-face interaction, and displays only what each person chooses to present publicly (Chou & Edge 2012). They found that the longer (in years) students had been using Facebook, the more they thought that others were happier than themselves and the less they agreed that life is fair. Hours spent using Facebook each week also predicted thinking that others were happier than themselves. Furthermore, the more Facebook friends they had whom they did not know personally, the more they felt that others had a better life than themselves. In contrast, the more hours they spent physically meeting and going out with friends each week, thereby engaging in face-to-face interaction, the more they disagreed that others had a better life or were happier than themselves.

Chou and Edge (2012) speculated that spending a great deal of time on Facebook might lead people to perceive and store a disproportionate number of positive events about their Facebook friends. As a result, this disproportionately heightened availability of positive events about others may lead people to judge that others' lives are overall better and happier than one's own. Given the possibility of such adverse downstream effects of the availability heuristic, it may be important for us to consider more deliberately how we control our own exposure to different sources of information.

The representativeness heuristic

Availability (or rather, accessibility) is only one of the types of information we use to make likelihood judgments under uncertainty. Recall the example from the beginning of this chapter: You've just been introduced to a new person at work, and you don't know whether that new person is a co-worker or a boss. To help you judge which is more likely, let's say you use your own, previously stored mental representation of the typical boss. If your mental representation of the typical boss is a person who is older, not younger, than you, then you might estimate whether this new person is older or younger than you and then make an inferential leap – a guess – about whether "co-worker" or "boss" is more likely to be the right label to apply. Or your mental representation of the typical boss might be more detailed than this. If the image that leaps to your mind when you hear the word "boss" is a sixty-something person wearing a suit and having a neat, conventional appearance, and the new person appears to be twenty-something and is sporting surfing shorts, lime green hair, and a nose piercing, you may judge the likelihood of her being a co-worker as being greater than the likelihood of her being your boss. (Of course, you could be wrong, and that again illustrates the nature of heuristics: They allow you to make very fast judgments that may turn out to be correct, but that can also lead you badly astray in individual cases.)

In the above case, you have made your judgment on the basis of the **representativeness heuristic**, in which "an event A is judged more probable than an event B whenever A appears more representative than B" (Kahneman & Tversky 1972, p. 431). **Representativeness** itself, Kahneman and Tversky (1972) went on to propose, is tricky to define, but in essence, it can be thought of in terms of two criteria. First, representativeness refers to how similar an example is to members of its class (e.g., how similar Joan's appearance is to the class of all bosses). Note again that your perception of how similar Joan's appearance is to the class of all bosses depends upon your own mental representation of bosses in general. According to Kahneman and Tversky (1972), this similarity judgment is the basis for your judgment about how likely she is to be a member of that class. For judgments about people, the mental representation may often essentially be a **stereotype** about the class; for judgments about objects and living kinds other than people, the representation can be thought of as a **prototype** or averaged representation of that class.

Second, representativeness can be a reflection of what people assume randomness looks like (Kahneman & Tversky 1972). If you ask people to create a random sequence of hypothetical fair coin toss outcomes, they tend to think that it should not contain any repeating patterns (e.g., H T T H T T H T T might typically be perceived as non-random; Kahneman & Tversky 1972). People also expect that ultimately, after a huge number of fair coin tosses, there will have been approximately the same number of heads and tails. More importantly, they expect that a smaller, representative sample of coin tosses should also contain approximately equal numbers of heads and tails (e.g., H H H H H H H H H would not be perceived as representative of the full set of fair coin tosses; Tversky & Kahneman 1971). This latter belief is known as the **law of small numbers**. However, because each coin toss is independent of the next, both of the above sequences of coin tosses are equally likely to occur. Tversky and Kahneman (1971) contrasted the law of small numbers with the **law of large numbers**, wherein one can reasonably expect a huge sample (e.g., of a trillion coin tosses) to be representative of the population (e.g., of all the coin tosses that have ever occurred). In the law of small numbers, people similarly assume that very small samples (e.g., a set of 9 coin tosses) should look representative of the population too, but in reality, this absolutely need not be the case.

The Tom W. problem

The representativeness heuristic has been demonstrated across a number of different paradigms. Kahneman and Tversky (1973) randomly assigned American university students to one of three experimental conditions in a now-classic study. One group of students was asked to consider 9 different areas of specialization in graduate training:

- Business administration
- Computer science
- Engineering
- Humanities and education
- Law
- Library science
- Medicine
- Physical and life sciences
- Social science and social work. (Kahneman & Tversky 1973, p. 238)

They were asked to estimate the percentage of all first-year U.S. graduate students currently enrolled in each of these 9 areas. That is, they were asked to give their estimates of the **base rates** of U.S. graduate students in these specializations.

A second group of students was given a description of the personality of a particular student named "Tom W." The student was described as follows:

> Tom W. is of high intelligence, although lacking in true creativity. He has a need for order and clarity, and for neat and tidy systems in which every detail finds its appropriate place. His writing is rather dull and mechanical, occasionally enlivened by somewhat corny puns and by flashes of imagination of the sci-fi type. He has a strong drive for competence. He seems to have little feel and little sympathy for other people and does not enjoy interacting with others. Self-centered, he nonetheless has a deep moral sense. (Kahneman & Tversky 1973, p. 238)

These students then rank-ordered the 9 above areas of specialization for how similar they thought Tom W. was to a prototypical graduate student in each of those areas (Kahneman & Tversky 1973). In other words, they judged how *representative* Tom was to their mental representations of what graduate students in those areas are like.

The third group of students read the same description of Tom W. Then, they were told that this description had been written when Tom was in high school, and that Tom was currently enrolled in graduate school. This group was asked to rank-order the 9 areas of graduate specialization with respect to how likely they thought it was that Tom had enrolled in that area (Kahneman & Tversky 1973). The driving question was whether perceived base rates (as measured in the first group) or representativeness (as measured in the second group) predicted judgments of the likelihood (as measured in the third group) that Tom W. belonged to a particular area of graduate specialization.

The results were quite striking: There was an almost-perfect positive correlation between judgments of the *likelihood* that Tom W. was in each area of graduate specialization and *how representative* Tom W. was thought to be of graduate students in each area of specialization (Kahneman & Tversky 1973). In contrast, base rates did not positively correlate with likelihood judgments – in fact, there was a strongly negative correlation between base rates and likelihood judgments. This was the case in part because the description of Tom W. was judged dissimilar, for example, to those studying humanities or the social sciences; yet these were two of the areas of specialization with the highest perceived base rates. Kahneman and Tversky (1973) suggested that people neglected their knowledge of base rates in making likelihood judgments, preferring instead to base their likelihood judgments on representativeness. Of course, it is possible that people did so on the assumption that the description of Tom W. was provided because the experimenters wanted them to use it. We'll return to this possibility later in this chapter.

The Linda problem

In a further test of the representativeness heuristic, Tversky and Kahneman (1983) presented the following description to university students in Canada:

> Linda is 31 years old, single, outspoken and very bright. She majored in philosophy. As a student, she was deeply concerned with issues of discrimination and social justice, and also participated in anti-nuclear demonstrations. (p. 297)

The students were then asked to choose which of the two options below was more probable:

> Linda is a bank teller.

> Linda is a bank teller and is active in the feminist movement. (Tversky & Kahneman 1983, p. 299)

Tversky and Kahneman (1983) argued that the correct answer is that the first statement is more probable than the second, citing the **conjunction rule**: The probability of two things *in conjunction* cannot be higher than the probability of either thing alone. In the case of Linda, the probability that she is both a bank teller and a feminist activist cannot be greater than the probability that she is a bank teller. The reason becomes apparent when you realize that the set of bank tellers *includes* bank tellers who are feminist activists. That is, the set of bank tellers comprises all bank tellers regardless of whatever else they also are. So if we suppose that at least some bank tellers out there are not also feminist activists, the set of bank tellers is going to be larger than the set of bank tellers who are also feminist activists. Yet 82% of participants in this study thought that the statement "Linda is a bank teller and is active in the feminist movement" was *more* probable than "Linda is a bank teller," a finding that Tversky and Kahneman (1983) called the con-junction fallacy.

However, as you may have noticed, people might very reasonably have read the statement "Linda is a bank teller" and interpreted it in this context to mean that "Linda is a bank teller (and is NOT active in the feminist move-ment)." If they made this assumption, then the conjunction rule should not apply. That is, they would have been simply judging whether, among all bank tellers, more are feminist activists than not. Tversky and Kahneman (1983) ruled out this possibility by conducting another version of the study in which they replaced the first statement, "Linda is a bank teller," with the statement "Linda is a bank teller whether or not she is active in the feminist movement." Yet a majority of participants in this version of the study *still* judged the statement "Linda is a bank teller and is active in the feminist movement" to be more probable than "Linda is a bank teller whether or not she is active in the feminist movement," again demonstrating the conjunc-tion fallacy.

Tversky and Kahneman (1983) also acknowledged that people frequently use connectives (e.g., or; and) in a way that is different from how they are used in formal logic (and in their studies). To address this issue, in one study, they asked American students in 1980 to imagine that the legendary Swedish tennis player Bjorn Borg would reach the Wimbledon finals the following year. The students were asked to predict the results of that hypothetical future match. At the time they were presented with this problem, Borg had just won Wimbledon for the fifth time and was considered the most dominant player in men's tennis. When asked to rank what was more likely to occur, that Borg would lose the first set or that Borg would lose the first set but win the match, they judged the second to be more probable, sug-gesting support for the representativeness heuristic. However, Tversky and

Kahneman (1983) wondered whether people were simply reading the second option – that Borg would lose the first set but win the match – in a different way than they had intended. It was possible, for example, that people were instead assuming that this meant either Borg would lose the first set OR win the match, or that Borg's losing the first set implied that he would win the match, or that he would lose the first set if he won the match. Any of these interpretations, among others, would mean that their judgments were technically correct and not necessarily the result of relying on representativeness.

To rule out this possibility, Tversky and Kahneman (1983) presented another group of American students with sequences depicting the hypothetical results of different five-set matches. For example, in one sequence, Borg was described as having lost the first set, won the second and third sets, lost the fourth, and won the fifth set and the match. Then, people were asked to judge whether any of these sequences were consistent with the statement "Borg would lose the first set but win the match." As it turns out, the only sequences they judged to be consistent with the statement were ones that met both conditions, with Borg both losing the first set *and* winning the match. Given these findings, Tversky and Kahneman (1983) argued that people did understand the intended meaning of the conjunctive sentence, and held to their argument that people were using the representativeness heuristic to make these likelihood judgments.

The representativeness heuristic: Alternative views

Hertwig and Gigerenzer (1999), however, presented a thoughtful alternative spin on the representativeness heuristic, offering some challenges to Tversky and Kahneman's (1983) interpretation of the classic studies on the Linda problem. A key question they raised was how people, when asked to judge which statement about Linda is more probable, interpret the word "probable" (Hertwig & Gigerenzer 1999). Tversky and Kahneman (1983) meant for people to interpret that word in the mathematical sense (e.g., pertaining to "certainty," "frequency," etc.). In contrast, Hertwig and Gigerenzer (1999) suspected that people instead tend to interpret the word "probable" in a non-mathematical sense (e.g., pertaining to "possibility," "correspondence," "applicability," etc.). If people tend to interpret the word "probable" to have a non-mathematical meaning, such that they believe they are being asked to judge whether being a bank teller and a feminist activist to be more "applicable" to Linda than just being a bank teller, then there is nothing wrong with their judgments per se.

To test this possibility, Hertwig and Gigerenzer (1999) first asked students in Germany to give their responses to the Linda problem. Then, they showed the students a list of mathematical and non-mathematical interpretations of the word "probable" and asked them to indicate which reflected what they understood the word to mean in the Linda problem. Overall, 18% of responses were mathematical, and most were non-mathematical. Of the 15 students who gave the typical response to the Linda problem itself (i.e., judging Linda's being a bank teller and active in the feminist movement to be more probable than Linda's being a bank teller), 12 did not give a mathematical meaning for the word "probable." Hertwig and Gigerenzer (1999) suggested that the apparent use of the representativeness heuristic in Tversky and Kahneman's (1983) work may instead be attributed to reasonable responses made by people inferring a non-mathematical meaning of the word probable. This work opens an interesting avenue for further discussion and inquiry. Since there have also been many demonstrations of the representativeness heuristic outside the Linda paradigm, additional research is needed to determine how broadly this alternative account can be appropriately applied.

The representativeness heuristic and stereotypes

The above-described classic literature on the representativeness heuristic has close ties with social psychological work on how stereotypes influence our judgments about other people. In early work, Bodenhausen and Wyer (1985) suggested that stereotypes themselves operate as a heuristic, or quick rule of thumb, that we use to figure out other people's behaviors. In one study, they presented American students with one of two cases of convicted criminals. One, "Ashley Chamberlaine of Cambridge, Massachusetts," was so named by the researchers to evoke Americans' stereotypes of a non-Hispanic white upper-class female; the other, "Carlos Ramirez of Albuquerque, New Mexico," was named to evoke their stereotypes of a Hispanic male. Pre-testing showed that another sample of people from this same population thought "Ashley" to be more likely to have committed forgery than assault (thereby establishing how people were likely to stereotype her case). The same people expected "Carlos" to be more likely to have committed assault than forgery. Bodenhausen and Wyer (1985) further found that these stereotypes operated as the initial basis for people's judgments about Ashley's and Carlos' likely future behavior if the crime was congruent with their stereotypes. That is, if they read that Ashley had in fact committed forgery, they thought she was more likely to commit the same crime again than if they read that she had committed assault. If they read that Carlos had committed assault, they thought he was more likely to relapse than if they read that he had committed forgery. This reliance on stereotype-congruent behaviors to make predictions about future behavior held true even when other reasonable explanations were given for the behavior (e.g., "experiencing great frustration in his personal life").

Although Bodenhausen and Wyer (1985) did not directly claim that there was any conceptual overlap between their conclusions and the representativeness heuristic, it is clear that they are fundamentally quite similar in at least one respect. In both, the general idea is that a person's apparent *representativeness* of a particular group (e.g., the supposed similarity of "Ashley Chamberlaine's" name to people who are female, relatively wealthy, and non-Hispanic white) is used for judging how likely that person is to behave in ways one believes to be typical of that group (e.g., to be the kind of person more likely to commit forgery more than once than to commit assault more than once). In general, it appears that the vast literature on stereotyping can add significantly to our understanding of how assumptions about representativeness may influence our everyday judgments.

The representativeness heuristic and WEIRD psychology research

Finally, it is important to consider how the representativeness heuristic might guide the reasoning of researchers who study judgment and decision-making and other human behaviors and cognition. The majority of researchers conducting studies on the human mind carry out their work in Western, industrialized countries, and it seems inevitable that they must be influenced by assumptions of representativeness. That is, in the majority of research on human behaviors and cognition, the assumption has often been that people in Western, educated, industrialized, rich, democratic countries (i.e., WEIRD; Henrich, Heine, & Norenzayan 2010) represent the prototypical human being, and that we can extrapolate from such populations to human beings in the rest of the world.

In an extensive review of a number of different fields of study in psychology and related fields (e.g., visual perception, moral reasoning, categorization, etc.), Henrich et al. (2010) reported that the results of studies can differ depending on the population (e.g., country) upon which the study is conducted. For example, well-known visual illusions such as the Müller-Lyer illusion are not found in populations living in spatial environments that differ from those living in WEIRD societies. They also found that in comparing the results of very similar studies conducted across countries, the results of those conducted in WEIRD societies are often extreme outliers, rather than at the median. For example, Henrich et al. (2010) reviewed work on economic decision-making across cultures, in which it is clearly apparent that lay people's opinions about what constitutes a fair deal differ quite radically across countries. On the basis of this finding and numerous others, they argued that WEIRD study participants are actually quite profoundly *un*representative of the world's population of humans, whereas they have often been assumed by researchers to be representative (Henrich et al. 2010).

Again, it is likely that the majority of researchers in psychology and related fields are themselves members of WEIRD populations, living and working within WEIRD societies. It stands to reason that even the questions about human behavior that these researchers choose to study are based on their observations and findings about WEIRD populations (Henrich et al. 2010). Bennis and Medin (2010) pointed out that WEIRD people are not necessarily *especially* unrepresentative of humans, as it stands to reason that they would perform as outliers on a task that was especially designed within a WEIRD culture to study that particular population. If tasks were designed within non-WEIRD cultures to study non-WEIRD populations, it would not be surprising to find that those populations also seemed to be apparent outliers on those tasks when expanded across populations. Yet the overall message from this work is clear: In conducting research about human behavior, it matters what assumptions we make about the representativeness of the population one is studying, the research questions we are choosing to ask, and most importantly, the conclusions we are drawing from the data. We will return to the logic of scientific inquiry in Chapter 12.

Questions for discussion

1. Henrich et al. (2010) argued that it is important for researchers and students to avoid assuming that study participants from WEIRD societies are necessarily representative of humans more generally. Note that in the literature on the availability and representativeness heuristics, many (though not all) study participants were even more narrowly sampled from WEIRD university students. Do you think a broader sample of lay adults might change the results of any one of the studies discussed in this chapter? If so, how and why?

2. Consider again Hertwig and Gigerenzer's (1999) challenge to Kahneman and Tversky's (1983) evidence for the conjunction fallacy. Which side of the debate holds up more strongly, in your opinion, and why? What questions remain to be examined in this debate?

3. Follow up on the conjunction fallacy debate by reading the original Kahneman and Tversky (1983) and Hertwig and Gigerenzer (1999) papers. What issues has each of these research teams examined that the other did not?

Suggestions for further reading

Henrich, J., Heine, S. J., & Norenzayan, A. (2010). The weirdest people in the world? *Behavioral and Brain Sciences, 33*(2–3), 1–75.

Hertwig, R., & Gigerenzer, G. (1999). The "conjunction fallacy" revisited: How intelligent inferences look like reasoning errors. *Journal of Behavioral Decision Making, 12,* 275–305.

Tversky, A., & Kahneman, D. (1973). Availability: A heuristic for judging frequency and probability. *Cognitive Psychology, 5*(2), 207–232.

Tversky, A., & Kahneman, D. (1983). Extensional versus intuitive reasoning: The conjunction fallacy in probability judgment. *Psychological Review, 90*(4), 293–315.

3 Anchoring and Primacy Effects in Judgment

Learning Goals

By the end of this chapter, you will have:

- Considered again the central problem of how people intuitively make likelihood judgments under uncertainty; specifically, whether information received first has a disproportionate influence on such judgments.
- Critically evaluated empirical evidence for primacy effects and for anchoring-and-adjustment effects on judgments.
- Understood and evaluated the claims of the belief-adjustment model, an influential cognitive process model describing how people's beliefs are updated to account for new evidence.
- Considered evidence for boundary conditions (i.e., limitations) on anchoring, including the nature of the anchor and the manner in which it is presented.
- Evaluated whether and how anchoring effects play a role in judgments outside the laboratory (e.g., medical diagnosis; sales and marketing), and what consequences they might have.
- Considered potential ways to eliminate anchoring and possible directions for future research.

Key Terms

Primacy effect	Attribute substitution
Belief-adjustment model	Selective Accessibility Model
Anchor	Numeric priming theory
Anchoring-and-adjustment	Cross-modal anchoring effect
Heuristic (updated definition)	Cross-scale anchoring effect

Suppose that you have graduated from school, have been working for a few years, and are attempting to manage your finances as well as possible. You own a small condominium and, thinking that you might be able to unload it for a profit, plan to put it up for sale on the real estate market. But you find conflicting information on the internet regarding the best strategy for choosing a listing price. Does the listing price – the price at which the condo will be advertised – sway people's judgments of the likely true value of your home and, in turn, affect how much they are willing to pay? Is underpricing the best strategy, in that it might attract more people to look at your condo, or will overpricing help elevate the price at which it is eventually purchased?

Or suppose that a close friend has invited you for a visit during a short school holiday. After a journey of several hours, you disembark from your train and await your friend outside the station. Minutes tick by. You approach a newspaper vendor and purchase a newspaper marked with the date: December 20. As you glance at the date, you wonder how much longer you are going to have to wait before your friend shows up. Having just read the number 20, will it influence your intuitive estimate of how much longer you are likely to have to wait? For example, will you guess that you'll have to wait a little less than 20 minutes, starting from 20 minutes and then taking into account your knowledge that your friend has usually been on time in the past? Or does the number 20 have no influence of your estimate at all, given that you are perfectly aware that it is just a date printed on a newspaper, having absolutely nothing to do with your friend's arrival?

Finally, suppose that you have landed an interview for your dream job, and you are preparing for the big day. Everyone from your grandparents to your taxi driver tells you that first impressions matter. If this is true, then what exactly is happening in your interviewers' minds when that initial impression is made? How does this early mental representation continue to influence how they process new, additional information about you? How does this mental representation ultimately affect their judgments of how likely you are to be competent, hardworking, or a good match for the position? In each of these examples, and throughout the current chapter, we ask whether, and how, initially presented information disproportionately affects likelihood judgments under conditions of uncertainty. Just as for the availability and representativeness heuristics considered in Chapter 2, the effects of initial information on likelihood judgments have been described as Type 1 reasoning under the organizing framework of dual-process models (Kahneman 2003, 2011; Chapter 1). Later in this chapter, we'll also consider ways in which Type 2 reasoning might be leveraged to counteract such effects when they are unwanted.

Early work: The primacy effect in impression formation

In 1946, Solomon Asch famously observed that people are able to develop an impression of another person immediately and very easily, and he asked how a single global impression of a person is integrated from the different things we know about the person. For example, we might be told that a person is cheerful, practical, and selfish. This list of traits helps us create an overall impression of that person, leading us to make inferences about the kind of person this is and how he or she probably generally behaves.

Asch (1946) asked whether the same set of traits would always give rise to the same overall impression no matter what, or whether the order in which one learns about the person's traits matters. He asked one group of people to listen to the following traits in this order: *intelligent, industrious, impulsive, critical, stubborn, envious*. Another group listened to the exact same traits read in the opposite order: *envious, stubborn, critical, impulsive, industrious, intelligent*. People were then asked to give an overall description of this person. Their descriptions, according to Asch (1946), suggested that the first traits that they read became the background context against which the other traits were then interpreted. Specifically, those who first heard that the person was intelligent and industrious immediately thought the person was likely to be quite accomplished, and when they heard the latter negative traits, they tended to say that these were probably a consequence of the initial, positive traits. For example, they might say that the person tends to be critical and stubborn because he is smart, knows what he is talking about, and therefore knows when other people don't make sense. In contrast, those who first heard that the person was envious and stubborn tended to speculate that the person was unsuccessful and poorly adjusted overall, and that the positive traits would probably be overwhelmed by the person's negative traits.

Asch (1946) also asked people to indicate whether they thought the person would also have a number of traits not mentioned at all in the list (e.g., *humorous; good-looking*). In this task, people's judgments also sometimes differed quite radically depending on the order in which they had heard the person's traits. When judgments did differ, the *intelligent*-first order generally lead people to endorse positive traits more than did the *envious*-first order. For example, 52% of those who heard the *intelligent*-first order thought the person would also be *humorous*, whereas only 21% of those who heard the *envious*-first order endorsed this trait. And 74% of those hearing *intelligent* first thought the person would be *good-looking*, as opposed to only 35% of those hearing *envious* first. Keep in mind that people in both order conditions were hearing identical traits, differing only in the order presented. These findings suggest not only that people's general global impressions of the person were influenced by the order of presentation of traits, but also that people were willing to infer the presence of other traits that matched these global impressions in terms of general positivity or negativity.

An important remaining question was whether people are still influenced by the order in which they learn about traits when they realize that order is being manipulated, or whether they override the effect of primacy. To examine whether this is the case, Asch (1946) also ran a within-subject version of the study, asking the same people to read both versions and make the same judgments after each. Interestingly, 14 of 24 people who read the same list of traits in the two different orders simply reported that their impressions of the person changed across the two readings. One commented: "You read the list in a different order and thereby caused a different type of person to come to mind. This one is smarter, more likeable, a go-getter, lively, headstrong" (Asch 1946, p. 271). That is, they seemed to be aware of the influence of primacy but did not seem to compensate for it. Those who did not report changing impressions, in contrast, tended to report that they had tried to avoid making any judgments until after they had heard the entire list of traits (Asch 1946). Coincidentally, this latter finding suggests a possible strategy for overriding the effect.

Asch's (1946) essential findings were replicated by Anderson and Barrios (1961), who showed that the first traits heard about another person have a disproportionately strong influence on people's overall favorability ratings of that person. To examine more precisely how this so-called **primacy effect** comes about, Anderson (1965) used a tightly controlled experimental design, systematically varying the order in which the positive and negative traits describing a person were presented. In one set of experimental conditions, three positive traits were presented together in unbroken sequence, placed among three negative traits. The positive traits began either in the first position (ending in the third), second (ending in the fourth), third (ending in the fifth), or fourth (ending in the sixth). In yet another set of experimental conditions, the three negative traits were instead presented together in unbroken sequence, in the above positions (Anderson 1965). Participants viewed the traits and then separately judged how favorably they felt about the person and how much liking they felt for the person, both on 1–8 Likert scales.

The results showed a relatively clean linear effect of primacy. That is, the influence of the group of three positive (or negative) traits in each condition was strongest when they were presented first, next strongest when presented second, and so on, such that its influence dropped by about the same amount for each step it was removed from the first position (Anderson 1965). Anderson (1965) suggested that a weighted-average model could account for this pattern of data, meaning that the weight or importance of each group of three positive (or negative) traits is systematically decreased depending on presentation order. The earlier a trait is mentioned in the sequence, the more influence it has on the final overall impression one forms of the person (Anderson 1965).

As Asch (1946) noted, which strategy people adopt in making judgments can determine whether a primacy effect occurs. Stewart (1965) expanded upon Asch's (1946) findings, asking American undergraduates to complete a modified version of Anderson's (1965) task. All participants completed ratings for a total of 72 sets of traits, each set describing one person. For half of these sets of traits, they made repeated favorability ratings (0–8 scale) for the person, once after each trait was presented. For the other half, they made a single favorability rating (same 0–8 scale) for each person only once, after all the person's traits had been presented (as in the previous studies described). Also, for each set of traits, either all positive traits were presented first, followed by an equal number of negative traits, or vice-versa. Finally, Stewart (1965) reran the study to test whether any effects found would be replicated. He found that when people made a single favorability rating only after all traits were presented, the primacy effect was found both times that he ran the study. In contrast, when favorability ratings were repeatedly made after each trait was presented, the primacy effect was no longer reliable, and in fact, a recency effect was found (though this latter effect was found only in the first run of the study and was not replicated in the second run).

Taken together, Anderson's (1965) and Stewart's (1965) studies confirmed that there is a reliable primacy effect of early-presented traits on people's overall favorability judgments. However, neither directly addressed the other part of Asch's (1946) claim – that traits presented earlier change how people interpret the meaning of the traits presented later. Hogarth and Einhorn (1992) adopted and tested this latter idea in their **belief-adjustment model** – a descriptive, more general model of belief updating based on the idea that impressions are formed from initial evidence and then updated as new information comes in. In their model, three subprocesses influence how people make their overall judgments: (1) How the evidence is *encoded* (i.e., whether it is encoded relative to a current, but changing, prior belief, or whether it is encoded relative to a constant value); (2) whether the evidence is *processed* piece by piece as it is received or only once after all the evidence has been received; and (3) how the *adjustment* or updating process is carried out (Hogarth & Einhorn 1992). Let's unpack each of these subprocesses in more detail.

In the encoding process, people start out with initial beliefs (i.e., the **anchor**), and whenever they receive new evidence, it is received in the context of those existing beliefs (Hogarth & Einhorn 1992). They might then apply this new evidence toward achieving their own immediate goals. If their goal is to use that evidence to *test a hypothesis* (e.g., suppose that a manager hypothesizes that a particular job candidate is the right person to hire), then the new evidence is encoded as either confirming or disconfirming the hypothesis under consideration (e.g., the job candidate has versus does not have the right experience). Accordingly, that new evidence will either increase or decrease belief in the hypothesis (whether that candidate is right for the job; Hogarth & Einhorn 1992). (Hypothesis testing is further discussed in detail in Chapter 12.) If, instead, their goal is to *make an estimate* given that evidence (e.g., gauging how much they like a person), then their estimates will shift either up or down depending on the relationship of the evidence to the liking they already held for that person (i.e., the anchor; Hogarth & Einhorn 1992). For example, if the evidence is only mildly positive (e.g., the person smiles just a little bit more than the average person) and they already liked the person a great deal, it might actually bring down liking a little bit. If the evidence is mildly positive and they already strongly disliked the person, it would increase liking (e.g., they might then only moderately dislike the person).

It also matters, according to Hogarth and Einhorn (1992), exactly how the evidence is processed (i.e., the second subprocess in the belief-adjustment model). That is, it matters whether the evidence is processed as each new piece is received, or whether it is only processed a single time after all evidence has been received, just as we saw in the previous section (Stewart 1965). In the first case, people's overall judgment (e.g., of how much they like the person) anchors on the initial piece of evidence and is then adjusted in response to each piece of new evidence that comes in. In the second, their impression is automatically anchored on the initial piece (or perhaps first few pieces) of evidence, and then the remainder of the evidence drives a single adjustment based on some aggregate, or summarizing, of that evidence. Hogarth and Einhorn (1992) also suggested that the latter mode of processing might be more computationally taxing than the first, and that people may switch to the first mode if they find they don't currently have the cognitive resources to carry out the full computation (e.g., if they are tired, or pressed for time).

Finally, the adjustment subprocess itself may matter: Hogarth and Einhorn (1992) made a *contrast assumption*, suggesting that the degree of contrast between the anchor and a new piece of evidence predicts how much impact that evidence has on people's estimates. For example, if people's prior belief (i.e., anchor) in a hypothesis is weakly positive, and a piece of evidence comes in that is strongly negative, this will affect their position (pulling it away from endorsement of the hypothesis), but not radically. In contrast, if people's prior beliefs were already strongly positive, and the same piece of strongly negative evidence was presented, the large degree of contrast between the initial position (anchor) and the new evidence can be expected to more radically affect their position (Hogarth & Einhorn 1992). For a piece of strongly positive evidence, the reverse was predicted to occur: It would affect a weakly positive prior belief in the hypothesis more than it would affect a strongly positive prior belief. In sum, the belief-adjustment model suggests that early evidence provides a starting point against which later evidence is assessed, a notion echoed in the parallel literature on the anchoring-and-adjustment effect.

Early work: Seminal demonstrations of anchoring-and-adjustment

When people are asked to estimate numerical answers to problems, they appear to be similarly affected by the order in which information is presented; that is, they are disproportionately influenced by information presented first. In a seminal study of quick estimates, Tversky and Kahneman (1973) gave Israeli high school students 5 seconds to provide an answer to a mathematics problem. Some of the students were asked to estimate $1 \times 2 \times 3 \times 4 \times 5 \times 6 \times 7 \times 8$; the rest were asked to estimate $8 \times 7 \times 6 \times 5 \times 4 \times 3 \times 2 \times 1$. The first group gave a median estimate of 512; the second group a median estimate of 2,250. Tversky and Kahneman (1973) initially interpreted these results to suggest that the students were making use of availability, but later reinterpreted it as a demonstration of **anchoring-and-adjustment**, a separate heuristic in its own right (Tversky & Kahneman 1974). They defined this heuristic, simply, as one in which "people make estimates by starting from an initial value that is adjusted to yield the final answer" (Tversky & Kahneman 1974, p. 1128). They noted that relying on this heuristic can be problematic when an insufficient adjustment is made from that initial anchor, and that this may occur quite frequently. Also worth noting is that in the above problem, the answer is 40,320. The fact that both groups of students radically underestimated the correct answer is easily explained in that *both* conditions provided an anchor that was much, much smaller than 40,320 (i.e., anchors of 1 and 8, respectively).

More profoundly, an anchor value affects judgments even when there is no rational reason to think that that value is even relevant to the task. This is evidenced by people's judgments on the wheel of fortune task (Tversky & Kahneman 1974), which revealed that the anchor does not even need to be relevant to the problem to influence judgments. People in this study were asked to make percentage-based estimates of different quantities (e.g., the percentage of member countries of the United Nations that were on the African continent).

For each estimate, the experimenter first spun a "wheel of fortune," which would land on a number between 0 and 100. Each person had to say first whether his or her estimate was higher or lower than that number, and then to make a specific estimate. Despite the arbitrary nature of the number provided by the wheel of fortune, these anchors still affected people's estimates. For example, in estimating the percentage of countries in the United Nations located in Africa, people for whom the wheel of fortune gave 10 as a starting point estimated 25 on average. In contrast, people for whom the wheel of fortune gave 65 as a starting point estimated 45 on average.

Box 3.1: Is Anchoring-and-Adjustment a Heuristic?

Anchoring-and-adjustment is no longer technically classified as a **heuristic**, according to Kahneman and Frederick (2002). In this paper, they gave a new definition of the term heuristic, explaining that a clear definition was never given in the seminal Tversky and Kahneman (1974) paper. Specifically, they argued that "judgment is mediated by a heuristic when an individual assesses a specified target attribute of a judgment object by substituting another property of that object – the heuristic attribute – which comes more readily to mind" (Kahneman & Frederick 2002, p. 53). In other words, we can say that a heuristic is influencing a judgment when people try to answer a hard question by instead answering an easier one.

Representativeness and availability, described in Chapter 2, are both heuristics by this definition. Suppose you are asked to make a complex probability judgment (e.g., estimate the likelihood that Alex, a quiet person, is a librarian). The availability heuristic would come into play if you swap probability information that is hard to think about (e.g., estimates of the base rate of librarians in the world; estimates of the likelihood that a person is a librarian if known to be quiet; etc.) for easily available information (e.g., if you are easily able to call to mind a couple of quiet librarians you've known in the past, you might give a rather high estimate). The representativeness heuristic would be said to influence your judgments if you swap the above complex probability information for representative information (e.g., you have a stereotype of librarians as introverted folks, and Alex is a quiet person, so you make your judgment accordingly). Thus, you can say that your judgment was influenced by a heuristic when you (knowingly or unknowingly) engage in **attribute substitution** – that is, when you substitute an attribute that is easier for you to think about for the attribute you are supposed to be judging.

Given the new definition, Kahneman and Frederick (2002) and Kahneman (2003) suggested that anchoring-and-adjustment, the third of the original three heuristics named in Tversky and Kahneman (1974), should not be classified as a heuristic per se. After all, anchoring-and-adjustment involves no attribute substitution, but instead involves making a particular value of the attribute being judged seem more possible. For example, when estimating the proportion of United Nations member countries in Africa, people might never have thought it could be as low as ten, but when that number was presented by the wheel of fortune, it seemed more possible that it *could* be on the lower side. Kahneman and Frederick (2002) suggested that the affect heuristic (Slovic et al. 2007; see also Chapters 1, 5, and 14), in which a person's negatively or positively valenced feeling of emotion is substituted for other information in making judgments, should be listed instead as the third major cross-cutting heuristic. Even so, anchoring-and-adjustment remains an extremely robust phenomenon that has a powerful impact on judgments by making particular values temporarily salient (Kahneman 2003).

Anchoring-and-adjustment: Understanding the adjustment process

One alternative account of the classic findings above is that there may not actually be an adjustment process per se (Chapman & Johnson 2002). Instead, according to this alternative account, the Selective Accessibility Model, what may be happening is that when the anchor value is presented, associated information is also made temporarily more accessible (Bahník & Strack 2016; Strack & Mussweiler 1997). For example, if you are trying to guess the height of the Burj Khalifa in Dubai, and you are presented with the number 15, you may retrieve many memories of relatively small buildings and come up with an estimate that falls far short of the correct answer (830 meters or 2,722 feet). That is, the information you retrieve from memory to help you make the estimate tends to be information that is consistent with the anchor. As a result, your estimate will be disproportionately close to that anchor. As you can see, by this account it is possible that no adjustment from the anchor actually takes place.

Epley and Gilovich (2001) suggested, however, that whether adjustment takes place depends on whether you are given an anchor (e.g., the experimenter suggests a value) or you come up with the anchor yourself. When you are *given* an anchor, you first have to consider whether it is itself the correct answer. In contrast, people might think differently about anchors they came up with themselves. For example, suppose you are asked to estimate the freezing point of vodka (Epley & Gilovich 2001). You will probably first, and quite easily, dredge up your own factual memory of the freezing point of water (0°C/32°F). In this case, you've self-generated your own anchor. You may also, along with many others, already know that the freezing point of alcohol is lower than the freezing point of water (Epley & Gilovich 2001). The only point at which you are actually reasoning about the estimate is when you are trying to figure out *how much* lower the freezing point of vodka might be than the freezing point of water. At no time thus far did you actually think that you knew the freezing point of vodka and could retrieve it directly from memory (i.e., you always knew that the anchor of 0°C/32°F was not itself the correct answer, and that an adjustment had to be made; Epley & Gilovich 2001). Accordingly, Epley and Gilovich (2001) suggested that when people generate their own anchors – as in the freezing point of water in the example above – the anchoring effect comes from an insufficient adjustment from that anchor, just as Tversky and Kahneman (1974) originally proposed.

To test this claim, they asked American undergraduate students to make four estimates. Epley and Gilovich (2001) expected two of those estimates to cause the students to automatically come up with anchors. For example, we can reasonably expect the question "When was Washington elected president?" to lead American students to automatically think of the year 1776, when the U.S. declared its independence, given that Washington was America's first president (Epley & Gilovich 2001, p. 392). It is also reasonable to expect these students to know that Washington would have become president after, not before, the Declaration of Independence, as these are facts that American children are generally taught in primary school.

The other two estimates were presented along with an experimenter-given anchor (e.g., "What is the mean length of a whale?" [69 feet]; Epley & Gilovich 2001, p. 392). After making each of these four estimates, the students explained the process by which they had decided on each estimate. Among those who reported coming up with the expected self-generated anchors (e.g., the year 1776), almost all reported an adjustment process (94%; Epley & Gilovich 2001). For the estimates in which the experimenter provided an anchor (e.g., 69 feet), significantly fewer participants explicitly described an adjustment process (22%; Epley & Gilovich 2001).

Exactly when the adjustment process can be expected to occur and the precise nature of the process have also been debated over the years (Wilson,

Houston, Etling, & Brekke 1996). The traditional "insufficient adjustment" account is that people start from the anchor and adjust from that starting point, but that they tend not to adjust quite far enough to be accurate (Tversky & Kahneman 1974). Others have suggested, following Lopes (1985), that an averaging process may best explain adjustment; that is, any new value is integrated with the old value such that the estimate will fall between the two (Wilson et al. 1996), though it may not be psychologically plausible to expect people to automatically calculate such averages. Quattrone, Lawrence, Finkel, and Andrus (1984), in contrast, proposed that the adjustment process essentially shifts the estimate from the anchor to fit just within a plausible range. Despite these slight variations regarding the exact calculation underlying adjustment, all of these proposals have in common the fundamental argument that there is an adjustment process most frequently triggered by self-generated anchors, and that it involves attempting to come to a moderate estimate, tempered by the anchor.

Anchoring-and-adjustment: Boundary conditions

Although anchoring-and-adjustment is easily demonstrated, it has been a trickier task to identify the precise conditions under which the influence of anchors is particularly strong versus weak. As we saw, Tversky and Kahneman's (1974) initial demonstrations showed that random numerical anchors (e.g., the number spun on a wheel of fortune) that are irrelevant to the judgment being made (e.g., an estimate of the number of African countries in the United Nations) nonetheless produce anchoring effects. However, it was still not clear from this work whether the degree of irrelevance of the anchor to the judgment predicts the degree to which it influences judgments. Because of this, one central theme of follow-up work has been to assess whether there are boundary conditions on anchoring-and-adjustment.

Extreme or implausible anchors

Even extreme anchors – those that are so high or so low that they are absolutely implausible – have been shown to influence people's estimates. Strack and Mussweiler (1997) presented German university students with both plausible and implausible anchors for a variety of judgments. Before this, in pre-testing, they determined which values fell within a standard deviation of people's mean estimates, and which values were ten or more standard deviations from those means. The former served as the plausible anchors, and the latter served as the implausible (extreme) anchors. For example, when people were asked to estimate the age to which Mohandas Gandhi lived, they were first given either a plausible anchor of 64 or 79 years old, or an implausible anchor of 9 or 140 years old, and asked to say whether they thought Gandhi's age was above or below that number. They were then asked to provide a numerical estimate of Gandhi's age. Strack and Mussweiler (1997) found a strong anchoring effect overall. Much more astonishingly, they also found that the effect of anchors on judgments did not differ for plausible versus implausible anchors; both types of anchors influenced judgments.

Other studies replicated the finding that both plausible and implausible anchors affect judgments, although some of this work also indicated that plausibility does moderate the strength of the effect. Chapman and Johnson (1994), for example, tested between several hypotheses regarding the relationship between anchor extremity and the strength of the anchoring effect (see also a more comprehensive review; Chapman & Johnson 2002). One hypothesis was that the more extreme the anchor, the greater the influence on judgments (linear function). A second hypothesis was that as the anchor approaches the extremes, the increase in its influence is attenuated, such that the effects of anchors reach an asymptote. Finally, a third hypothesis was that anchors at the extremes create a contrast effect: The extremeness of the anchor is so implausible that judgments are skewed in the opposite direction to that of the anchor.

Chapman and Johnson (1994) tested between these three hypotheses by presenting American undergraduate students with a series of lotteries (e.g., a lottery in which one either had a 53% chance of winning $22.91 USD or a 47% chance of winning $67.13 USD). For each lottery, students considered an anchor that was either extreme (i.e., fell outside the range of values one could win in that lottery; e.g., $4.37 USD or $83.02 USD) or reasonable (i.e., fell within the range of values one could win in that lottery; e.g., $30.58 USD or $56.30 USD). Students first indicated whether they would sell the lottery for the anchor amount exactly, more than that amount, or less than that amount. Then, they were asked to report the minimum amount of money they *would* accept in exchange for that lottery. The results showed a pattern of results most strongly consistent with their second hypothesis: Extreme anchors do affect judgments, but their effect is diminished relative to that of more reasonable anchors.

Subliminally presented anchors

The anchoring-and-adjustment effect is so robust (Furnham & Boo 2011) that the question arose as to whether it might even appear for anchors that are not consciously perceived. If found to be true, such an effect could have intriguing implications for swaying people's judgments without their knowledge. Past research suggested that anchoring can occur when people see the anchor but are not asked to make any deliberate comparison at all (Wilson et al. 1996). Other research exploring the boundary conditions of anchoring showed that the anchor does not necessarily have to be presented to a person just before the judgment, as people are also influenced by widely known numerical landmarks even when these do not directly answer the question. For example, recall that Epley and Gilovich (2001) showed that when American undergraduates were asked to judge the year in which George Washington was elected as the first president of the U.S., they first anchored on the date that is much more well known among Americans (1776, the signing of the Declaration of Independence) and adjusted to a mean estimate just a few years later than this. The majority of students in their study, when asked to explain how they arrived at their answer, described an anchoring-and-adjustment process (Epley & Gilovich 2001).

Thus, pushing still further at the boundaries of the anchoring effect, Mussweiler and Englich (2005) directly tested whether even subliminally presented anchors might influence judgments. They presented German university students with subliminal primes of an anchor while they were in the process of making a specific estimate. Students in their study were asked to fixate on the middle of a computer screen while they were thinking about the answer to a question. They were presented with the question on the screen for 3 seconds ("What is the annual mean temperature in Germany?"). A nonsense string of letters (*MBUTGEPL*) was then presented for 60 seconds. During that 60 seconds, a single anchor value (i.e., either 5 or 20) was presented for 15 milliseconds (i.e., too briefly to be consciously registered) every 6 seconds. They then gave their estimate in response to the initially presented question. In pre-testing with another group of German students, Mussweiler and Englich (2005) found that unanchored responses to this question had a mean of 13.6°C. They chose the low and high anchor values (i.e., 5 and 20) around this mean.

Participants were probed for their awareness of the subliminal anchor with seven questions that first asked generally whether they noticed anything particular about the study and then became more and more specific, revealing the purpose of the study (Mussweiler & Englich 2005). For example, in the last of these questions, participants were told that numbers were presented when the letter string was on the screen, and they were asked if they saw those numbers and whether they could say what the numbers were. Only two participants reported any suspicions regarding the apparent "flickering of the letter string." The results, whether calculated with or without the data from those two participants, showed that people made significantly higher judgments of temperature in the high subliminal anchor condition (mean judgment of 14.9°C) than in the low subliminal anchor condition (mean judgment of 12.8°C; Mussweiler & Englich 2005). Follow-up work showed that this result was replicated for another judgment (i.e., estimating car prices; Mussweiler & Englich 2005).

Perhaps the most likely explanation for subliminal anchoring effects such as these is that the anchor works as a prime: When presented, the anchor value may be temporarily more accessible (Reitsma-van Rooijen & Daamen 2006). According to the **numeric priming theory** of anchoring, people then come up with an estimate that is some weighted combination of the anchor value and other potentially relevant values that have also been primed or activated (Reitsma-van Rooijen & Daamen 2006). An assumption of numeric priming theory is that the anchor only has to be primed, and does not necessarily have to be consciously considered, to affect estimates (Reitsma-van Rooijen & Daamen 2006). Many such values may be primed – for example, when a person living in Germany is asked to estimate the mean annual temperature in that country, that person might automatically activate a number of temperature values previously experienced around the year and around the country. If given some time to respond, the person might activate quite a lot of temperature values that are, along with the anchor, combined into a final estimate (Reitsma-van Rooijen & Daamen 2006). Among so many different values, the subliminal anchor would not be expected to influence the estimate a great deal. On the other hand, if the person has very little time to come up with the estimate, then very few additional values may be activated and combined into the estimate. Under these conditions, the subliminal anchor would be expected to have a stronger influence on the estimate.

Reitsma-van Rooijen and Daamen (2006) tested these latter claims by asking Dutch university students to make a difficult estimate; some were asked to do so under time pressure, and the rest were not. Specifically, they were told that there had been an epidemic of a disease of the lungs in another country, and they were asked to estimate how likely it was that this epidemic would recur within the next year. Anchors, either low or high (i.e., 10 or 90 [percent]), were presented subliminally and repeatedly in 17-ms bursts and immediately masked with a fixation point and nonsense letter string (e.g., *MJFqRe*). Students' estimates were interactively influenced by the manipulations of anchor (low or high) and time pressure (present or absent). That is, under time pressure, they made significantly higher estimates with a high anchor ($M = 39\%$) than with a low anchor ($M = 20\%$). When there was no time pressure, estimates were not significantly influenced by the anchor ($M = 26\%$ in the high anchor condition and $M = 32\%$ in the low anchor condition). That is, a subliminally presented anchor only affected estimates under time pressure, as predicted by numeric priming theory.

More recently, Oppenheimer, LeBoeuf, and Brewer (2008) asked whether an anchor can prime a more general sense of large versus small (i.e., not necessarily attached to a particular number) that could affect judgments across domains. They called this hypothesized effect the **cross-modal anchoring effect**. In one of their experiments, they gave American undergraduate students a packet of single-page tasks, supposedly unrelated to one another. Two tasks were of interest in this packet. In one task, people were asked to copy three lines as accurately as possible. Oppenheimer et al. (2008) manipulated between subjects whether the lines, which were all presented horizontally on the page, were long (3.5 inches) or short (1 inch). Then, in the task presented on the following page in the packet, they were asked to estimate how long the Mississippi River is (followed by several other estimates to obscure the experimenters' hypothesis). People who were given long lines to draw gave significantly longer estimates than those given short lines to draw (mean estimates of 1224 and 72 miles, respectively; Oppenheimer et al. 2008).

In a follow-up study, Oppenheimer et al. (2008) tested more directly whether the effect was cross-modal. Specifically, they asked whether anchors for length (i.e., long versus short) would influence estimates in another domain (i.e., temperature, such that length anchors influenced temperature estimates to be higher or lower). They recruited people on the street in San Francisco, California, to complete the same task as in their first study, except that they asked people to give estimates of the average July temperature of Honolulu, Hawaii, instead of estimates of length. People who saw long lines estimated the July temperature of Honolulu to be significantly higher than did people who saw short lines (mean estimates of 88°F and 84°F, respectively). Given these findings, Oppenheimer et al. (2008) argued that people show a cross-modal anchoring effect, although the influence of the cross-modal anchor was not quite as strong as in their unimodal anchoring study.

Similarly, Strack and Mussweiler (1997) showed that anchoring effects are strengthened when the anchor and the judgment to be made both refer to the same dimension. For example, suppose one is asked to estimate the height of a well-known national landmark. In this judgment, anchoring effects are stronger if the anchor provided is also about height than if the anchor is about width. (The same was true if one was asked to estimate width; anchoring was stronger if the anchor was about width rather than about height; Strack & Mussweiler 1997.) Note that referring to the same dimension does not guarantee that the anchor is relevant to the judgment (e.g., when the anchor is the height of a Volkswagen sedan).

Furthermore, other work has shown evidence for a **cross-scale anchoring effect**. People making hypothetical credit card payments show a classic anchoring effect, choosing to make lower payments if a minimum payment amount is specified than if it is not (Navarro-Martinez et al. 2011; Stewart 2009). By manipulating whether the minimum payment on a statement was expressed in dollars (e.g., $38.74 minimum payment for a $1937.28 bill) or as a percentage (e.g., 2% of a $1937.28 bill), Harris and Speekenbrink (2016) tested whether the same anchor expressed on a different scale still yields an anchoring effect on payment decisions. As in Oppenheimer et al.'s (2008) findings, both types of anchors led people to show an anchoring effect, and the same-scale anchor (e.g., $38.74) had a stronger effect than the cross-scale anchor (e.g., 2%).

Taken together, the findings described in this section suggest that the influence of anchors on estimates may be even more widespread than has traditionally been supposed. Anchors need not be perceived consciously to have an effect on estimates, and they need not pertain to the same kind of measurement, or be on the same scale, as the estimate being made.

Anchoring effects in everyday life

Anchoring effects in medical diagnosis

Given the wide scope of the anchoring effect in the laboratory, a critical question is whether they actually influence important judgments in people's lives. For example, do initial anchors influence clinicians deciding between possible medical diagnoses for their patients? In medical diagnosis, Elstein (1999) proposed a normative model for how new information ought to influence clinicians' likelihood judgments of possible diagnoses. The model specifies that clinicians should ideally start from the initial probability of the diagnosis being considered. That is, they should ask: How rare or common is that diagnosis in general? The clinician should either seek out the initial probability (e.g., from published research data) or have a reasonable guess as to what it might be (e.g., from experience or by consulting an experienced colleague). Then, clinicians should run an available diagnostic test to gain more information about this particular patient (Elstein 1999). Unless the test is 100% diagnostic (in which case no calculations are needed, because the test alone can give the answer), clinicians should then factor in the strength of the evidence given by the test. Specifically, they would need to know the outcome of the test (e.g., positive or negative) and how accurate the test is (e.g., if you do have a particular disease, how often does it correctly detect it; if you don't have the disease, how often does the test correctly show this). (See Chapter 5 for a more comprehensive discussion of this calculation in medical diagnosis.)

Although this model of diagnostic reasoning may seem reasonably straightforward, Elstein (1999) pointed out that clinician error can occur at each of the two major steps: (1) Figuring out the initial probability of the diagnosis and (2) assessing the strength of the test. In the first step, he noted that clinicians may often start with the wrong anchor – for example, relying on representativeness or availability to determine a starting point when they do not know the true initial probability of a diagnosis (Elstein 1999). Although doing so may work much of the time, it cannot be foolproof. In addition, in the second of these steps, the degree to which test results influence diagnostic judgments may depend on whether those results are obtained early or late in the diagnostic process.

Anchoring-and-adjustment may also come into play earlier in the diagnostic process, when the clinician is first examining the patient and generating an initial set of possible diagnoses. Gorini and Pravettoni (2011), for example, suggested that during a patient's initial examination, the clinician may often be drawn to the most salient feature or features (e.g., a startling skin rash). The attention-drawing feature – acting as the anchor – may disproportionately affect the clinician's eventual diagnosis decision despite subsequent tests and other information suggesting a different diagnosis.

Spaanjaars, Groenier, van de Ven, and Witteman (2015) went back still further in the diagnostic process, asking whether reading referral letters that suggest a possible diagnosis disproportionately influence clinicians' final diagnoses. In their study, clinicians read a clear-cut case history of depression after reading a referral letter that either suggested depression or anxiety as a diagnosis. Clinicians with an intermediate level of expertise (i.e., 2–10 years in practice) showed an anchoring effect to the suggested diagnosis, whereas very experienced clinicians (i.e., 11–50 years in practice) did not. Spaanjaars et al. (2015) speculated that this may have occurred because only the less experienced clinicians felt that both depression and anxiety were plausible diagnoses for the case. Additional work will be needed to determine whether this is indeed the case.

These results are compatible with classic findings by Wilson et al. (1996), who also reported that having expertise in the domain relevant to the judgment being made predicted weaker anchoring effects. From a practical standpoint, however, Spaanjaars et al. (2015) noted that their findings could be good news *or* bad news for less experienced clinicians, depending on the situation. Their results suggest that when the referral letter directed clinicians toward the correct diagnosis (i.e., depression), only the less experienced clinicians benefited from this information and were more likely to anchor on the correct diagnosis (Spaanjaars et al. 2015). As with other cognitive shortcuts, anchoring effects in practice are only damaging when they happen to direct the reasoner away from the correct response.

Yet clinicians may go so far as to distort incoming information to be coherent with a hypothesized diagnosis. In one striking demonstration, Kostopoulou, Russo, Keenan, Delaney, and Douiri (2012) asked practicing family physicians in the U.K. to consider several case studies. Each case opened with a presenting problem (e.g., fatigue) that was then followed by an information cue intended to orient them toward one of two common diagnoses (e.g., either diabetes or depression). The physicians were then presented with more information cues. For each of the three case studies, they saw neutral cues that did not strengthen the likelihood of either diagnosis per se (e.g., slight weight loss over the last several months). At the end of the third and final case study only, they also saw several negative cues that supported the opposite diagnosis as the initial cue given in that case.

When physicians in the study saw each information cue (e.g., slight weight loss), they were first asked to rate how much it supported one diagnosis versus the other (e.g., diabetes or depression), or neither (Kostopoulou et al. 2012). Then, they rated the likelihood of one versus the other diagnosis considering what they knew about the case so far. To figure out how much the physicians distorted the meaning of the cues that followed the initial cue, the experimenters also asked a control group of physicians to simply rate each cue for how much it supported one versus the other diagnosis (e.g., diabetes or depression) without ever having seen the initial cue or presenting problem. These ratings were used as the baseline rating for each cue. The experimenters calculated distortion by subtracting the absolute value of how each physician rated each cue from the baseline rating for that cue. They then assigned that number a positive or negative valence (i.e., positive if physicians more strongly endorsed the diagnosis they had been leaning toward just before they saw that information; negative if it went the other way). Physicians reliably distorted information in support of the hypothesis they were favoring. Furthermore, the more strongly they believed in a particular diagnosis when receiving a new piece of information, the more they distorted the meaning of that information (Kostopoulou et al. 2012). Taken together, these findings suggest that when anchors fall away from the correct diagnosis, decision-making can be very adversely affected.

Anchoring effects in real estate pricing

Similarly, a striking example of anchoring effects in decision-making is in the domain of real estate. As a person's home typically represents an enormous percentage of his or her savings, sometimes even well over the total net worth of the household (Flavin & Yamashita 2002), this issue is of deep relevance to potential owners and buyers. Interestingly, conventional wisdom does not necessarily point to any single best strategy for pricing a home on sale. The reasoning behind simply *listing the price that is thought to be the true worth of the house* rests on the assumption that prices are market-driven; that is, they are rationally derived from the features of the property (e.g., the location, size, and so on; see Bucchianeri & Minson 2013). This view suggests that people are generally only willing to pay for what's there, canceling out any attempts to artificially manipulate buying behavior with the listing price. A common justification for *underpricing the house*, on the other hand, is that doing so is expected to drive up the price by igniting a so-called "bidding war." In a bidding war, potential buyers are initially attracted to what seems an apparent bargain, and then make offers above the listing price in the hope of beating out other bidders. When other potential buyers see that some initial offers have been made, they too assume that the price must be reasonable, and make bids of their own (an example of so-called "herding" behavior; Bucchianeri & Minson 2013). In contrast, the idea behind *overpricing the house* is to establish a relatively extreme anchor, in the hope that buyers will insufficiently adjust downward from the anchor and make a higher offer than they would have made with a less extreme anchor or a fair listing price (Bucchianeri & Minson 2013).

First, let's consider the possible effects of overpricing a home on the real estate market, and whether potential buyers (e.g., university students) and experts (e.g., real estate agents) are susceptible to anchoring from the listing price. In a classic study, Northcraft and Neale (1987) asked business school students and experienced real estate agents to visit a local home for sale. They were allowed 20 minutes to look over the home and surrounding area. They received a portfolio of information, including the listing sheet describing the important features of the home, listing sheets for other homes for sale in the neighborhood, and information about real estate sales in that neighborhood and the whole city for the prior 6 months. The critical manipulation was the price on the listing sheet for the home. The (actual) appraised value of the home was $74,900 USD, but the experimenters manipulated whether it was listed above or below that value. In four between-subjects conditions, they listed the price as either 4% above or below the actual value (moderate anchors), or 12% above or below the actual value (extreme anchors; Northcraft & Neale 1987). (The real estate agents were only given the extreme anchors, as they were more difficult to recruit and constituted a smaller sample.)

All the study participants were asked to give estimates of (1) the house's appraisal value, (2) an appropriate listing price, (3) what price would be reasonable for a seller to pay for the house, and (4) what lowest price they would accept if they were selling the house. Students were influenced by the anchors across all four judgments. Their price suggestions were generally highest for those who saw the high extreme anchor and proportionately lower for those who saw the other anchors (e.g., lowest for the low extreme anchor; Northcraft & Neale 1987). The real estate agents also showed a clear anchoring effect for all four judgments. Interestingly, those who saw the high extreme anchor came quite close to the actual value of the home, whereas those who saw the extreme low anchor tended to undershoot the actual value. However, students were significantly more likely than real estate agents to report having taken the listing price (i.e., anchor) into account in making their judgments (Northcraft & Neale 1987). That is, students adopted anchoring as a deliberate reasoning strategy much more often than did real estate agents.

The idea that potential buyers/sellers and real estate agents alike are susceptible to anchoring from listing prices is supported by large-scale analyses on real estate purchases (Bucchianeri & Minson 2013). Using a dataset of over 14,000 real estate transactions over a 5-year period in 3 U.S. states, they found a small but highly reliable increase in the eventual sale price for homes with overpriced listing prices. The degree to which sale prices were increased was even higher for extreme anchors (i.e., list prices of more than 20% above market value) than for more moderate anchors (i.e., list prices of 10–20% above market value). This finding is not due to such extraneous factors as home quality, time on the market, time of year, neighborhood (i.e., zip code), or the real estate office listing the home, as these were all controlled for in the analyses. Bucchianeri and Minson (2013) did not find any evidence that herding effects occur, even in hot markets where there are relatively few properties and relatively many potential buyers. Thus, their analyses strongly suggest that overpricing is the superior home selling strategy.

Interestingly, in contrast to the above evidence, Bucchianeri and Minson (2013) found that real estate agents tended to recommend underpricing. In a separate study, they asked local realtors to consider six homes listed for sale in that area, and to give a listing price that they would recommend. In 70% of cases, the agents recommended underpricing. Of course, whether this finding is a good thing or a bad thing depends on one's point of view – underpricing is desirable for the buyer; undesirable for the seller. But it appears that sellers seeking to maximize a sale price should generally seek to set an extreme overpriced anchor.

Countering effects of anchoring

Because the desirability of the anchoring effect can differ across points of view and different situations, it seems worthwhile to try to equip people with ways to counter the effect themselves when needed. Interestingly, the anchoring effect has proved very difficult to eliminate. For example, simply informing people about the effect of an anchor is not sufficient to attenuate the anchor's effects on judgment (Chapman & Johnson 2002). Whyte and Sebenius (1997) also found that the anchoring effect remained robust regardless of whether estimates were made by individual people or groups of people, and tended to appear across different levels of expertise in the domain of judgment.

One attempt to help people reduce their own anchoring effects was to provide them with decision support systems (George, Duffy, & Ahuja 2000). George et al. (2000) created a decision support system intended to help people estimate the value of homes on the real estate market while countering any effects of anchoring from the listing price. The students in their study were presented with a variety of pieces of information about a property (e.g., photos, rooms, size, amenities, etc.) and were asked to make the same four estimates of the home's value as did the participants in Northcraft and Neale's (1987) study, described in the previous section. The anchor (listing price) was either high or low, and the decision support system either warned or did not warn participants when their estimates came too close (i.e., within 10% or within 20% of the anchor) to the listing price. They found that people using the decision support system showed the anchoring effect just as robustly as in previous work (George et al. 2000). People who received warnings when their estimates were close to the anchor changed their estimates more often than did people who didn't receive warnings. However, the degree to which they ultimately showed the anchoring effect was not reduced.

Some evidence suggests that simply experiencing positive affect may reduce the effect of anchoring by reducing how much people rely on superficial or heuristic-based reasoning overall (Estrada, Isen, & Young 1997). Estrada et al. (1997) manipulated positive affect in a group of physicians by randomly assigning them to either receive a little bag of candies or nothing. They were then asked to consider a written case study of a patient and to think aloud in coming to a diagnosis. Independent raters read and coded transcripts of the physician's thoughts on the diagnosis, rating the degree to which the physician showed anchoring effects. Anchoring was identified when the physician mentioned an incorrect diagnosis early on and failed to adjust (e.g., by ordering different diagnostic tests) even when clear evidence pointed toward a different diagnosis. Those physicians in the positive affect (i.e., candy) condition showed significantly less anchoring in their think-aloud reasoning than did those in the control condition (Estrada et al. 1997). Future research may need to focus more on such general interventions that reduce reliance on heuristics overall, rather than try to address specific features of the anchoring effect itself.

Questions for discussion

1. When you go on a job interview, according to the research described in this chapter, exactly what impact does the first impression you make have in the minds of your interviewers? Is there anything you could do to manage this process to your benefit, and if so, what?

2. The main take-home message from the research described in this chapter is that the anchoring-and-adjustment effect is extremely reliable and robust. But are the effects described in the different domains (e.g., medicine; real estate) likely to influence people's lives? Justify your answer, whether yes or no, by drawing on research described in this chapter.

3. Under what conditions or situations is anchoring undesirable? Are there conditions or situations in which it is actually desirable?

4. The research described in the last section suggests that it is not easy to get rid of the anchoring effect. Propose a possible new technique or manipulation for reducing the effect, and briefly describe a study designed to test whether it would work.

Suggestions for further reading

Asch, S. E. (1946). Forming impressions of personality. *The Journal of Abnormal and Social Psychology*, *41*(3), 258–290.

Chapman, G. B., & Johnson, E. J. (2002). Incorporating the irrelevant: Anchors in judgments of belief and value. In T. Gilovich, D. Griffin, & D. Kahneman (Eds.), *Heuristics and biases: The psychology of intuitive judgment* (pp. 120–138). Cambridge, UK: Cambridge University Press.

Tversky, A., & Kahneman, D. (1973). Availability: A heuristic for judging frequency and probability. *Cognitive Psychology*, *5*(2), 207–232.

PART II

Judgments of the Past and the Future

Hindsight Bias

Learning Goals

By the end of this chapter, you will have:

- Considered the cognitive and motivational processes by which we recreate our past states of knowledge, giving rise under some conditions to hindsight bias and creeping determinism.
- Evaluated different ways of measuring hindsight bias.
- Mapped conceptual relationships between hindsight bias and other important phenomena, including reverse hindsight bias, visual hindsight bias, outcome bias, and epistemic egocentrism or the "curse of knowledge" effect.
- Applied the concept of hindsight bias to situations in daily life and considered potential cross-cultural differences and similarities.

Key Terms

Hindsight bias	Cue values
Creeping determinism	Causal model theory
Memory paradigm	(of hindsight bias)
Hypothetical paradigm	Reverse hindsight bias
Determinism	Visual hindsight bias
Selective Activation, Reconstruction	Outcome bias
and Anchoring (SARA) model	Theory of mind
Reconstruction After Feedback with	Epistemic egocentrism
Take the Best (RAFT) model	Curse of knowledge effect
Probability cues	

As we have seen so far, one important way in which we try to anticipate future and unknown events is to make informal judgments about how likely different outcomes are to occur. In the months and days leading up to a major political election, citizens and news pundits form opinions regarding which candidate is most likely to win. When a major corporation cuts jobs in a restructuring plan, stock traders try to predict what the restructuring will do to the company's profits. When two people are dating, they (and sometimes others outside the relationship) think about how likely it is that the relationship will last.

The major driving question in this chapter is how well we remember these past judgments – and how well we remember what knowledge we possessed at the time we made those judgments – once we learn how events actually unfold. For example, after it was revealed in 2013 that Angela Merkel had been re-elected Chancellor of Germany, or that PepsiCo's early 2012 corporate restructuring was followed by short-term earnings losses, how well did those who had made predictions about the likelihood of those events retain their original memories of what they had predicted before the fact? After it was reported that famed Bollywood actress Shilpa Shetty and businessman Raj Kundra had gotten married, how accurately were Ms. Shetty's fans able to gauge whether or not they really saw it coming?

What is hindsight bias and how is it studied?

Informally, **hindsight bias** is often described as the erroneous judgment that one "knew all along" that a particular outcome would occur. Formally, there are several important components of the definition of hindsight bias, as Fischhoff (1975) first described. First, retroactive judgments of the probability of a specific outcome (e.g., how likely South Korea was to make it to the semifinal round of the 2002 World Cup, especially given that they had never before won a single match in previous World Cup tournaments) shift upwards once that outcome has actually been achieved. In other words, when we know the actual outcome, and are trying to remember our past judgment of how likely that outcome was, our remembered judgments tend to drift toward the actual outcome. We do the same thing when we are trying to make that judgment from the perspective of someone who does not know the actual outcome – we can't seem to shake completely free of what we personally know to be the actual outcome. Second, once a specific outcome has occurred, people tend to judge that the outcome was relatively inevitable – that it was always going to happen that way. We'll discuss this phenomenon, called **creeping determinism** (Fischhoff 1975), in more detail later on. Third, people tend not to be consciously aware that their judgments have changed after the fact.

The very first controlled experimental reports of hindsight bias were focused on people's judgments of current events. In February 1972, U.S. President Richard Nixon, who was widely known at the time for his anti-communist policies, made a highly publicized visit to China to normalize relations and open up commerce between the two countries. Fis-chhoff and Beyth (1975) saw that trip as an opportunity to set up a formal test of hindsight bias for the first time. Shortly before the trip took place, they asked university students in Israel to rate how likely it was that various outcomes would take place (e.g., that Nixon and Chairman Mao Zedong would meet together at least once; that the U.S. would establish a perma-nent diplomatic mission). Then, a couple of weeks after the trip took place, they were asked to remember their earlier answers to the same questions. They were also asked to report what they believed had actually happened (e.g., whether Nixon and Mao had actually met together at least once). This method of testing for hindsight bias – by asking people to recall the likeli-hood judgments they made before knowing the outcome – is known as the **memory paradigm**. Sure enough, Fischhoff and Beyth (1975) found that people's recollections of their original likelihood ratings shifted after the fact to be closer to what they now believed to be the actual outcome.

Fischhoff (1975) also demonstrated hindsight bias using an alternative method known as the **hypothetical paradigm**. One group of Israeli students was asked to read a long paragraph about an event (e.g., a battle between the British and the Gurkhas in the year 1814) and then to predict the likelihood of several alternative outcomes (e.g., a British win; a Gurkha win; stalemate with or without a peace agreement). A second group of students was presented with the long paragraph plus the definitive outcome (e.g., they were explicitly told that the Gurkhas won this battle), and they were then asked to rate the likelihood of the same outcomes *as if* they did not know the actual outcome. Fischhoff (1975) found that people who knew the outcome – those making the probability judgments in hindsight – gave probabilities closer to that out-come than did people who didn't know the outcome (i.e., those making prob-ability judgments in foresight). That is, once again, people making judgments in hindsight seemed unable to let go of their knowledge of the actual outcome in making likelihood judgments. More strikingly, they seemed to be unaware that they were doing so. Self-centered overconfidence cannot fully account for this finding, either; Fischhoff (1975) found that people also overestimated other people's ability to make accurate probability judgments in foresight.

Fischhoff (1975) and Fischhoff and Beyth (1975) pointed out that in life, outcomes are often very difficult to predict before the fact. In complex situa-tions, the available evidence will often point to multiple possible outcomes. However, the pervasiveness of hindsight bias suggests that people will have a difficult time learning to be prepared for surprising outcomes. When a per-son makes a prediction that is far off the mark, he or she *should* become more cautious about making predictions in the future, learning from this direct experience that outcomes can really be very hard to predict. Instead, that person is much more likely to push the botched prediction aside, tending to believe – erroneously – that he or she really "knew it all along."

The phenomenon of hindsight bias has been shown over the years to be remarkably robust (Pohl, Bender, & Lachmann 2002). From these first demonstrations by Fischhoff (1975) and Fischhoff and Beyth (1975) to the present day (see Roese & Vohs 2012, for a review), the fundamental finding has not changed across a wide variety of measurements and experimental paradigms. The seminal studies on hindsight bias that we just discussed focused on current *events or episodes*, an approach that has remained popular in hindsight research. Events or episodes may map most realistically to the kinds of hindsight problems people face in the world, but other kinds of materials have also been used to maximize experimental control (Pohl 2007). Some studies feature *two-alternative-forced-choice questions*, such as Fischhoff's (1977) classic question, "Is absinthe (a) a liqueur or (b) a precious stone?" People are asked to pick a response and then to rate their confidence in this response, for example, on a half-scale from 100% (absolutely certain) to 50% (complete guess). In other studies, people make true-false judgments about factual *assertions*, such as "Harare is the capital of Zimbabwe," and then make a confidence rating. Still others ask people to make numerical estimates of an *unknown quantity* (Pohl 2007), such as "How long is the Great Wall of China?" or "What percentage of Australia's landscape is covered by woods?" This wide range of materials and dependent measures has helped establish the reliability and robustness of hindsight bias.

Creeping determinism

In philosophy, determinism refers to the explicit belief that when some-thing happens, that occurrence was *absolutely* inevitable given those par-ticular circumstances. In contrast, the idea of creeping determinism in hindsight bias is that once one knows what has happened, that occurrence seems *relatively* more inevitable than if one had not known what happened. In this way, Fischhoff (1975) intended the concept of creeping determinism to be something like a less stringent version of philosophical determinism. Sure enough, in Fischhoff's (1975) experiments, people making judgments in hindsight ("as though" they did not know the actual outcome) tended to give lower likelihoods to alternative possible outcomes than did people making judgments in foresight (who truly did not know the actual outcome). Fischhoff's (1975) original idea of creeping determinism has held up well over numerous subsequent studies, even those centering on events of some direct importance to the reasoners.

Box 4.1: Competing to Host the Olympic Games

In July of 2012, 10,820 athletes from 204 nations converged upon London as the Olympic Games began. Preparations for the event began more than 8 years beforehand: Even before the giant stadiums were constructed and the intricate opening and closing ceremonies were planned, these Olympic Games were prefaced by an arduous process in which cities around the world submitted detailed applications, along with a substantial application fee, to the International Olympic Committee. Each city made its best case to the committee to convey that it was capable of pulling off such an enormous event. On May 18, 2004, nine cities that had applied to be the host city for the 2012 Olympic Games – Havana, Istanbul, Leipzig, London, Madrid, Moscow, New York, Paris, and Rio de Janeiro – learned which five had been selected to be on the International Olympic Committee's shortlist for the final round of consideration. Leipzig, though it was the smallest of the cities competing, had scored well on nearly every one of the IOC's measures (being a small city, it was lacking only in infrastructure; the city attempted to present this as an advantage by unveiling a bold plan to convert the entire city, in essence, into an Olympic village). Going into the announcement, it was widely believed to have a strong chance to become one of the finalists.

Yet to the great disappointment of many in Leipzig, the cities of Havana, Istanbul, Rio de Janeiro, and finally Leipzig were cut from the shortlist. When the decision was read to an eagerly waiting crowd in the central market square of Leipzig, they learned that Leipzig had been placed 6th, just missing finalist status. *Did Leipzig ever really have a chance after all? Was this result inevitable given the circumstances?*

Blank and Nestler (2006) ran a timely study in which they capitalized on Leipzig's situation to test for creeping determinism (which they called "necessity impressions"; like creeping determinism, this term reflects the general idea that in hindsight, people can form the impression that the outcome absolutely had to occur given the circumstances). They asked Leipzig residents to rate a number of statements regarding the inevitability of the eventual outcome *before* the news was announced (e.g., "nothing can influence the outcome of this decision"; "an unexpected event might still influence the outcome of the decision") and *after* the news was announced (e.g., "nothing could have influenced the outcome of this decision"; "an unexpected event might still have influenced the outcome of the decision"). Leipzig residents' responses to all of these questions became significantly more deterministic after the outcome was known. In other words, in hindsight, they came to believe more strongly that the outcome was never going to be any different than it was.

Theories explaining how hindsight bias occurs

Theories that attempt to explain exactly how hindsight bias occurs can be roughly broken down into two broad categories: (1) Cognitive theories, which can be further subdivided into memory accounts and causal model theory, and (2) motivational theories.

Cognitive theories: Memory accounts

Some cognitive theories are adaptations of existing process models of the human memory system to explain how hindsight bias occurs. As you might expect, memory models are based on hindsight research using the memory paradigm (as described above, in this paradigm, people are asked to recall the likelihood judgments they made before knowing the outcome). In general, memory models suggest that hindsight bias occurs because people are not always able to directly retrieve memories of judgments they made before the fact. Instead, they sometimes need to reconstruct those memories, and as is well documented, the reconstructive process is prone to distortions (Schacter, Guerin, & St. Jacques 2011).

For example, one prominent memory model of hindsight bias, known as SARA (Selective Activation, Reconstruction and Anchoring; Pohl, Eisenhauer, & Hardt 2003), is based on the idea that memory consists of associated networks of item-specific information units. The model suggests that when people are asked to answer questions about unknown quantities (e.g., "How old was Nelson Mandela when he became the president of South Africa?"), words in the question itself activate associated units of information in memory. For example, upon hearing this question, a person might automatically recall general knowledge of the approximate average age at which presidents are elected, and another stored memory of seeing a picture of Nelson Mandela with white hair. When the actual answer (e.g., 75 years old) is revealed, the information that was most relevant to the correct answer (e.g., the mental image of a white-haired Nelson Mandela) becomes even more strongly activated. So when the person is next asked to reconstruct her earlier estimate in hindsight, this reconstructed estimate is more heavily influenced by the pieces of information that are most strongly activated at that moment – that is, the information that turned out to align with the correct answer. This is how, according to SARA, the person's estimate after the fact will move closer to the correct answer, showing hindsight bias.

Another memory-based model, known as **Reconstruction After Feedback with Take the Best** (RAFT; Hoffrage, Hertwig, & Gigerenzer 2000), assumes that hindsight bias simply happens to be a side effect of an adaptive learning process (Hawkins & Hastie 1990). RAFT was designed to show how people make hindsight judgments about two-alternative-forced-choice questions in which two things are compared to each other in terms of some numerical measurement (e.g., "Which city is larger: Hamburg, Germany or Heidelberg, Germany?"). In this model, making a judgment in hindsight is a three-step process. First, people will try to recall their original estimate from memory. If – and only if – they can't directly retrieve this memory, then they will try to reconstruct the memory by making the judgment over again (see also Erdfelder & Buchner 1998). Second, to make this judgment again, people will try to recall the **probability cues** and **cue values** that they used to make the initial judgment. Probability cues are pieces of information that correlate with the judgment people are trying to make. For example, one probability cue is that a city with a professional, premier league soccer team is likely to have a large population; another probability cue is that a city with a large exhibition center is likely to have a large population. The cue values are the information that is associated with each of the items being compared. For instance, a person might be moderately confident that Hamberg has a premier league soccer team and that Heidelberg does not. Third, once people learn the correct answer to the original question (e.g., that Hamburg does, in fact, have a larger population than Heidelberg), the cue values in their knowledge base may be automatically and non-consciously updated to correspond more closely to the correct answer. For example, now that they know Hamburg has the larger population, they may feel even more highly confident that Hamberg has a premier league soccer team and that Heidelberg does not. So when people try to recreate their original judgment, they may actually be working with updated probability cues (e.g., with strengthened confidence), and may not be aware that they have updated them. Whenever this happens, people's reconstructed memory of their own original response can become skewed toward the correct answer, showing hindsight bias.

Cognitive theories: Causal model theory

A third cognitive theory about the mental process underlying hindsight bias aims to explain how people show hindsight bias in studies using the hypothetical paradigm (again, these are studies in which the judgments of people ignorant of the outcome are compared to the judgments of people who know the outcome but are asked to judge as if they do not). Because the hypothetical paradigm does not involve remembering a previous response, the memory models we have just discussed cannot explain how hindsight bias appears in this paradigm. To fill this gap, Fischhoff's (1975) original ideas set the stage for the **causal model theory** of hindsight bias, which was originally introduced by Wasserman, Lempert, and Hastie (1991) and further shaped by ideas reported in Hawkins and Hastie (1990), Hölzl and Kirchler (2005), Pezzo (2003), and Nestler, Blank, and von Collani (2008). Suppose again that one is asked to read about an event or episode (e.g., a battle between the British and the Gurkha in the year 1814), and then to predict the likelihood of several alternative outcomes (e.g., a British win; a Gurkha win; stalemate with or without a peace agreement). When one is explicitly told that the Gurkha won this battle, let's suppose that one, knowing the outcome, then mentally highlights those parts of the battle description that would make a Gurkha win make more sense (e.g., the Gurkhas' use of guerilla tactics). Wasserman et al. (1991) proposed that having these kinds of causally relevant pieces of information available allows people to build a commonsense causal bridge to the outcome, making the outcome seem (in hindsight) more inevitable.

Nestler et al. (2008) further proposed that when people read about scenarios like the British–Gurkha battle in the hypothetical paradigm, they are naturally motivated to try to explain why it is that the outcome of any given event occurred (e.g., why the Gurkha won this battle). In other words, people go through a stepwise process of sense-making (Pezzo 2003). First, people try to find potential causes of the outcome (e.g., the Gurkhas' use of guerilla tactics), a process that Nestler et al. (2008) called the *search* for causal antecedents. Then, people think more carefully about whether those potential causes really do explain the outcome well or not, in an *evaluation* of those causal antecedents. If one or more causes is thought to explain the outcome well, then creeping determinism sets in, and people show hindsight bias.

In support of the idea that causal reasoning is necessary for hindsight bias to occur in the hypothetical paradigm, Yopchick and Kim (2012) still further found that when the description of the event (e.g., the battle) is stripped clean of potential causes of the outcome, people do not show hindsight bias. That is, simply knowing the outcome is not enough for hindsight bias to occur. Only when a plausible, relevant cause is provided does hindsight bias clearly and reliably show up in the hypothetical paradigm.

Motivational theories

Generally speaking, the field has reached an overall consensus that hindsight bias is primarily driven by cognitive factors, in the sense that people do appear to undergo memory or causal belief updating (Pezzo 2011). However, hindsight bias does depend, to a lesser degree, on personal motivations. For example, one might be personally motivated to reinforce one's self-image as a knowledgeable person, inching one's hindsight judgments toward the actual outcome (Pezzo & Pezzo 2007). Another way in which motivation may affect hindsight bias was identified by Walster (1967), who proposed that people have the need to feel as though they are in control of important events. She asked people to read about a momentous decision (e.g., deciding to buy a house) and then told them the outcome of that decision (e.g., whether a little or a lot of money was gained or lost). People who rated how confident they were that they could have predicted that outcome ("I knew it all along") showed greater confidence for more extreme, or more important, consequences.

One might also reason that a self-serving bias, or the tendency for people to attribute their successes to internal, personal factors and their failures to external, situational factors (Miller & Ross 1975) might accordingly interfere with (or exacerbate) hindsight bias. If the outcome is of positive personal relevance, then a self-serving bias might attribute that positive outcome to one's own merit, and hindsight bias should be strengthened (i.e., if the outcome was within one's control, then one must have seen it coming). If, instead, the outcome is negative, then a self-serving bias will attribute that undesirable outcome to external factors outside one's own control, and hindsight bias should be weakened (i.e., if the outcome was not within one's control, one could not have seen it coming).

Mark and Mellor (1991) were among the first to investigate the last of these cases: Whether negative self-relevant events elicit a self-serving bias that overrides the hindsight bias. In their study, they recruited union workers who had been laid off from work, most of whom had not been notified until the very day or week of their layoffs. They also recruited two comparison groups, union workers who had not been laid off and community members who were not members of the union. All three groups were comparable on a number of basic demographic variables (e.g., age, gender, level of education). Everyone in the study was asked to rate the predictability of the recent layoffs in their local union (thus, everyone was rating the same set of layoffs). They chose from the following options: (1) "I'm not sure I ever saw it coming," (2) "I wasn't sure, but I suspected it was coming, or (3) "I saw it coming all the way." Mark and Mellor (1991) found that the community members reported having the most accurate foresight ("I saw it coming all the way"), followed by union workers who survived the layoffs, followed by those who were laid off ("I'm not sure I ever saw it coming"). In other words, those who were actually directly affected by the layoffs were least likely to claim that they saw the layoffs coming – that is, they showed the least hindsight bias.

Mark and Mellor (1991) argued that the layoffs activated a self-serving bias in those who were laid off; this self-serving bias was so strong that it counteracted or inhibited any hindsight bias that might otherwise have appeared.

Finally, our motivation to understand surprising events can influence hindsight bias. For example, Pezzo (2003) pointed out that when an outcome is very surprising, we are more motivated to try to make sense of why it happened than if the outcome was expected. A student who studies very hard for an exam and goes in feeling relaxed and well-prepared may feel quite surprised upon receiving a poor grade, triggering a search for understanding and explanation. If you noticed that this line of thinking builds nicely into the causal model theory of hindsight bias, you're absolutely right. Pezzo (2003) further suggested that when the outcome is surprising, motivating people to undergo a sense-making process, people will show hindsight bias if they find a reasonable explanation for the outcome. Conversely, if the outcome is not surprising at all, then there is no need to search for an explanation at all, and no hindsight bias will occur.

To test these predictions, Pezzo (2003) asked people attending college basketball games to predict the outcome before the fact. Overall, supporters of the home team strongly expected their team to win. After the home team did indeed win (an unsurprising outcome from their perspective, prompting no need for sense-making), they showed no hindsight bias. In contrast, visiting team supporters did not expect the home team to win in foresight, so when the home team did win, they showed hindsight bias, as predicted, presumably because that result was relatively surprising to them. Once the outcome occurred, supporters of the visiting team, motivated by their surprise, thought about reasons *why* the home team might have won, ultimately shifting their judgments in hindsight (Pezzo 2003).

In what they called a model of "motivated" sense-making, Pezzo and Pezzo (2007) further proposed that the sense-making process itself can be driven by motivation to preserve one's self-image. They suggested that when an outcome is both negative and self-relevant (e.g., a worker handling the x-ray scanner at an airport fails to detect a large knife in a passenger's suitcase), a person (e.g., the worker) will selectively search *only* for explanations that do not place blame for the outcome on the self. There are several different possible outcomes to this search for explanations, according to this model. (1) If the worker is successful in finding a situational, non-personal cause of the outcome (e.g., it was the end of an unreasonably long and exhausting work shift; some co-workers were arguing loudly nearby), then the worker will show hindsight bias. This occurs because having identified a cause strengthens the perception that the outcome was inevitable (Tykosinski 2001). (2) A second possible outcome to this search is that the worker cannot find a legitimate external cause, but is still able to, in self-defense, dismiss any possible internal causes (e.g., "It can't be that I wasn't paying attention, because I was"). In this case, no hindsight bias should be expected to occur. The self-serving bias interferes with the appearance of the hindsight bias, and the worker will probably conclude that one never could have seen it coming (Mark & Mellor 1991). (3) A third possible outcome is that the worker cannot find a legitimate external cause, and accepts an internal cause ("I wasn't looking carefully enough"; "I was not doing my job well"), taking on blame for the outcome. In this case, the worker is predicted to show hindsight bias ("given how careless I was being, it was pretty inevitable that I would miss a weapon that came through"; Pezzo & Pezzo 2007).

Phenomena related to hindsight bias

A number of important psychological phenomena across fields of study are closely related to hindsight bias, and to at least some degree, will be easier to understand now that we have become more familiar with the principles of hindsight bias. These phenomena include reverse hindsight bias, visual hindsight bias, outcome bias, and epistemic egocentrism (also known as the curse of knowledge effect), among others.

Reverse hindsight bias

Under certain conditions, reverse hindsight bias has been known to occur. That is, sometimes after learning the outcome of an event, instead of showing hindsight bias, people do the opposite, disproportionately believing that they "never would have seen it coming." In reverse hindsight bias, people's likelihood estimates of the actual outcome after the fact are even lower than estimates given by people who did not know the outcome at all. That is, not only are they failing to show hindsight bias, but their judgments are actually going in the opposite direction.

The appearance of reverse hindsight bias is relatively predictable, occurring under specific conditions. For example, unexpected events can produce reverse hindsight bias, presumably due to the element of surprise (Ofir & Mazursky 1997). Specifically, Ofir and Mazursky (1997) proposed that for extremely surprising events, people will show reverse hindsight bias, whereas for moderately or mildly surprising events (as in the other research we have discussed so far), they may instead show classic hindsight bias. In one study, all participants first read about a patient going in for a heart bypass operation and learned that 2% of people going in for such an operation die from the operation itself. Then, a third of the study participants were told that the patient had died from the operation, and they were asked to judge the likelihood of the operation's success as if they did not know the actual outcome. Another third of the participants were told that the patient had died from the operation and were asked to rate how surprising this outcome was. The remaining third of participants were not given the outcome, and they were asked to rate the likelihood of the operation's success in foresight. People were, of course, extremely surprised at the outcome, and compared to those rating the likelihood of success of the operation in foresight, people making judgments in hindsight expected it to be significantly more successful – showing reverse hindsight bias (Ofir & Mazursky 1997).

What makes an event surprising in the first place? Of course, as in Ofir and Mazursky's (1997) example above, an outcome with a very low prior probability of occurring (2%) is going to be very surprising. In other cases, even if prior probabilities are not known, causal factors can lead people to expect one outcome, eliciting great surprise when an alternative outcome occurs instead. In one study by Yopchick and Kim (2012), people read about hypothetical events or episodes (e.g., about a double homicide case that went to trial in 1998). They were asked to judge the likelihood of two possible outcomes (e.g., that the prosecuting attorney would win or lose the case). If a plausible, relevant, potentially causal statement was provided prior to the judgment (e.g., the murder weapon was found) and the outcome made sense given that statement (e.g., the prosecuting attorney won the case), then people showed hindsight bias. However, if the same causal statement was given prior to the judgment (e.g., the murder weapon was found) and the outcome was the opposite of that expected given the causal statement (e.g., the prosecuting attorney lost the case), reverse hindsight bias appeared. In other words, when causally relevant factors lead more plausibly to the outcome that did not occur than to the actual outcome, we can reasonably expect to see reverse hindsight bias (Yopchick & Kim 2012).

Visual hindsight bias

One might ask if the hindsight bias phenomenon is entirely verbal in nature – as might seem to be the case given the nature of all the hindsight bias methodologies we have discussed so far – or not. In a clever play on a hindsight bias task in the hypothetical paradigm, Bernstein, Atance, Loftus, and Meltzoff (2004) first asked people to recognize and name pictures on a computer screen. These pictures were line drawings of common objects (e.g., a fish) that were first shown as very degraded (blurry) and then gradually became more and more sharply focused. In their study, the same people saw some objects in a foresight condition and others in a hindsight condition. When people were looking at objects in the foresight condition, they only saw the degraded-to-focused presentation of each drawing and named the object as soon as they recognized it. When people were looking at objects in the hindsight condition, they first saw the object in full, clear focus and were asked to name it. Then, they were shown the degraded-to-focused presentation of the drawing, and they were asked to imagine that a peer named "Ernie" was looking at it. People in the hindsight condition were asked to name the object as soon as they believed "Ernie" would recognize it. Bernstein et al. (2004) found that people reliably showed **visual hindsight bias**: Those who already knew the identity of the object tended to think their hypothetical peer Ernie would recognize the object at a more degraded level of focus than they themselves recognized it in foresight. Not surprisingly, this finding has been nicknamed the "I saw it all along" effect!

Outcome bias

Suppose you are told about a person who was forced to quit a great job because of a heart condition. If the person has a particular type of bypass operation, life expectancy could be increased, although 8% of people who undergo this operation do not survive it. The person's physician decides to move forward with the bypass operation. Now, suppose that instead of being asked to judge the likelihood of the operation's success (as in hindsight bias research), you are instead asked to judge the quality of the physician's reasoning process in deciding to go ahead with the operation. That is, you are asked: Does the physician's judgment seem sound?

Let's take it one step further. Suppose that before you judged the quality of the physician's reasoning, you were informed that the patient actually died after the operation. Does the quality of the physician's reasoning process seem different now? If it does, then your perception is no different from those of the participants in Baron and Hershey's (1988) classic studies. But keep in mind that it was the exact same reasoning process whether or not the outcome was known. In other words, the physician's reasoning process itself cannot truly be of different quality depending on the outcome, because at the time the physician was reasoning through the problem, *given the information available*, it was a sound decision.

Baron and Hershey (1988) called this phenomenon **outcome bias**. Specifically, outcome bias refers to people's tendency, when judging the quality of a decision, to take the outcome into account in a way that is actually quite irrelevant to decision-making quality. They pointed out that it is not reasonable to insist that being clairvoyant is a necessary trait of good decision-making. If the judgment is sound given what one knows in foresight, then it doesn't make much sense to denigrate the same judgment in hindsight. Neither is it reasonable, argued Baron and Hershey (1998), to over-apply the simple decision rule that a bad outcome must reflect poor decision-making.

Outcome bias can appear in any of a number of different contexts, including evaluation of the decision-making of corporate executives, tax auditors, politicians, and intelligence agents. It can be particularly salient when the outcome is strongly negative, as when a politician loses an election by a slim margin, a businessperson fails to complete a potential company-saving business deal, a tax auditor fails to identify a person hiding a large portion of income, or an intelligence analyst fails to see a large-scale terrorist attack coming. And of course, "Monday Morning quarterbacks" have been (rather unfairly) criticizing the play and decisions of losing sports teams and their coaches in hindsight quite possibly for as long as team sports have been played.

Epistemic egocentrism/Curse of knowledge effect

Hindsight tasks using the hypothetical paradigm rely heavily on people's possession of theory of mind – the understanding that other people have different minds (and know different things) than themselves (Birch & Bernstein 2007). In tasks especially designed to test theory of mind, one is asked to answer a question from the perspective of another person – in particular, a person who only knows outdated information (i.e., does not know the same updated information that one knows). In this sense, both theory of mind tasks and hindsight tasks in the hypothetical paradigm involve reasoning about a state of the world that one knows no longer exists (Stanovich & West 2008). In the case of hindsight tasks in the hypothetical paradigm, the state of the world that no longer exists is one in which the outcome is unknown (Fischhoff 1975). In theory of mind tasks, the state of the world that no longer exists is often about the location or existence of objects, such as where a child has hidden a marble (Baron-Cohen, Leslie, & Frith 1985) or whether a closed box of candy actually contains any candy at all (Perner, Leekam, & Wimmer 1987). Furthermore, both theory of mind tasks and hindsight tasks in the hypothetical paradigm involve taking on the point of view of a person who does not know the current state of the world. In hindsight tasks in the hypothetical paradigm, that person is oneself in the past; in theory of mind tasks, it is another hypothetical person. To the extent that hindsight tasks in the hypothetical paradigm closely overlap with theory of mind tasks, the demonstrations of hindsight bias in the research described in this chapter can also be interpreted as demonstrations of a relative failure in theory of mind.

This argument may seem surprising at first, given that a key finding in the theory of mind literature is that most young children, certainly from about the age of 4.5 onwards, are able to pass classic theory of mind tasks (Leslie 1987). Yet in fact, it has been well documented that even adults have trouble performing perfectly on more challenging versions of the original theory of mind tasks. This phenomenon is known as **epistemic egocentrism** (Royzman, Cassidy, & Baron 2003) or the **curse of knowledge effect** (Birch & Bloom 2007). Studies on epistemic egocentrism and the curse of knowledge effect generally show that when adults are asked to take the perspective of another person, they have a tendency to underestimate how likely it is that the other person holds a belief that is not consistent with the actual state of the world (that is, they underestimate the likelihood that the other person could have a false belief). This occurs even though the adults know for certain that correct beliefs about the state of the world have been shown only to them and not to that other person. In fact, Birch and Bloom (2007) showed that the curse of knowledge effect only appears in adults when it is possible to easily explain how the false belief relates to plausible background knowledge about the world. This finding aligns well with the causal model theory of hindsight bias, which, again, suggests that the ease with which we can causally connect outcomes to prior events drives us to show hindsight bias.

Hindsight bias over the lifespan

Studies on hindsight bias over the lifespan are quite rare, but those that have been conducted suggest that no one, no matter what age, seems to be immune to hindsight bias. In one study, Pohl, Bayen and Martin (2010) asked 9-year-olds, 12-year-olds, and adults to complete foresight and hindsight tasks in the memory paradigm. They first answered a variety of unknown quantity questions (e.g., "How many months are elephants pregnant?"). To measure judgments in foresight, they were only asked to recall their answers to half of the questions and were not given the actual answers (e.g., "What was your previous answer?"). To measure judgments in hindsight, they were then given the answers to the other half of the questions and asked to recall their earlier estimates (e.g., "The correct answer is 21 months. What was your previous answer?"). To make this a strong test, they were explicitly asked to try to remember their answer exactly, and to avoid allowing the correct answer to influence their recall. Yet all three groups of people showed hindsight bias, such that their estimates shifted toward the correct answer in the hindsight but not the foresight tasks. Nine-year-olds believed more strongly than the other two groups that they had actually known the correct answers all along.

In a similar approach, Bayen, Erdfelder, Bearden, and Lozito (2006) compared performance on hindsight tasks in the memory paradigm between younger (i.e., undergraduate students) and older adults (i.e., adults living in retirement communities). In one study, they asked people to try to memorize the correct answer for a later test, and also to report their original response. In another, people were not asked to memorize the correct answer, but only to report their original response. They found that whether younger adults showed more or less hindsight bias than older adults depended on whether they were also trying to memorize the correct answer. When people were trying to memorize the correct answer, older adults showed more hindsight bias than younger adults. When they were not, younger adults showed more hindsight bias than older adults. Bayen et al. (2006) suggested that all the adults knew that being asked to memorize the correct answers was irrelevant to being able to report their initial responses, and that the correct answers needed to be inhibited or suppressed when reporting their original responses. Thus, their findings suggest that older adults are not as good as younger adults at inhibiting/suppressing information (i.e., the correct response when they were asked to memorize it), but have no such deficit in accessing information (i.e., their original response when they weren't trying to inhibit the correct answer) compared to younger adults.

The most comprehensive single study of hindsight bias across the lifespan to date included children ages 3–15, young adults ages 18–29, and older adults ages 61–95 (Bernstein, Erdfelder, Meltzoff, Peria, & Loftus 2011). The experimenters set up a verbal hindsight bias task that they believed would be interesting and relevant to the entire age range. Note that because most hindsight tasks are verbal problems, it is extremely difficult to run the exact same verbal tasks on 3-year-olds as on older children and adults. For example, Bernstein et al. (2011) noted that the results for preschoolers should be interpreted with caution, because the answers to all the questions fell between 1 and 100, and the youngest children in the sample could not reliably count past 30. To help counteract this problem, they also made use of the visual hindsight bias task, discussed in the previous section, which only requires study participants to say at what point they can recognize and name a line drawing (versus guessing when a peer, "Ernie," can identify it).

Interestingly, Bernstein et al. (2011) found that over the lifespan, the degree to which people show hindsight bias can be described as a U-shaped function. The youngest children (3- and 4-year-olds) showed very strong hindsight bias and were the only group to completely replace their recollection of their prior response with the hindsight response. The preschoolers were also the only group to consistently insist that they (or their hypothetical naïve peer) "knew it all along." This finding, Bernstein et al. (2011) argued, is of particular importance for education in that it highlights one way in which hindsight bias can interfere with young children's assessments of their own rate of learning. That is, if they really feel that they always knew information that, in reality, they had never heard before, they may be more likely to maintain the illusion that they have relatively little to learn.

Hindsight bias was less strong, though still present, for the older children and younger adults. Interestingly, it remained quite stable between ages 5 and 29. Older adults, however, showed hindsight bias that was stronger than that shown by older children and younger adults. The experimenters suggested that older adults may more often fail to recall their initial responses, making it more frequently necessary for them to reconstruct their estimates (Bernstein et al. 2011). As we have seen, it is in the reconstruction process that distortions are particularly likely to occur.

Hindsight bias around the world

Although research on cross-cultural comparisons of hindsight bias is also rare, the studies conducted so far have produced intriguing results. Pohl et al. (2002) attempted to test for hindsight bias across a broad multi-national sample, recruiting participants from Europe, North America, Asia, and Australia. They selected 20 unknown quantity questions (e.g., "How many different kinds of insects inhabit the Antarctic?") in the hypothetical paradigm that were designed to be as equally relevant as possible between cultures. Interestingly, they found that hindsight bias was nearly universal (missing only in Germany and the Netherlands) and appeared to about the same degree across countries and continents. Because hindsight bias has previously been shown many times in German participants (e.g., Blank & Nestler 2006; Hoffrage et al. 2000) and the Dutch sample in this study only contained six participants, Pohl et al. (2002) suggested that these latter findings may have been something of a fluke, and it does seem reasonable to suppose that few behavioral effects would emerge with such a small sample (i.e., low power).

Yet there may still be cross-cultural differences in hindsight bias under certain conditions. A particularly interesting hypothesis is that people from collectivist cultures (e.g., Korea, Mexico, China, Kenya) have been argued to view situations more holistically, attending to more complexity (Choi & Nisbett 2000). As such, they might more easily make sense of surprising outcomes than people from individualist cultures (e.g., the U.S., Canada, Great Britain, Germany). Choi and Nisbett (2000) tested this hypothesis by presenting a highly improbable outcome to an event or episode to Korean and North American participants. Korean participants reported being less surprised and, accordingly, showed more hindsight bias than did North American participants.

In line with Choi and Nisbett's (2000) hypothesis, the collectivist-individualist difference in the strength of the hindsight bias may only be expected to occur in cases where the sense-making process is driving the bias. Heine and Lehman (1996) presented Canadian and Japanese participants with hindsight bias tasks using assertions (e.g., "The liver is the largest organ in the human body") in both the hypothetical and memory paradigms. Overall, they found that both Canadian participants and Japanese participants showed hindsight bias, but not to a significantly different degree. And in nearly all cases in the research described in this section, although culture might moderate the strength of the bias, it almost always did appear.

Conclusions

The study of hindsight bias is particularly important because in some sense, it is the study of how we think about our past versus our future. Hawkins and Hastie (1990) observed that "events in the past appear simple, comprehensible, and predictable compared to events in the future" (p. 311). Events in the past *are* in fact simpler in that they have already been constrained to what actually happened (e.g., Rei received a promotion at work at this year's performance appraisal). In contrast, the future contains the full set of possible events that could occur. In the 2012 film *Men in Black 3*, an alien named Griffin has the ability to perceive all possible alternative futures simultaneously and in detail, as though they have already occurred ("it's a gigantic pain in the ass, but it has its moments," Griffin comments). Although we cannot foresee our possible futures to the same level of detail, we can, without much mental strain, immediately see that there are a range of reasonable possible outcomes in any given situation (e.g., Rei might receive a promotion; Rei might be passed over for the promotion; Rei might be fired; Rei might receive a salary raise but not a promotion; etc.). The question is whether we are able to look back and accurately recall our experience of the uncertainty that once characterized our future – now that it has moved into our past.

The study of hindsight bias can also fundamentally be interpreted as the study of how people find it difficult to re-enact their own past states of knowledge. As we have seen, the knowledge we now have always seems to color our recollections of past knowledge. This tendency is reflected across a wide range of mental phenomena. It is robust across the lifespan and appears in many different countries (although the degree to which it appears throughout life and cross-culturally can depend on which mental processes are driving the bias in that instance). In the next two chapters, we will consider how we make judgments about possible events in the future, and how those judgments affect our choices in the here and now.

Questions for discussion

1. Compare the different ways of measuring hindsight bias: (a) hypothetical and memory paradigms; (b) event/episode, two-alternative-forced-choice, assertions, and unknown quantity materials; (c) verbal and visual tasks. What are the advantages and disadvantages of each? Does any one method tell us anything that the other methods do not?
2. This chapter outlined some ways in which epistemic egocentrism, or the curse of knowledge effect, overlaps with hindsight bias. How exactly, if at all, is hindsight bias *different* from this phenomenon?
3. In this chapter, we considered how normal memory processes can account for many hindsight phenomena. Given the entire body of research covered in this chapter, however, can hindsight bias be described as a purely memory-based phenomenon? If so, how does each piece of evidence reflect the workings of memory? And if not, what pieces of evidence reflect mental processes that have little or nothing to do with memory per se?
4. In hindsight after reading this chapter, do you find it surprising that we show the hindsight bias? Or did you know it all along?

Suggestions for further reading

Fischhoff, B. (1975). Hindsight ≠ foresight: The effect of outcome knowledge on judgment under uncertainty. *Journal of Experimental Psychology: Human Perception and Performance, 1*(3), 288–299.

Pezzo, M. V. (2011). Hindsight bias: A primer for motivational researchers. *Social and Personality Psychology Compass, 5*(9), 655–678.

Roese, N. J., & Vohs, K. D. (2012). Hindsight bias. *Perspectives on Psychological Science, 7*(5), 411–426.

5 Risk Perception

Learning Goals

By the end of this chapter, you will have:

- Considered evidence for how people make decisions about risks, how people weigh risks against benefits, and what factors influence risk perception in the world.
- Thought critically about how the presentation of statistical information, combined with lack of knowledge about statistics, can distort risk perceptions.
- Gained a better understanding of how to educate people to assess risk given a diagnostic test, comparing the relative ease with which we can calculate the likelihood of an outcome using natural frequencies versus using Bayes' Theorem.
- Developed additional concrete ideas about how to become an educated consumer of statistical information about risk.
- Considered potential causes of irrational judgments in high-stakes decisions about risk, and how these might be mitigated.

Key Terms	
Risk perception	Absolute risk
Risk-benefit analyses	Conditional probability
Unknown risks	False positive
Known risks	Bayes' Theorem
Dread risks	Natural frequencies
Rational	High-stakes decisions
Relative risk	Status quo bias

*But in this world nothing can be said to be certain, except death
and taxes.*

(Benjamin Franklin, American politician and inventor,
in a letter dated November 13, 1789)

The daily news provides constant reminders of undesirable events or
situations that could potentially happen at any time. An entire region could
suddenly be subjected to a power outage. An unexpected roadside accident
could abruptly change a person's life on an otherwise unremarkable day.
A tsunami could render thousands homeless and subject to dangerously
unsanitary conditions. Researchers of **risk perception** ask how we judge
risk, the likelihood of events for which past relevant numerical data are
available (Knight 1921). They ask how we attempt to take as much control
as possible over our uncertain future by trying to gauge our risk for negative
events, outcomes, and situations, and what steps we take to avoid these
undesired events if we feel we are at unacceptably high risk. The psychology
of risk perception also describes what kinds of risks people are willing to
take, and how much risk people tend to be willing to accept. It highlights
how people's informal risk perceptions do not always line up with evidence.
A person who strongly opposes hazardous conditions in the workplace
might simultaneously think nothing of driving without wearing a seat belt,
smoking, or neglecting to get any exercise, even if the latter behaviors are
much more likely to end a person's life prematurely than those particular
work conditions.

Risks versus benefits

Public policy makers frequently carry out **risk-benefit analyses**, in which
potential harms are weighed against potential benefits to determine whether
a particular action should be taken. Should a new pharmaceutical drug be
put on the market when research shows it will prevent a serious illness in
some people but also cause significant side effects in many others? Should
a highly efficient nuclear power plant be built, knowing that with proper
safeguards in place, the risk of accidents or meltdowns is infinitesimally
small? Should the speed limit on a major highway be increased, given that
millions of commuters will be able to reach their destinations more quickly
over many years, although a small number of additional fatal accidents are
likely to occur?

Starr (1969) was among the first to observe that risk-benefit analyses could
be conducted to balance societal benefits of any activity against the acci-
dental deaths expected to result from partaking in that activity. Starr (1969)
estimated societal benefits in terms of the monetary value of the activity

(either the money spent on an activity or the money earned from performing that activity) and risks in terms of the number of deaths expected per hour of exposure to that activity. For example, the benefit of being able to reach a certain destination in the convenience of one's car can be considered against the risk of being in a fatal car accident; the benefit of earning salary by working in a coal mine can be weighed against the risk of dying in an accident in that coal mine. Starr's (1969) analyses suggested that as risk increases for an activity, people are exponentially more willing to spend money (or require exponentially more pay) to engage in that activity. Interestingly, the analyses also suggested that people were willing to take on about 1000 times more risk for voluntary activities – such as downhill skiing – than for involuntary ones with the same monetary value per hour of exposure (e.g., eating food with preservatives).

However, the results of other studies and methodological approaches suggested a more complicated picture. Starr's (1969) approach was advantageous in that it used concrete behaviors as estimates of societal benefits and risks; that is, it was based on measurements of what people are really paying for or earning from engaging in an activity and the actual death rate (as accurately as could be gathered) resulting from engaging in that activity. This is important, of course, because people's actions don't necessarily correlate with the actions they think or say they are likely to take. However, a disadvantage of this approach is that it cannot tell us how people's attitudes toward that activity would change if they were presented with alternative courses of action. Suppose a person is working in a coal mine at a certain level of risk of death, but doesn't realize that some additional safety measures could cut that risk of death in half. Once the option for additional safety measures is presented, that person might then feel strongly that the mining company should put those safety measures into place.

To learn how people think about risk when allowed to consider not only actual situations, but ideal ones as well, other researchers tried a different approach, asking people directly to make *judgments* of the benefits and risks of a variety of activities (e.g., mountain climbing; using motor vehicles; using pesticides), and calculating their levels of tolerance for risk (Slovic, Fischhoff, & Lichtenstein 1982). This direct questioning approach also provided an opportunity to ask people about the level of safety they believed each activity *should* have, and their preferences regarding the implementation of new rules and regulations to reduce risk. In one of these early, groundbreaking studies, Fischhoff, Slovic, Lichtenstein, Read, and Combs (1978) found that people wanted most risks to be lowered by deliberately increasing rules and regulations for those activities, such that the riskiest activity was no more than ten times as risky as the safest activity. People's responses in this study suggested that they believed Starr's (1969) estimates (i.e., showing that benefits should increase exponentially as risk increases) describe the ideal state of affairs, but not the actual state of affairs in the world. In contrast, people felt that in reality, there was no way to predict the risk of an activity given its benefits or vice-versa; for example, they believed that any given high-risk activity is just as likely to have low benefits as high benefits in the world. But they felt that rules and regulations should be put in place so that high-benefit activities would allow for people to take higher levels of risk, and that low-benefit activities should *not* be allowed to incur high levels of risk. For example, they might advocate accepting greater levels of risk given the immense societal benefits of childhood vaccinations and also support the notion that regulations must be put in place to eliminate situations in which people must work in unsafe conditions for very little pay.

In addition, early research focusing on people's judgments of benefits and risks showed that there are at least two major characteristics of potential dangers that people take into account when deciding how much risk they are willing to take. The first has to do with the degree to which they feel they understand the risk. For example, some risks are new, not well understood by science, unobservable, and unknown to those exposed to it. Slovic (1987) has called risks falling along the high end of this dimension **unknown risks**. Examples of such risks include those posed by newer technologies, such as exposing food to radiation to sanitize it, and diseases not yet well understood, such as Ebola. **Known risks**, in contrast, are older, well-researched, observable, and known to those who have been exposed (e.g., risks posed by choosing to fly as a passenger in a commercial airplane).

Another characteristic of potential dangers that affects people's risk perceptions is how much the potential danger gives people a feeling of dread. Risks falling along the high end of this dimension are called **dread risks** in the literature; these risks have "catastrophic" potential, will result in fatalities, and are seen as being uncontrollable, and the risks and benefits are not seen as being fairly distributed between individuals (Slovic 1987). Risks that people rate as strongly characterized by dread include risks from nuclear power and the risk of bioterrorism. Risks falling along the low end of the dread-risk dimension are characterized by the absence of such a feeling (e.g., risks posed by driving to work every day or by foregoing an annual flu shot). According to Zenko (2012), an average of about 29 Americans were killed by terrorists annually between 2001 and 2012; this is comparable to the average number of Americans killed annually by falling televisions or furniture. Nonetheless, people find the feeling of dread to be very compelling.

Dread risk

Based on their research on dread risk, Slovic and colleagues (Slovic et al. 1982; Slovic 1987) developed a theory describing what motivates people to act to reduce risk. The higher the dread felt toward any given activity or technology, the more risky people believe it to be, and the more they want to see it strictly regulated to reduce risk. In particular, people feel strongly about avoiding situations in which there is a slight possibility that something catastrophic could happen (e.g., living near a nuclear power plant), whereas they seem to care comparatively little about avoiding situations in which there is a much greater likelihood that a less negative outcome could happen (e.g., driving to work every day; Gigerenzer 2004). Interestingly, the psychological power of dread risk appears to manifest itself primarily in lay people. Experts in the field making risk assessments are influenced more purely by knowledge of mortality rates expected from the activity or technology (Slovic 1987). That is, in a statistical sense, experts are more rational in their perceptions of risk. Lay people, on the other hand, are swayed by the psychological perception of dread and the feeling that they lack adequate knowledge about the risk. It seems that, lacking statistical knowledge, lay people use emotion as a guide to action, and tend to err on the side of safety, simply avoiding dread-risk situations that they feel they don't understand. When it comes to making public policy, however, it nearly always matters what lay people think. Experts will certainly be consulted, but in most cases it is difficult to enact public policy changes that do not cohere with the beliefs and perceptions of the lay public (e.g., policies to counteract global warming; Weber 2006). The bottom line is that public policies are often calculated to reduce fears rather than solely to optimally regulate risks. In some sense, this is disturbing because we often have in hand the statistical information necessary to implement policies that will probably save more lives than the policies we currently have. It is also important to consider people's emotional comfort, but the fact that there is a tradeoff is worthy of discussion.

As we saw earlier, negative affect or emotion (e.g., experienced as fear or worry) may be a strong motivating factor underlying the tendency to overprotect ourselves from dread risks. The interesting flip side is that when we don't feel negative affect toward a particular risk, we tend to be relatively apathetic about it (Peters & Slovic 2000). One case that nicely illustrates the latter situation is the difficulty of enacting governmental policies to slow global warming. Scientists had long reached an overwhelming consensus on the dangers of global warming (Ding, Maibach, Zhao, Roser-Renouf, & Leserowitz 2011), but few governments took significant steps to address it (Weber 2006) until recently. Drawing upon the distinction between Type 1 and Type 2 reasoning (see Chapter 1), Weber (2006) proposed that in most cases, the only exposure lay people have to information about global warming is in abstract, statistical format, which she argued tends to influence Type 2 disproportionately more than Type 1 reasoning. For example, reports aimed at the lay public emphasize facts about hotter temperatures and higher sea levels in recent years compared to those over the Earth's history. The second part of her proposal is equally important: That Type 2 reasoning, driven by abstract and numerical information, is far less likely to motivate people to take drastic action for change than Type 1 reasoning, which is driven by fear and anxiety. According to Weber (2006), this is why climate change experts, who in many cases have observed in person the real phenomenon of melting glaciers and the resulting disruption to surrounding life, believe global warming to be a severely anxiety-inducing phenomenon. That is, the information that climate change experts receive includes direct, vivid experiences, which influence Type 1 reasoning and are most likely to motivate action for change. In contrast, most members of the lay public have not had this direct experience, and their Type 1 reasoning is not triggered (Weber 2006).

Additional support for this claim comes from a recent study showing that lay people who believed they had personally experienced global warming (e.g., by observing changes in the seasons, weather, lake levels, animals and plants, or snowfall) also had elevated estimates of the risk of global warming relative to people who did not believe they had personally experienced global warming (Akerlof, Maibach, Fitzgerald, Cedeno, & Neuman 2013). This difference in risk estimates could not be fully accounted for by differences in the two groups' political affiliations, demographics (e.g., gender, family income, education, race, ethnicity), or prior personal beliefs about the effectiveness of national policies to control climate change. Interestingly, although only 27% of the people in this study reported personally experiencing global warming, the types of evidence they most frequently described (e.g., shorter winters; higher frequency of storms) were indeed supported by actual climate data from the region, as recorded by the U.S. National Oceanic and Atmospheric Administration (NOAA; Akerlof et al. 2013).

Many researchers have pointed out that our extreme avoidance of dread risks can lead us to engage instead in activities that are actually more risky and more likely to result in death. On September 11, 2001, terrorists hijacked four American commercial jets and flew two into the twin towers of the World Trade Center in New York City and a third near the Pentagon, the military headquarters in the U.S. capital city of Washington, D.C. The fourth jet was retaken by civilian passengers and crashed in a rural area, and the entire set of attacks resulted in at least 3,250 human casualties. The attack dominated U.S. news reporting for many days and was therefore highly salient in Americans' minds, potentially triggering the availability heuristic (Chapter 2). Thus, one question for risk perception researchers was how heightened *fear* of the dread risk of terrorism after the 9/11 attacks resulted in even more casualties in subsequent days.

Even taking into account the disastrous events of 9/11, air travel remains, statistically, among the very safest modes of travel. Yet Myers (2001) speculated that a second toll of lives might have occurred *after* the 9/11 attacks were over. Specifically, he asked whether large numbers of people avoided air and train travel to avoid the dread risk of terrorism, choosing instead to use a statistically more risky (dangerous) mode of travel: Driving a car. In fact, Sivak and Flannagan (2003) estimated that the risk of dying while driving the same distance as the average U.S. plane flight is 65 times greater than the risk of dying as a passenger on that average U.S. flight! This estimate even included the casualties of September 11, 2011. According to Sivak and Flannagan (2003), a catastrophic event of the magnitude of the September 11 attacks would have to occur approximately *every* month for the risk of flying to equal the risk of driving.

Gigerenzer (2004) reasoned that three pieces of indirect evidence would support Myers' (2001) speculation if found to occur simultaneously: (1) air travel decreased, (2) road travel increased, and (3) road fatalities increased, all in the months immediately following September 11, 2001. Data from the U.S. Department of Transportation and the Air Transport Association provided the first two pieces of evidence, indicating dramatic decreases in the monthly number of miles traveled by passengers by air and marked increases in the monthly number of miles driven, respectively, in the three months following the September 11 attacks. For the third piece of evidence, Gigerenzer (2004) tracked the number of fatal car accidents for each of the 12 months in the years 1996–2000, and compared these numbers to the number of fatal car accidents for the year 2001. The number of fatal car accidents in the final four months of 2001 (that is, immediately following the September 11 attacks) dramatically exceeded the average from the preceding five years for each of those four months, and always either matched or exceeded the very highest number of accidents in those preceding years. By adding up the apparent surplus of crashes per month following September 11, 2001, and multiplying by the number of lives lost on average per fatal crash, Gigerenzer (2004) estimated that about 350 additional Americans may have lost their lives because they were trying to avoid potential terrorism on planes by driving. This second toll of lives has gone virtually unnoticed in the public eye, but it is a fascinating and disturbing potential consequence of our strong motivation to avoid highly available dread risks, even at the cost of introducing different, sometimes more dangerous risks.

A replication of Gigerenzer's (2004) analysis in Spain illustrates that although avoiding dread risks may be a universal tendency, the practical outcome of this avoidance may not always be the same across cultures and countries. In 2004, terrorists bombed four commuter trains in Madrid, Spain, killing 191 people and injuring 1,800, according to the BBC. In an analysis similar to Gigerenzer's, López-Rousseau (2005) asked whether avoiding commuter trains following the Madrid train attacks resulted in a higher death toll via car accidents. Interestingly, López-Rousseau (2005) found that the data met the first condition; people in Spain did indeed reduce commuting by train in the months following the March 11 attacks. However, neither of the last two conditions was met. In Spain, people simultaneously also *decreased* their driving, and car fatalities were actually *reduced* following March 11, relative to the same months in previous years. In other words, people in Spain avoided the dread risk of terrorism on trains, but did not replace that risk with the risk of car accidents.

Why the latter two results were different in Spain in 2004 than in America in 2001 is a matter of pure conjecture, but the possibilities are quite interesting. López-Rousseau (2005) speculated that Americans are relatively unused to experiencing terrorism on U.S. soil, whereas Spain has been subjected to terrorism for decades and therefore no longer treats terrorism as a dread risk. This account does not seem to acknowledge, however, that people in Spain did in fact avoid the dread risk of terrorism on trains following the March 11 attacks, reducing the number of miles they traveled on trains relative to the same months in previous years. López-Rousseau (2005) also observed that the U.S. is more of a car culture than Spain, which seems to more directly address the fact that people in Spain did not increase car travel following the attacks. Yet another possible explanation is that in Spain, the impact of dread risk may have expanded to include all commuter travel, not just train travel. Different empirical approaches will be needed in future research to determine the reasons for the different results in the U.S. and Spain, but the analyses at this point suggest that avoidance of dread risks seems to be consistent, though the consequences of that avoidance may differ across cultures and situations.

A reasonable outstanding question is whether the avoidance of airline and train travel in the U.S. and Spain, respectively, might be partly due to the fact that fewer flights were running in the U.S. and that train lines in Spain also operated on a reduced schedule in the weeks and months immediately following the terrorist attacks, and therefore was not entirely driven by people's *voluntary* avoidance of the dread risk of terrorism. That is, maybe people would have taken more flights and train rides if they had been available. A more recent analysis by Prager, Asay, Lee, and von Winterfeldt

(2011) addressed this issue; they studied subway travel patterns on the London Underground following the suicide bomb attacks on July 7, 2005, that resulted in the deaths of 52 civilians and injuries to over 770 civilians in Britain. In their statistical analysis, Prager et al. (2011) not only accounted for reduced service due to structural damage following the attacks, but also economic conditions, weather, and the fact that London students were on summer holiday following the attacks. Even so, they found that about 82% of people's reduced travel on the London Underground could not be accounted for by any of these factors. Instead, the avoidance of dread risks (in this case, the dread risk of terrorism) seems to strongly influence people's travel patterns, above and beyond those other factors. Overall, the research on people's avoidance of dread risks suggests that fear of certain kinds of risks can lead people to behave in ways that do not optimize their chances of survival.

Understanding risk by the numbers

It might be tempting to think that if people were simply aware of the relevant statistical information, then they would behave much more rationally than they do, avoiding statistically high-risk behaviors and preferring less risky ones. However, a massive body of research indicates instead that even when people are provided with numerical risk information, they find it very difficult to use (Reyna, Nelson, Han, & Dieckmann 2009) and often will ignore it completely (Kunreuther et al. 2002). Some of the most striking studies demonstrating this phenomenon center on people's difficulty in understanding medical screening test results (Reyna, Lloyd, & Whalen 2001). As an illustrative example, consider the hypothetical case in Box 5.1.

How do people think about risk by numbers? As we will see in this section, people's perceptions of risk are strongly influenced by the *format* in which numerical risk information is presented (Miron-Shatz, Hanoch, Graef, & Sagi 2009). For example, Hannah (see Box 5.1) is told at various times that her baby (1) is at eight times the average risk of having Down syndrome, (2) has a less than 1% chance of having Down syndrome, and (3) has a 1 in 125 chance of having Down syndrome. There are three key points to take away from the current research literature on risk perception. The first is that these formats are all mathematically accurate in describing the same situation (more on this in a moment). This is why physicians will often use these formats interchangeably when telling patients about their test results, and why any given physician may use a description that is quite different from another's.

The second key point is that each of these formats creates a very different affective response, which guides people's inferences about the level of risk for the baby, which in turn can lead people to make very different medical

Box 5.1: **The Case of Hannah: Interpreting Screening Test Results**

Suppose that "Hannah," a 30-year-old adult, is pregnant for the first time. On a routine obstetric check-up, she is offered a standard blood test to screen for Down syndrome, a genetic abnormality, in her unborn baby. There is no chance that the blood test could harm Hannah or her baby physically. Hannah agrees to the screening test, and the blood is drawn. A week later, her doctor calls with the test results: Her baby is at "elevated risk" for Down syndrome. Hannah isn't sure what this means. Does her baby have Down syndrome? Or, does her baby have it to some degree? "A baby either has Down syndrome or doesn't have it. Your baby is just more likely to have it than we had assumed, but it is still not highly likely," her doctor explains. "To be precise," her doctor says, "given the blood test results, your baby's risk of having Down syndrome is nearly eight times higher than babies of the average woman your age."

Hannah takes the doctor's advice to discuss her situation with a genetic counselor. The genetic counselor further explains that the doctor's explanation is correct, but that Hannah could alternatively look at her test results this way: The baby has a less than 1% chance of having Down syndrome; a 1 in 125 chance, to be exact, whereas the average woman her age has a 1 in 1000 chance of having a baby with Down syndrome. There is a way to find out for sure whether or not the baby has Down syndrome; undergoing another diagnostic test, called an amniocentesis, that involves drawing some fluid from the womb. Unfortunately, the genetic counselor warns, there is a 1 in 200 chance that the procedure will accidentally abort the baby, who is actually more than 99% likely to be perfectly healthy. However, because Hannah is more likely to have a baby with Down syndrome (1 in 125) than the amniocentesis is to harm the baby (1 in 200), the genetic counselor recommends having the amniocentesis for a definitive diagnosis.

Hannah feels uncomfortable with this course of action, but she hates the feeling of uncertainty, and there are five months left before the baby will be born. She is not sure what to make of all the numbers that describe her test results, and she is not sure what to do. *If you were Hannah, what would you do, and why?*

decisions. That is, none of these formats is mathematically wrong, but people find it harder to accurately process some formats than others. For this reason, a person is more likely to form a distorted overall impression of risk for some formats than for others. For example, the first description above (saying simply that Hannah's baby is at eight times the average risk of having Down syndrome), as one might guess, makes one feel that Hannah is at very great risk of having a baby with Down syndrome. The second two descriptions, in contrast, make one feel that the odds are actually quite strongly in favor of a perfectly healthy baby.

The third and final key point is that research has uncovered ways in which risk information can be most accurately conveyed and processed. This research has strong implications for improving health, personal decisions, business decisions, and so on. However, this research is just beginning to be implemented outside the laboratory. In medicine, change has been slow (or in many places non-existent), in part because of a lack of awareness of the evidence (Smith 2011). For the moment, it falls to consumers of health care to learn for themselves how to properly understand, use, and navigate statistical information in medicine. Unfortunately, most people do not sufficiently understand the meaning of screening and diagnostic tests, and therefore they make important health decisions without being adequately informed (Siegrist, Cousin, & Keller 2008).

Becoming an educated consumer of statistical health information

One critical weapon for consumers of health information is basic knowledge of how statistical information is calculated, and knowledge of how to convert it into a format that allows us to best understand it. Gigerenzer and Gray (2011) and their colleagues have developed a compelling body of research showing that people have a much easier time accurately judging health risks when they are presented with "absolute risks instead of relative risks ... and natural frequencies instead of conditional probabilities" (Gigerenzer, Gaissmaier, Kurz-Milcke, Schwartz, & Woloshin 2008, p. 53). Let's consider each of these in turn.

Thinking about absolute risks instead of relative risks

In the mid-1990s, studies were conducted showing that for every 7,000 women taking a new contraceptive, two women developed dangerous, potentially fatal blood clots in the legs or lungs. In contrast, for every 7,000 women taking the old contraceptive, only one woman developed such blood clots. What is interesting is the way in which the U.K. Committee on Safety of Medicines chose to make an emergency announcement reporting these findings to the media. Specifically, they announced that the new contraceptives led to a "twofold" increase in the incidence of life-threatening blood clots (Gigerenzer et al. 2008). This is of course perfectly true; two women is indeed twice as many women as one woman. But as you might expect, when the public was given only the "twofold increase" statistic without mention of the overall rarity of such clots, the natural result was disproportionate public fear. Women were afraid to take their contraceptives as diagnosed and were subsequently more likely to become pregnant, and many of these people terminated pregnancies that were unwanted.

In a large-scale statistical analysis, Furedi (1999) estimated that the format in which the information was announced led to about 13,000 additional abortions performed in England and Wales during the year following the scare. Interestingly, pregnancies and abortions are associated with elevated rates of potentially fatal blood clots that are actually higher than the rate of blood clots associated with the new contraceptive pill (Gigerenzer et al. 2008). It seems highly unlikely that this would have occurred if the public had been told the same information in a different format; specifically, that two in 7,000 women had clots with the new contraceptive as opposed to one in 7,000 with the previous contraceptive (Gigerenzer et al. 2008).

Gigerenzer and colleagues (2008) pointed out that a key difference in these two formats is that the first format ("twofold increase") tells us the **relative risk** increase, and the second format ("two in 7,000 versus one in 7,000") tells us the **absolute risk** increase. In this case, the relative risk of developing serious blood clots is an increase of 100% when taking the new contraceptives compared to the old. At the same time, the absolute risk is quite small; only one additional woman in every 7,000 taking the new contraceptives is expected to develop clots. Motivated to produce eye-catching headlines, the popular press takes some pains to present research findings in their most sensational light, and authors of original research articles, additionally motivated by the prospect of increasing the impact and reach of the research they publish, may often be susceptible to doing the same. These outlets commonly present research findings in terms of relative risk increases, which have the immediate effect of capturing attention and inducing fear.

Additionally, it is not uncommon for pharmaceutical companies to present data on the effectiveness of their drugs in terms of relative risk increases (e.g., "this medication reduces the chance of heart attacks by 36%") and to present data on side effects in terms of absolute risk increases (e.g., "7 out of 100 people taking this medication experienced an irregular heartbeat compared to 5 out of 100 people who were not taking this medication"). This allows them to present their products in a manner that people will perceive in the most positive way possible, while still remaining perfectly truthful (though rather deliberately misleading).

Some researchers argue that consumers' best defense against such statistical manipulations is to become more knowledgeable about statistics – understanding what statistics are and how they should be interpreted (Gigerenzer et al. 2008), and in this case, knowing the difference between absolute risk and relative risk. For example, having read the information earlier in this section, you should know enough to respond with caution when an advertisement claims that taking aspirin cuts the risk of heart attacks in half. (You might immediately ask: Out of every 10,000 people who do not take aspirin, how many are expected to have a heart attack? And out of every 10,000 who do take aspirin, how many have a heart attack?) Similarly, in the case of Hannah at the beginning of this section, a 1/125 chance of having a baby with Down syndrome can be equated to an 8/1000 chance, which is more easily compared to the 1/1000 chance for the average woman of her age. That is, her risk is indeed higher than the average, yet it is still very low.

Thinking about natural frequencies instead of conditional probabilities: The mammogram problem

Lay people are not the only adults who find it difficult to understand probabilistic information about risk. A rather disturbing study by Eddy (1982) first showed that the vast majority of physicians in that study did not understand how to correctly interpret the results of a mammogram, the standard screening test for breast cancer. Eddy's study presented mammogram results to physicians using conditional probabilities or percentages, the format typically used in medical education and medical textbooks. A **conditional probability** is the probability of X given that Y has occurred. This is denoted as P(X|Y); for example, P(Dilly committed the crime|An ex-spouse accused Dilly of committing it). In this case, the probability of actually having breast cancer given a positive mammogram is denoted as P(Having breast cancer|Positive mammogram).

Eddy (1982) presented physicians with the following information: 1% of women taking a routine breast cancer screening actually have breast cancer; among women who do have breast cancer, there is an 80% chance of a positive mammogram (that is, that the breast cancer will be successfully detected); among women who do not have breast cancer, there is a 10% chance of a positive mammogram (that is, that there will be a **false positive** result). Then, physicians were asked to suppose that a woman has a positive mammogram: What is the probability that she really has breast cancer? In Eddy's (1982) study, 95 of 100 physicians estimated this probability at between 70% and 80%, most likely confusing the probability of really having breast cancer with the probability of having a positive mammogram. However, the correct answer is dramatically lower. There are two important things to keep in mind that will lead us to the correct answer. First, we need to take into account the base rate of breast cancer (1%; see also Box 5.2). Second, it is important to note that the probability of having breast cancer given that one has a positive mammogram, P(Cancer|Positive), is not the same thing as the probability of having a positive mammogram given that one has breast cancer, P(Positive|Cancer). One way to understand the probability mathematically is to use **Bayes' Theorem**, where ~Cancer denotes that breast cancer is not present:

$$P(Cancer|Positive) = \frac{P(Positive|Cancer) * P(Cancer)}{P(Positive|Cancer) * P(Cancer) + P(Positive| \sim Cancer) * P(\sim Cancer)}$$

Again, Eddy (1982) told physicians that the overall probability of having breast cancer, P(Cancer), is 1%, or .01. The probability of not having breast cancer, P(~Cancer), is therefore 99%, or .99. We know that the probability of having a positive mammogram given that one has breast cancer, P(Positive|Cancer), is 80% or .80, and the probability of having a (false) positive mammogram given that one does not actually have breast cancer, P(Positive| ~Cancer), is 10%, or .10. If we plug all these numbers in the above equation, we get (.80 * .01) divided by (.80 * .01 + .10 * .99), which equals .008 divided by .107, which equals about .075, or 7.5%. That is, a woman who has a positive mammogram actually has only a 7.5% likelihood of having breast cancer!

If you find this line of reasoning and calculation very easy to understand intuitively, you are very much in the minority. Time and again, research has shown that people do not generally find reasoning with conditional probabilities to be *at all* intuitively straightforward. And as you just saw in the study above, even domain experts such as physicians, whose job it is to explain to patients what their mammogram results mean, grossly overestimated the likelihood of cancer given a positive mammogram. Now for the fun part: Mentally reformatting those conditional probabilities into **natural frequencies** (e.g., the number of women out of every 1000) turns out to make these kinds of problems much easier to understand and solve (Hoffrage & Gigerenzer 1998), not only for physicians, but also for lay adults. In other words, instead of thinking about "80% of women," we're going to think about 800 women out of every 1000. So let's go back and translate Eddy's (1982) original problem into natural frequencies as follows: Out of every 1000 women taking a routine breast cancer screening, 10 actually have breast cancer (1% of 1000 women is 10 women). Of the 10 women who do have breast cancer, 8 will have a positive mammogram (80% of 10 women is 8 women). Of the remaining 990 women, who do not have breast cancer, 99 will have a positive mammogram (10% of 990 women is 99 women). This means that out of the original set of 1000 women, 8 + 99 = 107 women in total will have a positive mammogram. Only 8 of those 107 women, however, actually have breast cancer (quick check: 8 divided by 107 = .075, or a 7.5% probability that a woman has breast cancer given a positive mammogram, the same result given by Bayes' Theorem above).

In laboratory studies, teaching physicians to convert conditional probabilities to natural frequencies before thinking about the meaning of diagnostic test results has been quite successful. In fact, based on such evidence, Hoffrage and Gigerenzer (1998) suggested that medical schools should teach physicians to quickly translate percentages and conditional probabilities to natural frequencies, instead of implicitly hoping that the physicians they train will remember and apply Bayes' Theorem in practice. In fact, Sedlmeier (1997) found that teaching people to convert percentages to natural frequencies leads to much more accurate reasoning than people who were taught to apply Bayes' Theorem, and that this difference still persisted in a follow-up test five weeks after training. To date, however, not many physicians have been trained to convert percentages to natural frequencies (Wegwarth & Gigerenzer 2011). See Box 5.2 for another well-known example of how converting probabilities to natural frequencies dramatically increases the ease of reasoning.

Box 5.2: Base-Rate Neglect: The Taxicab Problem

Bar-Hillel (1980) presented the following problem:

Two cab companies operate in River City, the Blue and the Green, named according to the colors of the cabs they run. 85% of the cabs are Blue and the remaining 15% are Green. A cab was involved in a hit-and-run accident at night. An eyewitness later identified the cab as Green. The court tested the witness's ability to distinguish between Blue and Green cabs under nighttime visibility conditions (identical to the time of the accident). The witness was able to identify each color correctly 80% of the time, but confused it with the other color 20% of the time. What do you think is the probability that the cab in the accident was Green, given what the witness claimed? (pp. 211–212)

It would seem easiest to simply take the information about how accurate the witness tended to be – about 80% accurate – and assume that to be the correct answer. In fact, 36% of the participants in Bar-Hillel's (1980) study did just that, and only 10% of participants came anywhere close to the correct answer (see below). The problem is that using only the 80% figure ignores the fact that there are many more Blue cabs (85%) in the city than Green cabs (15%) – the *base rates* of Blue and Green cabs. Why does this matter? Let's try converting everything into natural frequencies to see.

Out of every 100 cabs in the city, 85 are Blue and 15 are Green.

If the witness gives the right color 80% of the time and confuses it with the other color 20% of the time, then when viewing the 85 Blue cabs, she will say correctly that 85 * .80 = 68 are Blue and incorrectly that 85 * .20 = **17** are Green.

Out of the 15 Green cabs, she will say correctly that 15 * .80 = **12** are Green and incorrectly that 15 * .20 = 3 are Blue.

So out of 100 cabs, she will identify 12 + 17 = 29 as Green, and will be correct only 12 of those times. Because 12 / 29 = .41, the probability that the cab in the accident is Green is 41%, not 80%.

As we also saw in the mammogram problem, one of the key problems seems to be noticing and using base rates in making these probability judgments. Using natural frequencies is simply one user-friendly way to see why base rates matter without having to whip out Bayes' theorem or, in most cases, even a calculator.

High-stakes decision-making

So far, the vast majority of the kinds of risks we have discussed – the risk of sustaining a terrorist attack on a building; the risk of having cancer given a routine screening test; the risk of having a child with a severe genetic abnormality – are characterized by their low base rates and their potentially extremely serious, life-changing outcomes. Decisions made to prepare for such risks are known in the literature as high-stakes decisions. **High-stakes decisions** are defined as problems of choice in which there is the potential for very significant, enormous financial and/or emotional losses, and in which the costs associated with changing a decision once made are also very significant.

In a comprehensive review, Kunreuther et al. (2002) outlined the following six key ways in which people's actual high-stakes decisions appear to deviate from normative decisions as calculated by the application of expected utility theory (Chapter 8): (1) People often behave as though rare outcomes with high-stakes losses have a probability of zero, resulting in a total lack of preparation. Normatively, however, the undesirability of such outcomes (e.g., terrorist attacks at sporting events) is so high that it is rational to accept the relatively modest costs of time and expense to prepare even for the slim possibility that they might occur. (2) Numerous studies have shown that decision makers tend to be shortsighted, overweighting concerns about the immediate future, which is more salient, and paying relatively little attention to the extended future (e.g., Kunreuther, Onculer, & Slovic 1998). Such shortsightedness likely contributes, for example, to people's lack of action to counteract global warming – even in individuals who believe that global warming will ultimately have extremely negative consequences. (3) Affect or emotion is a major player in swaying high-stakes decisions, especially when the decision is complex, involving many tradeoffs, and when the optimal course of action is not immediately clear. This general tendency, known as the affect heuristic (see also Chapters 1, 4, and 14), can disproportionately contribute to decisions in such cases (Finucane, Alhakami, Slovic, & Johnson 2000). (4) High-stakes decision situations induce stress, which has been shown to alter decision-making in systematic ways. For example, stress tends to lead people to use more simplifying heuristics, although it is not yet clear from research whether decisions are actually less normative under stress (Kunreuther et al. 2002). (5) Because high-stakes decisions are so rare, people seldom have direct prior experience reasoning about them and tend to rely heavily on social cues. For example, people will tend to follow procedures already in place, or do what they know another person did in a similar situation. However, following the lead of others is risky in that people might be replicating poor decisions already made. (6) When faced with high-stakes decisions, or more generally any difficult decisions, people quite often succumb to the **status quo bias** (see also Chapter 7); that is, they opt to do nothing. However, in many cases, a reasonable course of action often has a higher expected utility than complete inaction, and people are bypassing the opportunity to offset potentially catastrophic outcomes (Kunreuther et al. 2002).

Perhaps what makes high-stakes decisions so difficult is that there is very little room to learn. Those catastrophic negative outcomes are extremely rare, so there are few previous cases to consider, and in most cases, people will never receive feedback about their actions, as they will never be put to the test. For example, a new security system installed in a local elementary school to prevent the very slim possibility of massive gun violence is in fact highly unlikely to *ever* be put to the test by an armed assailant attempting to enter the building. However, feedback can come over longer periods of time in the aggregate. For example, it can ultimately be assessed whether schools across the country with security systems were in fact more safe than those without, after controlling for additional factors such as local population density and violent crime rates. Kunreuther et al. (2002) pointed out that normative models of decision-making, taking into account the above non-normative tendencies in human reasoning, can be used to develop prescriptive models to provide to those making high-stakes decisions. Using such prescriptive models, and becoming better informed about statistics and probabilistic thinking (Gigerenzer & Gray 2011), can help us optimize our decisions about risk.

Conclusions

As we have seen, in some very important ways, people tend to take a very reasonable approach to risk. They believe that when the risks of an activity go up, the benefits should go up exponentially. If risks and benefits do not have this relationship, people believe that regulations should be put into place to ensure adequate safety to offset risks.

Yet there are also many critical ways in which people's treatment of risk information is not normative (see Chapter 1). We are disproportionately afraid of dread risks – those that could potentially result in large-scale catastrophes – and those that we don't understand well to the point of taking on even riskier activities to avoid them. We are strongly affected by the format in which we are given risk information; we are confused by relative risks and conditional probabilities but are really quite good at understanding absolute risks and natural frequencies. Finally, when faced with high-stakes decisions, we may often fail to make normative judgments.

In large part, the study of risk perception focuses on how our understanding of probabilities and risks guides our decisions and behaviors in the here and now. In the next chapter, we will consider how we use available information to try to predict future events – whether those events are the onset of a severe tropical storm, an episode of a debilitating mental disorder, or even simply the way one will feel about one's job in the future.

Questions for discussion

1. If you were in Hannah's situation (Box 5.1), what would you do, and why? Come up with a creative way to implement this solution in clinical practice to help people make better medical decisions.
2. Gigerenzer and Gray (2011) are strong advocates for required statistics training in primary and secondary school, for physicians, and for news reporters. What do you think of this suggestion? Would a deeper understanding of statistics make people better consumers of risk information in daily life? If the goal were to help people make better medical decisions throughout their lives, what content would an ideal course of this kind include?

3. After reading this chapter, work out the solution to the taxicab problem (Box 5.2) on your own. Why is base-rate information crucial? Why do you think people tend to neglect it?

Suggestions for further reading

Gaissmaier, W., & Gigerenzer, G. (2012). 9/11, Act II: A fine-grained analysis of regional variations in traffic fatalities in the aftermath of the terrorist attacks. *Psychological Science, 23,* 1449–1454.

Gigerenzer, G., Gaissmaier, W., Kurz-Milcke, E., Schwartz, L. M., & Woloshin, S. (2008). Helping doctors and patients make sense of health statistics. *Psychological Science in the Public Interest, 8,* 53–96.

Slovic, P. (1987). Perception of risk. *Science, 236,* 280–285.

Prediction 6

Learning Goals

By the end of this chapter, you will have:

- Closely considered two prescriptive models of predictive judgments: Expert (also called clinical) intuition versus statistical prediction.
- Compared the accuracy of clinical intuition to statistical prediction in empirical work across a variety of domains including clinical and medical diagnosis, criminal profiling, baseball players' performance, and weather forecasting.
- Explored a variety of biases in decision-making that have been associated with affective forecasting and intertemporal choice, and considered their potential impact on judgments in daily life.
- Thought critically about the conceptual, practical, and ethical difficulties involved in end-of-life decision-making, and how understanding this issue can advance the study of prediction.
- Evaluated the current efficacy and future promise of modern interventions designed to improve prediction, including decision support systems and avatars imbedded in virtual reality environments.

Key Terms

Sabermetrics	Emotional evanescence
Criminal profiling	Focalism
Clinical intuition	Living will
Statistical prediction	Instructional advance directive
MMPI; MMPI-2	Palliative care
Face validity	Projection bias
Blind empiricism	Peak-end rule
Decision support systems	Intertemporal choice
Affective forecasting	Temporal discounting
Impact bias	

Clinical intuition versus statistical prediction

The bestselling book *Moneyball: The Art of Winning an Unfair Game* (Lewis 2004) describes the use of **sabermetrics**, the analysis of baseball statistics, to predict individual players' future performance. As Lewis (2004) explains, the traditional way of picking baseball players to draft onto a major-league U.S. baseball team has been to rely on the intuitive judgment of professional scouts. Expert scouts visit a player, often a college student, and carefully note many different aspects of the player's performance, reputation, and physical appearance. They also have information about the player's past performance record. With this information in mind, the scouts form an overall, intuitive impression regarding which players they think are most likely to continue to play well in the major leagues.

In contrast, making predictions about players' future performance based on sabermetrics is less reliant on intuition. In fact, decisions can be made using this method without ever even seeing the player in person. The enormous database of individual players' performance statistics is analyzed to determine which particular traits, which were demonstrated in the college or high school performances of the players, are the best predictors of major-league success. For example, statistical analyses suggested that the percentage of the time in which a player is able to get on base is the most important *predictor* of success in the major leagues (Lewis 2004). In the sabermetrics approach, players are picked solely on the basis of whether they possess these predictors. For example, a high on-base percentage will be favored regardless of whether the player has a stereotypically athletic physical appearance.

In baseball, a very lively debate still continues over which method is superior, and interestingly, similar debates have long existed in many different domains. Suppose you read in the news that the local police are trying to figure out who is carrying out a series of murders in your area. To reassure the public, they announce that a criminal profiler has been assigned to the case to help predict the killer's likely next step and his or her personal characteristics. In **criminal profiling**, the characteristics of the unsolved crimes are used to try to infer characteristics of the criminal such as age, educational level, and other demographics, along with behavioral tendencies and psychiatric symptoms. What approach should the profiler take? Out of the many possibilities, one very common approach is for the profiler to first read over the case files of the crimes that have been committed by this unknown person. Then the profiler will draw upon his or her expert knowledge to make predictions about the person's characteristics. Many profilers rely on intuition to make this judgment (see Homant & Kennedy 1998). An alternative possibility is for the profiler to instead enter the features of the case files (e.g., location, facts about the victims, etc.) into a computer program. The program will compare the features of the current case file against the features of cases from the past, drawing upon a massive national criminal database going back for decades. If the program detects a pattern of features in this case that are similar to patterns seen in other past cases, it will make predictions on the basis of those other past cases. Some profilers, in fact, do carry out such statistical analyses using large databases of similar past criminal activity (e.g., Kocsis, Cooksey, & Irwin 2002).

Or suppose that you are a psychiatrist seeing a new client and you need to figure out which psychiatric diagnosis is most appropriate for the client, if any. As in the criminal profiling situation, there are many ways in which a psychiatrist might approach this client case. However, let's again consider the contrast between two different approaches of how one might go about making these predictions. On the one hand, a psychiatrist might listen to the client, ask questions, and gradually form an intuitive opinion about the patient's disorder and likely prognosis. This opinion is presumably based on some combination of the psychiatrist's experience with past patients, past clinical training, and an intuitive assessment of the current patient as an individual. In contrast, the psychiatrist might instead ask the client to fill out a standardized questionnaire. The client's responses can be compared to the responses of thousands of other people who have also completed the same questionnaire. Then the psychiatrist can look at patterns of responses on test items that were previously shown in empirical research to indicate a particular disorder.

The baseball situation, the criminal profiling situation, and the clinical diagnosis situation all illustrate a contrast in approach. **Clinical intuition** generally refers to approaches in which people with experience and expertise in the domain make intuitive predictions for individual cases (Dawes 1994; Meehl 1954/1996). That is, experts consider the information available and make the decision themselves. The overall claim is that the expert is able to understand the dynamics of the individual case (e.g., how the different aspects of it fit together), and that once one understands the case, one should be able to make more accurate predictions about it (Meehl 1973). That is, the expert decides, based on intuition, what features of the case are most important for making the prediction. In contrast, **statistical prediction** refers to approaches in which predictions about a particular case are made solely on the basis of empirical evidence and/or a statistical comparison to data drawn from a large sample (Dawes 1994; Dawes, Faust, & Meehl 1989; Meehl 1954/1996). Here, the intuitive decision maker takes a back seat to a statistical analysis, or a mathematical formula that is used to compute predictions from data. The broad claim from those endorsing this approach is that the most accurate predictions, on average, are made from empirical data.

Box 6.1: **Statistical Prediction in Mental Health: The *MMPI* and *MMPI-2***

Perhaps by far the most well-known example of the statistical prediction approach in clinical diagnosis is the *Minnesota Multiphasic Personality Inventory*, both in its original and revised versions (*MMPI*, Hathaway & McKinley 1940; *MMPI-2*, Butcher, Dahlstrom, Graham, Tellegen, & Kreammer 1989). The inventory is a large questionnaire that includes both questions that obviously relate to behavioral health and ones that do not clearly relate to behavioral health in any way (i.e., they lack **face validity** in that they do not seem like they measure what they are measuring). A famous example of the latter type of item in the original *MMPI* asked people whether they preferred U.S. President Washington or Lincoln. (This item was removed in the *MMPI-2*, as it is too culture-specific to the U.S.; Butcher, Atlis, & Hahn 2003.) The general idea is that it doesn't really matter what the *content* of the question is; what matters is whether a particular answer to that question statistically *predicts* a particular behavior trait or disorder. If people's answers on a question help predict behaviors or disorders, then the question is useful, even if it doesn't make sense on its face. This is the fundamental philosophy underlying the test construction method sometimes called **blind empiricism**.

In the current MMPI-2 (1989), there are 567 questions, each answered with a true-or-false response (Drayton 2009). In accord with the blind empiricism approach, questions were included as long as they could help distinguish between responses of people with specific disorders or other traits (e.g., depression; schizophrenia; low self-esteem; familial discord) and "normative" (i.e., control) responses (Butcher et al. 2003). Normative responses were determined by asking 2600 people from six different areas of the U.S. to complete the inventory. Butcher et al. (1989) attempted to recruit a normative sample of participants across genders and ethnicities, such that they were relatively proportional to the demographics of the U.S. Some of the items in the inventory were designed to predict untruthful responses (e.g., lying to look more well-adjusted than they are, lying to exaggerate psychopathology, etc.; Butcher et al. 2003). Furthermore, the lack of face validity on some items helps make it less likely that people can deliberately manipulate the outcome of the inventory (Drayton 2009). From a practical standpoint, does it matter for clinical practice that the *MMPI-2* (Butcher et al. 1989) lacks face validity? Why or why not?

Meehl (1954/1996), in a famous book considering the relative accuracy of clinical intuition versus statistical prediction, offered a nuanced analysis of this debate. Meehl, a practicing psychotherapist who was strongly sympathetic to the clinical intuition viewpoint, was simultaneously a psychometrician at the University of Minnesota, an institution well known for its commitment to more statistically based approaches (Meehl 1954/1996, 1986). From this unusual perspective, he attempted to provide a truly balanced consideration of the different merits and downsides of each approach. A clinical intuition approach, in which the clinician interviews the client one-on-one, provides a richer, fuller set of information about the client, from which a causal story can be assembled (see Chapter 11; Meehl 1954/1996). In contrast, a statistical approach allows one to compare an individual client to a database of information about similar others; this, too, allows one to make use of a large set of potentially useful information (Meehl 1954/1996). Perhaps, then, the best way to evaluate whether statistical prediction is more or less accurate than clinical intuition is to examine empirical studies pitting the accuracy of one approach against the other. Interestingly, such studies have overwhelmingly emerged in favor of the statistical prediction approach (Grove, Zald, Lebow, Snitz, & Nelson 2000). Meehl (1986) wrote:

> There is no controversy in social science that shows such a large body of qualitatively diverse studies coming out so uniformly in the same direction as this one. When you are pushing 90 investigations, predicting everything from the outcome of football games to the diagnosis of liver disease and when you can hardly come up with a half dozen studies showing even a weak tendency in favor of the clinician, it is time to draw a practical conclusion, whatever theoretical differences may still be disputed. (Meehl 1986, p. 374)

A meta-analysis by Grove et al. (2000) on studies of prediction in behavioral and medical domains further supports this general claim. Among a total of 136 studies conducted between 1966 and 1994, 46% indicated considerably higher accuracy using statistical prediction, 48% showed no difference in accuracy between the two approaches, and only 6% indicated a significant advantage for clinical intuition (Grove et al. 2000). The date of publication of the studies, type of training, level of experience, and the particular predictions being made (e.g., medical diagnosis or prognosis; future job or academic performance; future criminal activity) had no bearing on the core results (Grove et al. 2000). It is interesting to note that most of the studies included in the meta-analysis used even less information for the statistical prediction approach than for the clinical intuition approach; in one case, even a two-variable equation made more accurate predictions than experts making intuitive decisions given many sources of information.

Nonetheless, it turns out to be very hard for people to let go of clinical intuition entirely, replacing it with statistical prediction, especially in such high-stakes domains as medical diagnosis and criminal justice (e.g., parole decisions). Meehl (1986) himself found it difficult to intuitively favor the statistical approach over the clinical intuition approach when seeing clients, but given the empirical data, he considered this to be "an irrational thought, which I should attempt to conquer" (p. 375). Thus, despite all of the research that has been conducted in this area, we still do not see algorithms and databases fully replacing physicians, judges, and juries in practice. And as Dawes (1994) pointed out, of course sometimes algorithms and databases generate predictions that turn out to be wrong. These errors can be especially salient to us when they are very clearly at odds with our intuitions (that is, when they are errors that any reasonable human would have caught). Because the kinds of errors that machines make are not necessarily the same as the ones that humans make, this further solidifies our mistaken impression that the machines, overall, are not as good as humans in making such predictions.

Alternate solutions are needed, and one reasonable direction has been to consider how clinicians might themselves become more efficient aggregators of statistical information. Westen and Weinberger (2004) suggested that it has been a mistake for researchers in this field to claim that clinicians themselves should be entirely cut out of the equation. Meehl (1954/1996) and Dawes et al. (1989) clearly defined statistical prediction as a *method* of aggregating data, and as such, expert clinicians should be perfectly capable of making use of statistical prediction. That is, the originators of this debate never claimed that clinicians themselves were inherently bad decision makers; rather, they were comparing the different methods that clinicians can use. Westen and Weinberger (2004) suggested that the real debate ought to center around whether clinicians (or non-experts) using more intuitive versus more statistical prediction methods make more accurate decisions. In addition, they pointed out that statistical prediction, at some point, often ultimately overlaps with clinical judgment. For example, statisticians carrying out factor analyses of data are making interpretations (intuitions per se) about the meaning of the factors that emerge from the data. And even when people are responding to questions in the *MMPI-2* (Butcher et al. 1989) itself, they are making intuitive judgments about their own thoughts and feelings regarding each item.

Others have pointed to a more practical solution in line with these arguments: Domain experts need not carry out the statistical predictions themselves in order to use them; the predictions can be provided to them. Then, they can use a combination of the two approaches, where the expert can see what the statistical prediction method has generated, but where the expert also has the final say. Computer-based decision support systems in medicine, for example, are software tools designed to compare a patient's characteristics and symptoms against past cases in a database (Hunt, Haynes, Hanna, & Smith 1998). The decision support system provides a recommendation and/or diagnosis for that particular patient, which the physician can then consider in making his or her own judgment. In fact, a systematic review found that many decision support systems have a beneficial influence on clinicians' judgments (Garg et al. 2005). Some of the specific features of decision support systems that positively affect clinical judgments have also been identified. In particular, decision support systems with a substantial positive effect on clinical judgments tend to be computerized, are built in as an automatic part of the clinician's workflow right at the time that decision-making takes place, and provide both diagnoses and recommended actions (Kawamoto, Houlihan, Balas, & Lobach 2005).

Forecasting, expertise, and feedback

A consistent and perhaps surprising finding in the literature is that clinicians do not always become more accurate with experience. In fact, Garb (1998), in a review of the relationship between clinical experience and the validity of predictions, suggested that the two are generally not related. In particular, differences are generally not found when comparing the judgments of experienced clinicians to those of either graduate trainees or relatively inexperienced clinicians. The null effect of experience on accuracy holds true over a variety of different clinical intuitions, including clinical judgments of the risk of mental disorder and clinical judgments of the likelihood of future criminal behavior (Garb 1998).

Einhorn and Hogarth (1978) suggested that a major reason why experience does not necessarily lead to accuracy is that feedback on performance is really necessary for learning to occur. In particular, corrective feedback that ultimately directs the clinician's attention away from invalid predictors and toward valid ones is critical (Einhorn & Hogarth 1978; see Chapter 12). For example, after seeing some cases of strep throat co-occurring with soreness of the throat, a medical student might begin to form the erroneous idea that throat soreness is a necessary predictor of strep throat. If the student's supervisor explicitly denies that this is the case, or if the student has an experience with a contradictory case in which a patient tests positive for strep without having a sore throat at all, such corrective feedback may lead the student to revise these views. If, on the other hand, the student gains experience without receiving any such corrective feedback, the student will not be able to improve. Yet he or she will still tend to gain a false sense of confidence as information is gathered, even without an increase in accuracy (Oskamp 1965).

Interestingly, it turns out that experience does lead to more accurate predictions in the domain of weather forecasting. In weather forecasting, feedback is frequently, consistently, and relentlessly given: After a prediction is made, we have only to wait a short time to see how the weather turns out. Weather forecasters also gain enormous amounts of practice by making daily projections, and base-rate information is highly accessible to them, thanks to years of records on hour-to-hour atmospheric conditions and the resulting weather (Monahan & Steadman 1996). Stewart, Roebber, and Bosart (1997), for example, showed that weather forecasters' temperature forecasts were highly accurate (although precipitation forecasts were generally not quite as good), and that accuracy differed very little for 12- versus 24-hour forecasts. They also found that agreement among forecasters was higher than is typically seen in other domains (e.g., clinical prediction; Stewart et al. 1997). Weather forecasters have often been held up as a model of expert prediction, and some have called for cross-domain training that capitalizes on the strengths of weather forecasters (Monahan & Steadman 1996).

Predictions about our future selves

For personal decision-making, being able to accurately judge how much we will value something in the future has crucial implications for making the best decisions now. For example, having clear insight into how much we will value being cancer-free later in life should, if we are being rational, influence our decisions now regarding what kinds of foods to eat and whether to exercise. But how good are we at predicting what we ourselves will value in the future? When we make predictions, one might think that we would be most accurate when making them about ourselves. After all, continuously consciously experiencing our own thoughts, behaviors, and feelings throughout life constitutes quite a lot of direct experience from which to draw inferences.

Early research by Kahneman and Snell (1992) measured how accurately people are able to predict how much they would like a specific experience in the relatively near future. In their study, people ate a serving of plain low-fat yogurt in the lab and rated how much they liked it (on average, it was very slightly disliked). They then committed to eating a serving (3/4 cup) of it 7 days in a row at home (at least 2 hours after their last meal each day), rating each time how much they liked it. On the 1st day (in the lab), they also predicted how much they would like the yogurt on the 2nd and 8th days of the study. By comparing the prediction ratings to the actual liking ratings for the 2nd and 8th days, we can get a clear picture of the accuracy of people's predictions over time. Interestingly, *actual* liking of the yogurt was much lower on the 2nd day relative to the first serving eaten in the lab, but then steadily rose through the 8th day (Kahneman & Snell 1992). In contrast, people *predicted* that they would like the yogurt about the same on the 2nd day as the first, but that they would like it less and less until the 8th day – almost an exact reversal of their actual liking for the food over time. Kahneman and Snell (1992) speculated that an anchoring effect (Chapter 3) drove predictions for the 2nd day, as people failed to adjust sufficiently from their initial experience tasting the yogurt in the lab.

It is fascinating that predictions about how much we will like something in the future could be far off the mark, even under such highly constrained conditions (e.g., predicting one's liking of a single, simple food the next day and over only a single week). Yet it seems that some of the most important predictions we make about our own likes, feelings, and values are much farther into the future, and are potentially about much more complicated things, some of which we haven't previously experienced. For example, how sad would it make you to get fired from your current job in a few years or to experience a breakup with your romantic partner? How happy would it make you to unexpectedly inherit a small fortune? When you make judgments such as these, you are carrying out **affective forecasting**: Making predictions about how some possible future event would make you feel.

Research suggests that we are quite good at predicting whether hypothetical far-away future events will cause us to experience positive versus negative feelings overall (Wilson & Gilbert 2005). A substantial body of research has shown that we have a much harder time predicting *how long* that event would make us feel that way and *how intensely* we would feel that way (Wilson & Gilbert 2005). Are we more likely to overestimate or underestimate how intensely and how long a future event will make us feel a certain way? Although both have been shown to occur, overestimation is far more common, and is known as the **impact bias** (Gilbert, Driver-Linn, & Wilson 2002). The problem with overestimating how long and intensely a future event will make you feel is that you'll be disproportionately motivated to make it happen (if it is positive) or to prevent it (if it is negative). Yet it is not likely to affect your future feelings quite so much as you think (Wilson & Gilbert 2005). So, if you go out of your way to facilitate or prevent that event, this might not be the best use of your time. Furthermore, the intensity of the emotion you feel appears to fade over time, a phenomenon called **emotional evanescence** (Wilson, Gilbert, & Centerbar 2003).

One of the major causes of impact bias may be **focalism**, in which people, when thinking about a specific possible future event, overestimate how much that event itself would affect their feelings, and underestimate how much other circumstances and events that would occur around the same time would affect their feelings (Wilson & Gilbert 2005). In other words, when we mentally attend to a particular event (e.g., unexpectedly inheriting a fortune one day), we might only focus on the money itself and neglect to take into account other events (e.g., whether disliked former friends and distant relatives will then come out of the woodwork to persistently ask you for money; tax headaches).

A second major cause of impact bias, according to Wilson and Gilbert (2003), is a sense-making process (e.g., see also Chapters 4, 10, 11). Wilson and Gilbert (2005) argued that we are particularly susceptible to the impact bias when the future event is very personally relevant but not easily explained (e.g., unexpectedly inheriting a fortune). Research suggests that we can expect such events to capture our attention (e.g., all our attention is on our good fortune) and then cause us to react emotionally (e.g., with happiness). Then, we will try to make sense of the event (e.g., who left the inheritance to us, and why?).

Most critically, the idea is that once we figure out how the event came about, making sense of it, we will then feel less strongly about the event. That is, once we *make sense* of the event, it seems more normal, ordinary, and expected to us (Wilson & Gilbert 2005). The general tendency to judge events or behaviors to be more normal when we are able to explain them in a way that makes sense has been dubbed the "understanding it makes it normal" effect and has also been documented in mental health assessment (Meehl 1973). Once people believe they understand another person's bizarre or disordered behavior, they judge it to be more normal (Ahn, Novick, & Kim 2003). In accord with the impact bias, people report feeling less negative stigma toward others when their disordered behavior has been satisfactorily explained and is, therefore, better understood (Weine, Kim, & Lincoln 2016). In sum, it is important for people to be made aware of the impact bias when planning for the future. Knowing about the impact bias might make us better able to compensate for the bias to make more optimal decisions (Wilson & Gilbert 2005).

End-of-life decision-making

In the book *Being Mortal*, physician Atul Gawande relates stories of terminally ill patients and their decision-making struggles at the end of life. In one case described by Gawande (2014), a patient had become paralyzed from a malignant cancer that had spread to his spine, and chemotherapy had been unsuccessful. The patient was presented with a choice: Let the disease take its course, with medications to manage his pain, or undergo surgery to remove some of the cancerous tissue around the spine. The surgery would not improve his health, change his paralyzed condition, or prolong his life much, and was in fact quite likely to do serious harm, as his doctors warned. He chose the surgery and passed away in the hospital shortly afterward, connected to machines – the very situation he had previously stated that he wanted most of all to avoid (Gawande 2014). Were the patient's choices optimal? Or would it have been better to maximize life quality (e.g., focusing on pain management) at the end?

This case illustrates a common, major end-of-life decision-making dilemma. Some have suggested that end-of-life decision-making can be aided by having each patient make a **living will**, or **instructional advance directive**. This refers to a legal document in which the person expresses his or her preferences for end-of-life medical care. In some countries (e.g., the Netherlands; Belgium), people may also express their preferences regarding euthanasia (i.e., assisted suicide to relieve pain and suffering). Its purpose is to let your physicians and caregivers know how you want to be medically treated, in case you aren't able to express or recall this yourself (e.g., when unconscious in the middle of surgery; in an advanced state of dementia; in a coma).

For caregivers, having a living will can greatly reduce the stress of trying to guess what the patient would have wanted; for example, whether the patient would want to be kept alive by machines regulating breathing, feeding, or kidney function (Ditto, Hawkins, & Pizarro 2005). It can also help prevent patients from receiving treatment that harms more than it helps or has no redeeming value, as in the case of the surgery we just considered (Scott, Mitchell, Reymond, & Daly 2013). A comprehensive review of the literature suggested a net positive impact of living wills on the quality of care at end-of-life (Brinkman-Stoppelenburg, Rietjens, & van der Heide 2014). Specifically, having a living will increased the chances that end-of-life care was carried out in accord with the patient's wishes, and increased the use of **palliative care**, which focuses on the effective management of stress, pain, and other symptoms, and improving the quality of life for terminally ill patients and their families (Lo, Quill, & Tulsky 1999). Living wills also reduced hospitalizations and being kept alive by machine intervention (e.g., tube feeding, cardiopulmonary resuscitation [CPR], etc.; Brinkman-Stoppelenburg et al. 2014).

However, there are major decision-making challenges inherent to creating living wills. First, it is not clear whether we can expect people's choices to remain consistent over time. Given the literature on affective forecasting, for example, it seems very likely that when making a living will, we may not always know the relative intensity with which we will react to different treatment options in the future (Ditto et al. 2005). In fact, a third of people asked to provide their treatment preferences for the end of life changed their minds at least once over the course of the next 2 years (Ditto et al. 2003).

Other closely related biases may also influence people's preferences for end-of-life care. Loewenstein (2005) suggested that the **projection bias** strongly influences people's advance medical decision-making. In the projection bias, people essentially project their current mental and emotional state into the future. For example, suppose you are planning a trip for leisure that will take place more than a year from now. If you are currently feeling very ill with motion sickness from a long plane ride just taken for work, you might be most likely to plan a trip close to home. Or if you have just been cooped up for several days in an unusually heavy snowstorm, you might be most likely to plan a trip far away. In each of these cases, your decisions are strongly influenced by your current (and possibly temporary) preferences. Ultimately, you might be relatively happier with the trip if you instead plan according to how you most typically feel about vacations, or if you attempt to make an educated guess regarding how you are likely to feel at that particular time in the future. Analogously, in the case of medical preferences at the end of life, Slevin et al. (1990) described a study in which only 10% of healthy study participants but 42% of cancer patients stated that they would undergo chemotherapy for an additional 3 months of life.

Yet it remains unclear whether the normative choice for any specific person *should* be based on the preferences given while well and fully functional, or if they should be based on preferences that were given closer to the end of life, when these preferences diverge (Ditto et al. 2005). Pain, for example, is extraordinarily salient when currently experienced, but it is rather quickly forgotten in retrospect, and it is difficult to imagine when never previously experienced (Christensen-Szalanski 1984). For example, in one study, pregnant women preferred not to have anesthesia for childbirth when asked a month before labor and also during early-stage labor. During active labor, the peak period of pain, their preferences shifted to favor anesthesia. Yet, and most interestingly, they had shifted back to their original preferences when asked again one month following labor (Christensen-Szalanski 1984).

Additional research suggests that when remembering a past episode of pain, we tend to think only of how much it hurt at the peak period of pain, and how much it hurt at the end of the episode. The average of the two turns out to be a relatively robust predictor of people's decisions about future actions (Redelmeier & Kahneman 1996). These two points in time may dominate our evaluations of the painful period, overriding even the duration of pain. Suppose you experience two different episodes of the same amount of unpleasant pain; in one episode, it stops after a minute, but in the other episode, the pain continues for an additional half-minute, during which it gradually reduces a bit. People prefer to re-experience the longer episode when choosing which to undergo again in future – essentially choosing *more* total pain (Kahneman, Fredrickson, Schreiber, & Redelmeier 1993). This phenomenon, in which people remember past pain as the average of the pain at its peak and at the end of the pain session, is known as the **peak-end rule** and may have important implications for patients' decision-making (Redelmeier & Kahneman 1996). It might, for example, lead us to select a longer, more painful treatment we have experienced over a shorter, less painful treatment if the peak-end average of the longer treatment is lower. Yet as we have seen, such decisions would not be optimal.

One promising approach to addressing the complex business of end-of-life decision-making is to create computerized decision support systems for patients, families, and physicians (e.g., Rid & Wendler 2014). A simplified approach to creating such a decision support system would be to poll people of a wide range of ages and different genders, races, and ethnicities for their treatment preferences, and to make predictions for any given patient based on such demographic variables (Rid & Wendler 2014). Such a tool would also need to draw upon large medical databases for common major medical conditions, tracking the likelihood of success for each possible treatment path. This may be most fully achievable in countries with a centralized system of health care, in which such data are more likely to have been gathered and accessible (Rid & Wendler 2014).

Investing for the future: Money and health

Both medical intervention decisions at the end of life and decisions about personal money management are decisions of intertemporal choice. **Intertemporal choice** refers to choosing between an immediate outcome (e.g., spending your paycheck now so you can enjoy wearing a shiny new outfit today) and one in the future (e.g., saving your paycheck for retirement, or perhaps toward an even shinier, more expensive new outfit to be worn in several months; see Chapman 1996). A steadily growing body of research on intertemporal choice has shown that the farther away the future gains, the less value people place on those gains, a phenomenon known as **temporal discounting** (Green, Myerson, & McFadden 1997). As people disproportionately undervalue future resources relative to those that can be used now, they generally find it challenging to make current sacrifices for future gains (e.g., eating less sugary foods now to promote greater health in the future). Temporal discounting appears across the lifespan but to a lesser degree with increased age (Green, Fry, & Myerson 1994). It has long been observed by economists and psychologists and plays an important role in models of future-oriented decision-making (Chapman 1996).

One intervention aimed at reducing temporal discounting was designed to influence the intentions of young adults (e.g., in their early 20s) to save more of their money for future retirement. In general, people have a hard time thinking of their future selves as themselves; people tend rather to think of the future self as a different, distinct person (Parfit 1971). Showing a young adult how she or he might look 50 years later might help one feel more connected to one's future self. To do so, Hershfield et al. (2011) created personalized avatars for study participants that had been digitally aged. Across several studies, Hershfield et al. (2011) showed that people who were shown digitally aged avatars of themselves, whether viewed in a virtual "mirror" or in photographs, allocated more money to a hypothetical retirement fund than when they were shown same-age avatars of themselves. The idea behind the aged-avatar intervention is that when we decide how much money to save for the future, we will feel a little more as though it is still really for ourselves, not for some hypothetical older person somewhat tenuously connected to ourselves.

Similarly, Fox and Bailenson (2009) used an immersive virtual environment technology to show American university students what might happen over time if they exercised versus did not exercise. Participants across two of the study conditions saw an avatar, created to look like the participant. In one condition, people watched the avatar losing weight as the person exercised in the first phase of the study, and in the second phase, people stood still while watching the avatar gain weight. In a second condition, other people also exercised in the first phase and stood still in the second, but the avatar they watched throughout did not change shape. Finally, people in both conditions were allowed to either choose to continue to exercise or to stop. Those who viewed the avatar losing or gaining weight in conjunction with exercise or inactivity, respectively, exercised more than those who saw the avatar maintain a constant shape regardless of exercise or inactivity (Fox & Bailenson 2009). Presumably, seeing one's avatar slim down gives one at least some immediate reward for efforts made in the present, rather than having to go for months before seeing returns. As in the retirement savings research by Hershfield et al. (2011), interventions such as this may have exciting potential to influence health behaviors by helping people feel more in sync with their future selves.

Conclusions

In this chapter, we considered the ways in which people make predictions about the future and evaluated their accuracy. Statistical prediction techniques, which draw upon past data to predict the future, have generally been found to be superior or equal to the intuitions of expert judges. Whether judges become more accurate with experience strongly depends on whether they receive corrective feedback on their predictions; receiving constant feedback has helped weather forecasters to be among the world's most accurate predictors. When people predict their feelings in the future, they tend to misjudge how strongly or how long they will feel that way. This phenomenon poses serious problems for future-oriented decision-making, including medical decisions for the end of life and daily decisions that will affect retirement and future health. Interventions that involve using decision support systems – which capitalize on statistical prediction techniques and finding ways to help people feel more connected to their future selves – are beginning to help solve these problems.

Questions for discussion

1. Suppose that a dear friend or close relative is having behavioral problems and wants to seek a diagnosis and professional help. You are asked to recommend a clinician who will do the best possible job of meeting these needs. Would you recommend a clinician who will administer the *MMPI-2* (Butcher et al. 1989; see Box 6.1); one who will sit down with your friend or relative, talking with him or her to figure out what the problem is; or one who will do both? Why?

2. Conduct an internet search to find a template for completing a living will or advance directive form in your area (or anywhere you choose). Discuss what might constitute optimal decision-making when completing this form. Are there additional issues and considerations not raised in the chapter that would need to be taken into account? How would you choose to deal with projection bias, temporal discounting, the peak-end rule, and people's changing preferences after the experience of pain?

Suggestions for further reading

Gawande, A. (2014). *Being mortal: Medicine and what matters in the end*. New York, NY: Metropolitan Books.

Meehl, P. E. (1954/1996). *Clinical versus statistical prediction: A theoretical analysis and a review of the evidence*. Northvale, NJ: Jason Aronson, Inc.

Wilson, T. D., & Gilbert, D. T. (2005). Affective forecasting: Knowing what to want. *Current Directions in Psychological Science, 14*(3), 131–134.

PART III

Decisions about Resources

Choice and Mental Accounting 7

Learning Goals

By the end of this chapter, you will have:

- Examined factors influencing the choices we make and our personal satisfaction with those choices, including the quantity of options available and what our end goals are.
- Considered the basic tenets of Simon's (1972) theory of bounded rationality and applied it to the problem of everyday choice.
- Evaluated research on the cognitive neuroscience of choice and critically considered how it contributes to our understanding of choice above and beyond purely behavioral research.
- Discussed how mental accounting differs from regular accounting and from traditional economic models, and considered how an understanding of mental accounting can better explain people's spending and saving behaviors.
- Compared arguments for and against libertarian paternalism across a range of situations, and formulated your own point of view.

Key Terms	
Choice	Principle of fungibility
Maximize	Sunk cost
Satisfice	Transitivity
Bounded rationality	Mandates and bans
Choice overload effect	Economic incentives and disincentives
Price primacy	Nudges
Product primacy	Libertarian paternalism
Mental accounting	Default rule
Behavioral life-cycle hypothesis	Status quo bias

Daily life is made up of a series of choices about whether and how to spend our *resources* of time, money, effort, and opportunity. In this section (encompassing Chapters 7, 8, and 9), we ask what factors influence how we choose to expend these resources, and whether or not those choices are ultimately consistent with our values and optimize our progress toward our own goals. In particular, we highlight research that integrates insights from marketing, management, and behavioral economics with the psychology of judgment and decision-making.

Choice

Choice refers to a selection made from among two or more options – for example, whether and what purchase to make in a clothing store, or which of several medical treatment options to pursue. Classic theories of rational choice (e.g., von Neumann & Morgenstern 1944/2007) traditionally tended to assume that people have complete knowledge about their choices and that they are capable of carrying out complex calculations to select the most optimal choice whenever faced with a decision (Simon 1972). Simon (1956), in contrast, pointed out that complex organisms do not need to strive exclusively for the best possible situations in order to survive, but rather need only find situations that are "good enough." That is, organisms need not **maximize** (and in fact rarely do); instead, they need only **satisfice**. Furthermore, he argued, it makes more sense to develop theories of choice that take into account people's limitations. For example, we are limited by our incomplete knowledge and finite computing power. These are theories of **bounded rationality**; that is, theories of human reasoning that account for uncertainty, lack of complete information about the choices available, and the complexity of the decision that is being made (Simon 1972).

Bounded rationality implies that people aren't really able to make optimal choices when faced with very complicated decisions. Yet many businesses appear to assume that having more options to choose from is better – that is, that more options allow for a greater degree of freedom and make it possible for people to get exactly what they want. This assumption is reflected in every large grocery store with many varieties of each item, and in specialty shops boasting hundreds of different wines, cheese, and meats. The question is whether having more choices really is better. For example, from a consumer's point of view, are we happier about our choices if we chose from among many options as opposed to a few? Or, to take a marketer's point of view, are consumers more likely to buy something if given a lot of choices rather than a few?

In 2000, Iyengar and Lepper published a paper empirically addressing these questions, reporting surprising results from several studies. One study was carried out on-site at a California supermarket, which already offered about 300 different selections of jams. Samples of various products for sale were routinely given out at booths inside the supermarket. At one of these booths, Iyengar and Lepper (2000) were able to manipulate the number of samples offered. For one 5-hour period on a Saturday, they offered six different free samples of jam for customers to taste; 242 customers passed the booth during this time. For the same length of time on a consecutive Saturday, 24 free samples were offered and 260 customers passed the booth. The experimenters found that people were more likely to stop by the booth that had 24 samples than six samples (60% and 40% of passersby, respectively), though they did not try more different flavors at one booth versus the other (1.5 and 1.4 jams on average, respectively; Iyengar & Lepper 2000). The truly surprising finding was that of those who tried samples, only 3% actually bought jam from the full shelf display (of 300 selections) after trying samples at the 24-sample booth, whereas 30% bought jam from the same shelf display after trying samples at the 6-sample booth (Iyengar & Lepper 2000). From a marketer's perspective, offering fewer choices actually yielded a better result (i.e., more sales), a finding generally known as the **choice overload effect**.

In a parallel investigation, students in a psychology course were offered the opportunity to complete an extra-credit assignment involving writing an essay. Some students were told they could choose from six essay topics, and others were told they could choose from 24 essay topics (Iyengar & Lepper 2000). Those students choosing from only six topics were more likely to complete the assignment than those choosing from 24 (74% and 60%, respectively). Furthermore, those choosing from only six topics produced better essays: Graduate teaching assistants, blind to the experimental conditions, rated the essays produced by those in the 6-topic condition more highly than the essays produced by those in the 24-topic condition in terms of both content and form (Iyengar & Lepper 2000). In this case, the students themselves benefited more when fewer choices were offered.

An important caveat is that we should not expect the choice overload effect to occur under all conditions. For example, Iyengar and Lepper (2000) suggested that the effect may not be found when people already strongly prefer one of the choices before they are presented with their alternatives. That is, the choice overload effect is most likely to happen when people aren't very familiar with the things they are choosing between. Scheibehenne, Greifeneder, and Todd (2010) conducted a meta-analysis encompassing many experiments conducted on the choice overload effect, as did Chernev,

Böckenholt, and Goodman (2015) more recently. Although Scheibehenne et al. (2010) did not find an overall choice overload effect, Chernev et al. (2015) simultaneously controlled for moderating variables and, indeed, found a statistically significant effect. Interestingly, these two meta-analyses identified very similar moderating factors that appear to influence whether or not the effect appears. The choice overload effect is more likely to occur when the decision task is difficult (e.g., when people are under time pressure). It is also more likely to occur when the options being offered are very complex, making it difficult to compare them, and (as Iyengar and Lepper [2000] suggested) when one doesn't know one's preferences ahead of time (Chernev et al. 2015; Scheibehenne et al. 2010). In addition, when people are actively trying to minimize the mental effort exerted in making their choice, they are more likely to show the choice overload effect (Chernev et al. 2015). In sum, the choice overload effect, like many decision-making phenomena, has important boundary conditions that allow us to predict when it can be expected to occur.

Within these boundary conditions, the literature suggests that limiting the number of choices available might actually lead to better outcomes, from the perspectives of both the consumer and the seller. Schwartz and Ward (2004) went so far as to assert that choice must be constrained to optimize satisfaction:

> Choice, and with it freedom, autonomy, and self-determination, can become excessive, and ... when that happens, freedom can be experienced as a kind of misery-inducing tyranny. Unconstrained freedom leads to paralysis. It is self-determination within significant constraints – within rules of some sort – that leads to well-being, to optimal functioning. (Schwartz & Ward 2004, p. 86)

Given findings such as Iyengar and Lepper's (2000), they argued, it might be better overall to have some degree of freedom, but not unlimited freedom, when under the conditions in which the choice overload effect occurs.

Schwartz and Ward (2004) further suggested that it may be easier to think about why limiting choices is beneficial if we consider the goals of making a choice. Specifically, maximizing and satisficing (Simon 1956) can be thought of as two different possible end goals of a choice (Schwartz & Ward 2004). If one has fewer options to choose from, one might feel that one has been given free rein to merely satisfice – to make a simple decision that will be good enough and that does not require one to do a lot of strenuous mental gymnastics or find out about and assess every choice possible. If one is given many options, this might encourage maximizing; with so much information available to be considered, one might feel pressured to make a best-quality decision. A homeowner who has committed to spend most of his savings on remodeling his kitchen might feel internally pressured to look at the entire paint color wheel and to consider hundreds of options for cabinet knobs, simply because those options are available for consideration.

The degree to which one might feel pressured to maximize rather than satisfice could also reflect differences between individuals. To study this possibility, Schwartz et al. (2002) developed a Maximization Scale to measure individual people's desire to maximize (e.g., as opposed to being fine with satisficing). Across 17 scale items, people are asked to rate their preferences for maximizing when making decisions in a range of domains (e.g., shopping, seeking to switch jobs, seeking out better relationships, changing TV channels, writing letters, etc.) and when thinking about maximizing in general (e.g., having high standards, not settling for less, etc.; Schwartz et al. 2002). They found that maximizing was positively correlated with feeling regretful and depressed and with being perfectionistic, and negatively correlated with feeling happy, feeling satisfied with life, being optimistic, and having high self-esteem (Schwartz et al. 2002). In other words, a tendency toward maximizing does not generally seem to predict satisfaction, although it is not clear from this correlational study why the two do not go together.

Schwartz et al. (2002) speculated that possessing the drive to maximize one's decisions makes it difficult to feel fully content with whatever the outcome may be. Simon's (1956) early notion – that satisficing enables one to get by perfectly well without exhausting oneself in trying to reach perfectionistic ideals – may extend to include people's feelings of satisfaction with their choices, once made. One is actually more pleased and content with one's choices *after* the fact if one was not trying to maximize them at the time that the choices were made. To the extent that maximizing *causes* dissatisfaction, or satisficing *causes* satisfaction, decision makers might do well to consider abandoning maximizing in favor of satisficing.

Purchasing decisions

To some degree, our discussion of choice so far has assumed that we make choices by thinking through the options. However, research on purchasing decisions has focused more broadly on *two* central influences: (1) People's feelings about the product and (2) their evaluations of its price, reflecting a dual-process model (see Chapter 1). In general, it seems worthwhile to consider how both affect and deliberate evaluation influence choice. As people are not necessarily consciously aware of exactly what factors influence their choices, researchers have turned to neuroimaging techniques, together with behavioral measures, to help identify plausible hypotheses about the underlying decision process. A number of such studies have suggested that seeing a product activates neural circuits associated with thinking about gains (i.e., nucleus accumbens), whereas seeing the price of the product instead activates distinct neural circuits associated with thinking about losses (i.e., insula; Knutson, Rick, Wimmer, Prelec, & Loewenstein 2007). Knutson et al. (2007) hypothesized that it should be possible to predict whether or not a person will choose to purchase a product by examining the pattern of neural activation in the nucleus accumbens and insula during the decision process. They also hypothesized that activation in the medial prefrontal cortex, previously associated with integrating gain and loss information (e.g., judging whether the cost or price is worth the reward to be gained from acquiring a particular product), could be used to predict actual purchasing decisions.

To test these hypotheses, Knutson et al. (2007) asked young adults to view products and decide whether to purchase them during an fMRI scanning session. The study participants were each given an "endowment" of USD $20, which they could either keep or use to purchase products during the session. Participants were told beforehand that one of the trials, which would afterward be selected randomly, was to be treated as "real." This meant that if the participant had purchased the product during that randomly chosen trial, the price would be deducted from the participant's endowment, and the product depicted would really be shipped to the participant. In this way, the experimenters ensured that the participant's decisions in this task would be more meaningful to them than if their purchases had been purely hypothetical. Each product (e.g., a box of chocolates) was presented for 4 seconds, followed by a 4-second display of the price of that product (e.g., USD $7), followed by a 4-second purchasing period. During the purchasing period, people indicated by pressing a key marked "yes" or "no" whether they had decided to purchase the product or not.

They found that if there was heightened bilateral activation of the nucleus accumbens while the product was presented, there was also an elevated likelihood that the person would purchase it (Knutson et al. 2007). This finding appears to be consistent with the idea that seeing the product leads people to think about gains, and while they are thinking about gains, they are more likely to purchase. In addition, they independently found that if the right insula showed heightened activation while the price was presented, people were less likely to purchase the product (Knutson et al. 2007). This result was also consistent with previous behavioral studies suggesting that price presentation triggers thinking about the money one would lose in making a purchase, lowering the likelihood of purchasing. When there was heightened bilateral activation of the medial prefrontal cortex while the price was presented, people were also more likely to purchase. Knutson et al. (2007) argued that an interpretation compatible with this result is that integrating product and price information (e.g., asking whether this is a good price, given the desirability of the product) might offset thinking solely about losses.

Neuroimaging methods have been further deployed to learn about the time course of choosing between options. Recall that in Chapter 3 we discussed how the primacy of information affects our likelihood judgments across domains. Primacy effects also influence choice: In particular, **price primacy** and **product primacy** in marketing refer to how being exposed to the price first or the product first, respectively, influences decisions regarding whether to purchase that product (Karmarkar, Shiv, & Knutson 2015). When one is initially attracted to the sight and smell of a juicy pie displayed on a stand in front of a bakery (product primacy), the choice of whether to buy it might be strongly influenced by affect – how one *feels* about the pie. When one instead is attracted to a bakery stand by a huge sign that reads "pies on sale – half price" (price primacy), the choice of whether to buy a pie might instead be strongly influenced by an analytical *evaluation* of whether this appears to be a good price for a pie. Although behavioral studies have been highly informative in piecing together how affect and analytical judgment influence choice in purchasing decisions, neuroimaging techniques have uncovered corroborating evidence.

For example, building upon past investigations of primacy effects, Karmarkar et al. (2015) asked in a neuroimaging study whether potential buyers are more strongly influenced by price when it is presented first, and also whether they are more strongly influenced by their feelings about the product when the product is seen first. First, regardless of whether the price or product was presented first, people bought roughly the same number of items and liked them about the same. The neuroimaging data, however, raised the new possibility that the *time course* of the mental processes underlying purchasing decisions might differ depending on whether the price or product was seen first. For the trials in which participants ultimately purchased the product and when the product was presented first, there was heightened activity of the nucleus accumbens right away. When the price was presented first, the nucleus accumbens showed heightened activation only after the product had also been presented. These findings are consistent with the notion that seeing the product triggers thinking about rewards (Karmarkar et al. 2015).

In addition, in the trials in which participants ultimately purchased the product and the product was presented first, the medial prefrontal cortex showed elevated activity when all the information had been presented (i.e., both product and price). In contrast, when the price was presented first, the medial prefrontal cortex did not show elevated activity until the purchasing choice was being made. In a follow-up study in which all the products presented were utilitarian in nature (e.g., batteries; a USB drive), Karmarkar et al. (2015) also found that people made significantly more purchases when the price was presented first than when the product was presented first. They suggested that price primacy may lead people to think more about whether the product is priced fairly or at a bargain rate when making purchasing decisions.

Findings such as these have important implications for understanding how people choose to spend their resources. For marketing purposes, for example, presenting prices first may be particularly effective for utilitarian products. In addition, as consumers, an awareness of research findings on price and product primacy could be useful in helping us figure out ways to spend our resources in a way that best meets our goals. Consumers, of course, may already be well aware that prices and feelings about the product influence decisions to purchase, but they may not be aware that what we attend to *first* can disproportionately influence how we think through those decisions.

Mental accounting

Our decisions about whether, and how, to spend our resources are influenced by where we think those resources came from in the first place. Studies suggest that how we personally track and handle our resources differs dramatically from how resources are formally tracked in business. Businesses and corporations have accounting managers who carefully keep track of the resources that come in and those that go out, and professional accounting is governed by a number of rules and regulations that have become standard practice over many years (Thaler 1999). In contrast, **mental accounting** – accounting carried out by individuals and households – does not appear to be governed by formal, explicit rules. Yet there are certain rules and tendencies that people seem to follow implicitly, without necessarily knowing that many other people do the same (Thaler 1999). One especially striking characteristic of mental accounting is that people tend to mentally categorize types of expenditures and types of income, and treat these categories differently from each other (Thaler 1999). A family that is reluctant to spend its hard-earned savings on a weeklong holiday trip may feel much better about the expense if they think they are paying for it not out of their savings, but rather out of a small bonus just received at work after a month of good sales. In contrast, perhaps a more rational way of thinking about one's money would be that it is simply money, regardless of where it came from or how it is now going to be used.

The behavioral life-cycle hypothesis

The behavioral life-cycle hypothesis (Shefrin & Thaler 1988) is a theory of how people save wealth. The behavioral life-cycle hypothesis factors in three characteristics of mental accounting that were not generally addressed by traditional economic theories. First, it reflects how people treat different categories of money differently in mental accounting. For example, people tend not to adhere to the economic **principle of fungibility**, which refers to being interchangeable or equivalent at a given time. Money is fungible in that someone in the U.S. could swap a USD $10 bill right now for any other USD $10; the two can be interchanged. People's mental accounting tends to violate the principle of fungibility (e.g., if one declines to exchange the very first USD $10 bill one ever earned for a USD $10 bill someone else received in change at a carnival ride). The behavioral life-cycle hypothesis, in fact, holds that people mentally divide their wealth into three accounts: *Current income*, consisting of paychecks and small bonuses; *current assets*, including nonretirement savings and large windfalls; and *future wealth*, including retirement savings and future income (Shefrin & Thaler 1988). This latter category may also include shorter-term savings for the future, such as college education funds set up for children until they go to college.

Second, the behavioral life-cycle hypothesis takes into account the fact that people will encounter temptations to spend their money instead of save it. It acknowledges that people's desire to spend will be in conflict with the exertion of their willpower, which in turn is costly in terms of the mental effort expended (Shefrin & Thaler 1988). That is, the behavioral life-cycle hypothesis assumes that people are influenced by two opposing goals. One side of a person wants to spend money now to acquire goods or services that he or she wants, and the other side wants to resist spending money to save for the future. It also assumes that when current income increases, expending willpower becomes relatively less effortful, and that expending willpower becomes generally less effortful when retirement is close at hand (Shefrin & Thaler 1988).

Finally, the behavioral life-cycle hypothesis accounts for the fact that whether or not people save is influenced by how the wealth is described, or framed (Shefrin & Thaler 1988). If one receives a substantial *salary increase* at work, it will be categorized differently than if it is framed as a substantial *bonus*, even if the total amount received is the same. A large salary increase will likely be mentally categorized as current income, whereas a large bonus is more likely to be thought of as current assets (i.e., non-retirement savings). This matters, according to the theory, because studies show that people are more likely to spend their current income than they are to spend their current assets. Shefrin and Thaler (1988) cited studies conducted in Japan, where bonuses are routinely given to most workers. These showed that people had a significantly lower propensity to spend from their bonuses than from their income, though this finding held only during regular, non-recession years (Ishikawa & Ueda 1984). Generally, the principles underlying the behavioral life-cycle hypothesis have been largely held up in experimental work, suggesting that they may be applied to shape people's spending and saving behaviors. For example, companies seeking to encourage their employees to build up a nest egg for future financial security might shunt funds meant for salary increases into routine bonuses instead.

Sunk costs

People also tend to treat money already spent on something as though it is a good reason to put down even more money for it – even if it is clear that the extra spending will not make them happier overall. Suppose a young couple decides to build a new home. Planning to spend all of their savings while avoiding debt, they agree upon a budget, purchase a small piece of land, and hire builders. The builders begin digging up the ground in order to lay the foundation for the house, and they soon find that there is a huge slab of underground rock covering much of the property. The rock must be removed in order to build the house – a very expensive and unforeseen cost. The couple now must choose how to proceed. They could cut their losses to date, sell the land, pay the builders for the work done so far, and start shopping for a different house or piece of land. Or they could take out a major bank loan, which they would have to pay off over 15 years with interest, using the proceeds to blast and remove the rock and go on with their original plans, hoping that no other problems will arise.

According to Thaler (1980) and Arkes and Blumer (1985), traditional economic theories would predict that this should be a straightforward decision, in which one considers the benefits and costs of each option for the *current* decision. A sum of money has already been spent on a service or good and is now gone – the sunk cost. So the current decision is not about what is past, but about future costs: Whether they should now go into major, unplanned-for debt to build a house or stay out of debt. That is, the rational thing to do according to such theories would be to walk away from the house-building scheme now, avoiding debt and further losses. As Arkes and Blumer (1985) bluntly stated, "sunk costs are irrelevant to current decisions" (p. 126). Given what we have learned about the hindsight bias (Chapter 4), in which people seem to have a difficult time reconstructing past states of knowledge, one might expect that they would easily be able to ignore or at least downplay sunk costs. Yet people often find it very difficult to walk away from what they have already spent toward achieving a goal, and may often even choose to spend much more money than originally planned toward achieving that original goal.

For example, in one classic experiment, Arkes and Blumer (1985) asked American university students to consider a scenario in which they had purchased non-refundable ski trips: $100 for a Michigan ski trip and $50 for a Wisconsin ski trip. In this scenario, the students read, they were expecting the Wisconsin ski trip to be more enjoyable. They then realized at the last minute, according to the scenario, that both ski trips were scheduled for the same weekend, and that they had to choose which to attend. Sunk costs appeared to influence people's decision-making: Only 46% of students chose the Wisconsin trip; 54% actually chose instead to take the trip they expected to enjoy *less* (presumably because it had cost them more).

In another famous scenario, students were asked to imagine that they were president of an airline building company, and wanted to build an airplane undetectable by radar (i.e., "radar-blank;" Arkes & Blumer 1985). Some students were told to suppose that they had already spent 9 million dollars on building the plane, which was almost done, but that another company had just developed a radar-blank plane that was vastly superior to theirs. They were asked whether they should spend an additional 1 million to finish their own plane. Others were told that they had not started building the plane yet and that another company had just developed a radar-blank plane that was vastly superior to the one they had planned to build. These students were asked whether they should spend 1 million dollars on building their own plane. In the first condition, in which 9 million dollars in sunk costs had already been spent, 85% of people thought that the plane should be completed with an additional 1 million. In the second condition, in which no sunk costs had been expended, only 17% thought spending 1 million dollars on such a project would be a good idea.

Interestingly, adults and older children appear to be more susceptible to the influence of sunk costs than younger children (Arkes & Ayton 1999). For example, in Tversky and Kahneman's (1981) classic studies in adults, they found that people were more willing to buy a $10 ticket to a play if they had lost $10 cash than if they had lost a previously purchased $10 ticket to that same play (presumably making them feel as though they were spending $20 on the new ticket). In a similar study, Webley and Plaisier (1998) asked children between the ages of 5 and 12 in Exeter, U.K. to pretend that they were at a fairground, holding one pound and 50 pence. They were asked to pretend that they then either lost the 50 pence coin or lost a merry-go-round ticket they had just bought with the 50 pence. They were then asked whether they would choose to spend 50 more pence of the remaining pound to buy a new merry-go-round ticket. The older children, like Tversky and Kahneman's (1981) adult study participants, were willing to buy a new ticket if they had lost 50 pence, but not if they had lost a 50 pence ticket. In contrast, the youngest children (i.e., 5–6 years old) were willing to buy a new ticket regardless of whether they had lost the money or the ticket (Webley & Plaisier 1998).

Why might older children and adults, but not young children, be susceptible to the influence of sunk costs? Arkes and Ayton (1999) argued that sunk cost effects occur because of a simple rule that adults and older children have been socialized to follow: "Don't waste" (p. 598). Although this is a perfectly reasonable rule to follow in general, Arkes and Ayton (1999) suggested that in the case of not wishing to "waste" sunk costs, people are overgeneralizing this rule. It is an overgeneralization because the loss of the resources (i.e., the sunk cost) is already in the past, and is not part of a decision to be made for the future. That is, the only waste people ought to be concerned with at the time of decision-making is whether resources will be wasted in the future. Younger children, suggested Arkes and Ayton (1999), have not yet been fully socialized to attend to this rule. Interestingly, it also seems to lead them to make more rational decisions about spending.

Time versus money

There is some evidence to suggest that people treat their different types of resources (e.g., time and money) differently when deciding how to spend them. The whole idea of work, of course, involves trading your time for money, and the notion of hiring services involves trading your money for time. A person might spend weekdays delivering boxes in exchange for a paycheck, and then pay some of that money to the teenager next door to mow the lawn on Saturday mornings so she can spend that time coaching her children's soccer team instead. One notable difference between money and time is that money can be held and saved but that time, by definition, passes by and is gone. Another is that people are used to keeping track of money (i.e., mentally accounting for it) and thinking of it as a valuable commodity, but they aren't necessarily used to doing so for time (Soman 2001).

Take, for example, a version of the sunk cost scenario in which time, rather than money, is the currency to be spent. Soman (2001) asked university students in Hong Kong to consider a scenario in which they had worked 15 hours for a professor to earn a ticket to a theater production and another 5 hours for a different professor to earn a ticket to a rock concert. Students were asked to imagine that they would enjoy seeing both, but thought that they would enjoy the rock concert more. Then, they were told that it turned out that both events were at the same date and time, and that they had to choose one. Fascinatingly, 95% of students chose the rock concert – showing that the sunk cost effect did not occur when it was time, not money, that had been expended (Soman 2001). In contrast, the sunk cost effect reappeared in a version of the same task in which money was expended instead of time. Specifically, when another group of students was told instead that they had spent more money on a theater ticket than on a rock concert ticket (i.e., HK$450 versus HK$150), only 38% of students chose the rock concert (Soman 2001). These differing results for money versus time are at least consistent with the possibility that people may not mentally account for time in the same way that they do for money.

Building upon findings such as these, Lee, Lee, Bertini, Zauberman, and Ariely (2015) further proposed that money and time, respectively, may preferentially activate each of the two types of processing in dual-process theories (see Chapter 1). In particular, they argued that money activates an analytical mode of processing, in part because when we think deliberately about economic exchanges, we most often do so in terms of money. Money, they speculated, tends to activate analytical processing simply because we have so much experience with this pairing. Time, in contrast, may activate an affect-driven mode of processing. Lee et al. (2015) further hypothesized that when people state their preference among two or more choices, their preference remains more consistent if this decision was based on affective processing than if it was based on analytical processing. The idea is that one is reasonably likely to *feel* the same about a preference at different points in time. For example, it seems reasonable to suppose that I will probably have about the same amount of liking for cauliflower today as I will tomorrow or the day after. In contrast, if I think analytically about whether or not to purchase a cauliflower, today I might give extra weight to the low sale price, tomorrow to the realization that I don't know any good cauliflower recipes, and the day after to the knowledge that cauliflower contains a good deal of vitamins C and B6, potassium, and fiber. In other words, the failure to consider or to weight different factors consistently in analytical thinking might lead to less stability in my preferences.

To test the hypothesis that our preferences are more consistent when considering expenditures of time than when considering expenditures of money, Lee et al. (2015) measured whether people showed violations of **transitivity** in their preferences. In mathematics, transitivity means that if a relationship (e.g., *more than*) holds between numbers A and B, and the same relationship holds between numbers B and C, then the same relationship must also hold between numbers A and C. For example, if Ace has more pencils than Bill, and Caro has more pencils than Ace, then Caro must also have more pencils than Bill. In observing people's preferences, the idea of transitivity is the same. Say that I am asked to choose between a doughnut and a piece of pie, and I prefer the doughnut. Then I am asked to choose between a piece of pie and a scone, and I prefer the piece of pie. When I am presented with a doughnut and a scone, and I prefer the doughnut, my preferences are characterized by transitivity (e.g., doughnut > pie > scone). In contrast, if I prefer a doughnut to pie, and prefer pie to a scone, but then prefer a scone to a doughnut, I am violating transitivity. Accordingly, transitivity violations can be taken as indicators of preference instability.

In their study, Lee et al. (2015) asked U.S. university students to consider nine different possible round-trip flights from the U.S. to a country in Asia. The nine flights were presented two at a time in different combinations for a total of 36 pairs of flights. For each pair of flights, people were asked to express which one of the two flights they preferred. In one between-participants condition (*control*), each of the nine flights was described in terms of its customer ratings for in-flight entertainment and for service. In another condition (*money*), these same customer ratings were presented along with the price of the flight. In a third condition (*time*), the customer ratings were instead presented along with the duration of the flight. Using participants' choices for each pair of flights, Lee et al. (2015) then determined how many transitivity violations they made. For example, if a study participant preferred Flight 1 to Flight 2, and Flight 2 to Flight 3, but then also preferred Flight 3 to Flight 1, that would be coded as a transitivity violation. The results revealed that people made significantly more transitivity violations (i.e., preferences were more unstable) in the *money* condition than in the *control* or *time* conditions. Furthermore, the number of transitivity violations in the *time* and *control* conditions did not differ from each other (Lee et al. 2015). In other words, preferences were significantly more stable for judgments based on time than they were for judgments based on money, supporting the experimental hypothesis. Money and time, though both are valuable commodities, may sometimes be treated very differently when we are deciding whether and how to spend them.

Nudges

Our decisions regarding whether and how to spend our *resources* of time, money, effort, and opportunity can be swayed by others' preferences in a number of ways. Others' preferences can be expressed at a societal or group level through mandates and bans, economic incentives and disincentives, and nudges (Sunstein 2014). **Mandates** and **bans** explicitly state that one is required to make certain choices, such as not importing genetically modified crops into a country for production and sales (e.g., France and Scotland are among the countries that have implemented bans). **Economic incentives and disincentives** encourage people to make certain choices by linking monetary gains or losses to decisions. For example, a major problem for public health is that once a country experiences a rising percentage of its citizens with health-threatening obesity, the trend does not reverse on its own (Roberto et al. 2015). To take more definitive measures toward stemming this tide, a number of countries have implemented taxes on some of the foods that help drive obesity (e.g., Mexico's tax on sugary beverages). Similarly, countries routinely impose economic sanctions against other countries making displays of aggression. For example, a country may refuse to import specific goods produced by another country until it stops conducting tests for the development of nuclear warheads.

Finally, there are **nudges**. Sunstein (2014) defined these as "liberty-preserving approaches that steer people in particular directions, but that also allow them to go their own way" (p. 583). Nudges are the means by which Thaler and Sunstein (2008) suggested that societal institutions can carry out **libertarian paternalism**, the notion that institutions can influence people's behavior while still fundamentally upholding people's rights to liberty and free choice. Nudges, in the framework of libertarian paternalism, are intended to encourage people to do things that would be good for them (e.g., having fewer sugary drinks) and/or for society (e.g., donating one's organs upon death). The idea is that individual liberty is still preserved as long as it is easy for the person to opt out of the nudge-directed choice, and that opting out is not costly (in terms of time, effort, money, etc.) to the person.

Thaler and Sunstein (2008) argued that the influence of nudges on behavior cannot be escaped, even if the nudges are not intentionally placed. For example, if fatty foods with relatively low nutritional value (e.g., French fries) happen by chance to be placed at the eye level of children in the school cafeteria, more students will choose them than if they were placed higher up. If instead bananas or carrot sticks happen to be placed there, more children will choose those than if they were placed elsewhere. One way or another, the children's choices are influenced by the structure of the environment – even if the placement of the foods was done without any deliberate plan whatsoever (e.g., if it was only done because the worker who brings out the fries is shorter than the worker who brings out the fruit in one cafeteria). So even if one tries to argue that the foods should be randomly placed, wherever the foods happen to fall will still affect choices. This can lead, eventually, to unintended effects such as leading kids in one school to eat more healthily than in another school (Thaler & Sunstein 2008). They argued that rather than leave this to chance, we might as well implement nudges that will guide people toward decisions we know to be more beneficial, rather than toward decisions that we know will be relatively more harmful. In fact, one could argue that leaving an unintentional nudge in place that would probably increase harmful choices is ethically questionable (Thaler & Sunstein 2008). Basically, once we know that food placement matters, we cannot un-know it, and whether we act or do not act upon that knowledge, one could argue that we have become to some degree responsible for the consequences.

When one does choose to act, there are many different types of nudges that can be implemented. One type of nudge, the **default rule**, sets the default to the desired response (Sunstein 2014). This nudge capitalizes on the **status quo bias**, or people's strong tendency to choose to do nothing (Samuelson & Zeckhauser 1988). For example, a country that wants to encourage its citizens to donate their organs to medicine upon death might have donation be the default. That is, every citizen will donate their organs by default, but they are free to officially opt out at any time before their deaths. Similarly, employers wishing to convert to electronic rather than paper pay stubs may announce that electronic pay stubs will be provided by default but that any employee may easily request paper stubs by clicking a box on an online screen.

Another type of nudge is one that increases the ease or availability with which a choice is made apparent (Sunstein 2014). For instance, to encourage children to choose fruits and vegetables in the lunch line, these might be placed first, at eye level. To encourage people to buy locally farmed produce, a grocery store might place it at the front entrance, where it is most likely to be seen by everyone coming in. To encourage more people to vote in political elections, a city might open up additional voting locations and hire extra staff to ensure that people are able to vote quickly and easily, without standing in long lines. A third type of nudge is educational in nature. Such nudges seek to provide people with factual information about different choices, such as the most likely consequences of those choices, findings from research, and so on (Sunstein 2014, 2015). For example, warning labels on artificial sweeteners and cigarettes in some countries explain that a preponderance of research studies have demonstrated these substances to be carcinogenic.

Notice that the principle of libertarian paternalism assumes that it is possible for a societal institution, such as the government of a country, to know what daily choices would be best for its citizens. Some critics have called this assumption into question. For example, White (2013) suggested that it is impossible for others to know the factors that drive an individual's choices. We might know that, in general, people buy chocolate bars because the sight of them at the checkout counter triggers brain-induced cravings for simple carbohydrates. But the reason a given person is buying a chocolate bar today could be hard for others to guess. One person might use it to teach sixth-grade science students the concept of a melting point. Another might give it to a child as the agreed-upon prize for having cleaned out the garage. For the third, it might be the vital secret ingredient in a recipe for spicy beef chili. The point is that individuals themselves, as White (2013) argued, are generally going to be better at figuring out what choices would be best for themselves than outsiders, because they are likely to have more mental access to the reasons why they are making their choices.

Yet Anomaly (2013) argued that one cannot generally state that individuals are always better at judging their own best interests than others. For example, sometimes individuals are not fully informed about the different consequences of each choice. Scientists who spend a lifetime studying the effects of tobacco are likely to know more about it than people who do not, and many nudges are educational in nature. In addition, sometimes people are not fully mentally capable of making their own choices, such as when inebriated or in the later stages of dementia (Anomaly 2013). Furthermore, a large body of research in implicit cognition suggests that people do not necessarily have conscious access to why they made the decisions that they did (e.g., Nisbett & Wilson 1977).

White (2013) also pointed out that people learn from the consequences of their bad choices, and that in a way, putting nudges in place prevents us from forming a more fully developed knowledge of how things work. In some ways, by not letting us make mistakes, nudges are indeed paternalistic in the sense that they seem to assume that we cannot find things out for ourselves. As mentioned above, however, Sunstein (2014) argued that nudges do not undermine freedom of choice as long as opting out of the nudge is not costly to the decision maker. In other words, under a libertarian paternalism approach, people are still free to make bad choices and learn from them, and relatively little will be done to stop them from doing so.

That said, a libertarian paternalism approach would probably not always be able to set up individualized nudges in practice (White 2013). If research shows that the vast majority of children would be better off eating more bananas and apples and fewer French fries, then the choice architecture of a school cafeteria would be set up to encourage these patterns of eating. Of course, one might suppose that some subset of children may have excellent metabolism, and it does not matter much for the health of those children whether they eat fruits or fried foods. In this choice architecture, they too would be nudged toward fruits and away from fries indiscriminately, though they might have enjoyed the fries much more. As you can see, the idea of libertarian paternalism is essentially utilitarian; that is, it aims to act for the good of many, without necessarily attending to the more specific needs of individuals (Sunstein 2015). For these reasons, it is important for people to be aware of the choice architecture of their environments, and for governments to be transparent about them.

Conclusions

In daily life, we are always deciding how to spend our resources of time, money, effort, and opportunity. Under certain conditions, we tend to be happier with those decisions when there were fewer options to choose from in the first place, and when we see the goal of choice as satisficing rather than maximizing. When deciding whether to make a purchase, seeing the product primes us to think about rewards, seeing prices primes us to think about losses, and seeing both makes us think about whether we are getting a good deal. We keep track of our wealth, or endowment, by categorizing it into mental accounts. And in a departure from rational economic models, we treat each of those accounts differently, and we are more willing to spend from some mental accounts (i.e., income) than from others (i.e., savings). The architecture of the choice environment also nudges our choices in a certain direction, whether it was deliberately constructed to do so or not. Because no choice environments are truly neutral, it is crucial to consider how they influence us and to what degree free choice is possible. In Chapters 8 and 9, we will further consider how the manner in which information is framed more generally affects our decisions and inferences about how to expend our resources.

Questions for discussion

1. Complete the Maximization Scale for yourself (see Schwartz et al. 2002, p. 1182), answering each of the 17 items on a 1–7 Likert scale, where 1 = completely disagree and 7 = completely agree. Do your judgments seem to differ across items, or do they stay relatively constant? Sum up your score and compare your score and individual judgments to those of some of your classmates. Do you see little or a lot of variability between individuals? Complete the scale again in a week, not looking at your old ratings. Then, compare your two sets of scores. Do your scores stay constant over time? What might all of these different kinds of variability (or consistency) mean?

2. In this chapter, we reviewed research showing that considerations of money affect our choices differently than do considerations of time. These findings, however, do not make claims about what would be a normative model for making decisions about money versus time. What might such a normative model be (i.e., how people *should* be making decisions about money versus how they should be making decisions about time), in your opinion? Could these findings be used to make better decisions in daily life?

3. In 2004, Johnson and Goldstein reported on the ramifications of default values for organ donation in a number of European countries. For example, Germany had an opt-in system for organ donation and Austria had an opt-out system; almost 100% of Austrians consented to donate organs in the opt-out system, but only 12% of Germans in the opt-in system. Both ethically and practically, which type of system is preferable (and for whom)? Or does there exist another alternative that is better than these? Justify your answer using information from this chapter and your own research.

Suggestions for further reading

Schwartz, B., & Ward, A. (2004). Doing better but feeling worse: The paradox of choice. In P. A. Linley & S. Joseph (Eds.), *Positive psychology in practice* (pp. 86–104). Hoboken, NJ: Wiley and Sons.

Simon, H. A. (1972). Theories of bounded rationality. *Decision and Organization, 1*(1), 161–176.

Thaler, R. H., & Sunstein, C. R. (2008). *Nudge: Improving decisions about health, wealth, and happiness.* New Haven, CT: Yale University Press.

8 Expected Utility Theory

Learning Goals

By the end of this chapter, you will have:

- Gained a conceptual and concrete understanding of expected value theory, expected utility theory, and multi-attribute utility theory/multiple-criteria decision-making.
- Practiced thinking through calculations of expected value, expected utility, and multi-attribute utility according to normative models for various gambles and choices.
- Evaluated the limitations of these models, including theoretical limitations, challenges to the claim that they are normative models (Chapter 1), and practical difficulties in applying these models to real-world decisions.
- Compared the strengths and weaknesses of expected value theory, expected utility theory, and multi-attribute utility theory/multiple-criteria decision-making.
- Compared and contrasted the advantages of multi-attribute utility theory/multiple-criteria decision-making with those of one-reason decision-making and robust satisficing.

Key Terms

Descriptive microeconomics	Multi-attribute utility theory (MAUT)
Expected value theory	Multiple-criteria decision-making
Utility	(MCDM)
Expected utility theory	One-reason decision-making
Expectation principle	Take the Best
Fair gamble	Robust satisficing

On June 23, 2016, more than 30 million people in the United Kingdom voted in a referendum (known as "Brexit") to determine whether their country would remain part of the European Union or leave it, launching the legal process to begin its withdrawal (Dorling 2016; Wheeler & Hunt 2016). As one might expect, first-person comments made by voters suggested that a range of individual decision-making strategies may have been carried out in choosing which way to vote. Some seem to have considered multiple consequences of each option (i.e., remain versus leave) for issues ranging from work agreements to free trade. Others may have been largely driven by a single overarching concern, such as the desire for the U.K. to maintain more control over its own borders, or dislike of European Union regulations imposed on U.K. businesses. A few may have voted more haphazardly, in the belief that their votes would not count for much. An intriguing question, not only with respect to the Brexit referendum but also more generally, is whether there was actually an ideal, "correct" vote for each individual person given his or her own personal preferences, values, and goals. That is, was there actually a *right* decision for each person that, with the correct tools and formulas, could be figured out based on everything known before the fact about the "remain" versus "leave" options? In this chapter, we will closely consider normative models of decision-making, which purport to do just this for decisions regarding how to expend our resources of time, money, effort, and opportunity. As we discussed in Chapter 1, normative models are intended to represent ideal, gold-standard, rational decision-making. We will consider whether they can tell us the best way to make a decision given our own personal needs and wants, how these answers can be calculated, and what limitations these models have.

In 1959, Herbert Simon argued for the need to better understand **descriptive microeconomics**, or how individual people decide what to do with their money and goods. In fact, every individual economic decision can be seen as a choice task. For example, a small child standing in a candy shop with her monthly allowance in her pocket can imagine at least several different possible states of the world that she can bring about (Edwards 1954). She could leave the store with a little candy and a little less money. She could leave with quite a lot of candy and no money. She could also leave with her allowance intact and no candy. The type of candy with which she could leave the store is also under consideration (e.g., fruity, chocolaty, and so on). One could say that choosing between these potential states of the world is her current decision task.

The earliest models of choice were designed to advance our understanding of descriptive microeconomics, but they assumed that people are (1) completely rational, (2) fully informed, and (3) infinitely sensitive

(Edwards 1954). Being completely rational means, at the very least, that people are capable of ranking their choices (e.g., based on their respective values) and that they will prefer the choice with the highest rank. Being fully informed means that people are aware of all the choices they have and the various costs and benefits of each. Being infinitely sensitive implies that people care about incremental differences; for example, that people's decisions are influenced by miniscule differences in price between choices (Edwards 1954). A large body of behavioral research has since shown quite clearly that real people are none of these things, as we will consider in detail in Chapter 9. However, the early models might still be useful if we think of them as *normative* rather than descriptive; that is, they might be said to represent ideal decision-making, or how one might make choices if one were indeed rational, informed, and infinitely sensitive.

Expected value theory

One classic, normative model of rational choice that has received much attention from researchers in both economics and psychology is **expected value theory**. The general idea behind expected value theory is that the most rational choice to make between options is the choice that will maximize value over the long run (see overview in Harless & Camerer 1994). We can illustrate with a gambling example. Suppose you are choosing between two gambles. In Gamble A, there is an 80% chance you will win nothing and a 20% chance you will win USD $500. In Gamble B, there is a 20% chance you will lose $100 and an 80% chance you will win $200. Putting aside for the moment what gamble you would personally wish to choose, let's figure out what the normative choice would be according to expected value theory.

First, let's look at what Gambles A and B look like in formal notation. (Do take note of this notation, because it will make it much easier to read research articles on this subject.)

Gamble A: (.80, $0; .20, $500)

Gamble B: (.20, −$100; .80, $200)

In Gamble A, for example, *.80, $0* refers to an 80% chance of winning nothing, as described above. The probability and its outcome are separated by a comma, and different probability-outcome pairs are separated by a semicolon.

The expected value (EV) of each gamble is the average of the outcomes you would expect to have over many, many plays of the gamble; that is, how much money on average you would be making (or losing) per gamble. This can be calculated by multiplying the value of each possible outcome by its given probability and summing these together. For Gamble A, this means we should first multiply winning nothing by its probability (80%) and add it to the product of winning USD $500 by its probability (20%):

$$\text{EV (Gamble A)} = (\$0 * .80) + (\$500 * .20)$$
$$= \$0 + \$100$$
$$= \$100$$

That is, the expected value of Gamble A, over the long run (i.e., on average, if one were to see Gamble A played many, many times), is $100. For Gamble B, we can do the same:

$$\text{EV (Gamble B)} = (-\$100 * .20) + (\$200 * .80)$$
$$= -\$20 + \$160$$
$$= \$140$$

Because the expected value of Gamble B ($140) is greater than the expected value of Gamble A ($100), expected value theory suggests that it is more *rational* to choose Gamble B. The expected value of any monetary gamble can be calculated by applying the same formula. For example, suppose that two of your school friends each try to launch a new business. Each of these two friends asks you to invest a minimum of EUR €1000, but you are only willing to invest in one company. Your friend Bernard wants you to invest in franchising a very widely known fast-food restaurant; he estimates that there is a 90% chance you will get it back, along with EUR €50 in interest, and a 10% chance you will not get any of it back. Your friend Elizabeth wants you to invest in a more risky internet technology start-up; she thinks there is an 80% chance you will never get it back and a 20% chance you will double your investment. These gambles are notated as follows:

Bernard: (.90, €50; .10, −€1000)

Elizabeth: (.80, −€1000; .20, €1000)

Assuming that these probabilities and outcomes are accurate, the expected values can be calculated as detailed below.

$$\text{EV (Bernard)} = (€50 * .90) + (-€1000 * .10)$$
$$= €45 + -€100$$
$$= -€55$$

$$\text{EV (Elizabeth)} = (-\text{€}1000 * .80) + (\text{€}1000 * .20)$$
$$= -\text{€}800 + \text{€}200$$
$$= -\text{€}600$$

Bernard's company, according to expected value theory, is the better investment, as losing €55 is less bad than losing €600. However, as the expected values of both investments are negative, you would actually be best off declining to fund either company.

Note that expected value theory has some serious limitations. First, as Edwards (1954) pointed out, such early models assume that people are fully informed about their choices. In reality, when choosing between different investments, the probabilities would be unknown and estimated quite subjectively, as would the exact possible outcomes. For example, Bernard and Elizabeth gave you their best possible estimates regarding what might happen to your investment, but there is no way for them to really know if these probabilities and outcomes are accurate.

Second, the expected value of a gamble is a weighted average (i.e., each possible outcome is weighted by its probability) taken across many plays of the gamble over the long run. It can be mathematically shown that as the number of times you play that gamble approaches infinity, that weighted average should indeed be achieved. But in real life, your choice will often result in a single play (or relatively small number of plays) of a gamble yielding a single, not an averaged, outcome. For example, if you choose to play Gamble B above, you will either lose $100 or win $200. The expected value of that gamble, $140, is only an average of hypothetical plays over time, and is not an actual possible outcome if you are only playing the gamble once.

In addition, because the expected value of a gamble is represented by a single number, it does not by itself tell us how risky the gamble is. That is, simply knowing the expected value of a gamble limits the amount of information you have about the gamble. For example, Gamble B above has a higher expected value than Gamble A, but if you take Gamble B, you could actually lose $100, a potential issue if (for example) you simply cannot afford to lose money at this time.

Expected utility theory

Despite these issues, expected value theory provides an easily calculated and straightforward normative framework for choosing between well-defined gambles. One early question was whether expected value theory could be expanded into a more versatile model for calculating normative decisions; for example, whether it could be applied even when the possible outcomes do not include monetary values. Suppose that you are looking at two paintings of the same monetary value on the market. You may simply like one painting much more than the other (e.g., it makes you feel more relaxed; it matches your living room furniture better; it strikes you as more aesthetically pleasing). We can express any given person's *preference* numerically, and call it the utility (instead of the monetary value) of the painting. The dictionary definition of utility is "usefulness," although von Neumann and Morgenstern (1944/2007) described utility as how preferable a person found an outcome or item to be. Others, such as Bentham (1789/1907) and Mill (1861/1998), conceptualized utility as a continuum between pleasure (i.e., positive utility) and pain (i.e., negative utility). Generally, we can think of utility as how *desirable* something is, subjectively determined by a given person or group (Briggs 2015). For example, we would say that you personally find one painting (i.e., the preferred one) to be of greater utility (i.e., desirability) than the other. So we can only legitimately compare the utilities of different options if they were assigned by the same person or group.

There are three main features of **expected utility theory** (Kahneman & Tversky 1979). First, the **expectation principle** is that we can calculate the utility of any gamble by taking each possible outcome of that gamble, multiplying the utility of that outcome by its probability, and adding these products together. That is, expected utility can be calculated just like expected value, except that the utility (subjectively assigned by the decision maker) of each possible outcome is used in the calculation instead of the value of each outcome. Expected utility theory is also analogous to expected value theory in that it assumes that the decision maker's goal in making a choice is to *maximize* utility (just as the goal in expected value theory is to maximize monetary value; Edwards 1954).

A classic example of an expected utility calculation is that of deciding whether or not to carry one's umbrella when leaving the house. Imagine that early one morning, the weather report states that there is a 30% chance of rain. (This really means that given atmospheric conditions, there is a 30% chance that a measurable amount of rain will fall somewhere within the forecast area – in this case, your city; Gigerenzer, Hertwig, Van Den Broek, Fasolo, & Katsikopoulos 2005.) Based on the weather report, you decide to assume that there is a 30% probability it will rain on you today, and a 70% probability it will not rain on you (this is an approximation of the actual meaning of the forecast; we'll make this assumption to simplify the calculation). Then, you consider the utilities of the different possible outcomes. If you carry your umbrella and it *rains*, you will stay dry, which is good. On the other hand, you will also be burdened throughout the day with an umbrella, which is a little bothersome but not terrible. So on a 1–5 scale of desirability, where 1 is extremely undesirable and 5 is extremely desirable, suppose you would personally rate this outcome a 4, taken as a whole. Again, note that you make these judgments for yourself, and that in the original models, the utilities were not meant to be compared across different people's judgments (von Neumann & Morgenstern 1944/2007). If you carry your umbrella and it *doesn't* rain, you will also be dry and burdened with an umbrella for the day. Because this outcome is essentially identical to the former (i.e., in terms of being dry but carrying an extra burden), let's say that it also rates a 4 in your opinion. In sum, if you carry your umbrella today, you are pretty much guaranteed an experience that you feel rates a utility of 4.

Now, let's consider the alternative course of action: Not carrying your umbrella. Suppose that after deciding not to carry your umbrella, it ends up raining. You will be wet (and perhaps quite uncomfortable), though unburdened by any umbrella. Suppose that you would rate this overall situation a 1, as you would really dislike spending the day soaked through. The final possible outcome is that you decide not to carry your umbrella, and it does not rain. In this most glorious and ideal of situations, you would be both dry and unburdened by the weight of an umbrella, and you rate this a 5.

Just as in expected value theory, you can now calculate the expected utility (EU) of each gamble (i.e., carrying versus not carrying your umbrella), given the utility ratings you assigned above, and your approximations of the probabilities of being rained upon (30%) versus not rained upon (70%), given the weather forecast:

$$EU \text{ (carry umbrella)} = (.30 * 4) + (.70 * 4)$$
$$= 4$$
$$EU \text{ (leave umbrella)} = (.30 * 1) + (.70 * 5)$$
$$= 3.8$$

According to expected utility theory, and assuming that the probabilities you are using are correct and that the assigned utilities accurately reflect your true preferences, you would do better to carry the umbrella, as 4.0 is a higher expected utility than 3.8.

The second important feature of expected utility theory is that it assumes that a person will accept a given gamble when the expected utility of the gamble, given the person's current "wealth" or holdings, is higher than the person's current wealth without the gamble. That is, the assets that a person already holds when a gamble is offered affects whether or not the person should take that gamble. For example, the utility calculations we just carried out above regarding whether or not to carry an umbrella would have to be completely redone if we learned that you already have a waterproof poncho tucked into your pocket. You might feel, for example, that the umbrella provides no added utility under these circumstances, and in fact might decrease utility because of the added burden of carrying the umbrella around for no good reason.

The third and final important feature of expected utility theory is that it assumes that people are fundamentally risk-averse, generally preferring relative certainty over relative risk across the board (Kahneman & Tversky 1979). For instance, you might choose to put your savings into a low-yield savings account, which pays only 1% in interest annually, rather than risk losing those savings in stock market investments (even if the stock market investments have a somewhat higher expected value). Risk aversion is also demonstrated when people refuse to play a **fair gamble**. A fair gamble is one whose expected value is zero. For example, suppose that you are offered the chance to play a gamble in which you have a 50% chance of losing GBP £100 and a 50% chance of winning £100, with an expected value of £0. You would be said to be risk-averse if you repeatedly and consistently rejected the chance to play this gamble.

A person's risk aversion can be measured by asking him or her to assign subjective values to gambles. Suppose you are offered a gamble (.50, £0; .50, £100) in which you would have a 50% chance of gaining nothing and a 50% chance of gaining GBP £100. The expected value of this gamble is (.50 * £0) + (.50 * £100) = £50. Now, suppose that you could trade in the opportunity to play this gamble for a sure payoff of money instead. If you would be willing to exchange a play of this gamble for a sure payoff of any amount less than its expected value of £50, you are showing risk aversion. For example, you are demonstrating risk aversion if someone offers you this gamble and you are willing to trade it for £40 cash. Your acceptance of a payoff lower than the expected value of the gamble shows that you consider *certainty* (i.e., of the sure payoff) to be of added value. That is, a lump sum payoff with 100% certainty (e.g., £40 for sure) is treated as though it has extra utility beyond its monetary value (e.g., it is treated as though it has an expected value of £50 compared to an uncertain gamble with an expected value of £40).

From risk information to action

Expected utility theory can also aid us in better understanding the case of Hannah (Box 5.1), who was informed that testing has shown that she is at elevated risk for having a child with Down syndrome. We saw in Chapter 5 how the numerical presentation of the information can affect how she interprets that information, and that thinking about absolute, not relative, risk can help her understand the information more accurately. Now, the question is: how should she translate this knowledge into a course of action, given her own goals and the information she has received (i.e., should she proceed with the amniocentesis test, given that the procedure will give a definite diagnosis but also has a small chance of accidentally aborting the baby?).

This question is made more straightforward by applying expected utility theory. Hannah's decision regarding whether or not to get an amniocentesis will rest upon her personal goals and priorities, and how much risk she feels that she is willing to take. This suggests that expected utility theory should be able to provide normative solutions for whether or not a given person should take a calculated risk in a given situation – for example, whether to move ahead immediately with more invasive diagnostic tests such as an amniocentesis.

For example, in a refreshingly practical paper published in the journal *Chance*, statisticians Fan and Levine (2007) explained how they applied expected utility theory to calculate the optimal decision regarding whether to have an amniocentesis given their own personal situation. In their case, Fan and Levine's (2007) screening test for their own unborn child revealed a 1 in 80 chance of Down syndrome; they opted to have an amniocentesis and, as it happened, their child did not have any genetic abnormalities. They pointed out, however, that the normative decision for a parent in any particular case depends not only on the probability of Down syndrome for that particular pregnancy, but also crucially on how the parent rates the relative desirability of miscarrying a normal fetus (a outcome that may be more likely if having an amniocentesis) versus having a child with Down syndrome (an outcome that may be more likely if not having an amniocentesis). The higher perceived utility of one outcome relative to the other could flip the optimal choice for that parent. For this reason, it could be argued that applying expected utility theory to one's own goals and situation is more rational than taking advice from others, even if they have had similar experiences in the past.

Applying expected utility theory to such decisions may also have the added benefit of giving people more confidence in their decisions and, presumably, more peace of mind. Bekker, Hewison, and Thornton (2004), in a randomized controlled study, offered pregnant women who had initial abnormal screening test results either a routine genetic consultation session or a session in which they were also presented with several decision aids. For example, one aid was a decision analysis tree making it clear what decisions had to be made and the possible outcomes stemming from each decision. The second was a series of prompts asking women to choose between continuing or terminating the pregnancy based on hypothetical likelihood values (e.g., a 50% chance of Down syndrome). They were also presented with a graph that could help them identify the course of action with the greatest expected utility given the results of their diagnostic test. Although this information did not seem to change the women's ultimate decisions, they found that women in the decision aid sessions felt more comfortable with their decisions and had a more realistic understanding of their actual risk for having a baby with Down syndrome (Bekker et al. 2004).

Expected utility: A normative model?

As we have described so far, some have argued that expected utility theory is a normative model of choice because it is designed to help people optimize the likelihood of achieving their own goals, desires, and preferences (see review in Galotti 2007). That is, rather than merely optimizing the highest monetary return over the long run, the idea behind applying expected utility theory is to optimize one's own preferences (i.e., outcomes of high utility in your own judgment) over the long run. Although in the past it was often implicitly treated as a descriptive or predictive model of economic behavior, a large body of subsequent behavioral research, which we will consider in detail in Chapter 9, suggests that expected utility theory may be better characterized as a normative model (Briggs 2015).

In particular, in line with the idea that expected utility theory is a normative theory, there are several ideal conditions or axioms under which the theory holds true (von Neumann & Morgenstern 1944/2007). In essence, these axioms offer a definition of how a rational decision maker would behave, and, taken together, state that a rational person has very clear and reliable preferences between outcomes. One of these axioms refers to the *completeness* of the decision maker's system of preferences: That is, the decision maker has to be able to state a preference for one of two outcomes, or that they are equally preferred (von Neumann and Morgenstern 1944/2007). Another axiom states that the decision maker's preferences must be *transitive*; that is, they should be consistently rank-ordered (see Chapter 7). For example, if the decision maker prefers peanuts to cashews (P > C) and prefers cashews to almonds (C > A), then she or he should also prefer peanuts to almonds (P > A). A third axiom is that even if one potential outcome is very desirable, its influence in decision-making should be insignificant if it is extremely unlikely to occur. For example, suppose again that the decision maker prefers peanuts to cashews (P > C) and prefers cashews to almonds (C > A). If the person is now given a choice between (1) cashews and (2) almonds (but there is an extremely negligible chance for peanuts instead of almonds), (1) should still be preferred to (2) as long as the chance of peanuts is very,

very small (see von Neumann and Morgenstern 1944/2007). These axioms define the conditions under which it is possible for expected utility to be calculated mathematically.

In practice, however, many of the limitations of expected value theory also apply to expected utility theory. For instance, sometimes the probabilities of different outcomes really are unknown, and even in ideal cases, they are often only estimated (e.g., as in the weather forecast example described earlier). Expected utility theory maximizes utility over the long run, such that the more times one makes the same choice, the more likely it is that the expected utility of the choice will be achieved. However, for many decisions in life to which a utility calculation might be applied, it is not even possible to play the identical gamble many times. For example, people generally only get married a small and finite number of times (sometimes one). Even among those who remarry, each time they get married the circumstances are different, so those marriages cannot be treated as the same gamble being played over and over again (Briggs 2015). Finally, decision makers estimate their own utility ratings, and how accurate they are at doing this depends in part on how well they consciously understand their own preferences. Expected utility theory itself does not assist decision makers and stakeholders in coming up with those utility ratings.

Multi-attribute utility theory and multiple-criteria decision-making

In addition, for simplicity we have assumed so far that there is only a single attribute to consider in making any given choice. This may be true in some situations; for example, in deciding whether to buy a painting, the single attribute you might have considered was how much you like it or in deciding whether to take a gamble, you might only consider how much money you might win. However, many choices in life are likely to involve taking multiple attributes into account at the same time (Ramesh & Zionts 2013). For example, suppose that you are choosing between two job offers. One pays considerably more than the other, but there are other meaningful attributes to consider besides salary. The one that pays less is also in a city where your sibling, who is also your best friend, currently lives, and the one that pays more is in a city in which you currently know no one. It seems likely that you would want to take both of these factors (and probably others as well) into account in choosing which job you will take. Suppose also that the higher-paying job comes with both a higher rank and more responsibilities than the other job. These might also be important attributes to take into account, and how you rate them in terms of utility depends on your personal goals and preferences.

The question is whether there is a systematic, mathematical way to make normative choices while considering more than one attribute at once across your different options. **Multi-attribute utility theory (MAUT)** and **multiple-criteria decision-making (MCDM)** are approaches to decision-making that are designed to do just this, with the core aim of identifying the best possible decision that maximizes your goals (Dyer, Fishburn, Steuer, Wallenius, & Zionts 1992; Ramesh & Zionts 2013). It has been shown that these approaches are normative under specific conditions; for example, when we can reasonably assume that the attributes are independent of each other and that all the options that you are considering have been included in the analysis (Galotti 2007). MAUT and MCDM, as fields of study, were launched approximately 5 years apart and initially were somewhat distinguishable, but the differences have become less marked over time, and of recent years they have often been referred to interchangeably (see Dyer et al. 1992; Wallenius et al. 2008). For the most part, in this chapter I will refer to MAUT for simplicity.

There are many variants of MAUT (Velasquez & Hester 2013), but let's first consider a general overview of these approaches to get an overall idea of how it works. To identify the choice most likely to help you achieve your goals under MAUT (e.g., when choosing between job offers), several fundamental steps are involved. You would first need to list what attributes matter to you and decide how important each attribute is relative to the others (Galotti 1995). For example, you might first decide that you generally care about four key attributes in a job, ranked from most to least important in your opinion: (1) Proximity to family, (2) Rank of the position, (3) Salary, (4) Level of responsibility. You would then need to assign each attribute a numerical weight according to how important you think it is. Next, you would need to list all of the actual options (e.g., job offers) you are considering. For example, suppose that in this case your options are a job offer in Columbus, Ohio, and a job offer in Des Moines, Iowa. You would need to rate the utility of each of the four attributes with respect to each of these two job offers (Galotti 1995). For example, if you really want to be close to your family, and your dearest relative currently lives in Columbus, then you might give the job in Columbus the highest possible utility rating on proximity to family. The utility rating you assign for proximity to family should be comparatively lower for the job in Des Moines, because you don't know anyone who lives there. (Note, of course, that if your personal goal is instead to increase independence from family, then you would give the job in Columbus a relatively low utility rating on proximity to family.)

Then, based on this information, you would need to construct a formula to calculate the utility of each option you are considering (Fishburn 1970).

This calculation is valid, and also most straightforward, if we can correctly assume that our preferences for each of these attributes are independent of each other (Fishburn 1970). In cases where it is reasonable to consider the attributes separately (e.g., we might be able to consider the rank or position one will hold in one job separately from whether it is located in a city close to family), we can apply MAUT pretty straightforwardly. Specifically, for each option (e.g., for the job in Columbus), you would multiply the utility rating for each attribute by the weight or importance you are giving to that attribute, and sum these products together. (Notice that this is much like an expected utility calculation, except that instead of using the utilities of possible outcomes, you are using the utilities of the various attributes of each option, and instead of weighting these utilities by their probabilities, you are weighting them by how important they are to you.) After you calculate the total for each of the options available, the option with the highest total is the best one to choose (Galotti 1995).

MAUT is somewhat unique in that it has been developed by scholars working in a wide array of countries in addition to those in Western Europe and North America (Dyer et al. 1992). Two of its most striking applications have been in business management and in aiding governments (i.e., local, regional, and national) in carrying out highly centralized decision-making (Dyer et al. 1992). Such applications illustrate how implementing a MAUT analysis can be very complex and challenging in practice. The difficulties inherent to implementing a MAUT analysis are in some ways analogous to those found in applying expected value theory and expected utility theory.

For example, consider the problem of air pollution control in 1970's New York City (Keeney & Raiffa 1993). A key question for the mayor at that time was whether the city should impose stricter limits on the amount of sulfur dioxide contained in the fuels that were burned for heat and power in the city. Ellis (1970) carried out a full MAUT analysis of this problem to help the mayor address this question. First, the mayor came up with a list of objectives that he wished to achieve in making this decision. His key goals were to reduce pollution-related health problems for the city residents, reduce psychological problems for the city residents, reduce negative economic effects on residents, reduce negative economic effects on the city, and come up with the most politically desirable solution possible. This last objective had to do with maximizing legislative and public support for any course of action and considering potential effects on the mayor's future in politics (keep in mind that these are the individual decision maker's goals; Ellis 1970).

Then, they had to determine the value of each attribute (i.e., determine the degree to which each of the mayor's five objectives could be met) for each of two options: (1) Maintain the status quo versus (2) reduce the legal limit on sulfur dioxide in fuels (i.e., from 1.0% to 0.4% for oil and 0.7% for coal; Ellis 1970). Only these two options were considered, which greatly simplified the MAUT analysis and made it more feasible to carry out. Figuring out the value of each objective for each option was in and of itself extremely challenging. For example, in cases where there were no data directly pertinent to an objective, Ellis (1970) had to substitute a more readily available proxy. For example, there were no data on city residents' psychological well-being available. One option might have been to collect survey data, but this was not practically feasible at that time. Instead, Ellis (1970) used data on the daily level of pollution as a proxy for psychological well-being (i.e., making the assumption that the higher the pollution level, the more adverse effects on psychological well-being). Data substitutions like this can make carrying out the MAUT calculation more feasible, although ideally, one would wish to have the most directly pertinent data possible for as many attributes under consideration as possible.

In this particular case, Ellis' (1970) full MAUT analysis, whose results were in favor of implementing tighter restrictions on sulfur dioxide in fuels, was presented to the New York City Council as it deliberated over whether to approve this change. The new restrictions were ultimately signed into city law, and Ellis was retained as an independent consultant to the city (Keeney & Raiffa 1993). Carrying out the quantitative MAUT analysis on this city-wide issue was an enormous, multi-year endeavor, as identifying the mayor's key objectives, the options for action, and the values of the attributes associated with each option forced Ellis (1970) to think very critically about what was at stake in the decision and exactly what could be expected from each option (Keeney & Raiffa 1993). That is, in addition to coming up with a mathematically based recommendation, undertaking a MAUT analysis enabled Ellis (1970) to really understand the problem, the options, and their implications in depth. Overall, having gained this in-depth qualitative understanding itself may improve decision-making, and almost certainly made it more feasible for Ellis (1970) to convince the city council to implement the new law (Keeney & Raiffa 1993).

There has been some question regarding whether it is realistic to use MAUT as a normative model; that is, whether ordinary people could possibly carry out anything resembling it. In decision-making in the real world, at least for relatively major personal decisions, it seems that people are indeed able to consider multiple attributes, and that they do so quite regularly. For example, in a review, Galotti (2007) described a number of studies in which she examined whether multiple attributes influence real-life decision tasks (i.e., high school juniors deciding which college to attend; college students choosing a major; pregnant women choosing a birth attendant;

kindergarteners' parents deciding between a number of school options for first grade). Across five studies, she found that the mean number of attributes that people considered ranged from 3 to 9, and that the mean number of options they considered ranged from 2 to 5. Over time, people considered fewer options, most likely having ruled the other options out, but people did not tend to reduce the number of attributes they were considering over time. Ultimately, they tended to make decisions that correlated moderately to strongly positively with the predictions of linear models such as MAUT. This suggests that MAUT might serve not only as a normative model for decision-making under uncertainty but also as a descriptive model, at least for personal decisions.

Alternative approaches

For large-scale, complex decisions such as in the pollution regulation example, however, applying MAUT in real life can be daunting. As we saw, some simplifications, estimates, and substitutions often need to be made to carry out the calculations. Schwartz, Ben-Haim, and Dacso (2010) further explained that MAUT calculations are actually even more complicated than we have considered so far, even for personal decisions, because we also ought to account for uncertainty. For example, in choosing between job offers in Columbus, Ohio, and Des Moines, Iowa, you might assign Columbus the highest possible value on the attribute of proximity to family because your sibling lives there. However, suppose your sibling is thinking about switching careers. That is, there is some uncertainty regarding whether your current information about Columbus will stay accurate over the next few years; your sibling lives in Columbus now, but might not in the near future. There is also some uncertainty in how important that attribute will continue to be to you over time (Schwartz et al. 2010). Right now, you feel that you value physical proximity to your sibling very highly, but in the coming years you might make some new close friends and feel less dependent upon your sibling, or one or both of you might have children and start putting a higher value on the quality of the preschools and elementary schools in the area.

In addition, you are trying to predict how you will feel about the job in the future if you take it, and in general, people can be relatively decent at predicting whether they will feel generally positive or negative about something but quite poor at predicting how strongly they will feel that way, or for how long (see Chapter 6). Finally, some aspects of the job are not possible to know for sure in advance (Schwartz et al. 2010), such as whether you will fit into the company culture, whether you will get along well with your boss, or whether you will find your co-workers on major projects to be highly competent and easy to work with. In sum, MAUT seems to make sense as a normative model but can be challenging to implement in practice, perhaps both for personal decisions and for larger-scale decisions involving multiple people.

There are alternatives to MAUT that attempt to get around some of these complexities in practice. For example, **one-reason decision-making** can be surprisingly accurate, particularly when conditions are uncertain and when predictions are being made about the future (Gigerenzer 2007; Katsikopoulos & Gigerenzer 2008). That is, instead of grappling with multiple attributes and their tradeoffs, the idea is to identify the single attribute that matters most, and base the entire decision upon that one attribute. For example, you might be best off choosing a job based solely on salary if your ultimate dream is to build a nest egg that will allow you to travel all over the world. People also keep track of their secondary priorities in one-reason decision-making, using them only to break ties (Gigerenzer 2007).

One-reason decision-making, according to Gigerenzer (2007), is carried out by means of a heuristic called **Take the Best**. In Take the Best, a single reason you have identified as the best attribute or cue to a good job drives the choice (Gigerenzer 2007). (Gigerenzer and Goldstein [1999] noted that when we rank-order these attributes or cues, we may or may not be correct, so that issue applies here just as it does for the other models discussed in this chapter.) Suppose you have decided to rank-order the attributes as follows: Salary is most important, followed by proximity to family members. In applying Take the Best, you simply see whether the salary is highest for one option (say, the job in Columbus, Ohio). On the basis of this one attribute, you then stop the decision process and make the decision to take the job in Columbus. If both job options offer the same salary, then you would move on to consider the second most important attribute or cue that you have identified (e.g., is the job close to family members?). This sequential process continues, considering exactly one attribute at a time in the order that you believe to be appropriate, and stopping and making a final decision immediately when one option is better than the other regarding the attribute you are considering. For example, given that the salaries of both job offers are the same, and then given that you have family in Columbus, Ohio, and none in Des Moines, Iowa, you would then choose the job in Columbus and decision-making would be done. Over a series of studies, the results suggested that when making predictions about an uncertain future, using Take the Best can have superior accuracy to other, more complicated formulas taking multiple attributes into account (Gigerenzer 2007). In contrast, when reasoning in hindsight about events in the past, other formulas are likely to outperform Take the Best (Gigerenzer 2007).

Another alternative to MAUT was offered by Schwartz et al. (2010). The goal of MAUT is to identify the best choice for the decision maker; that is, the choice with the highest utility assuming everything goes as currently expected. Schwartz et al. (2010) instead suggested that when it is very uncertain how things will actually turn out (e.g., when choosing a college or job), it might make more sense to have a different goal, based on the idea of satisficing (see Chapter 7). The goal of Schwartz et al.'s (2010) normative model of robust satisficing is to choose the option that you are the most confident will still be good enough even if some things happen to go wrong. In robust satisficing, the goal is to maximize this confidence in being good enough, rather than to maximize utility per se (Schwartz et al. 2010).

The process of robust satisficing is somewhat simpler than MAUT and involves first asking and determining what outcome would be good enough (i.e., this is the satisficing part; Schwartz et al. 2010). After identifying which options (e.g., job offers) would enable this good-enough outcome, you'd then choose the option that you believe would do so under the most different possible conditions. That is, supposing all the different things that could go wrong, which is the option that would still enable you to achieve the "good enough" outcome over the most different scenarios (Schwartz et al. 2010)? Robust satisficing is a particularly interesting model in that it breaks away from the assumption that a normative model has to involve thinking about the individual attributes of different options. More research is needed to show which of these normative models yields the most ideal choices across many different contexts (or in which particular contexts a given model yields the most ideal choices).

Conclusions

In this chapter, we considered some major normative models of decision-making; namely, expected value theory, expected utility theory, and MAUT. We also discussed some promising alternative models that have been argued to yield superior decisions, especially under conditions of uncertainty and for predictions about the future (i.e., the Take the Best heuristic; robust satisficing). A critical remaining issue that needs to be explored in more detail is whether, and to what extent, people actually make decisions in these ways. That is, do people actually make normative decisions along the lines of these models? Or do they deviate from them in systematic ways? If people do deviate from normative models, what implications do those deviations have for the decisions that they make? In Chapter 9, we will directly address all of these questions, considering evidence for descriptive models of decision-making. In particular, we will focus on a detailed exploration of prospect theory, a highly influential descriptive model of decision-making that takes into account the ways in which people systematically fail to reason along the lines of expected utility theory. For example, manipulating the framing or mere presentation of a problem can change people's preferences even when the choices being considered are identical with respect to expected utility.

Questions for discussion

1. Applying expected value theory, choose between Gamble 1 (.8, $100; .2, –$50) and Gamble 2 (.3, $15; .7, $0). Show your calculations. Then discuss whether you would really want to make the choice indicated by your calculations, and why or why not.
2. Applying expected utility theory, choose between Gamble 1 (.8, win a large pepperoni pizza; .2, read an extra article for this course) and Gamble 2 (.3, win a stick of gum; .7, go about the rest of your day). Remember that you personally assign the utility rating to each outcome. Be sure to consider each rating carefully so that your decision is as accurate as possible in achieving your goals over the long run.
3. Choose a major political or personal decision, either past or future (e.g., Brexit; an upcoming political election; the choice of your major; the choice of a summer job; etc.). Given what you have learned in this chapter, discuss generally how you might go about setting up a MAUT analysis for this decision. Feel free to limit your options to two to simplify the process. Explain your reasoning to a classmate. Does this method seem likely to yield the ideal decision?
4. In theory, assuming that accurate data are available, do you agree that (1) expected utility theory and (2) MAUT are normative models that should yield the best possible decisions given your goals and preferences over the long run? Why or why not?
5. Compare MAUT, Take the Best, and robust satisficing. Does one seem more appealing as a normative model than the others? Why or why not?

Suggestions for further reading

Briggs, R. (2015). Normative theories of rational choice: Expected utility. In E. N. Zalta (Ed.), *The Stanford encyclopedia of philosophy*. Retrieved from http://plato.stanford.edu/archives/win2015/entries/rationality-normative-utility.

Galotti, K. M. (2007). Decision structuring in important real-life choices. *Psychological Science, 18*(4), 320–325.

Gigerenzer, G. (2007). *Gut feelings: The intelligence of the unconscious*. New York, NY: Penguin Group (USA), Inc.

9 Framing Effects and Prospect Theory

Learning Goals

By the end of this chapter, you will have:

- Identified and considered a number of ways in which people's actual decision-making tends depart from expected utility theory. These include framing effects, reference dependence, loss aversion, non-linear preferences, and source dependence.
- Examined how some of these effects may help advance the science of persuasion.
- Become familiar with the tenets of prospect theory, a descriptive model of risky choice, and the precise ways in which it differs from expected utility theory.
- Considered the ways in which prospect theory accounts for how people's judgments systematically violate some of the predictions of expected utility theory.
- Examined some of the challenges in applying prospect theory to economic theory, and considered possible solutions that have been proposed to address these issues.

Key Terms

Principle of invariance	Certainty effect
Framing effects	Allais Paradox
Risk-averse	Framing phase
Risk-seeking	Valuation phase
Procedure invariance	Overall value (V)
Reference dependent	Decision weight (w)
Prospect theory	Subjective value (v)
Prospects	Endowment effect
Loss aversion	

In Chapter 8, we examined how models such as expected utility theory aim to maximize the possibility that we will achieve our own goals by deploying our resources of time, money, effort, or opportunity accordingly. Although expected utility theory was, for many years, widely assumed to be a descriptive model of how people actually make decisions, many behavioral studies have since shown that people violate the predictions of expected utility theory reliably and in many different ways (Kahneman & Tversky 1979). In this chapter, we will consider these studies and how they provide evidence for descriptive models of how people *do* choose to deploy their resources. We will also consider how these choices depart from expected utility theory, and how expected utility theory is better thought of as a normative model.

Framing effects

Throughout most of Theodore Seuss Geisel's (1960/1988) classic children's book *Green Eggs and Ham*, the narrator refuses to try the title foods. The manner in which the green eggs and ham are presented does not matter to the narrator; the choice remains the same. The narrator's consistency in preference, regardless of presentation, illustrates the **principle of invariance** (see Tversky & Kahneman 1986). The principle of invariance is a critical part of a rational theory of choice, because the manner in which choices are presented, or framed, really should not matter if the different choices essentially amount to the same thing. In this case, green eggs and ham are still green eggs and ham wherever they are served. It would not be rational, for example, if the narrator decided that green eggs and ham would taste better if only they were eaten in a house, or while sitting next to a mouse. Being consistent is rational under these circumstances.

Yet it turns out that people appear to violate the principle of invariance in a number of different ways. In Chapter 7, for example, we saw that people are less willing to buy a $10 ticket to a play if they had just lost another $10 ticket they had purchased earlier than if they had just lost $10 in cash (Tversky & Kahneman 1981). Framing effects are another particularly striking violation of the invariance principle. According to Kahneman (2003), framing effects can be said to occur when people show a systematic preference for one choice in a choice task, but when they think about the offered choices deliberately, they consider those choices to be identical. For example, some people might have a strong preference to eat gummy candies out of a box rather than out of a bag when at the movie theater. But if they stop to think about it, they admit that it is the same candy regardless of how it is packaged.

Perhaps the most well-known demonstration of framing effects was achieved by asking people to read a vignette describing a potential disease outbreak. Students at Canadian and American universities were asked to consider the same problem framed in one of two different ways (Tversky & Kahneman 1981). Here is the first:

Problem 1. Imagine that the U.S. is preparing for the outbreak of an unusual disease, which is expected to kill 600 people. Two alternative programs to combat the disease have been proposed. Assume that the exact scientific estimate of the consequences of the programs are as follows:

If Program A is adopted, 200 people will be saved.

If Program B is adopted, there is 1/3 probability that 600 people will be saved, and 2/3 probability that no people will be saved.

Which of the two programs would you favor? (Tversky & Kahneman 1981, p. 453)

In the above example, both programs are framed in terms of gain – that is, lives that would be saved by the corresponding program. Program A indicates a definite outcome with no uncertainty, and Program B involves taking a major gamble. The expected value of 100% certainty of saving 200 people is equal to the expected value of a 1/3 chance of saving 600 but 2/3 chance of saving 0. Yet people did not actually treat the two programs equally, as they overwhelmingly chose Program A (72%) over Program B (28%; Tversky & Kahneman 1981).

These findings can be contrasted with those from the second problem, in which a different set of participants was asked to consider the following:

Problem 2. Imagine that the U.S. is preparing for the outbreak of an unusual disease, which is expected to kill 600 people. Two alternative programs to combat the disease have been proposed. Assume that the exact scientific estimate of the consequences of the programs are as follows:

If Program C is adopted, 400 people will die.

If Program D is adopted, there is 1/3 probability that nobody will die, and 2/3 probability that 600 people will die.

Which of the two programs would you favor? (Tversky & Kahneman 1981, p. 453)

Again, the expected values of Programs C and D are the same, and are equal to the expected values of Programs A and B. Like Program A, Program C is a sure thing, and like Program B, Program D is a gamble. The difference is that Programs C and D are presented in terms of losses; that is, people are asked to consider the numbers of people dying instead of people being saved. Loss framing gave rise to the opposite pattern of results: 22% chose Program C and 78% chose Program D (Tversky & Kahneman 1981).

There are at least two very important take-away conclusions from the "disease outbreak" experiment. First, in general, we can see that framing influences preferences between choices even when the choices are equivalent in expected value. Second, the results of this study suggest that framing choices in terms of gain (e.g., saving people) leads people to be risk-averse. That is, we saw that in the gain-framed Problem 1, people overwhelmingly chose the program with the certain outcome of at least saving some lives, not wanting to take the gamble. In contrast, framing choices in terms of loss (e.g., people dying) leads people to make risk-seeking decisions (Tversky & Kahneman 1981). In the loss-framed Problem 2, by far the more popular choice of the two was the program involving taking a major gamble, presumably in the hope of losing no lives.

Framing effects and health messaging

These conclusions have been replicated many times and are relatively consistent across different domains and tasks. For example, consider research on framing effects conducted in the health domain. One of the most important goals of health messaging research is to figure out how to get people to make changes in their behaviors that will increase health and extend life (e.g., avoid sunburn; get tested for HIV). A highly influential idea by Rothman and Salovey (1997) was to carefully design health-promoting messages to capitalize on known framing effects. In particular, they proposed to design health messages reflective of the finding that gain framing causes risk aversion, and loss framing causes risk-seeking. Because behaviors aimed at *preventing* health problems (e.g., lowering the likelihood of contagion) reduce risk, their model predicts that gain framing will be more effective than loss framing at getting people to carry out such behaviors. Also, because behaviors aimed at *detecting* health problems (e.g., screening for disease) might feel risky to people in the sense that they might find out about something bad, the model predicts that loss framing should be more effective than gain framing for increasing that behavior.

Rothman and Salovey's (1997) model has been tested across a number of different areas of health. In one classic study, Rothman, Martino, Bedell, Detweiler, and Salovey (1999) asked whether oral health behaviors could be influenced in accord with the model. They asked students at a U.S.

university to read a pamphlet explaining why they should use a mouth rinse. Either one of two types of mouth rinse was described. A *disclosing rinse* is used to detect gum disease or plaque, whereas a *plaque-reducing rinse* is used to lower the chance of gum disease by removing plaque (Rothman et al. 1999). Both rinses are used by swishing a small quantity in the mouth and then spitting it out. People read either gain-framed or loss-framed messages regarding one of the rinses. Gain-framed messages highlighted either the benefits of locating plaque on the teeth to prevent it from building up (detection) or the benefits of safely removing plaque with a rinse (prevention). Loss-framed messages focused on either the risk of being unable to locate areas in which plaque had built up (detection) or the risk of missing out on a safe way to remove plaque (prevention). People reported stronger intent to purchase and to use a *plaque removal* rinse if they read a gain-framed pamphlet than if they read a loss-framed pamphlet, whereas they more strongly intended to purchase and to use a *disclosing* rinse if they read a loss-framed pamphlet than if they read a gain-framed pamphlet (Rothman et al. 1999). It appears that being able to predict people's choices given framing may be useful in designing the most persuasive possible messages.

Choosing versus rejecting

The framing of the choice task itself may even influence choice decisions. Shafir (1993), for example, reported a framing effect that occurs when we think of the choice task as one in which we are choosing an option versus rejecting an option. For example, suppose you are a jury member on a child custody case in which one parent must be ruled the primary caregiver. The judge might ask you to decide which parent you choose for this role, or the judge might instead ask which parent you reject for this role (Shafir 1993). A framing effect occurs when one of the parents has average attributes (e.g., weak pros and cons) and the other has extreme attributes (e.g., strong pros and cons). For example, in the child custody case above, Shafir (1993) showed people descriptions of two parents. One had rather neutral descriptors, such as average health, average working hours, average income, and moderately strong bond with the child. The other had more extreme descriptors, both positive and negative, such as minor health issues, a lot of travel for work, high income, and very strong bond with the child. Strikingly, when people were asked to award custody, they awarded it to the second parent (64%), whereas when people were asked to deny custody, they tended to deny it to the second parent (55%; Shafir 1993). Thus, the framing of the question affected people's judgments; if it had not, then these two percentages would have added up to 100%. Shafir (1993) argued that depending on which task people think they are carrying out – which is really the same task framed two different ways – they give different weight to the different characteristics of each choice. When awarding custody, people give greater weight to the highly positive traits, and when denying it, they give greater weight to whichever traits were strongly negative.

Note that Shafir's (1993) classic findings lend themselves well to better understanding how people choose from among candidates in political elections, especially when one candidate is characterized by extreme positive and negative traits and the other is more mildly positive or rather average. In such cases, it matters whether we think of the choice task as voting for one candidate versus voting against one candidate, even when there are only two candidates in total. In one study, a hypothetical candidate with a strong track record of political experience and charity work who also bragged about having affairs and would not reveal any personal tax records was chosen by 21% but rejected by 92% in a matchup against a candidate with traits closer to average. Again, we can interpret a total in excess of 100% as evidence of a framing effect (Shafir 1993).

Overall, Shafir's (1993) studies indicate that people violate the rational principle of **procedure invariance**. There is procedure invariance when people's preferences between choices do not change depending on whether they are asked to make the choice in one way or in another way that is essentially the same as the first. Showing people two options and asking them to either choose one or reject one are equivalent tasks, but people's judgments show that they are making different choices depending on the task.

Shafir (1993) suggested that people's violations of procedure invariance have interesting implications for marketing. If a potential rug buyer is torn between a plain, less expensive option and an elaborate, more expensive option, the seller would be better off encouraging the person to choose one rug now to purchase than allowing the person to buy both rugs and return one later. When the buyer is looking for reasons why one of the rugs should be *chosen*, that buyer will focus on the beauty of the second rug compared to the first, increasing the chances of buying it. If the buyer has bought both and is looking for reasons to *return* one of them, that buyer will attend to the high expense of the second rug, increasing the chances of returning it. Shafir (1993) also noted that the size of the choice set and how many options need to be selected might lead people to implicitly assume that their task is either to choose or reject. For example, if there are 30 applicants for a graduate program and only 5 are to be accepted, the evaluators are likely to think of this as a task to choose 5. If, on the other hand, there are 30 applicants and 25 are to be accepted, the task might likely be interpreted as choosing 5 to reject. In sum, even though this particular framing effect may only occur when the choices are of a particular nature (e.g., some with average traits; others with very positive and very negative traits), it seems likely to apply to a range of potential situations in life.

Prospect theory

Studies further suggest that people's decisions are **reference dependent**; that is, our decisions depend on what reference level we are using as a standard of comparison. In an analysis of the emotional reactions of Olympic medalists, for example, Medvec, Madey, and Gilovich (1995) suggested that the medalists' happiness depended strongly on comparisons between what occurred and what they felt could easily have occurred instead. Videotapes of silver medalists and bronze medalists were taken both immediately after their performances and while they were on the medal stand, and independent raters judged how happy or unhappy they appeared to be on a 10-point Likert scale. Surprisingly, the researchers found that silver medalists appeared significantly *less happy* than bronze medalists, perhaps because silver medalists were thinking that they had come so close to winning the gold but didn't, whereas bronze medalists were thinking that they had been extremely close to not medaling at all but had managed to pull it off (Medvec et al. 1995). That is, their evaluations of their respective situations may have been reference dependent.

Similarly, one's judgment of the utility of a particular price or state of wealth depends on one's own current state of wealth (Kahneman 2003). A few coins for a cup of tea is judged to be not much if one is wealthy and quite a lot – too much – if one has almost no money at all. People's tendency to be reference dependent created a profound problem for understanding decision-making because it could not be easily reconciled with the predictions of expected utility theory (Kahneman 2003; see Chapter 8). To describe how people show reference dependence, how we violate the principle of invariance, and how we depart from expected utility theory in a number of additional ways, Kahneman and Tversky instead proposed an influential descriptive model of risky choice called **prospect theory** (Kahneman & Tversky 1979; Tversky and Kahneman 1992). The **prospects** in this theory refer to the different gambles between which people choose when carrying out risky decision-making (e.g., whether to adopt program C or D in the disease outbreak problem; Tversky & Kahneman 1981).

Prospect theory accounts for the following major characteristics of people's choices under uncertainty, all of which have been replicated many times in experimental studies (Tversky & Kahneman 1992):

- First, it incorporates *framing effects* of the type described in the previous section. We know from this work that how a problem is described can change people's preferences systematically, even if they themselves would admit that the different descriptions are essentially equivalent.
- *People want to avoid losses more strongly than they want to gain gains*, a phenomenon known as **loss aversion**. For example, Kahneman, Knetsch,

and Thaler (1990) showed that people who were given a pen to keep valued keeping that pen far more than potential buyers of that pen valued buying it (more on this later in the chapter).

- *Under certain conditions people very reliably tend to be risk-seeking.* This phenomenon is not traditionally accounted for in economic models of decision-making, which generally assume across-the-board risk aversion (see Chapter 8). Specifically, when a choice is framed in terms of losses, people overwhelmingly and reliably prefer a gamble to a sure thing (e.g., as we saw in the classic disease outbreak problem, Tversky & Kahneman 1981, and as also observed earlier by Markowitz 1952). Even with respect to gains, people prefer a gamble in which there is a very small chance they could win something big over receiving the expected value of that gamble with complete certainty (Tversky & Kahneman 1992). This latter finding can be observed on a daily basis in people's purchases of lottery tickets. For example, the odds of winning USD $1,000,000.00 in the Powerball lottery are less than 1 in 11,000,000. That means that this particular gamble has an expected value of less than $0.09 (i.e., 1 / 11,000,000 * $1,000,000.00). Yet many people willingly pay $2.00 for each opportunity to play.

- *People have non-linear preferences in risky choice.* In expected utility theory, outcome probabilities are *linear* in the sense that they are simply the product of the utility of an outcome and its probability; that is, the products are not distorted in any way. However, people's actual preferences are systematically *non-linear*; that is, we don't always personally place value on items at their exact monetary value. For example, we tend to disproportionately prefer certain (i.e., sure thing) outcomes to probable ones (the **certainty effect**), as we saw in Chapter 8. That is, we value a certain lump sum payoff more than a gamble even if they have equal expected values. People's non-linear preferences also drive the **Allais Paradox** (Box 9.1; Allais 1953, 1990).

- *People's willingness to choose a risky option is influenced by the source of uncertainty* (Tversky & Kahneman 1992). For example, Heath and Tversky (1991) found that people prefer to bet on uncertain events in a domain in which they feel they have some competence or expertise, even if they believe the other betting options to have the same likelihood of success. In one study, Heath and Tversky (1991) recruited people who self-identified as very knowledgeable in only one of two categories (i.e., either knowledgeable in politics but ignorant regarding football, or knowledgeable in football but poorly informed in politics). Then, both groups were asked to make predictions about upcoming election outcomes and upcoming football game outcomes and rate how likely they thought each of their predictions was to be correct. Twenty bets were presented to all the study participants; in each bet, they could choose whether to bet on one of their own predictions in football, one of their own predictions in politics, or on a device that would select a prediction by chance. Each bet was constructed so that the participant thought the three options had equal likelihoods of success. Expected utility theory would therefore predict that people should be equally likely to pick any of them. Instead, people strongly preferred to place bets on their own predictions in their area of expertise (Heath & Tversky 1991).

Kahneman and Tversky (1979) argued that all of the above behavioral findings show that expected utility theory does not work well as a descriptive model of risky decision-making. Their original alternative model, prospect theory, suggests that choice unfolds in two stages (Kahneman & Tversky 1979): an editing or **framing phase** and a **valuation phase** (Tversky & Kahneman 1992).

Kahneman and Tversky's (1979) original model suggested that in the framing phase, people tend to simplify each of the different prospects to make the choice less complex. For example, people might recode the outcomes of each prospect in terms of gains or losses. People define gains and losses with respect to a reference point, which can most simply be thought of as what wealth the person currently has (Kahneman & Tversky 1979). Sometimes, people also recode the outcomes to separate certain outcomes from risky outcomes. For instance, Kahneman and Tversky (1979) asked people to imagine a gamble in which you have an 80% chance of gaining 300 of something (say, packs of gum) and a 20% chance of gaining 200 packs of gum. Notice that if you were to take this gamble, there is actually a 100% chance you will gain at least 200 packs of gum. On top of that, there's an 80% chance you'll get yet another 100 packs of gum, and a 20% chance that you won't get any more. So the idea is that people would recode the gamble as follows: If I take this gamble, I'll get 200 packs of gum for certain; in addition, there is an 80% chance of getting 100 more packs and 20% chance of getting no more.

The model further specifies that in the framing phase, identical outcomes with identical probabilities cancel out across prospects. For example, if prospect A includes a 30% chance of winning a giant bag of candy and prospect B also includes a 30% chance of winning a giant bag of candy, then we will ignore this component of each prospect when choosing between the two. That is, the identical components in both prospects won't help us differentiate between them, so we remove them from consideration in the framing phase. The model also suggests that we edit out outcomes with extremely low probabilities in this phase (Kahneman & Tversky 1979). For example, if the above prospect A includes a 0.01% chance of gaining a free water bottle, we may choose to ignore this entirely in choosing between prospects A and B. In sum, the framing phase involves simplifying the choice we are trying to make, just as in the application of heuristics (Tversky & Kahneman 1992; see Chapter 3, Box 3.1).

Second, in the valuation phase of prospect theory, the **overall value** of each prospect (represented by the variable V) is computed, and one prospect, the one with the highest overall value (V), is chosen. As in expected utility theory, prospect theory accounts for how much the person values each possible outcome of a prospect and how likely it is. But because prospect theory is meant to be a descriptive model, the value of each possible outcome (expressed by the v function) and the likelihood of that outcome (expressed by the w function, also known as the π function) are modified to reflect people's actual decision-making. It's useful and interesting to see how the theory works, so I'll unpack it now.

First, the w function expresses how much the *probability* (P) of each outcome affects the overall value of the prospect (Kahneman & Tversky 1979). Having this function is necessary for a good descriptive model of risky choice, because people don't treat probability at face value (e.g., as can be seen in the Allais Paradox; Box 9.1). Instead, we are influenced by probabilities in distorted but predictable ways; that is, the way in which people treat probabilities is non-linear. The w function basically describes how people are *actually* influenced by probabilities ranging from 0 to 1 (i.e., 0% to 100%). In this way, the w function can be thought of as the **decision weight** – the amount of influence each outcome has on people's evaluations of a given prospect. Specifically, the w function describes how we tend to overweight low probabilities and how we tend to underweight everything else (i.e., moderate to high probabilities). This turns out to be true whether we are thinking about gains or losses (Tversky & Kahneman 1992) and has held up well across numerous experiments (see Barberis 2013 for a review). The w function is illustrated in Figure 9.1.

Zeckhauser's example (as cited in Kahneman & Tversky 1979) illustrates how our treatment of probabilities is non-linear. Suppose you are being forced by some evil person to play a game of so-called Russian roulette, and you are offered the opportunity to take one more bullet out of the loaded gun. How much are you willing to pay for that opportunity? Kahneman and Tversky (1979) argued that it quite probably depends on how many bullets are already in the gun. If there is only one, you would probably pay quite a lot to reduce the number to zero. If there are four, reducing the number of bullets to three also seems worth a lot but perhaps not quite as much. In each case, the probability of getting shot is being reduced by 16.67%, but getting the probability all the way down to zero has an additional appeal of its own, as it represents certain safety.

The **subjective value** or v function, in contrast to the w function, expresses how much people subjectively value each outcome of the

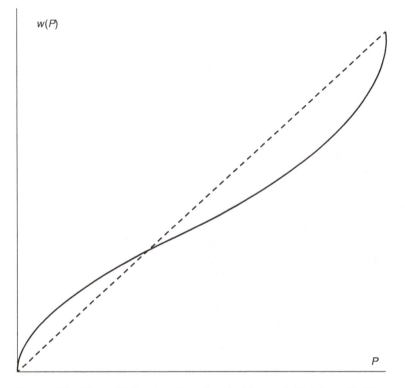

Figure 9.1 The *solid line* describes the decision weight (*w*) applied to an outcome in prospect theory, expressed as a function of the given probability (P) of that outcome from 0 to 1 (Kahneman & Tversky 1979; Tversky & Kahneman 1992). Specifically, $w(P) = (P^{0.65}) / (P^{0.65} + (1 - P)^{0.65})^{(1/0.65)}$. The *dotted line* depicts what the function would look like if people treated the given probability of an outcome straightforwardly. Adapted from Kahneman and Tversky (1979).

prospect (Kahneman & Tversky 1979). Values in prospect theory are expressed as gains or losses relative to the starting point, rather than as final total wealth as in expected utility theory. Prospect theory also describes our decision-making as being somewhat nearsighted, focusing most strongly on what is at stake in the present (Kahneman & Tversky 1979). As we have just seen in the many demonstrations of framing effects, our subjective values of outcomes are systematically distorted relative to their actual monetary values. Specifically, the subjective value we place on an outcome depends on whether we are considering gains or losses (i.e., such that we become risk-averse when thinking about gains and risk-seeking when thinking about losses). Subjective values also depend on what reference point we use: Winning USD $100 in a raffle is probably quite a bit more exciting to a person who only had USD $100 to begin with than to a person who already had USD $10,000.

Finally, the *v* function also illustrates loss aversion, such that it rises more slowly for gains (i.e., is concave) than it drops off for losses (i.e., is convex; Kahneman & Tversky 1979). The *v* function is illustrated in Figure 9.2. Note that negative affect may not be the driving force behind loss aversion. For example, Tom, Fox, Trepel, and Poldrack (2007) asked what brain circuitry might be involved in deciding whether to accept gambles and whether

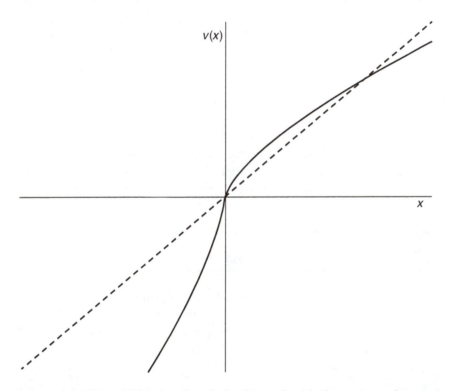

Figure 9.2   The *solid line* describes the intuitive value (*v*) of an outcome in prospect theory, expressed as a function of the monetary amount *x* (Kahneman & Tversky 1979; Tversky & Kahneman 1992). For gains (greater than or equal to zero), the *v* function illustrates how people treat *v* as the dollar amount *x* to the α power, or $v(x) = x^{\alpha}$. For losses (below zero), it suggests that people treat $v(x) = -2.25\ (-x)^{\alpha}$. Kahneman and Tversky (1992) estimated from experimental data on people's decision making that $\alpha = 0.88$. In the *solid line* in this figure, however, I set $\alpha = 0.70$ to more clearly visually illustrate the concave nature of the *v* function for gains and the convex nature of the *v* function for losses. The *dotted line* depicts what the function would look like if people treated each unit of money in a linear fashion; that is, without over- or under-weighting it. Adapted from Kahneman and Tversky (1979).

different circuitry is activated when considering potential gains versus losses. In particular, they wondered whether people are particularly averse to potential losses because they trigger a negative affective response not found when considering potential gains. People were asked to consider gambles, one at a time, with a 50% chance of either gaining money (ranging from USD $10 to $40) or a 50% chance of losing money (ranging from USD $5 to 20). They purposely chose a smaller range for losses because of loss aversion; that is, they expected people to be much more sensitive to potential losses than to potential gains (Tom et al. 2007). The results were not consistent with the idea that there are separate neural circuits for considering potential gains and losses. In fact, no brain areas associated with negative affective responses (such as fear or discomfort) showed elevated activation while considering the range of potential losses. Instead, a number of the same areas coded for both gains and losses (e.g., in the striatum and ventromedial prefrontal cortex), with greater activation for gains and decreased activation for losses.

The final part of prospect theory addresses exactly how the w function and the v function collectively express V, the subjective value of the prospect. Recall from Chapter 8 that in expected utility theory, the utility of each possible outcome of the prospect is multiplied by its given probability. The sum of these products is the expected utility of the prospect. Analogously, in

Box 9.1: The Allais Paradox

The Allais Paradox (Allais 1953, 1990) is just one example of how people's preferences are non-linear. It was one of the earliest and most striking findings showing how decision-making does not adhere to expected utility theory. The problem goes something like this. Suppose that you are asked to choose between two gambles:

- In Gamble 1, there is a 100% chance you will win EUR €1000.
- In Gamble 2, there is a 10% chance you will win EUR €5000, an 89% chance you will win EUR €1000, and a 1% chance you will win nothing.

Which would you would choose, Gamble 1 or Gamble 2?

Now, consider another choice between two gambles:

- In Gamble 3, there is an 11% chance you will win EUR €1000, and an 89% chance you will win nothing.

- In Gamble 4, there is a 10% chance you will win EUR €5000, and a 90% chance you will win nothing.

Which would you would choose, Gamble 3 or Gamble 4?

———————————

It turns out that generally, in the choice between Gambles 1 and 2, people have a tendency to prefer Gamble 1. In the choice between Gambles 3 and 4, people tend to prefer Gamble 4. Yet according to expected utility theory, people who are choosing rationally should either choose both Gambles 1 and 3, or they should choose both Gambles 2 and 4. But don't take my word for it; there are two parts to the mathematical proof for this claim.

Proof, Part I. Let's say that the utility of winning EUR €5000 is some value A, the utility of winning EUR €1000 is B, and the utility of winning EUR €0 is C. Now we can calculate the expected utilities of Gambles 1 and 2, respectively, plugging in the probabilities and utilities into the gambles described above:

- EU (Gamble 1) = B
- EU (Gamble 2) = $0.10A + 0.89B + 0.01C$

Now, let's go back to the data. People systematically preferred Gamble 1 over Gamble 2, which can be expressed with this inequality:

$$EU \text{ (Gamble 1)} > EU \text{ (Gamble 2)}$$

Plugging in the expected utilities we just calculated, we can express the inequality as follows:

$$B > 0.10A + 0.89B + 0.01C$$

Now we can simplify this a little bit by subtracting $0.89B$ from each side of the equation:

$$B - 0.89B > 0.10A + 0.89B + 0.01C - 0.89B$$

Which comes out to:

$$\mathbf{0.11B > 0.10A + 0.01C}$$

Let's come back to this after we walk through Part II of the proof.

Proof, Part II. Now, let's consider the expected utilities of Gambles 3 and 4, plugging in the probabilities and the utilities A, B, and C into the gambles described above:

$$EU \text{ (Gamble 3)} = 0.11B + 0.89C$$

$$EU \text{ (Gamble 4)} = 0.10A + 0.90C$$

As we saw in the data, people preferred Gamble 4 to Gamble 3, which can be expressed in this inequality:

$$0.10A + 0.90C > 0.11B + 0.89C$$

To simplify this equation, we can subtract 0.89C from each side, as follows:

$$0.10A + 0.90C - 0.89C > 0.11B + 0.89C - 0.89C$$

Which comes out to

$$0.10A + 0.01C > 0.11B$$

Bringing together the two parts of the proof, to sum it all up. When people say they prefer Gamble 1 over Gamble 2, they are saying the following:

$$0.11B > 0.10A + 0.01C \text{ (this is the final equation in Part I)}$$

When people say they prefer Gamble 4 over Gamble 3, they are saying:

$$0.10A + 0.01C > 0.11B \text{ (this is the final equation in Part II)}$$

Note now that these two equations are exactly the same except for the direction of the inequality sign. Regardless of what utility each person holds for the values of A, B, and C, people should either consistently prefer 0.10A + 0.01C over 0.11B or they should consistently prefer the opposite 0.11B over 0.10A + 0.01C. That is, their preferences should be consistent if they make decisions according to expected utility theory. Actually, Allais (1990) pointed out that this so-called "paradox" is only really a paradox if we *expected* people's choices to fall in line with expected utility theory. From the perspective of prospect theory, which accounts for people's choices in the above problems, this inconsistency is simply described as what people tend to do.

prospect theory, the subjective value v of each possible outcome of the prospect is multiplied by its decision weight w (Tversky & Kahneman 1992). The sum of these products is the subjective value of the prospect. To recap, the major ways in which prospect theory differs from expected utility theory are that v and w are non-linear, meaning that people distort both values and probabilities in systematic ways, and that people are assumed to edit and simplify their representations of each prospect before considering the valuation of each (Tversky & Kahneman 1992).

Prospect theory and economic theory

It is useful to think about how prospect theory might be applied to economic theory. As noted above, some tenets of prospect theory have had a strong influence on message framing research, particularly in health and medicine (Rothman & Salovey 1997). In addition, as we saw, Shafir (1993) discussed how people's different treatment of gains and losses could lead to relatively straightforward applications to sales. For example, sales staff might be well advised to take into account when they want the customer to be risk-seeking versus risk-averse and how to bring this about.

In the field of behavioral economics, prospect theory was considered to be so influential that Daniel Kahneman was a recipient of the 2002 Nobel Prize in Economics (see Kahneman 2003). Yet Barberis (2013) suggested that economic theory has been somewhat slower to adopt the tenets of prospect theory than might have been expected, even though the behavioral data were replicated in follow-up experiments. A major reason for this relatively slow adoption, according to Barberis (2013), is because it was not always immediately clear exactly how prospect theory should be applied in economic theory. A number of additional studies have since been conducted to clarify these ambiguities, making its application more feasible.

One example of such ambiguities is that it is relatively difficult to figure out how the reference point should be defined. As we discussed earlier, we need a reference point to determine what would count as gains versus losses (Barberis 2013). Although in theory it seems pretty straightforward to assume that the reference point is equal to the person's current wealth, investment behaviors from a finance perspective can be quite a bit more complex. For example, investors usually make decisions about an entire investment portfolio, rather than choosing between single gambles in isolation (Barberis 2013). For this reason, it is unclear whether investors would tend to think of gains and losses with respect to the value of the entire portfolio or with respect to individual stocks within that portfolio (and/or outside it). Another tricky question is whether the investor thinks of gains and losses as being defined within the short term (e.g., today, or over weeks or months) or over a longer period (e.g., years). For these questions, the answers may depend on what the investor is primarily concerned with at the time of decision-making. Even so, you can see how these ambiguities might need to be resolved before using prospect theory to predict investor behaviors.

One line of research partially addresses the issue of defining the reference point by proposing that investors think of gains as increases in wealth beyond what one *expected* to earn in the stock market (Barberis 2013). Kőszegi and Rabin (2006), in an influential proposal, suggested that the reference point is set by people's expectations given events in the recent past. If investors have, for example, been steadily earning 4% interest annually on an investment, they will treat a year in which they receive 2% as a relative loss and a year in which they receive 6% as a relative gain. Or suppose that an employee expected to receive EUR €70,000 in salary this year but instead received only €55,000 due to the company's financial difficulties. The employee is likely to perceive this year's salary as a relative loss (i.e., a salary cut).

Ericson and Fuster (2014) suggested that prospect theory may work best at describing people's behavior if it can account for the fact that people probably use multiple reference points. For example, let's consider how prospect theory can account for the endowment effect depending on different possible reference points (Kahneman et al. 1990; Thaler 1980). The **endowment effect** occurs when people value what they already own more than they would if they did not yet own it, even if ownership was randomly determined (Thaler 1980). Thus, people will go to more trouble to avoid losing something they already have than they will to gain that same thing if they did not yet have it. Thaler (1980) gave the hypothetical illustration of a man who bought a case of wine at the cost of USD $5 per bottle. The value of that wine then went up dramatically over time. Some time later, a wine merchant offered to purchase the case of wine for USD $100 per bottle. The man declined the offer, preferring to keep the wine, although at USD $100 per bottle it was far more valuable than any other wine he had ever purchased. The idea, again, is that he valued the wine all the more *because* he already owned it. Similarly, because of the endowment effect, we can expect people to respond positively when given government-funded health benefits, but to respond with disproportionately strong negativity when those same benefits are taken away (Bernstein 2013).

In a seminal experiment demonstrating the endowment effect, Kahneman et al. (1990) presented every other university student sitting in a classroom with small items (e.g., ballpoint pens in boxes) labeled with university bookstore price tags (e.g., USD $4). These students were told that they now owned the items. The remaining students in the room were not given the items, but could see the items, as each was sitting next to a student who owned one. Each student who owned a pen (i.e., the "sellers") were then asked to report the minimum price at which they would sell it. Each student who did not own a pen (i.e., the "buyers") were asked to report the maximum price they would pay to own one. The median price that the buyers were willing to pay for a pen was less than half of the median price sellers would accept for the same pen, demonstrating the endowment effect (Kahneman et al. 1990). That is, sellers – who already owned the item – placed much more value on that item than did buyers. Note that the endowment effect occurred even though the students had had no say in whether they had received a pen in the first place: Simply owning an item increases one's valuation of it, even if one did not seek it out.

Now, let's say that the endowment effect can be explained in terms of loss aversion (i.e., wherein people are disproportionately unwilling to lose what they already own; Ericson and Fuster 2014). Say that what you already own is often treated as the reference point against which gains and losses are evaluated. But consider a slightly different situation, which may warrant a different way of determining the reference point. For example, when people already intend to trade away what they already own (e.g., as merchants do), these people do not show the endowment effect (List 2004). This phenomenon – the disappearance of the endowment effect when people knew from the start that they did not have to keep their goods, and would have an opportunity to unload them – can still be explained within the bounds of prospect theory. The trick is to define the reference point with respect to people's expectations (Ericson & Fuster 2014): If people were *expecting* all along to trade (or sell) their own goods away, then they should not show loss aversion (as in Kőszegi & Rabin's 2006 model). That is, if they never planned to keep these goods, the goods will not be incorporated into the reference point.

By this reasoning, we can explain how people can be influenced to spend more on a particular good (e.g., corn flakes cereal) when it is typically priced more than the amount they think it is worth, but periodically goes on sale. Suppose that one day, knowing that sometimes it goes on sale, you go to the grocery store expecting to come home with a box of corn flakes. Even if it is not on sale that day, the plan you had to own that item will lead to loss aversion and higher valuation of the good (i.e., you went to the store with the concrete expectation of acquiring and owning the corn flakes; Barberis 2013). Because your plan to own the item set the reference point, you will be disproportionately reluctant to let it go, and willing to shell out more money for it than you otherwise would have. Overall, the idea is that the reference point is determined not only by what you have but also by what you *plan or expect* to have or not have (Ericson & Fuster 2014). With adjustments such as this, prospect theory seems better poised to account for a number of important complex phenomena outside the laboratory.

Conclusions

In this chapter, we considered evidence for multiple ways in which people's risky choice does not seem to be described well by expected utility theory. For example, we avoid risks when we are thinking about potential gains, and we tend to seek them when we are thinking about potential losses. How we define gains and losses in the first place depends on what reference point we adopt. This reference point can be the wealth we hold right now, but could also be partially determined by what we plan on owning or not owning in the near future. We dislike losses more than we like comparable gains, we do not value goods strictly by their dollar amounts, and we do not treat probabilities as they are given. Prospect theory aims to encompass all of these ways in which humans do not reason as predicted by expected utility theory. As prospect theory continues to be developed and refined in multiple domains, and is applied to not only issues in behavioral economics but also to such endeavors as improving health messaging, it seems likely to have continued impact on many fields of study. In Part IV of this text (Making Sense of the World), we will further consider how people tend to simplify their decision-making by creating coherent stories of how things work, drawing upon frameworks of knowledge to fill gaps in information, and ignoring details that do not fit into those frameworks.

Questions for discussion

1. Suppose you are a car salesperson hoping to sell a new car to a customer. Would it be easier for you to sell the car if you (1) offered a rebate worth 5% the price of the car, in which they would buy the car for full price and then receive the 5% in a separate check from your car dealership or (2) simply offered the car at a sale price for 5% off, in which they would only pay you 95% of the full price? Please use the *v* function of prospect theory (see Figure 9.2) to help you reason out your answer.
2. Considering Question 1 above, would it make a difference if the price of the car was equal to 50% of your customer's current wealth (i.e., your client is less wealthy), versus if it was equal to only 10% of your customer's current wealth (i.e., your client is more wealthy)? Please refer back to the discussion of reference points in this chapter.
3. Given what you know about the application of prospect theory to message framing, design and write the text of a brochure persuading people to stop texting while driving. Please justify, based on known research, why you framed the text as you did.

Suggestions for further reading

Barberis, N. C. (2013). Thirty years of prospect theory in economics: A review and assessment. *Journal of Economic Perspectives, 27*(1), 173–196.

Kahneman, D., & Tversky, A. (1979). Prospect theory: An analysis of decision under risk. *Econometrica: Journal of the Econometric Society, 47*(2), 263–291.

Tversky, A., & Kahneman, D. (1992). Advances in prospect theory: Cumulative representation of uncertainty. *Journal of Risk and Uncertainty, 5*(4), 297–323.

PART
IV

Making Sense of the World

Schemas and Framework Theories 10

Learning Goals

By the end of this chapter, you will have:

- Considered and compared distinct but somewhat compatible arguments in developmental psychology about the nature of people's background knowledge.
- Developed an understanding of how people's background knowledge about the world is organized and how it influences decision-making.
- Critically evaluated classic theories of schemas and scripts and considered their applicability to everyday life.
- Applied the notions of framework theories and schema theory to understanding and exploring important issues in legal and clinical decision-making.

Key Terms

Framework theories	Confabulation
Artifacts	Script
Stances	Errors
Modes of construal	Obstacles
Mechanical stance	Distractions
Design stance	Information integration theory
Intentional stance	Story model
Schema	Episode schema

Suppose you are the well-meaning parent of two children, each of whom is exhibiting behaviors that give you pause. Like many parents, you had no formal training in parenting and are figuring things out as you go. For the past 8 months, your 6-year-old has mostly ignored other children in favor of playing with an imaginary friend. Your 5-year-old pretends that every object is a gun, loudly play-shooting everyone from the elementary school principal to the local Catholic priest and announcing that they are dead. The potential issue at hand is whether something is just beginning to go *wrong* with your children; in other words, whether such behavior is not quite normal and whether you ought to intervene. For example, perhaps some one-on-one conversations with the children, new outlets for their attention such as soccer or swimming lessons, or the help of a child counselor, psychologist, or psychiatrist are needed (Yopchick 2012). Or perhaps these behaviors are among the many normal behaviors of childhood that come and go with age, and the children would be better off if you let them explore these kinds of behaviors on their own. From a judgment and decision-making perspective, there are at least two important and complex questions to be asked about the above scenario. First, what is the decision process by which people induce whether or not something is wrong with a person or situation and determine what to do about it (see also Chapter 6)? Second, what makes one suspect that there might be something wrong in the first place?

Although the obvious answer might seem to be that the information given in the descriptions of the children's behavior triggered the concerns, that information *alone* could not have told us that the behavior is suspect. Instead, that information taken together with at least two additional inferences may be critical. We may judge how likely these behaviors are to occur among children of this age – the very same type of judgment we spent considerable time discussing in Chapters 2, 3, and 4. And we may draw a mental comparison between these children's behavior and our *preexisting expectations* about what constitutes normal children's behavior. This latter possibility presumes that we intuitively hold commonsense knowledge about things in the world and how they operate (in this case, regarding what constitutes normal young children's behavior). This chapter is about such commonsense knowledge and how it influences the judgments we make. It launches a broader section (Chapters 10–13) examining how we make sense of the world against the backdrop of our existing knowledge in judgment and decision-making.

Framework theories

Consider the following questions. Which is more likely to catch a blood-borne disease from a mackerel fish: A shark or a deer? Suppose there is a bowling ball sitting on a carpet at a 0 degree incline. Will the bowling ball start moving when it is struck on the side by a slowly rolling glass marble? How do you think a hardworking manager might feel when she discovered that she was passed over for a promotion because a co-worker, one whom she had considered to be a close friend, spread lies about her? The most likely answers to these questions – *shark, no, upset*, respectively – may seem quite obvious. Yet the very fact that we can generate those answers so easily illustrates how heavily we rely on our commonsense background knowledge across at least several major domains: A minimum of a layperson's knowledge of the habitats of biological species is needed to answer the first, a rudimentary understanding of physics (mechanics) is needed for the second, and a basic understanding of psychology (human interaction) is necessary to answer the third.

An influential viewpoint in cognitive developmental work suggests that distinct sets of commonsense background knowledge and assumptions in these three broad domains – biology, physics, and psychology – enables us to carry out everyday thought. Wellman and Gelman (1992) argued that our intuitive knowledge about these three domains make up our commonsense **framework theories**. These develop very early in life and serve as an organizing foundation for our understanding of new information. Commonsense framework theories are analogous to the global, overarching theories used by scientists to define the problems of a field – for example, evolutionary theory in biology provides an organizing framework for the questions that scientists study, as well as for how living things are classified and categorized together. Wellman and Gelman (1992) proposed that lay people similarly have commonsense background knowledge and assumptions that help us understand what is going on in the world, and that each set of background knowledge is relatively specific to a particular domain.

Even young children can clearly distinguish between animals and **artifacts** (i.e., human-made items), and make different assumptions about each. For example, Keil's (1989) seminal research showed that young children (like adults) agree that animals (e.g., raccoons) are still themselves even if their appearance is changed (e.g., painted black with a white stripe down the back). Children also believe that artifacts can change identity when their appearance is changed (e.g., a coin melted down and made into a key that works). That is, children believe that things like appearance can be important for artifacts but aren't necessarily as important for animals. Interestingly, some other domains of framework knowledge take children longer to figure out. For example, children have difficulty developing the understanding that plants are alive, even though they have no problem understanding the same for animals (Richards & Siegler 1986; Stavy & Wax 1989). And as we will see in Chapter 13, even into adulthood, some core beliefs about how things work within a domain will sometimes be overextended to apply to an inappropriate domain. For example, people's understanding of the germ theory of disease within the biological domain may be overextended at times to apply to the social, or psychological, domain. (In one remarkable study, people behaved as though social status was "catching" and were accordingly more likely to shun people who happen to be standing near a person of lower social status than those standing farther away; Hebl & Mannix 2003.) That said, for much of the time, adults rely on framework theories quite appropriately to understand phenomena within these domains.

More broadly, our understandings of everyday events and phenomena may be influenced strongly by the kinds of explanations we generate for them. In particular, Dennett (1987) and Keil (1995, 2006) suggested that people adopt **stances** or **modes of construal** when coming up with such explanations. Stances or modes of construal are ways of explaining that are based on our existing knowledge. For example, you could explain a chipmunk's vocalizations in purely physical terms, describing them with respect to the vibrations of its throat structure and the acoustics of the oral cavity (i.e., taking a **mechanical stance**; Dennett 1987). Or you could explain the same vocalizations in terms of their purpose, or why they make the vocalizations. For example, you might conjecture that their vocalizations are for communication (taking a **design stance**). You could alternatively explain the chipmunk's vocalizations in terms of an **intentional stance**, presuming that the animal has beliefs and desires that drive this behavior – for example, you might say that the chipmunk is annoyed that you are standing near its store of food and is scolding you away. The explanations that we generate may then become part of the structure of our knowledge as it is stored in memory.

Schema theory

Under the umbrella of these broad framework theories, we also hold a great many different smaller categories of general knowledge, each of which is called a schema. Schemas are sets of general knowledge about what you have learned to expect in a particular kind of situation or thing. For example, your schema of a professor's office probably includes a desk, books, and chairs. Your schema of going to the grocery store includes aisles of products, selecting what you need, checking out, and making a payment. Because you've stored these sets of knowledge, you would expect these things in a new professor's office or grocery store that you had never been to before, and if it were missing any of these things, you would be surprised. Let's take an example to illustrate.

Please read the following sentence:

Agnes struggled slowly up the stairs for her doctor's appointment.

Then, please answer the following questions:

How old is Agnes?

Why do you think she is struggling to get up the stairs?

Why do you think she is going to see her doctor?

If you are a longtime resident of Canada or the U.S., you may be quite likely to guess that Agnes is elderly, that she has achy joints and perhaps arthritis, and that she is going to see her doctor for those reasons and perhaps also for any of a number of problems common to the elderly. If you are a resident of Denmark or Sweden, you might be less likely to make these specific assumptions. Think back to the name "Agnes," the first word in the sentence you read above. In Canada, the name "Agnes" was one of the 100 most common names given to newborn girls over most years between 1915 and 1945, but has not been particularly popular since (Williams 2015). "Agnes" also enjoyed great popularity in the U.S. for many years and was ranked among the top 100 most frequently given newborn girls' names from 1900 to 1920; however, it has not been among the top 1000 names for girls in any year since the early 1970s (Williams 2015; U.S. Social Security Administration 2015). This suggests that in Canada and the U.S., being named Agnes is a reasonably reliable statistical indicator of being an older adult and a rather poor indicator of being very young. In contrast, the name Agnes was listed among the top 50 names for newborn girls in Denmark every year from 2011 to 2014, and in Sweden it has been in the top 50 continuously since 1999, peaking at #3 in 2006 and #4 in 2014 (Williams 2015). Taken together, these trends suggest overall that the name is much less likely to be as exclusively associated with the elderly in Sweden and Denmark than it is in Canada and the U.S. Still further, the name may not be associated with any characteristics whatsoever in Korea or Japan, where it has been (I believe) unusual to be named Agnes at any point in time.

In short, we rely heavily on stored background knowledge, activated by even a single word, to make sense of new information. In normal conversation, we rarely explain everything as we go, but instead assume that other people have many small pockets of knowledge that they will call upon to help them make sense of the things we say. In the case of the sentence you read above about Agnes, for example, the name Agnes itself may activate a culture-dependent schema containing a person's background knowledge about humans of a specific age group to help impose additional meaning upon the sentence. If no schema is activated by the name, then we would expect quite a bit more variability in how different people interpret that sentence.

Bransford and Johnson (1972), in a set of seminal studies documenting effects of schemas on reading comprehension and memory, similarly presented high school students in the U.S. with a seemingly disjointed set of sentences or paragraph such as the following:

> A newspaper is better than a magazine.
> A seashore is a better place than the street.
> At first it is better to run than to walk.
> You may have to try several times.
> It takes some skill but it's easy to learn.
> Even young children can enjoy it.
> Once successful, complications are minimal.
> Birds seldom get too close.
> Rain, however, soaks in very fast.
> Too many people doing the same thing can also cause problems.
> One needs lots of room.
> If there are no complications, it can be very peaceful.
> A rock will serve as an anchor.
> If things break loose from it, however, you will not get a second chance.
>
> (Bransford & Johnson 1972, p. 722)

Some of the students in these studies were told the context of the above sentences, learning that they were all about "making and flying a kite" (Bransford and Johnson 1972, p. 723). Other students read the sentences without ever learning their context. The researchers also manipulated whether the students who learned the topic did so before or after they read the above set of sentences. The results showed that students who learned the topic – whether before or after they read the sentences – had higher comprehension scores than students who never learned the topic. Furthermore, students who learned the topic before they read the sentences had better recall of those sentences than did students who learned the topic after they read the sentences (Bransford and Johnson 1972). In other words, activating a schema (e.g., that of kite making and flying) improved both comprehension and memory in sentence processing, presumably by helping people organize incoming information into a set of knowledge already held in memory.

In addition to helping us navigate situations and places in the world by allowing us to draw upon our relevant background knowledge, schemas can also have powerful effects on how well people are able to learn and perform. Furthermore, not everyone has the same information contained in their schemas, and the nature of the content can matter for performance. Dweck, Chiu, and Hong's (1995) notion of implicit theories of human attributes (e.g., intelligence, moral character) illustrates the structure of two different schemas for intelligence. Each of these two schemas gives rise to a number of different inferences profoundly affecting people's learning and perseverance (Yeager & Dweck 2012). Specifically, those holding an entity theory of intelligence tend to view intelligence as a fixed and immovable trait, whereas those holding an incremental theory of intelligence see it as a flexible and changeable trait (Yeager & Dweck 2012). From these initial mindsets, school-aged children draw a wide spectrum of related inferences, influencing their goals for school, beliefs about what trying hard would do, how they tend to explain setbacks, and what strategies they adopt for learning (e.g., Blackwell, Trzesniewski, & Dweck 2007). Students' judgments on these four variables tend to be highly inter-correlated (Blackwell et al. 2007). For example, in a study of junior high students in the U.S., children who held entity theories of intelligence tended to be more interested in looking smart than in learning per se, believed that trying hard was something that only unintelligent people had to do, explained setbacks by either thinking they were not good at that sort of thing or not intelligent, and tended to give up or blame others when they failed. Children who were incremental theorists, in contrast, were more interested in learning something than in looking smart, believed that trying hard was an important part of what made a person smart, accounted for setbacks by thinking that they should have put in more effort, and tended to work harder and try different strategies when they failed (Blackwell et al. 2007). The content of our schemas guides how we make sense of current situations, even potentially influencing our performance in pervasive ways.

The importance of schemas for navigating through the world also becomes especially apparent when considering cases in which they don't operate as expected. Studies of human and animal memory are consistent with the hypothesis that the medial prefrontal cortex is implicated in schema representation and use (Ghosh, Moscovitch, Colella, & Gilboa 2014; Tse et al. 2011). Drugs that interfere with immediate early gene activity in the medial prefrontal cortex in rats prevent recall of information, as well as formation of new memories. Lesions to the ventromedial prefrontal cortex in humans can lead to the neurological disorder of **confabulation**, in which patients recall memories that are not correct without understanding that they are false. Most importantly for our current purposes, confabulation may be caused in part by a failure to activate only relevant schemas (Ghosh et al. 2014). For example, when waiting in the doctor's office for an appointment, a confabulating patient may activate the wrong schema (e.g., going to a restaurant) and may look around repeatedly, trying to find the menu. To document this phenomenon more systematically, Ghosh et al. (2014) asked patients with ventromedial prefrontal cortex lesions who were currently confabulating to view a series of words (e.g., toothbrush, thermometer) and quickly judge whether each was closely associated with a particular schema (e.g., going to bed at night). Then, they were asked to judge whether another series of words (some of which were repeated from the first set) were closely associated with a different schema (e.g., visiting the doctor). Compared to healthy control participants, the confabulating patients tended to have a very difficult time excluding words in the second round irrelevant to the current schema (Ghosh et al. 2014). This included words that were indeed part of the schema in the first round, but were not relevant to the schema in the second round. Such findings, along with anecdotal evidence, highlight the critical importance of activating a relevant schema to interpret what is going on in even the most common situations.

Scripts

One subtype of schema, known as a script, is a set of general knowledge for a highly routine *event* such as those described above (e.g., birthday parties, grocery shopping, doctor's office visits, going to a restaurant, etc.; Schank & Abelson 1977). Bower, Black, and Turner (1979) further suggested that scripts are well known by many people within a culture and can be measured and shown to facilitate learning and memory. For many scripts, there is a temporal sequence to the different components (e.g., going to a restaurant), whereas for others, the order of components in time is not necessarily relevant (e.g., cleaning house).

Evidence that scripts seem to have a generally agreed-upon set of components and (often) temporal order of those components within a culture is found in Bower et al.'s (1979) seminal work. In one study, they asked American students to describe what generally happens in a particular type of situation (e.g., going to a restaurant) in the temporal order in which they occur. Components mentioned were highly inter-correlated between people, and it was very rare for any given component to be mentioned by only one person. Some of the script items generated by the highest proportion of participants for going to a restaurant, for example, were as follows (Bower et al. 1979):

- *Be seated*
- *Look at menu*
- *Order meal*
- *Eat food*

Of course, the script for a given type of event can vary wildly across cultures and for different types of restaurants. Foreign tourists attempting to dine in casual noodle shops in Tokyo, for example, may experience complete bewilderment. This is because the restaurant script for this context, well understood implicitly within the culture, runs more along these lines:

- *Look at plastic food models of course offerings in front window*
- *Select button corresponding to your choice at touch screen mounted on wall*
- *Hand receipt to restaurant staff*
- *Food is delivered to table*
- *Eat food*

The idea is that these scripts are picked up over time by observation, and that our memories of them make it possible for us to quickly understand and know what to expect in many routine types of situations within that culture.

Of course, as Bower et al. (1979) pointed out, violations of scripts make stories (and life) more interesting by failing to meet those very expectations. Schank and Abelson (1977) discussed at least three broad types of violations to a script that may often occur. In **errors**, a typical component in a script is followed by a later component that ought to match the first, but does not. For example, a person might order coffee in a restaurant, but she is then served spaghetti instead. **Obstacles** are instances in which a typical component in a script cannot occur because of some problem. For example, a person is unable to order a meal in a restaurant because no one ever shows up to the table to take the order. Finally, **distractions** may occur; these are unexpected events that prevent the full execution of the script, sometimes pulling the character out of the script entirely (Schank & Abelson 1977). For example, the sight of a tow truck outside the restaurant, about to pull the person's car away, may have the person throwing money onto the table and sprinting out, effectively exiting the restaurant script.

Bower et al. (1979) also asked students to read several stories based on scripts that the experimenters had already gathered from other students from the same population. Each of these stories contained obstacles, errors, and interruptions as well as script-consistent components. After a 10-minute delay, students were asked to recall the stories in as much detail as they could. Bower et al. (1979) found that script violations were remembered better than were script-consistent components, perhaps because the former became the central point of each story by virtue of their unexpectedness within the script. Among the subtypes of script violations, interestingly, obstacles and distractions were both remembered better than were errors.

Bower et al. (1979) suggested that this may occur because obstacles and distractions interfere with the entire flow of the script; errors can be ignored while the script moves on, but obstacles and distractions bring the script to a standstill (whether temporary or permanent). The fact that violations capture attention suggests that we do indeed rely on scripts to make sense of events as they unfold, and that activating a script means activating a set of expectations about what should now happen.

Framework theories and schemas in legal decision-making

Framework theories and schemas play crucial roles in understanding how we reason through some of the most complex decisions that we face. One colorful example of this can be found in the domain of law. Framework theories and schemas can radically influence how jurors build explanations to understand a court case. In court cases, the juror's fundamental task is to base judgments upon an enormous amount of information presented during the trial. Early models attempting to describe the juror decision process made use of straight-forward algorithms (as reviewed by Pennington & Hastie 1988). For example, information integration theory suggests that each piece of information contributes a particular value regarding the guiltiness versus innocence of the person on trial, and that these can be weighted in terms of how impor-tant they are and calculated together for an overall assessment (Kaplan & Kemmerick 1974). A weighted average of this overall assessment and the juror's initial (prior to deliberation) judgment of the guilt/innocence of the person on trial yields the final decision by the juror. Such simple models are very powerful in that they can handle very large amounts of data and account for a number of behavioral phenomena.

Yet such models have important limitations, too, because court cases have a great deal of additional complexity that is not easily entered into such straightforward calculations. For example, the information jurors receive during a trial is not necessarily given in temporal order, and many pieces will be missing given that (1) each witness may have had limited access to the event and had a different point of view and (2) because of rules of law determining what pieces are and are not admissible (so some pieces may never be presented at all). In addition, the interpretation of many pieces of evidence depends on other pieces of evidence – some pieces can be linked together in a complex way, though they may not necessarily be presented as such by either the defense or the prosecution (Pennington & Hastie 1988).

The story model of juror decision-making (Hastie & Pennington 2000; Pennington & Hastie 1988, 1992) is a descriptive model that attempts to encompass these complexities for a fuller picture of how jurors make judgments about court cases. It suggests that jurors carry out such decisions in a three-step process. Specifically, they begin by attempting to construct a well-formed, structured story that makes sense of the evidence (i.e., that tells the story of what happened; Pennington & Hastie 1986, 1992). People do this, according to the story model, by organizing the court case information using an **episode schema**, which contains assumptions about the temporal ordering, or sequence in time, of events and circumstances. An episode schema may suggest that the event begins with some kind of initiating event and the physical state of the person under trial, which then lead that person to form goals and a psychological state, which then (either solely or conjointly with each other and with the physical state) lead to the person's actions and ultimately its consequences (Pennington & Hastie 1986, 1992; Hastie & Pennington 2000). For example, a juror might mentally reorganize the information in a wrongful death trial as follows after initially receiving it in scrambled temporal order:

1. *The person under trial was accosted in a bar by a belligerent acquaintance while his own blood alcohol level was high*
2. *This led to feelings of anger that he was unable to suppress due to his drunkenness*
3. *Simultaneously, he formed the goal of teaching the belligerent acquaintance a lesson*
4. *He acted by attacking the acquaintance with the fishing knife he usually carried*
5. *The acquaintance consequently died of a stab wound* (adapted from Pennington and Hastie 1986)

In a second step in the story model, people must learn the different verdict categories and what they mean. For example, they might need to learn the difference between first-degree and second-degree murder, manslaughter, and self-defense (i.e., not guilty), and what the qualifications are for each (Pennington & Hastie 1986, 1992; Hastie & Pennington 2000). Finally, they come to a decision by seeking a match between the temporally ordered story they have created and their new background knowledge of the different verdict categories (Pennington & Hastie 1986, 1992; Hastie & Pennington 2000).

In one study, for example, Pennington and Hastie (1986) sampled American jurors from a volunteer jury pool and asked them to watch a three-hour video that recreated a real-life murder trial. (Before the study, a separate group of judges and attorneys rated the video as highly realistic.) The jurors were told that they were to watch the trial as jurors and that they would be asked to make judgments afterwards. Jurors were asked separately to think about their decision while talking through it (i.e., a standard think-aloud protocol); their full responses were recorded and later transcribed for coding. Their final decisions were highly diverse: About equal numbers of jurors decided on first-degree murder, second-degree murder, and man-slaughter and self-defense combined, respectively. The fact that they came to such disparate conclusions after all watching the same video raises the question of exactly how each reasoned through the evidence (Pennington & Hastie 1986).

The think-aloud data from the study showed that jurors across the board drew explicit causal connections between pieces of information to make sense of them; they also temporally reordered the information to run in sequence (Pennington & Hastie 1986). The experimenters found that this process resulted in relatively clear stories that differed quite radically by verdict; major differences in story structure and in content were both found. In fact, 55% of the elements in their stories came directly from the testimony that they heard, but a full 45% were inferences that the pro-spective jurors made about the suspect's mental states and goals. This can account for how different jurors came up with completely different stories and, accordingly, different verdicts. Pennington and Hastie (1986) pointed out that, intriguingly, jurors with different background theories about how people generally tend to operate psychologically made very different inferences. For example, people who expressed aloud the belief that being baited by an aggressive acquaintance would generally lead to a fear reaction tended to infer that the suspect had been motivated by fear when striking out with a knife (suggesting self-defense). In contrast, people who mused aloud that the same circumstance would generally lead to a reaction of anger tended to infer that the suspect was motivated by the desire to teach that acquaintance a lesson (suggesting criminal intent). In other words, the background theories and schemas they already held guided their interpre-tation of what happened in that specific case, and appear to have radically influenced their verdicts.

In follow-up research, Pennington and Hastie (1988) asked American university students to read through a written version of the same court case and give a verdict decision. Then, students were given a surprise recognition memory test of pieces of evidence that had been presented in the court case. The students were more likely to correctly recognize pieces of evidence that were consistent with the verdict they had chosen than the pieces that were also true, but were instead consistent with a different verdict. They were also prone to falsely recognize incorrect pieces of evidence as having been pres-ent in the court case, but this tendency also followed an intriguing pattern.

Pieces of evidence not actually in the court case were more likely to be falsely recognized when they were consistent with the verdict the person had chosen than when they were consistent with a different verdict. These findings are strikingly similar to seminal findings in schema research, and point again to the importance of schemas in guiding inferences and influencing memories about what happened in a case.

Framework theories and schemas in clinical judgment

Like jurors, practicing mental health clinicians are faced with the task of making sense of a hodgepodge of information and drawing potentially life-altering conclusions. A patient's reported symptoms, current physical appearance, recent or significant life events and environment, and medical history may all factor into clinicians' diagnosis decisions. Lay people, too, often deal with the challenge of observing a friend or family member in attempting to determine whether that person's behavior is worrisome in a way that indicates the need for a professional evaluation. Potential patients face the same task given self-observation and knowledge of their own histories and environments. In all of the above situations, structured framework knowledge may form the backdrop against which a person's current behaviors and situation are compared. For example, you might compare your child's behavior to your understanding of how children generally behave at that age to get a sense of whether that behavior is normal. A clinician might compare a patient's behavior and history to prior beliefs regarding how symptoms and history tend to align into specific diagnostic schemas. In short, people with and without clinical training approach a case with existing pockets of knowledge, whether accurate or not, that guide their interpretation of the information at hand.

In a series of experiments conducted on mental health clinicians and lay people in the U.S., both groups were found to hold causal models of mental disorders (Kim & Ahn 2002a, 2002b). Clinicians and lay people read through the symptoms and associated characteristics of disorders and personality disorders from the *Diagnostic and Statistical Manual of Mental Disorders* (American Psychiatric Association 1994), both common (e.g., depression, anorexia) and more obscure (e.g., avoidant personality disorder). Clinicians showed significant agreement with one another on all but one of their causal models of disorder (the lone exception being schizotypal personality disorder, which has a relatively low prevalence; Pulay et al. 2009). Perhaps more surprisingly, clinicians' models also agreed to a significant extent with the models held by lay people (Kim & Ahn 2002b). The clinicians included people of different theoretical orientations (e.g., psychoanalysts, cognitive-behaviorists, etc.), but they still showed agreement regarding the fundamental cause-effect relationships within disorders. For example, regarding anorexia, clinicians agreed that the fear of being fat was more causally central than the refusal to maintain a minimal body weight, which in turn was more causally central than physical signs of starvation (Kim & Ahn 2002b).

Such background beliefs about the cause-effect relationships among symptoms of a disorder may influence clinical decision-making. For example, clinicians are more likely to diagnose hypothetical patients as having a disorder when the patients have causally central symptoms rather than effect symptoms in the clinicians' own causal models (Kim & Ahn 2002b). It is important to note that in the modern *Diagnostic and Statistical Manual of Mental Disorders* (American Psychiatric Association 2013) system, the symptoms are given equal weight in diagnosis in most disorders; that is, symptoms are neither stated nor implied to be more or less important than other symptoms within a particular disorder. Yet clinicians themselves make diagnosis decisions as though some are more important than others, in line with their own background knowledge and beliefs about the disorder in question. These findings in the domain of mental health suggest that causal models of disorders may operate as schemas to guide comprehension and decision-making.

Flores, Cobos, López, Godoy, and González-Martín (2014) further found that clinicians' reasoning and decision-making about case studies are influenced by the degree to which those cases are consistent with their schemas for the relevant disorders. In one study, they asked practicing clinical psychologists in Spain to consider 12 case studies. For half of these case studies, symptoms occurred in a temporal order causally consistent with the disorder schemas documented by Kim and Ahn (2002b); for the other half, symptoms occurred in a causally inconsistent temporal order (Flores et al. 2014). For example, in the causally consistent order for a case of anorexia, fear of being fat appeared first in the patient, followed later by the refusal to maintain a minimal body weight, followed lastly by physical signs of starvation. In the causally inconsistent order, these symptoms appeared in the patient in the reverse temporal order. As Flores et al. (2014) predicted, clinicians took longer to read cases in the causally inconsistent than in the causally consistent condition. Clinicians were also more likely to agree with the diagnosis provided (e.g., anorexia) in the causally consistent than inconsistent condition, despite the fact that the same symptoms appeared in each. Taken together, these results suggest that clinicians approach a case with *a priori* expectations for the temporal order of symptoms within a given disorder and that these expectations affect their diagnostic decisions (Flores et al. 2014).

Clinicians' knowledge structures of disorder, of course, extend beyond their *DSM-5* (APA 2013) symptoms and associated characteristics; a wide array of contextual information also appears to be organized within these disorder schemas, influencing decision-making. For example, De Los Reyes and Marsh (2011) presented U.S. clinicians with cases of adolescents that included extra content that did not itself indicate the presence or absence of any particular symptom. This extra content was either inconsistent with empirical investigations of conduct disorder (e.g., liked by friends' parents) or consistent (e.g., disliked by friends' parents). They found that this extra information, mentioned within a case description, strongly influenced clinicians' likelihood judgments of conduct disorder, such that they judged conduct disorder to be much less likely when inconsistent content was inserted into the case description than when consistent content or no extra content was inserted. Essentially, such content appears to be part of clinicians' schemas for conduct disorder, factoring into diagnosis judgments, even though it does not technically constitute symptoms of conduct disorder. Clinicians' diagnoses appear to be influenced broadly by schema-inconsistent information in addition to the presence or absence of symptoms per se.

When reporting their causal models for detailed cases of individual clients instead of for disorders in general, clinicians' responses tend to be quite diverse (de Kwaadsteniet, Hagmayer, Krol, & Witteman 2010), as are their recommendations regarding what treatment would be best for those clients. In an intriguing study, practicing clinical child psychologists in the Netherlands viewed individual case study descriptions of two different children, both showing signs of depression and one also showing features of other comorbid conditions, including attention-deficit/hyperactivity disorder (de Kwaadsteniet et al. 2010). For each case in turn, they were asked to identify all the problems in the case, along with all causal factors that influenced those problems. Then, they were asked to identify the causal relationships they felt to be present among those problems and causal factors. An intervention rating task followed, in which they ranked the likely effectiveness of ten candidate treatments (e.g., family therapy, medication, social skills training). They were then asked to identify what problems and causal factors would be impacted by each of their top five ranked treatments.

The results were striking: Although individual clinicians' causal models for specific cases were, again, quite variable, their recommended treatments could be reliably predicted by their causal models (de Kwaadsteniet et al. 2010). It may be that a particular clinician's causal models for individual cases are based on an overarching framework held by that clinician to explain how behavior problems emerge; additional follow-up research is needed to understand how models for specific cases map to frameworks of knowledge. Indeed, Berens, Witteman, and van de Ven (2015) further showed that when causal explanations for the same symptoms are systematically manipulated, Dutch clinicians' treatment plans were influenced accordingly. That is, clinicians' treatment decisions were not based on symptoms alone; the causal explanations given for them mattered (Berens et al. 2015).

Conclusions

As we have seen throughout this chapter, from an early age, people develop and store organizing structures for knowledge. These structures, in the form of framework theories (at a broader level) and schemas (at a more specific level), help us to learn new information and to retrieve relevant information that helps us explain and predict complex events. Decisions in the world are embedded in this culture-bound framework of existing knowledge whether or not that knowledge is correct, and in some cases, whether or not it is relevant. In the next chapter, we will consider in more depth how people make sense of the world by making inferences about causes and effects.

Questions for discussion

1. Let's return to the two examples of children's behavior described at the very beginning of this chapter. Do their behaviors violate your schemas of normal child development or not? How might cultural, family, and neighborhood influences on schema formation affect your judgment? How might they affect the decision their parent ultimately makes about whether to refer these children for professional help?
2. At www.youtube.com, search for funny commercials or stand-up comedy routines from the country with which you are most familiar. How do culture-specific schemas and scripts play into your ability to understand this humor? Then, search for funny commercials or stand-up comedy from another country where you have spent little or no time (subtitled if necessary). Is the humor harder for you to understand? Can you explain this in terms of schema theory?
3. How might different people's culture-bound schemas and framework theories influence the kinds of legal and clinical decisions discussed in the last two sections of this chapter?

Suggestions for further reading

Garb, H. N. (1998). *Studying the clinician: Judgment research and psychological assessment.* Washington, DC: American Psychological Association.

Hastie, R. (1994). *Inside the juror: The psychology of juror decision making.* Cambridge, UK: University of Cambridge Press.

Wellman, H. M., & Gelman, S. A. (1992). Cognitive development: Foundational theories of core domains. *Annual Review of Psychology, 43*(1), 337–375.

11 Judging Covariation, Contingency, and Cause

Learning Goals

By the end of this chapter, you will have:

- Understood and evaluated models of causal attribution that are based on how two events or things covary with one another.
- Critically considered sample summaries of covariation data in 2×2 contingency tables to better understand how people might think about causes.
- Examined how a variety of cues-to-causality may lead people to infer the presence of causal relationships.
- Compared theories of how people distinguish between types of causal learning (i.e., in carrying out diagnostic and predictive tasks) and between types of causes (i.e., cause, enable, and prevent relationships).
- Considered theoretical and practical ramifications of experiments demonstrating causal illusions in humans and apparent causal reasoning in non-human animals.

Key Terms

Covariation	Fundamental attribution error
Covariation principle	2×2 contingency table
Personal causality	Quackery
Impersonal causality	Causal field
Covariation model of attribution	Difference-in-a-background
Consensus	Cues-to-causality
Distinctiveness	Temporal order
Consistency	Contiguity in time and space
Probabilistic contrast model	Temporal binding
Correspondence bias	Causal mechanism

Similarity of cause and effect	Mental models theory
Simulation heuristic	Dynamics model
Counterfactual reasoning	Regression toward the mean
But for cause	Illusion of control
Blocking	Unrealistic optimism
Cue	Trap-tube task
Predictive learning task	
Diagnostic learning task	

Why did your friend suddenly burst into tears, running out of the room? Why did the caterer fail to deliver 200 promised doughnuts to a fundraising event? What is causing a painful rash and swelling on a patient's foot? It has been argued that causal thinking underlies the vast majority of judgments made under uncertainty (Hastie 2015). People are strongly driven by a desire to explain events, especially abnormal events (Hilton 2007), and the quest for explanation seems to powerfully motivate our behaviors, much like the quest for food and water in response to hunger and thirst (Gopnik 2000).

An interesting characteristic of causal explanation is that it requires people to go beyond the data that they have on hand (Hastie 2015). Suppose that we see a billiard ball roll toward another, and just after they make contact, the second ball starts to roll. We make the judgment that the first ball caused the second to move, but we did not actually *see* the causation directly (Hume 1739/2000). That is, all we could see was that the first ball moved, the balls made contact, and the second ball then began to move in the same direction. The *causal* story (i.e., that of the first ball causing the second to roll) is one that we mentally created; whether or not it is correct, it is a story that we built up from the visual data that we gathered. It has been argued that in general, we tend to create such explanations by which we tie events in the world to one another.

This process compounds when we are faced with more complicated scenarios to explain. We may try to explain why a friend is terribly frustrated with a housemate, or why someone broke into your car and not anyone else's nearby. We may ask why there was a partial nuclear meltdown at Three Mile Island, Pennsylvania, on the March 28, 1979, or why it was that Malaysia Airlines Flight 370 disappeared with its passengers and crew on March 8, 2014. In this chapter, we will come to a better understanding of causal reasoning, or the process of figuring out what causes what to occur in the world.

Judgments of covariation

Covariation occurs when two things tend to happen together. For example, you might notice that the more you pet your cat, the more it purrs, and the less you pet your cat, the less it purrs. When you try to figure out why a friend seems upset or why a professor fails to call on you even when your hand is raised, often much of the evidence you have to work with is covariation information. Heider (1958/2015) famously proposed that people use covariation information to try to figure out *why* other people said or did what they did. This is known as the **covariation principle**: "An effect is attributed to the one of its possible causes with which, over time, it covaries" (Kelley 1973, p. 108). In other words, we tend to create a causal story from covariation information. Heider (1958/2015) further suggested that people try to search for relatively stable properties of the person or situation that can generally be expected to cause certain effects. These stable properties help us to make predictions about how people will behave. For example, my belief that a friend has good common sense leads me to generally expect that friend to do and say things that are appropriate for the situation. My belief that a particular university is highly competitive leads me to expect to find many of its students studying in the library.

Heider (1958/2015) also drew a clear distinction between personal causality and impersonal causality. **Personal causality** refers to cases in which a person's intention was the force behind a particular action; **impersonal causality** is when the action occurs without having been intentional. For example, suppose that your professor did not call on you in class when your hand was raised. Personal causality can be attributed if she did so on purpose; for example, if you had just raised your hand in response to the previous five questions she posed to the class, and she hopes now to give others a chance to respond. Impersonal causality, in contrast, refers to cases in which she did not call on you, but this was not intentional. For example, say you seated yourself slightly behind a large load-bearing column running from the floor to the ceiling, and she never saw your raised hand, which was completely obscured from her view. Heider (1958/2015) argued that personal causality, in contrast to impersonal causality, is perceived to have a strong causal force that can be pinpointed to the person (e.g., the professor). As such, we tend to want to assign some causal force to the professor even if she *intends* to ignore you but fails to do so (e.g., say you insistently stand and jump up and down, waving your hand, and she finally calls on you to avoid making a scene). However, we tend not to assign causal force to the professor if your raised hand was hidden behind a large column.

Kelley's (1973) **covariation model of attribution** builds upon Heider's (1958/2015) analysis, suggesting that when we try to make inferences about other people, there are several specific kinds of covariation information that we take into account. One of these factors is consensus; that is, whether other people respond in the same way when presented with the same stimulus (Kelley 1973). For example, suppose that you just watched the latest superhero movie and found that you did not enjoy it at all – in fact, you very much disliked it. Consensus occurs when other people who went to see the same movie also disliked it. The second factor is distinctiveness: Whether you respond in this way only with this specific stimulus. We can see distinctiveness, for instance, if you have seen other movies recently and liked them, but that in contrast, you did not like this one. Finally, the third factor is consistency; that is, whether you respond in a similar way over time, across many experiences with the same stimulus. For example, your dislike of the movie has consistency if you rewatch it later, just to give it a fair shot, and find that you dislike it just as much as you did the first time you saw it.

Kelley (1973) argued that people think like scientists when making causal attributions for other people's behaviors, collecting the above covariation information and mentally running a naïve analysis of variance on the three factors. He acknowledged that this naïve analysis was probably not anywhere close to being a full statistical analysis (Kelley 1973), but argued that people are still able to draw some intuitive conclusions from the information. In particular, he proposed that different patterns of covariation information should lead to distinct, predictable causal attributions. For example, when there is low consensus (e.g., everyone else enjoyed the movie), low distinctiveness (e.g., you don't usually like movies, and this was no exception), and high consistency (e.g., upon rewatching the movie you disliked it again), we are likely to draw a person attribution for your response. That is, we will probably decide that you disliked this movie because *you* yourself are a person who tends not to like movies in general. If, instead, there is high consensus (e.g., everyone else also disliked the movie), high distinctiveness (e.g., you usually enjoy movies, but found this one to be singularly unenjoyable), and high consistency (e.g., upon rewatching the movie you disliked it again), we will probably draw a stimulus attribution. That is, we will most likely decide that the stimulus (e.g., the movie) caused your response: You disliked the movie because the movie itself was not good.

Cheng and Novick (1990) further expanded upon Kelley's (1973) analysis, proposing a normative model of the causal attribution process that they called the probabilistic contrast model. Kelley's (1973) model focuses only on main effects (i.e., making attributions to the person, to the stimulus, or to the occasion). A full analysis of variance, in contrast, includes not only main effects but also interactions. The potential importance of including interactions can be illustrated by reconsidering the example above. How you react to a particular movie may very well depend on the interaction of you in particular and that specific movie. Suppose that you happen to be a person who dislikes movies with close-up action scenes, as they make you feel dizzy, and the director of this movie took many such close-up shots. In this case, it was the *interaction* of your pet peeve with this particular stimulus that caused your dislike of the movie. Cheng and Novick's (1990) core insight was that people seem well able to mentally track and draw conclusions about such interactions as long as they do not become too complex.

However, note that making attributions about other people's behaviors may be something of a special case in causal attribution, as they can be distorted by the **correspondence bias**, also known as the **fundamental attribution error**. This bias refers to our tendency to make person attributions for behaviors that could be explained by the situation alone (Gilbert & Malone 1995). For example, in Jones and Davis' (1965) classic study, people were shown essays either supporting or criticizing Cuba's Fidel Castro. Even when people were told that the essay writers were assigned the topic they were to defend, and were given no choice in the matter, they still judged that the writers really believed, to some extent, what they had written. Gilbert and Malone (1995) suggested that one key mechanism underlying the correspondence bias may be a general lack of awareness of how situations, which are not always publicly visible, can have a strong causal force upon behaviors. For instance, when people criticize their politicians for having overly compliant and cowardly personality traits, these people may in some cases be succumbing to the correspondence bias, unaware of the myriad external pressures that have cornered these politicians into making compromises (e.g., concessions may need to be made to get enough votes to pass a piece of legislation). That is, any person placed into this exact situation might behave quite similarly, regardless of his or her personality traits.

Judgments of contingency

Contingency judgments can also help us figure out what causes what in the world. Suppose you want to determine whether eating monosodium glutamate (MSG) is causing your very frequent headaches. You read a research study, the results of which suggest that eating MSG can cause headaches in some people. The study, however, cannot tell you for sure whether eating MSG causes *your* headaches. Your doctor suggests that you collect more information by keeping track of what you eat and how you feel afterwards. Over the next 100 days, you keep a journal in which you record (1) whether or not you ate MSG that day and (2) whether or not you subsequently had a headache. These

Subsequent Headache?

		Yes	No
Ate MSG?	Yes	A: 58	B: 3
	No	C: 27	D: 12

Figure 11.1 A 2×2 contingency table of data compiled to help judge whether or not there is a relationship between your eating MSG and experiencing headaches. In this hypothetical example, observations were made over a total of 100 days.

data can be expressed in a 2×2 **contingency table** (see Figure 11.1), in which you summarize how frequently these factors co-occurred.

Notice in Figure 11.1 that the numbers in all four cells provide important evidence regarding whether eating MSG and then having headaches covaries in your case. Cells A and D can be treated as confirmatory evidence for a relationship between eating MSG and having headaches (see Lipe 1990). In cell A, you can see that on 58 days, you ate MSG and afterwards had a headache. In cell D, there were 12 days in which you didn't eat MSG and then had no headache. Both of these findings are *consistent* with the hypothesis that MSG causes your headaches.

The numbers in cells B and C tend to be taken as *possible* disconfirmatory evidence for this hypothesis, and can also be considered (Lipe 1990). In cell B, we can see that there were a few times in which you ate MSG but did not have a subsequent headache. Perhaps these instances could be taken to be disconfirm-atory evidence, though they were much less frequent than the confirmatory evidence found in cells A and D. (On a side note, it is also possible that some-thing more complicated is going on; this would only be possible to examine by collecting additional data. For example, it could be that a combination of MSG with another food gives you headaches, and if you don't eat that second food with the MSG, you don't get a headache. Most of the time you happen to eat those two foods together, but a few times, you only had the MSG and therefore no headache.)

Finally, the fact that you had headaches on 27 days in which you didn't eat MSG (cell C) needs to be considered. It could be that MSG does cause many of your headaches, but sometimes your headaches are caused by other things, such as not drinking enough water or reading without your glasses. Or perhaps all of your headaches were caused by something that wasn't MSG, and you just happened to be measuring MSG but failed to measure the other thing. The data you've collected cannot tell you exactly which of these possible alternatives (if any) is the true story, but from a practical standpoint they may cast some doubt on the claim that there is a clear-cut causal relationship between the two.

Of course, you can also conduct a chi-square statistical test, which (using the data in Figure 11.1) reveals that the null hypothesis – that MSG and your subsequent headaches are independent – should be rejected at the $p < .001$ level of significance. In other words, over the 100 days, you have gathered evidence that MSG and your headaches are not likely to be independent of each other. As we saw above, we still don't know the precise nature of their potential relationship, but a layperson might still find it quite reasonable to conclude that MSG probably plays some role in *causing* you to have headaches.

In fact, all four cells do tend to affect people's covariation judgments to some degree (Lipe 1990). Yet when people reason about such contingency information, they tend not to give equal weight to the four cells of the 2×2 contingency table. Studies have consistently shown that people give cell A the most weight, cell B the next most, cell C next to least, and cell D the least weight in drawing conclusions (Mandel and Lehman 1998). Furthermore, when people simplify judgments, they sometimes go so far as to attend only to cell A and ignore the rest, essentially adopting a purely confirmatory approach (e.g., Arkes & Harkness 1983).

Interestingly, knowing how people treat the cells in 2×2 contingency tables can help us understand how people come to develop erroneous causal beliefs. For example, a number of people believe in **quackery**, medical treatments unsupported by evidence that are passed off as scientifically based (Matute, Yarritu, & Vadillo 2011). In one study, Matute et al. (2011) asked internet users in Spain to observe 100 cases of hypothetical patients, all of whom were suffering from a fictitious disease. In each case, the patient was described as either taking a fictitious medicine called Batatrim or not taking it. Participants were informed whether each patient then felt better. Some participants were told that 80 patients took Batatrim and 20 did not, and 80% of each group felt better. The other participants learned that 20 patients took Batatrim and 80 did not, and 80% of each group felt better. In both conditions, the 100 cases showed that the medicine actually had no effect at all, as symptoms were equally likely to subside whether or not the medicine was taken (80% of the time in both cases). Yet people experienced an illusion of causality, such that they generally judged that the medicine made patients with the disease feel better (Matute et al. 2011). Matute et al. (2011) also found that the illusion of causality was much stronger for participants who saw 80 cases of patients taking Batatrim than for participants who saw only 20 such cases.

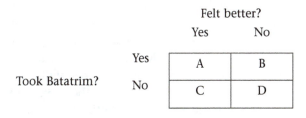

Figure 11.2 A 2×2 contingency table representing the data seen by participants in Matute et al. (2011).

Matute et al.'s (2011) findings can readily be explained using a 2×2 contingency table (Figure 11.2). As we discussed above, people generally tend to place the most weight on Cell A. The participants who saw 80 patients taking Batatrim (who felt better 80% of the time) saw a total of 64 patients out of 100 in Cell A. Those who saw only 20 patients taking Batatrim, who also felt better 80% of the time, saw a total of only 16 patients out of 100 in Cell A. Matute et al. (2011) pointed out that those who saw only 20 patients taking Batatrim were also able to view a great many cases (i.e., 64 in Cell C) of people who did not take the drug, yet felt better. These cases were probably highly salient (because there were so many of them), and in conjunction with the small number of cases in Cell A, people were less susceptible to the illusion that Batatrim heals the disease.

The role of plausibility

So far, we have talked about covariation information as though it alone can explain how we infer cause and effect from data. But covariation information is definitely not sufficient to explain the causal judgments we make. Suppose that three things tend to covary perfectly: Jo wears a pair of jeans, Jo steals a friend's dessert, and Jo's friend gets angry with Jo. When inferring why Jo's friend gets angry with Jo, we probably wouldn't think that her anger is just as likely to be caused by Jo's jean-wearing as by Jo's dessert-stealing. This example suggests that the causal relationships people *already believe to exist* influence how people receive and process covariation information.

Fugelsang and Thompson (2003) found support for this claim in a series of experiments. They told university students in Canada about a possible cause for an outcome; this possible cause was pre-rated as being either highly plausible or highly implausible. For example, insomnia was presented as a cause of fatigue (this was pre-rated as plausible), and taking iron supplements was presented as a cause of cancer (this was pre-rated as implausible). In the main study, students rated how likely it is that the possible cause (e.g., iron supplements) really causes the effect (e.g., cancer). They were then presented with covariation data that either supported or did not support the candidate cause. For instance, they might be told that out of ten patients taking iron supplements, nine developed cancer (supporting the candidate cause of iron supplements). Then they were asked to again rate how likely it was that the possible cause really causes the effect, taking both types of information into account. Fugelsang and Thompson (2003) found that the covariation data affected judgments of a potential cause more strongly if they already thought it made sense that it would cause the effect.

Goedert, Ellefson, and Rehder (2014) further showed that the prior plausibility of a cause influences the relative weights given to data in cells A, B, C, and D of the contingency table (e.g., Figure 11.1). They presented students in the U.K. and U.S. with cover stories in which the students were asked to investigate whether a candidate cause really caused a particular effect. They found that when the cause was plausible (e.g., *adding fertilizer* as a possible cause of *plant growth*), people gave significantly more weight to the covariation data in cells A and B than when the cause was implausible (e.g., *being in a blue pot* as a possible cause of *plant growth*). In contrast, the weight given to cells C and D did not differ regardless of whether the candidate cause was plausible (Goedert et al. 2014).

In follow-up studies, Goedert et al. (2014) gave people the opportunity to choose what covariation information they would see. Specifically, people could choose whether they would see the outcome of a particular case from cell A or B (in which the cause was present) or the outcome of a case from cell C or D (in which the cause was absent) when trying to figure out whether the candidate cause actually caused the effect. Goedert et al. (2014) found that people *chose* to seek out information from cells A and B (cause present) more frequently when the candidate cause was plausible than when it was implausible. In addition, they replicated their previous findings showing that cells A and B were given more weight when the candidate cause was plausible than when it was implausible, and that the weights given to cells C and D were not influenced by the candidate cause's plausibility.

Judging the plausibility of a cause

What leads us to consider a cause to be plausible in the first place? The research we have just considered suggests that it is more than just about covariation. One way in which people may judge a cause to be plausible is by judging how well it fits into their existing background knowledge (Chapter 10). For example, given evidence that the presence of a particular virus in utero tends to co-occur with low birth weight of the baby, we assume that the virus causes the low birth weight and not vice-versa because that causal direction is more compatible with our broader background knowledge about disease.

Einhorn and Hogarth (1986) further suggested that people decide on what counts as a cause by applying a number of rules. First, according to the philosopher Mackie (1965, 1974), we decide on what belongs in the background (i.e., the **causal field**) against which potential causes might operate. For example, one's birth and one's death covary 100% – everyone who has been born later dies at some point. But it doesn't seem quite right to conclude that birth *causes* death. Although death cannot happen without birth, we generally do not judge birth to be death's cause. According to Mackie's (1974) analysis, birth belongs to the causal field – it is part of the existing background conditions of a person's life. An event or factor that stands out as being quite different against that existing background is more likely to be seen as a cause. For example, if a person is born and grows up (the causal field), but one day suffers a heart attack and then dies, we will probably infer that the heart attack – salient against the causal field – was the cause of the death. In other words, the heart attack is judged to be a **difference-in-a-background**, to use Mackie's (1965, 1974) terminology, and we'll infer that it was the cause of the person's death.

Second, Einhorn and Hogarth (1986) suggested that people will see an event or factor as a cause when one or more **cues-to-causality** are present. One of these is the cue of *covariation*, already discussed above. By collecting data about the contingency of two events or objects, as depicted in Figure 11.1, people build up evidence that is relevant to judging whether one causes the other.

Another cue-to-causality is **temporal order**. For example, if in ordinary life people find that seeing a commercial for chocolates is very frequently followed by a craving for chocolate, the order in which these two things occur leads us to believe that the first caused the second, and not vice-versa. Einhorn and Hogarth (1986) suggested that people use temporal order as a cue to causality (and do so even when they shouldn't). For example, Tversky and Kahneman (1980) pointed out that the probability that a child has blue eyes given that her parent has blue eyes is equal to the probability that a parent has blue eyes given that her child has blue eyes. However, when people are asked to judge the likelihood of each of these probabilities, they judge the first to be more likely than the second (Tversky & Kahneman 1980). In other words, if they are thinking about the problem in temporal order, starting with the parent having blue eyes and inferring how likely it is that the child also has blue eyes, the relationship between the two seems more likely to them than when reasoning in reverse temporal order.

In fact, in a seminal study of juror decision-making (see also Chapter 10), Pennington and Hastie (1988) showed that in a court case, the order in which information is presented influences jurors' verdicts. They hypothesized that when the prosecutor or defense attorney presents court evidence in temporal order, making it relatively easy to infer the causal relationships between events and circumstances, jurors are more convinced by the story being told. To test this hypothesis, Pennington and Hastie (1988) manipulated whether the evidence from each side was presented in temporal order, or whether it was presented in a scrambled order. (Interestingly, the scrambled order was actually also the order in which evidence in the case had been presented in the real murder trial.) Study participants, who were American university students, were most likely to give the verdict "guilty" if the prosecuting attorney's case was presented in temporal order and the defense attorney's case was presented in scrambled order. They were least likely to give this same verdict when the identical evidence was presented in temporal order for the defense and in scrambled order for the prosecution. Such findings suggest that temporal order allows people to more easily build a causal story that makes sense of the evidence.

A third cue-to-causality is **contiguity in time and space** (Einhorn & Hogarth 1986): People may judge a cause to be present when the effect occurs soon after the cause, and when it is physically right beside the cause. In early studies by Michotte (1946/1963), people were shown "launching" displays showing the movements of two balls. Ball 1 moved toward Ball 2, Ball 1 stopped when it contacted Ball 2, at which time Ball 2 began moving. By varying the distance, direction, and speed of the balls' movements, Michotte (1946/1963) was able to identify the precise conditions under which people would judge that Ball 1 had caused Ball 2 to move. For example, he showed that the balls had to make contact, Ball 2 had to start moving almost immediately after contact (though more slowly than Ball 1 had been moving), and Ball 2 had to be moving in the same direction in which Ball 1 had previously been moving, in order for people to judge that Ball 1 *caused* the motion of Ball 2.

Note that people also make the opposite inference. When people first believe that two events are causally related (e.g., when they already believe that Ball 1 caused the motion of Ball 2), people then infer that the events happened closer together in time than they actually did (Buehner 2012). This phenomenon is known as **temporal binding**. A series of studies has shown that temporal binding occurs regardless of whether the effect was caused intentionally (e.g., by a person) or mechanically, without being intentional (e.g., by a machine; Buehner 2012).

Cause and effect can still be inferred without contiguity in time and space, but in such cases, some sort of **causal mechanism** (i.e., explanation or story) is necessary to fill the gap (Einhorn & Hogarth 1986). For example, suppose that a store marks down a display of children's toys to half-price, and a week or two later, we observe that the number of sales of those toys is beginning to rise. Even though the two events (i.e., marking down the prices; increasing number of sales) are not contiguous in time, we can still attribute the increased number of sales to the price markdown if we reason that it might take a while for word of mouth to get around about the discounted toys. In fact, Ahn, Kalish, Medin, and Gelman (1995) showed that when people are trying to figure out what caused an event (e.g., an airplane crash), they tend to ask for information about causal mechanisms. Furthermore, when they explain the event, they have a strong tendency to explain it in terms of mechanisms (83% of the time) rather than in terms of covariation (Ahn et al. 1995).

Fourth, the similarity of cause and effect can also cue people to infer a causal relationship. One way of thinking about similarity is in terms of physical appearance (Einhorn & Hogarth 1986). In the strain of folk medicine called the doctrine of signatures, popular in the sixteenth and seventeenth centuries, plants were chosen to treat ailments by their corresponding physical appearances (Pearce 2008). For example, plants that looked like ears were used to treat earache; those with parts shaped like a spleen or liver were used to treat disorders of the spleen or liver, respectively. A second way in which similarity is a cue-to-causality hinges upon the magnitude and duration of the cause compared to that of the effect. For example, the germ theory of disease was initially extremely difficult for people to accept because the cause was microscopically small and the effect was often enormous (e.g., large-scale outbreaks of disease and death; Einhorn & Hogarth 1986). Again, public acceptance of germ theory may only have been achieved when people better understood the causal *mechanism* by which the cause gave rise to the effect. In contrast, a powerful tsunami causing massive damage to a coastal town is less difficult to understand intuitively in terms of cause and effect.

There may also be cues-to-causality beyond those identified by Einhorn and Hogarth (1986). In their description of the simulation heuristic, Kahneman and Tversky (1982) suggested that people will often, after observing a past event, mentally simulate what might have happened instead under different circumstances. They suggested that people then use the outcomes of these mental simulations to make judgments about the future or the past (Kahneman & Tversky 1982).

Creating such simulations is one example of how people may evaluate potential causes using counterfactual reasoning. In counterfactual reasoning, people ask whether an event would have occurred if a particular factor had not (Spellman & Mandel 1999). For instance, let's say that a person met his future spouse at a charity fundraiser party. He wonders whether they would ever have met if he had not gone to that fundraiser on a whim, at the last moment. We then judge, accordingly, whether or not we think that factor (e.g., deciding to attend the fundraiser) caused the event (e.g., meeting his future spouse). In legal reasoning, a factor can be said to have caused an event if we can reason that the event never would have occurred *but for* that factor (referred to as a *but for* cause; Spellman 1997; Spellman & Mandel 1999). We might reason, for example, that a pedestrian would not have died *but for* the decision of the accused party to drive while intoxicated.

An important exception to this rule, however, is when the event is brought about by two separate causes, where each alone would have been sufficient to cause it. In one experiment by Spellman and Kincannon (2001), study participants read about a victim shot by two different people at the same time. Each individual shot was, in and of itself, fatal, and the victim died (Spellman & Kincannon 2001). Strictly making causal judgments on the basis of counterfactual judgments would lead to the conclusion that neither shooter had been the (*but for*) cause of the death. That is, if one shooter had not fired the shot, the victim would still have died, and if the other shooter had not fired, the victim would also have died. Yet college students judged both shooters to have caused the death, recommending significant prison sentences (i.e., a mean of 46 years). Studies such as these suggest that although counterfactual reasoning can assist our judgments of cause, it can be overridden by other cues-to-causality, such as proximity in time and space, and the availability of a causal mechanism (e.g., firing a gun).

Causal learning: Blocking

Classic experiments of non-human animal learning have been the basis for some of the earliest theories of human causal learning. Say that a rat first learns that hearing a tone predicts, with perfect accuracy, an electric shock to the feet (i.e., 100% of the time when the rat hears the tone, the electric shock is then experienced). Then, in a second learning phase, the rat both hears a tone and simultaneously sees a light, and 100% of the time, these are followed by an electric shock to the feet. Now, we can test what the rat has learned overall. Typically, such studies show that the rat is still afraid of the tone, but shows no fear to the light. In other words, the rat has already learned that the tone predicts the shock, and then fails to next learn that the light also perfectly predicts the shock, a phenomenon called **blocking**. Rescorla and Wagner (1972) proposed that blocking can be explained purely in terms of the associations that are learned. That is, the rat learns that the first cue, the tone, predicts the shock, and a strong association between the two is learned. When a second cue, the light, is placed in competition with the tone as a predictor of the shock, the rat fails to associate the light with the shock, as there is no need for it to do so: The tone already allows it to predict what will happen with 100% certainty.

Waldmann and Holyoak (1992) suggested that in people's causal learning, the meaning or context of what is being learned also matters; human causal learning is not only about associating two things with each other. For example, when a candidate cause (e.g., a person's appearance) is presented first, and your job is to determine whether or not it is causing a specific effect (e.g., others' emotional responses to that person), you are carrying out a **predictive learning task**. In predictive learning tasks, one learns that when the cause occurs, the effect (and any other effects of the cause) are likely to also occur. Conversely, when the effect (e.g., a person's appearance) is presented first and you are supposed to figure out if it is due to a particular cause (e.g., a disease that alters people's appearances), you are carrying out a **diagnostic learning task**. In diagnostic tasks, people judge whether the effect suggests that the cause has occurred. To recap, the information you can infer in a predictive learning task is different than what you can infer in a diagnostic learning task. When the cause is presented first, your task naturally involves thinking about whether the effect, along with any other effects, has also occurred. When the effect is presented first, you are thinking about whether it was due to a particular cause or by alternative causes.

In one of Waldmann and Holyoak's (1992) seminal studies, they asked students in Germany to carry out either a predictive or diagnostic learning task. Students taking the predictive learning task were first told of prior "research" showing that the physical appearance of a certain group of people causes others to have a novel physiological (emotional) response. In contrast, the students taking the diagnostic learning task were instead told that prior research revealed that a novel viral disease causes people's appearance to be affected. Both groups then completed the first training task, in which they were all shown the same individual descriptions of 48 people. All of these people were described as having "normal" perspiration, and then were said to have either "pale" or "normal" skin, and either "stiff" or "normal" posture. Students indicated whether they thought each person causes others to have the novel emotional response (in the predictive learning condition) or whether they thought each person has the novel viral disease (in the diagnostic learning condition). They were all given feedback on whether or not each judgment they made was correct. By the end of this first training session, students correctly learned from the information they were given that pale skin perfectly predicted (i.e., 100% of the time) the novel emotional response or the novel viral disease, respectively.

Then, the students completed a second training task. This time, they were shown the same 48 individual descriptions of people, except that each description had a fourth cue added: Every person described as having "pale" skin was also said to be "underweight," and every person described as having "normal" skin was said to have "normal" weight. As you may have already noticed, the new cue of weight is 100% redundant with the cue of skin paleness, just as the light, paired with the tone, was a redundant predictor of electric shock in Rescorla and Wagner's (1972) classic studies in rats. The results were striking: Blocking only occurred in the predictive learning task, and did not happen in the diagnostic learning task (Waldmann & Holyoak 1992). In other words, the cues (i.e., skin and weight) competed when people thought of them as causes; there was no cue competition when people thought of them as effects. This finding suggests that whether causal learning occurs is influenced by the causal structure of the situation.

Models of types/elements of causes

When we think of causes, we may most often think of the straightforward relationship in which a cause gives rise to an effect. Yet according to current major theories of causation, there are actually at least three major types of causal relationships that people consider: *cause, enable* (sometimes referred to as *allow*; this is a relationship that needs to occur in order for the cause to give rise to the effect), and *prevent*. How do people decide which of these types of causal relations applies to any two items or events, if any? Several prominent theories have been proposed to address this question.

Khemlani, Barbey, and Johnson-Laird (2014), in their **mental models theory** of causal composition, suggested that people first pick up covariation information, from which they form mental representations of each type of causal relationship. A *cause* representation is formed when people find that the first occurrence (e.g., Pat is mean to Lou) tends not to be observed without the second occurrence (e.g., Lou cries). That is, we observe times when Pat is mean to Lou and that Lou then cries (cell A, in terms of the 2×2 contingency table shown in Figure 11.3); we see times when Pat is not mean to Lou and Lou does not cry (cell D); and we see times when Lou cries without Pat having been mean (i.e., she may cry for other reasons; cell C); but we never see Pat being mean and then Lou not crying (cell B). To summarize, if we see a very low number (close to or equaling zero) in cell B, and positive numbers in the other three cells, we will likely infer a *cause* relationship between Pat's being mean and Lou's crying.

Allow, in the mental models theory, describes the situation in which the first occurrence is necessary for the second occurrence, but not sufficient to give

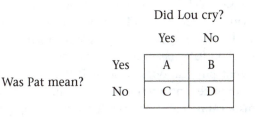

Did Lou cry?

		Yes	No
Was Pat mean?	Yes	A	B
	No	C	D

Figure 11.3   A 2×2 contingency table for representing a causal relationship between Pat being mean and Lou crying.

rise to the second occurrence on its own (Khemlani et al. 2014). For example, the first occurrence (e.g., Pat is mean to Lou) has to have happened in order for the second to also happen (e.g., Lou cries), but Pat's being mean doesn't make Lou cry per se. (Perhaps Pat is mean so often that it doesn't make Lou cry, but it might remove her happy mood.) We build up a mental representation of this overall idea when we frequently see the following: Lou crying after Pat is mean (cell A, Figure 11.3); Pat is mean but Lou does not cry (cell B); Pat is not mean and Lou does not cry (cell D); but we do <u>not</u> tend to see cases in which Pat was not mean but Lou still cries. That is, the model proposes that when the value of cell C is close or equal to zero, but there are positive numbers in the other three cells, we will tend to infer an *allow* relation.

Finally, when we tend <u>not</u> to see cases where both occurrences are present (but do see all other types of cases), we are likely to infer that there is a *prevent* relation such that one occurrence prevents the other (Khemlani et al. 2014). For example, if Pat's being mean prevents Lou from crying, we will tend not to see both happening together (e.g., the number in cell A is very low; perhaps Pat's being mean always makes Lou feel more emotionally detached from Pat, so Pat's being mean actually makes Lou much less likely to cry). In other words, we will tend to see cases where Pat is mean and Lou does not cry (cell B, Figure 11.3), and where Lou cries when Pat was not mean (cell C); we will also tend to see cases where neither occurs (cell D). In such cases, when the value of cell A is at or near zero, and there are positive numbers in the other three cells, we will infer a *prevent* relation. Overall, the mental models theory suggests that we build up distinct mental representations of the three major types of causal relations, based purely on co-occurrence information gathered through our own observations.

Another account, distinctly different from the mental models theory, is the **dynamics model**. The dynamics model proposes that people mentally represent causal relationships in terms of how they unfold in the physical world (Wolff 2007). For example, when Ball 1 strikes Ball 2, we can mentally represent the cause of Ball 2's movement as a physical force. In addition, we mentally represent the direction and distance in which Ball 2 is expected to move. Wolff (2007) also proposed that people represent non-physical causal relationships (such as Pat's meanness causing Lou's crying) in the same way that they represent physical ones (such as Ball 1 causing Ball 2 to move); that is, in terms of forces and a resulting direction. In this model, knowing a causal mechanism (Ahn et al. 1995) is critical in helping people understand how one thing could cause the other. For example, people may generally understand the intermediate steps between Pat being mean and Lou crying (i.e., the mechanism) as follows: Pat is mean; Lou hears Pat's words, comprehends them, and realizes that they were mean; Lou experiences a change in emotional state upon realizing this; tears come to her eyes.

According to the dynamics model, whether we judge the causal relationship between two things to be a *cause*, *enable*, or *prevent* relationship depends on three factors (Wolff 2007; Wolff & Barbey 2015). The first factor is the tendency of the second event to occur in the world – for example, does Lou generally tend to cry? The next factor is the tendency of the first event to oppose the tendency of the second event. That is, suppose that Lou generally tends not to cry. Does Pat's meanness run in opposition to Lou's tendency not to cry? The last factor is whether or not the second event happens. That is, did Lou cry? If Lou does not generally tend to cry, Pat's meanness is in opposition to this tendency, and Lou did cry, we represent this set of circumstances as a *cause* relation between Pat's meanness and Lou's crying. If Lou does tend to cry, Pat's meanness does not oppose this existing tendency, and Lou cries, an *enable* representation is formed (i.e., Pat's meanness enables Lou's crying). When Lou tends to cry, Pat's meanness is in opposition to this tendency, and Lou does not cry, a *prevent* representation is formed – that is, we judge Pat's meanness as preventing Lou from crying. (Again, a causal mechanism is helpful here if we want to understand how this could be: Perhaps Lou doesn't want to give Pat the satisfaction of thinking that Pat had the power to make her cry.)

Illusions of personal causal agency

So far, we have considered how humans, as well as non-human animals, are reasonably good at causal reasoning. However, the process is not without error. Tversky and Kahneman (1974) first noted that people may create "spurious causal explanations" (p. 1126) when they notice **regression toward the mean**. Suppose that one is trying to measure a variable (e.g., the performance of a professional basketball player). In regression toward the mean, an initial extreme value (e.g., the basketball player makes 77% of her shots in the first game) is often followed by a value closer to the actual mean (e.g., the same player makes 65% of her shots in the second game). Sports commentators might come up with causal mechanisms to explain this apparent change in percentages, saying that the player is now succumbing to pressure or showing signs of fatigue. Yet it might be more appropriate to simply say that the player's general level of performance is in the process of being measured over repeated observations, and that we should expect some variability over time.

In addition, a substantial literature suggests that we feel we have much more personal causal control over events than we really do. Being in uncertain situations can be psychologically uncomfortable, and one way in which people deal with such discomfort is by maintaining a somewhat distorted perception of personal control over events that exceeds the amount they actually hold. Langer (1975) first proposed the term **illusion of control** to refer to people's expectation that a given individual has a greater chance of personal success than probabilistic evidence supports. Even when it is clear that the outcome of an event will be determined by chance, people act as though they believe they have some causal control over the outcome.

For example, in one classic study, a randomly determined set of people was asked to choose a lottery ticket to purchase for $1 (Langer 1975). Another set of people was then presented with the exact tickets chosen by the first set of people. These people were asked to purchase the tickets for the same price, but were not given a choice; each person was simply handed one of the tickets. All the study participants were then individually approached and asked to sell their ticket to a third party who wanted a ticket but had been unable to obtain one. People who had not chosen their own tickets were willing to sell for about $2 on average. However, people who had chosen their tickets were only willing to part with them for over $8 on average, suggesting that they believed choosing the ticket had somehow made it more valuable (e.g., increased the likelihood that it would win; Langer 1975).

The general finding that people expect themselves to be more likely to experience positive events and less likely to experience negative events than the average person is known as **unrealistic optimism** (Weinstein 1980). Harris and Middleton (1994) asked university students to make judgments of risk for 15 different medical conditions over the next 5 years. They were randomly assigned to either make those judgments for themselves, an acquaintance, friend of a friend, or "typical" student at the same university of the same gender as the student. People rated themselves as less likely to contract the diseases than acquaintances, friends of friends, or "typical" students, as though they had special control over the occurrence of the disease (Harris & Middleton 1994).

Horswill and McKenna (1999) found that people given control over a situation are willing to take greater risks than people who do not have control. In their study, people were asked to view a variety of simulated driving tasks and make judgments about safe driving. For example, in one task they viewed a video, from the driver's perspective, in which the car was waiting to pull into traffic. Their task was to press a button at the moment when they felt it was too dangerous to drive into the traffic stream. The critical manipulation was that participants were randomly assigned either to imagine that they were driving, or to imagine that they were in the passenger-side seat. As predicted by the unrealistic optimism literature, those who imagined that they were driving (the perceived control condition) were willing to accept greater risks than those who imagined they were in the passenger seat (Horswill & McKenna 1999).

Causal reasoning in non-human animals

Some findings have suggested that non-human animals may carry out fundamental causal reasoning in some ways similar to that seen in humans. Blaisdell, Sawa, Leising, and Waldmann (2006), for example, reported a demonstration of possible causal reasoning in rats. In one study, they presented rats with a learning phase and a test phase. In the learning phase, rats observed numerous cases in which a light first came on, followed by two events that occurred at the same time as each other: a tone played, and food (a sugar solution) was dispensed. This sequence of events was intended to suggest a causal model in which the light is the common cause of both the tone and the food. (Notice that, incidentally, the tone also covaries with the food, but it appears at the same time as the food so there is no temporal order cue-to-causality.) After this, the rats experienced a test phase. In the test phase, some of the rats were provided with a new lever, which played the tone when they pressed on it. Furthermore, whenever each of these rats pressed the lever, the tone was also played for a different rat in another chamber, which did not contain a lever. In other words, some of the rats directly pressed on the lever and learned that it caused a tone to play, and the others simply experienced the tone playing now and then.

In general, we may assume that rats expect food if they frequently poke their noses into the place where it previously appeared. A key question was whether the rats who were pressing the lever (thereby playing the tone) were less likely to expect food to be dispensed upon hearing the tone than the rats who were only hearing the tone (Blaisdell et al. 2006). Such a finding would suggest that the rats learned the common-cause structure in the learning phase. Given that one cause (light) was shown to directly cause two other things (tone, food), there is now no reason to think that playing the tone will cause food to appear, as there was no evidence in the learning phase of a direct causal relationship between the tone and the food. In fact, this was exactly what Blaisdell et al. (2006) found: Rats who pressed the lever poked their noses fewer times into the place where the food previously appeared than rats who only heard the tone being played. Again, these findings are consistent with the idea that the rats learned the causal structure of the situation. However, a general debate continues regarding whether or not purely associative models of causal reasoning can account for findings such as these (cf. Haselgrove 2016).

Another task for non-human animals that has been argued to require causal thinking is the **trap-tube task** (Taylor, Hunt, Medina & Gray 2009). In this task, the animal is presented with an open tube, placed horizontally. Food (e.g., meat) is placed in the center of the tube, which the animal would only be able to reach by pulling or pushing it out of the tube with a stick. Two traps are embedded into the floor of the tube on either side of the food. One trap is functional, such that if the animal tries to pull or push the meat past it, the meat will fall down into the trap and the animal will not be able to access it anymore. The other trap is non-functional; that is, it is covered at the top so that the food can be pulled or pushed across it. To get the food, the animal needs to realize that it should pull or push the food over the non-functional trap and avoid trying to pass the food over the functional trap.

In one study of wild New Caledonian crows, Taylor et al. (2009) showed that three of six crows (though after many trials) figured out how to successfully and consistently solve the trap-tube task. Once these three crows learned how to solve the task, it was not the case that they were simply repeating the same actions over and over. The experimenters switched the position of the two types of traps between trials, so that this was not possible. In response, the crows would still solve the problem quickly in each trial; for example, they would move around to the other side, where they then pulled out the meat over the non-functional trap (Taylor et al. 2009).

However, it might be argued that these three successful crows did not really know why their solution worked. So Taylor et al. (2009) then presented the same three crows with a different task to see if their knowledge would transfer to the new task. This new task had the same underlying conceptual logic as the trap-tube task; the crows still needed to avoid pulling the meat over a functional trap. However, the new task had a different appearance (e.g., featuring long rectangular glass-top boxes instead of tubes). The question was whether the crows solved this new task very quickly, presumably transferring what they had learned about the logic of the first task to the new task. Incredibly, all three of the crows went straight to the correct solution in the new task (in an average of 10 out of the first 12 trials; Taylor et al. 2009). That is, it seems highly likely that the crows had learned that the functional trap was a causal feature of both tasks, giving rise to the loss of the meat. Taylor et al. (2009) made this claim, but stopped short of claiming that the crows had understood the deeper causal concept of gravity.

These claims by Blaisdell et al. (2006) and Taylor et al. (2009) are inconsistent with the more traditional claim that causal reasoning might be one of the important cognitive capacities that separate humans from non-human animals. On the contrary, we have seen in this chapter that non-human animals may be capable of drawing causal inferences from covariation data. We have also seen that humans, though equipped with the ability to come up with causal mechanisms connecting two events or things, are susceptible to causal illusions. In Chapter 12, we will continue in this vein, asking how people choose to *seek out* information that will help them explain the world around them. Namely, do people approach the world like scientists, systematically testing hypotheses, or do they use other intuitive strategies to explain and predict?

Questions for discussion

1. Suppose that you sometimes feel extremely tired mid-morning. You hypothesize that your mid-morning tiredness might be caused by skipping breakfast. How would you go about collecting evidence to help you figure out whether this is the real cause? How would you make sense of the data?
2. Come up with your own real-life examples of how people tend to infer a causal relationship given different cues-to-causality: Temporal order, contiguity in time and space, the availability of a causal mechanism, similarity of cause and effect, and counterfactual reasoning. Can you also come up with examples of when people have each of these cues-to-causality but do not conclude that there is a causal relationship present?
3. Consider the studies on rats and crows described in the last section of this chapter. Are you convinced that these studies demonstrate that these animals are reasoning *causally*? Why or why not?

Suggestions for further reading

Einhorn, H. J., & Hogarth, R. M. (1986). Judging probable cause. *Psychological Bulletin*, 99(1), 3–19.

Hastie, R. (2015). Causal thinking in judgments. In G. Keren & G. Wu (Eds.), *The Wiley Blackwell handbook of judgment and decision making, Vol. 1* (pp. 590–628). Chichester, UK: John Wiley & Sons, Ltd.

Sloman, S. (2005). *Causal models: How people think about the world and its alternatives.* Oxford, UK: Oxford University Press.

Hypothesis Testing and Confirmation Bias

12

Learning Goals

By the end of this chapter, you will have:

- Critically considered philosophical approaches to optimizing hypothesis testing and the basic assumptions underlying scientific inquiry aimed at understanding what is true in the world.
- Understood seminal research on the confirmation bias and analyzed the different conditions under which a positive test strategy is more versus less effective than a negative test strategy.
- Applied confirmation bias research to help better understand errors in scientific inquiry (i.e., in science research, criminal investigations, and medical misdiagnoses) and potential approaches to countering ideological extremism.

Key Terms	
Confirmatory evidence	Negative test strategy
Disconfirmatory evidence	2-4-6 task
Falsifiability	Consistency fallacy
Confirmation bias	Forensic confirmation bias
Positive test strategy	Bias blind spot

I had, also, during many years followed a golden rule, namely, that whenever a published fact, a new observation or thought came across me, which was opposed to my general results, to make a memorandum of it without fail and at once; for I had found by experience that such facts and thoughts were far more apt to escape from the memory than favourable ones. Owing to this habit, very few objections were raised against my views which I had not at least noticed and attempted to answer.

(Charles Darwin, English naturalist and scientist, 1876)

Hypothesis testing

How do we go about figuring out what is true in the world? In a recent online query, a teenaged student living in the U.K. asked readers from the world at large whether they thought that a particular friend was interested in him romantically. As evidence, he described a recent occurrence in which the friend walked up to him and gave him a hug. The responses he received online were fairly uniform in coming to the following conclusion: Maybe, but maybe not. To put this conclusion in slightly more specific terms: The hugging event is *consistent* with the hypothesis of romantic interest, but it is not, by itself, enough evidence to support any reasonable degree of confidence that this hypothesis is true. Some online commentators suggested that he needed to find more information relevant to answering his question, because this single piece of evidence was not sufficient.

Intuitively, this example seems quite straightforward: One does not have to be a philosopher of science to realize that the student's hypothesis has by no means been *proven* by this single confirmatory piece of evidence; nor has it even been very strongly supported. Yet in science research, many analogous scenarios have been the topic of much musing and discussion, perhaps because when a scientist is in the throes of investigation, it can be easy to lose sight of the underlying philosophy regarding what a given finding or piece of information should be taken to indicate. For example, suppose that a cognitive neuroscience researcher hypothesizes that a particular brain area (e.g., the hippocampus) is involved in carrying out a particular reasoning task. She shows, using brain imaging techniques, that there is greater blood flow/oxygen to the hippocampus during this task than when the person is at rest. Although it is easy for us to then leap to the conclusion that she has shown that the hippocampus is indeed involved in carrying out the reasoning task, notice that what we have here is a single piece of confirmatory evidence – not unlike in the case of the teenaged student wondering if his friend is romantically interested. That is, the imaging results are consistent with the hippocampal hypothesis, and are therefore potentially valuable evidence to report, but more evidence is needed. Some of the important questions one should ask in this case are what such evidence really shows, whether the brain at rest is the most appropriate control condition to use, whether other kinds of evidence in addition to this piece of evidence would be more powerful, and whether other ways of testing the hypothesis would be more promising. We will return to the issue of hypothesis testing in cognitive neuroscience research later in this chapter.

To begin, we will consider classic work in philosophy, in addition to essays and studies by science researchers themselves. These have been dedicated to considering very systematically what evidence would truly support a given hypothesis versus disconfirm it, and when (if ever) one can legitimately be confident that the hypothesis is true.

The logic of confirmation and disconfirmation in hypothesis testing

The philosopher Carl Hempel (1945) considered the problem of what really counts as evidence for or against a hypothesis by using an illustrative example. Suppose that you hypothesize that all ravens are black and want to discover whether or not this is really true. First, Hempel (1945) noted that the statement that (1) *all ravens are black* is logically equivalent to the statement that (2) *anything that is not black is not a raven.* But although the hypothesis is equivalent across the two statements, he argued, what evidence can be taken to support the hypothesis should be considered separately, because it can differ radically for each statement.

There are four main categories of evidence that may be presented in this case. First, suppose you find a piece of confirmatory evidence: That is, you find a single raven that is black. The existence of such a bird in the world is evidence consistent with the first form of the hypothesis, that *all ravens are black,* although it doesn't really say anything about the second form; that is, whether *anything that is not black is not a raven.* As Hempel (1945) pointed out, we should also note that although this piece of evidence is consistent with the hypothesis that *all ravens are black,* a single black raven doesn't seem sufficient as complete, slam-dunk evidence proving that the hypothesis is true. (Similarly, a single hug in the example described earlier is consistent with, but does not prove, romantic interest.)

A second category of evidence is disconfirmatory evidence. Specifically, suppose you are presented with a raven that is not black (e.g., a yellow raven). This evidence would be extremely useful in that it indisputably disconfirms both forms of the hypothesis; the existence of such a raven immediately topples the claim that all ravens are black and also directly refutes the claim that anything that is not black is not a raven. That is, this single piece of evidence would be powerful enough to disconfirm both forms of the hypothesis at once. Then you would know for certain that you should either abandon or modify the hypothesis, instead testing some other alternative or working on a different problem.

Third, suppose you are presented with something black that is not a raven (e.g., a piece of black licorice candy). This information is not useful; it does not tell you anything about either form of the hypothesis, neither confirming nor disconfirming either statement. It neither informs you about ravens (pertaining to the first form of the hypothesis) nor about things that are not black (pertaining to the second form of the hypothesis). This evidence is simply spurious.

Fourth, you might come across something that is neither black nor a raven (e.g., a red herring). The fact that this red herring exists *is* actually consistent with the hypothesis that *anything that is not black is not a raven*. Yet it doesn't really tell us anything about whether *all ravens are black* – that is, you would expect to find red herrings in the world <u>whether or not</u> it is true that *all ravens are black* (Mole & Klein 2010). In other words, the red herring, like the black raven, is consistent with one form of the hypothesis but provides no information about the other (Hempel 1945). And again, finding a red herring is consistent with the hypothesis that *anything that is not black is not a raven*, but this isn't enough by itself to really show definitively that even that second form of the hypothesis is true. Instead, our intuition is that such evidence seems not particularly useful to really finding out whether *all ravens are black / anything that is not black is not a raven*.

Popper (1959/1968) further argued that something more than just confirmatory evidence is needed to qualify as evidence for a hypothesis. He proposed that the scientific enterprise should generally be centered around the notion of **falsifiability**, rather than that of confirmation. In other words, one might quite reasonably conclude from Hempel's (1945) analysis that science ought to be built upon a philosophy of disconfirmation: As the yellow raven is the only piece of evidence that can definitely debunk the *all ravens are black* hypothesis in both its forms, we ought to be most actively seeking disconfirmatory, rather than confirmatory, evidence in science. Yet as we will see, seeking confirmatory evidence appears to be a general, intuitive strategy for hypothesis testing not only by lay people but also by scientists and diagnostic reasoning professionals.

Confirmation bias

Perhaps most notably, the confirmation bias is a heuristic that frequently comes into play when people are testing a hypothesis. According to Klayman and Ha (1987), **confirmation bias** can be thought of as taking a **positive test strategy**, in which "you test a hypothesis by examining instances in which the property or event is expected to occur (to see if it does occur), or by examining instances in which it is known to have occurred (to see if the hypothesized conditions prevail)" (p. 212). In testing the hypothesis that all ravens are black, actively looking for black ravens would constitute a positive test strategy. This strategy may be implemented without the researcher's awareness, and as we will later see, it can also appear in the reinterpretation of evidence to fit the hypothesis (Nickerson 1998). A positive test strategy can be contrasted with a **negative test strategy**, in which you instead try to run tests or find cases that might rule out or disconfirm your working hypothesis (e.g., looking for a raven that is any color other than black).

Seminal work on the confirmation bias

Classic studies on the confirmation bias clearly illustrate the contrast between adopting a positive test strategy and a negative test strategy in hypothesis testing. Probably the most well-known classic laboratory demonstration of the confirmation bias was produced by the so-called 2-4-6 task by Wason (1960). In his study, undergraduate students were first given the following instructions:

> You will be given three numbers which conform to a simple rule that I have in mind. This rule is concerned with a relation between any three numbers and not with their absolute magnitude, i.e. it is not a rule like all numbers above (or below) 50, etc. Your aim is to discover this rule by writing down sets of three numbers, together with reasons for your choice of them. After you have written down each set, I shall tell you whether your numbers conform to the rule or not, and you can make a note of this outcome on the record sheet provided. There is no time limit but you should try to discover this rule by citing the minimum sets of numbers. Remember that your aim is not simply to find numbers which conform to the rule, but to discover the rule itself. When you feel highly confident that you have discovered it, *and not before,* you are to write it down and tell me what it is. Have you any questions?
>
> (Wason 1960, p. 131)

They were then told that the sequence 2, 4, 6 conformed to the correct rule, and they were asked to begin trying to discover the correct rule. The rule that study participants had to discover was "three numbers in increasing order of magnitude" (Wason 1960, p. 130). Despite the fact that the study participants had been instructed to test sequences until they were highly confident that they had identified the rule, only 21% of participants ultimately came up with the correct rule. A closer look at their responses suggested that people had a tendency to use a positive test strategy to come up with sequences for testing. For example, a study participant who said she wished to test the hypothesis that the rule was a "progression of two" provided only number sequences consistent with that rule (e.g., 1, 3, 5 and 16, 18, 20) for the experimenter's feedback. In other words, study participants who failed to figure out the correct rule (and again, these were by far the majority of participants) did not seek to falsify the hypothesis they were testing, but rather sought information that would confirm it. If they had tried testing some sequences that didn't fit the hypothesized rule they were testing, they would have been more likely to find that their rule was disconfirmed. For example, if the person who thought that the rule was a progression by twos had tested a sequence that didn't fit that rule – for example, the sequence 5, 10, 15 – she would have unexpectedly received positive feedback. That is, the experimenter would have told her that the sequence 5, 10, 15 actually follows the rule, which would inform her that she should revise the hypothesis being tested (i.e., it is now clear that a progression of two is too restrictive to be the true rule, as both going up by twos and going up by fives fits the rule).

Klayman and Ha (1987), in a systematic analysis, further showed that whether a positive test strategy will work well depends on the relationship between the hypothesized rule and the actual rule. When the hypothesized rule (e.g., *three numbers in an upward progression by twos*) happens to be <u>more specific</u> than the true rule (e.g., *three numbers in increasing order of magnitude*), then a positive test strategy is particularly unhelpful. In this case, taking a positive test strategy by testing sequences that fit the hypothesized rule (e.g., *6, 8, 10*) can only provide confirmatory feedback from the experimenter and will never elicit disconfirmatory feedback, even if the hypothesized rule is wrong. In contrast, in this same case, where the hypothesized rule is more specific than the true rule, taking a negative test strategy can provide vital feedback. If one tests sequences (e.g., *5, 3, 1* or *5, 10, 15*) that one expects to be told do <u>not</u> fit the hypothesized rule (e.g., *three numbers in an upward progression by twos*), surprising feedback could be obtained (e.g., one will be informed that *5, 10, 15* fits the true rule). Such tests have the *potential* to disconfirm the hypothesized rule.

However, it is important to also understand that a positive test strategy is not always bad, and in fact can be <u>more</u> effective than a negative test strategy under certain conditions (Klayman & Ha 1987). Suppose that one came up with a hypothesized rule (e.g., *any three numbers all in increasing or all in decreasing order of magnitude*) that is more <u>general</u>, rather than more specific, than the true rule (e.g., *three numbers in increasing order of magnitude*). In this case, interestingly enough, a positive test strategy is going to be useful. If one tries testing a number of different sequences that one expects to confirm the hypothesized rule, it is possible in this case to elicit disconfirmatory feedback. For example, taking a positive test strategy, one might suggest the sequence *9, 6, 2* as a set of *any three numbers all in increasing or all in decreasing order of magnitude*, which fits the hypothesized rule. Given that the true rule is *three numbers in increasing order of magnitude*, the feedback that will be received is that the sequence *9, 6, 2* does NOT fit the true rule. This feedback will drive one to come up with a modified hypothesis, potentially enabling one to get a step closer to discovering the true rule (Klayman & Ha 1987).

Notice also in this particular case – where the hypothesized rule is more general than the true rule – that a negative test strategy is actually unhelpful. If one takes a negative test strategy, one will try to test sequences that one thinks will violate the hypothesized rule (e.g., *any three numbers all in increasing or all in decreasing order of magnitude*). For example, one would expect that if the hypothesized rule is true, then sequences such as *7, 2, 5* and *10, 98, 2* should violate it. One will then receive the expected feedback from the experimenter that neither *7, 2, 5* nor *10, 98, 2* fit the true rule, and one will feel with increased confidence that the hypothesized rule (e.g., *any three numbers in increasing or decreasing order of magnitude*) is indeed correct. However, it is not correct; in this case, the negative test strategy will be misleading.

In sum, the lesson to be drawn from Klayman and Ha's (1987) analysis is that we cannot generally state that a positive test strategy should always be avoided and that a negative test strategy is always best. The precise relationship between the hypothesized rule and the true rule – which one has no way of knowing in advance of having the correct answer – matters. As we will see in the next section, taking the strategy of doing both – seeking to both confirm a hypothesis and to disconfirm its alternative(s) – has been argued to be a better solution.

It's also worth noting that our discussion above pertains to figuring out what is true in the world. If one is instead simply concerned with what might work for a given situation (rather than seeking truth), then being influenced by the confirmation bias could be perfectly fine for one's purposes. For example, in the opening example of this chapter, if the teenaged student was not trying to find out whether his friend was romantically interested in him, but rather whether there was any possibility his friend might agree to attend a school dance with him, then using the hug as confirmatory evidence might be quite sufficient to act upon.

Confirmation bias: Research in the sciences

In scientific inquiry, seeking truth in the world is generally the central goal. Thus, science provides perhaps one of the clearest cases for striving to avoid the confirmation bias. For example, Mole and Klein (2010) described what they called a **consistency fallacy** in a subset of cognitive neuroscience research using functional brain imaging techniques such as fMRI. The consistency fallacy occurs when one misinterprets data that merely confirm a hypothesis without simultaneously disconfirming an alternative hypothesis, claiming that such data show the hypothesis to be true. Mole and Klein (2010) argued that sometimes, when describing increased activation of a particular brain area (e.g., amygdala) during a specific task (e.g., judging human face attractiveness), cognitive neuroscience researchers claim that this finding means that this brain area is involved in encoding such judgments. However, Mole and Klein (2010) suggested that the most that can be said about this increased activation is that it *is consistent with* the hypothesis that the brain area is involved in encoding such judgments. Just as the existence of a black raven is consistent with, not proof of, the hypothesis that all ravens are black, increased activation of the amygdala during this task does not, by itself, qualify as enough evidence to show the hypothesis to be true. Accordingly, they argued that it would be a consistency fallacy to claim that this increased activation demonstrates that, for example, the amygdala plays a role in judging human face attractiveness.

Instead, Mole and Klein (2010) argued, in order to show stronger support for a hypothesis that a particular brain area really is involved in carrying out a particular cognitive or behavioral function, confirmatory evidence (e.g., increased activation) must be paired with evidence disconfirming a corresponding null or alternative hypothesis. Generally, it is difficult to design fMRI research testing the hypothesis that a particular brain region plays a role in a particular cognitive function because it is not necessarily clear what the alternative is or how this would be disconfirmed (Mole & Klein 2010). They even argued that the hypothesis that a particular brain region is specialized for a particular function and not for a more generalized set of functions is not clearly testable by these criteria. Evidence generally taken to be consistent with such a hypothesis is that a particular cortical network is more engaged when carrying out that function than during other kinds of tasks. However, Mole and Klein (2010) argued that it is not clear what findings should be taken to *disconfirm the null hypothesis* (i.e., that this particular cortical network is *not* engaged in a broader range of functions). For example, although another, related task may not show the same patterns of activation, it may still be engaging the same cortical network (Mole & Klein 2010).

Coltheart (2013) expanded upon Mole and Klein's (2010) arguments in a discussion of the consistency fallacy in fMRI research. He, too, suggested that fMRI researchers must be very clear in specifying before the fact what patterns of data would be directly inconsistent with the hypothesis being tested, not only what pattern would be consistent with it. If fMRI researchers could (1) first specify what data patterns would be inconsistent with the hypothesis, and (2) it is plausible that such data patterns could conceivably be obtained, but (3) the experiment then shows that those data patterns were not in fact obtained, this would be more convincing evidence for the hypothesis. Such evidence, presented alongside other data that are consistent with the hypothesis, would allow one to avoid the consistency fallacy in Coltheart's (2013) view.

Whether or not one fully agrees with the specific philosophical viewpoints outlined in this section, it is clearly of critical importance for researchers to think very carefully about what their results mean and what conclusions they can legitimately draw. This may be especially important for fMRI research, given that it appears to have particular persuasive power. People tend to be more convinced by psychological explanations for behaviors when accompanied by descriptions of neuroscience evidence, even if irrelevant (Farah & Hook 2013; Weisberg, Keil, Goodstein, Rawson, & Gray 2008; Weisberg, Taylor, & Hopkins 2015). This finding has been replicated numerous times. In contrast, the hypothesis that brain *images*, as opposed to verbal *descriptions* of neuroscience findings, have particular persuasive power has not been upheld in the literature (Farah & Hook 2013; Michael, Newman, Vuorre, Cumming, & Garry 2013).

Confirmation bias: Issues in the law

As criminal cases also fundamentally involve hypothesis testing and evidence seeking, they are similarly subject to confirmation bias. Take, for example, the case of an innocent person who was falsely accused of terrorism (Kassin, Dror, & Kukucka 2013). After the Madrid terrorist attacks on commuter trains in 2004 (see again Chapter 5), a fingerprint found on a bag of detonators was identified by the U.S. Federal Bureau of Investigation (FBI) as belonging to an American attorney, Brandon Mayfield (U.S. Office of the Inspector General [OIG] 2006). According to the OIG (2006), Mayfield happened to be Muslim and had in the past worked in a child custody court case as the representative of a parent who was also a convicted terrorist. When three different American fingerprinting experts identified the print as Mayfield's, he was arrested as a material witness, though there was no other information connecting him to the Madrid bombings. Then, the Spanish National Police (SNP) revealed that they had instead positively identified the fingerprint as belonging to Ouhnane Daoud of Algeria. Upon reanalysis of the print, the FBI agreed that they had made a mistake and that it was definitely Daoud's (OIG 2006).

In a since-declassified retrospective review of the case, the OIG (2006) reported that confirmation bias may have played a critical role in the misidentification of the fingerprint as Mayfield's. It started with a coincidence; Mayfield's print was quite similar to the print on the detonator bag (though they were *not* identical). Then, confirmation bias set in: "Having found as many as ten points of unusual similarity, the FBI examiners began to 'find' additional features in LFP 17 [the print on the detonator bag] that were not really there, but rather were suggested to the examiners by features in the Mayfield prints. As a result of this process, murky or ambiguous details in LFP 17 were erroneously identified as points of similarity with Mayfield's prints" (OIG 2006, p. 7). In other words, the FBI examiners used Mayfield's known prints to identify specific features that were then mapped backwards to reinterpret ambiguous features of the print on the detonator bag. This circularity of reasoning was a major feature of the fingerprint experts' confirmatory approach that led to the ultimate error.

Cases such as this suggest that observers' prior expectations can influence how evidence is collected and interpreted in a criminal case. Kassin et al. (2013) dubbed this general effect the **forensic confirmation bias**. The forensic confirmation bias has been empirically examined across numerous studies and found to influence eyewitness testimony and the judgments of jurors, judges, interrogators, and forensic experts (Kassin et al. 2013). For example, although fingerprint expertise is highly respected in forensic science, studies of practicing fingerprint experts have shown that their identifications can be influenced by background knowledge they are told about the case (Dror & Charlton 2006). In a truly objective analysis, background knowledge about whether the suspect confessed or whether the suspect had an alibi should not influence the systematic visual judgments that a fingerprint expert makes when matching ridge patterns between two prints. Yet the fingerprint experts in Dror and Charlton's (2006) study, who had been led to believe they were carrying out real casework and were unaware that they were in a study, *were* consequently biased toward the conclusion matching the background information.

On the basis of findings such as these, Dror (2009) and Kassin et al. (2013) advocated for linear (as opposed to circular) processing of crime scenes. For example, in the case of the Madrid bombings, it would have been more objective for the fingerprinting experts to first analyze and document every aspect of the fingerprint found on the detonator bag. Having already completed that task in full, the experts would then have evaluated the degree of match between that print and Mayfield's print more objectively. That is, the degree of match could then be evaluated without going back and reinterpreting ambiguities in the detonator bag print to fit what was already known about Mayfield's print (again, this was where the circularity of reasoning was introduced). In fact, the linear procedure was added in 2011 to the FBI's standard operating procedures in direct response to the errors made in the Mayfield case (OIG 2011).

The conclusions to be drawn from this work regarding best practices in evaluating evidence, however, are still not very straightforward. The fact remains that it is the *job* of criminal investigators, by and large, to integrate all the evidence in a criminal case and make sense of it as a whole (Charman 2013). So to simply conclude that different investigators and experts must generally strive to avoid hearing about other pieces of the case does not seem realistic. Perhaps it would make better sense to try to analyze each piece of evidence independently, and then in a separate, subsequent step, attempt to integrate the whole. This, however, does not account for the reality that evidence may often come to light sequentially in a mixed temporal order, over an extended period of time. Nor does it take into account people's tendency to automatically attempt to make sense of information as it is provided (e.g., Hastie, Schroeder, & Weber 1990; Kunda, Miller, & Claire 1990). Yet taking certain achievable steps, such as adopting linear processing of crime scenes to the extent possible, may at least mitigate the effects of confirmation bias even if they cannot be fully eliminated.

Confirmation bias: Issues in medicine

An interesting parallel to the above cases can also be found in the field of medicine. Just as fingerprinting experts may reason in a circular manner by using specific features of the candidate print (e.g., the prints of Mayfield) to hunt for corresponding features in the print to be identified (e.g., the print found on the detonator bag), so also may clinicians when reasoning about patients. In trying to figure out what is wrong with a human system – that is, in making a diagnosis – clinicians may first come up with a hypothesized diagnosis based on an initial evaluation and then search in a confirmatory manner for the features that would support that diagnosis (Reason 1995).

Croskerry (2002) pointed out that especially when trying to diagnose an ambiguous or difficult medical case, finding any confirmatory evidence for one's working hypothesis feels rewarding to the clinician. Disconfirmatory evidence for that hypothesis, in contrast, indicates that putting in more mental effort is going to be necessary, or even that one must start from scratch in reasoning through the case (Croskerry 2002). In addition, confirmation bias in medical diagnosis may be particularly harmful when it is paired with an anchoring effect (Chapter 3). For example, a weak hypothesis formulated too early in the evidence-gathering stage may be bolstered, misleadingly, by a confirmatory search for additional supportive information (Croskerry 2002).

That said, it is important to note – as per our earlier discussion of positive and negative test strategies – that the confirmation bias does not always lead to error (Norman & Eva 2010). In fact, a clinician may use a confirmatory strategy most of the time and as long as the initial hypothesis is correct (which is reasonably likely, especially if the clinician starts with the most common possible diagnosis), there should be no problem with doing so. The only time the clinician may be chastised for susceptibility to confirmation bias is when she or he turns out to have been pursuing the wrong hypothesis. At other times, the exact same reasoning process may be praised for having been quite effective (Norman & Eva 2010). Indeed, as Tversky and Kahneman (1974) noted, heuristics are in general employed for efficiency and overall effectiveness, although under certain conditions they can produce error.

In psychiatry, however, there is some experimental evidence that confirmatory information searches in diagnosis may not be as likely to yield accurate judgments as disconfirmatory searches. Mendel et al. (2011), for example, asked German psychiatrists and medical students to carry out psychiatric diagnoses in an experimental task. After making a preliminary diagnosis, twice as many medical students (25%) as psychiatrists (13%) adopted a confirmatory search strategy in seeking out additional information about the case. Both psychiatrists and medical students who used a confirmatory strategy were much more likely to ultimately make the wrong diagnosis than those who used a disconfirmatory strategy, respectively. Furthermore, those who made wrong diagnoses made different treatment recommendations than those who made correct diagnoses, suggesting that this bias is likely to have a direct impact upon the experience of the patient. More work is needed within the context of clinical settings to more systematically map out what kinds of cases and under what precise conditions we can expect a confirmatory strategy to yield more diagnostic errors than a disconfirmatory one.

Combating extreme confirmation bias: An approach to ideological extremism

How can the confirmation bias be attenuated? Some suggestions come from the study of combating ideological extremism. Lilienfeld, Ammirati, and Landfield (2009) argued that the most deadly political movements worldwide in recent decades can be traced to a single root cause: Ideological extremism, a phenomenon that has been little studied in the field to date. Of particular interest for our current purposes is their proposal that the single cognitive bias most relevant to ideological extremism may be the confirmation bias (Lilienfeld et al. 2009). Specifically, they cited both the general tendency to seek out information in confirmation of one's working hypothesis and the tendency to downplay or reinterpret evidence in disconfirmation of it. Ideological partisanship – for example, between the major political parties within a country – may be driven by the same or similar processes, albeit in a milder and less violent form (Lilienfeld et al. 2009). In more extreme cases in which political regimes attempt to encourage confirmation bias by presenting only information that supports a single point of view while actively suppressing and eliminating evidence for all other points of view, ideological extremism can of course be expected to readily emerge. From a scientific perspective, it is interesting that people have shown themselves to be highly susceptible to such tactics across a great many different countries and regimes (Lilienfeld et al. 2009). It is far from being the case that people naturally tend to seek out disconfirmatory information and think like Popperian scientists (Nickerson 1998).

If Lilienfeld et al.'s (2009) analysis is correct, then it might make sense for researchers to work harder toward the goal of learning how to counteract the confirmation bias and related biases. They argued that although much attention has been paid to documenting the existence of biases, relatively little attention has been paid to uncovering and understanding effective methods of debiasing. So far, the most promising debiasing attempts have been designed to shift people from Type 1 to Type 2 thinking (Evans & Stanovich 2013; Kahneman 2011; Stanovich & West 2000) using deliberate strategies to pull oneself away from the confirmation bias. For example, the confirmation bias can be attenuated when one is asked to come up with an alternative point of view counter to the view that one has already chosen (e.g., Koriat, Lichtenstein, & Fischhoff 1980). Similarly, asking people to delay making a decision can reduce their susceptibility to the confirmation bias, presumably because they have been given more time to think critically and perhaps have more opportunities to encounter and consider alternative views (Spengler, Strohmer, Dixon, & Shivy 1995).

That said, Arkes (1981) has suggested that teaching people deliberate strategies is generally unhelpful, in part because people very often have no idea that they are biased when they are biased. Similarly, Pronin, Lin, and Ross (2002) proposed that people have a **bias blind spot**, tending to believe that others are more prone to biases than themselves. In one of Pronin et al.'s (2002) studies, American university students read about eight different well-documented biases (e.g., confirmation bias in assimilating new information). For each bias, they were asked to judge how much they themselves had that tendency and how much the average American had that tendency. Half of the students made these judgments for themselves first, and the other half made these judgments for the average American first. Overall, students rated themselves less susceptible to the bias than the hypothetical average American (Pronin et al. 2002). The bias blind spot does not appear to be solely an American phenomenon: These findings were replicated in travelers recruited in an international airport, who ranged widely in age and nationality, and who made ratings for themselves and for the average traveler at the same airport that day (Pronin et al. 2002).

Hansen, Gerbasi, Todorov, Kruse, and Pronin (2014) further showed that the bias blind spot can still occur when the person is engaging in deliberate, Type 2 thought processes. In one experiment, 80 photos of paintings from major art museums were first pre-rated by undergraduates who were not told who painted them. The 80 paintings were split into two groups of 40, each of which these undergraduates had pre-rated equally for quality. The 40 paintings in one group were assigned artist names from the phone book; the 40 paintings in the other group were labeled with highly recognizable names of artists (e.g., Picasso), using the true artist whenever possible (i.e., as long as the name was recognizable by this population). These materials were combined and presented to a new set of undergraduates to judge in terms of their artistic merit (i.e., quality). These students were either asked to choose to look at the name of the painter before making each artistic merit judgment or to choose *not* to look at the painter's name.

The results of Hansen et al.'s study (2014) showed that students who were asked to look at the painters' names judged the *strategy* to which they had been assigned to be more biased than did students who were asked not to look at the painter's names. However, students who were asked to look at the painters' names did not judge their *own* ratings to have been any more or less biased than did students who didn't look at the names. Moreover, students who were asked to look at the painters' names rated the artistic merit of the famous-name paintings more highly than they did the artistic merit of the phone-book-name paintings. In contrast, those who did not look at the painters' names gave artistic merit ratings that did not differ between the two groups of paintings. In other words, students showed the bias blind spot even when they knew they were purposely using a judgment strategy that they felt was relatively biased. Yet their own ratings of the paintings indicated that they were indeed biased. If such findings can be extrapolated to judgments under the effects of indoctrination, the implications would indeed be disturbing.

There are, of course, highly practical additional reasons why debiasing techniques may not ultimately be effective even if they are discovered. First, people who are currently immersed in a society in which they are being indoctrinated in a particular point of view (e.g., within a cult, in which the cult leader's words are taken to be divine truths) are not likely to be allowed to undergo debiasing techniques. Additionally, as Lilienfeld et al. (2009) argued, a common source of indoctrination information comes from the textbooks used to teach schoolchildren. Although introducing alternative viewpoints may be especially difficult in countries in which only state-approved textbooks are allowed, the selection of any textbook in any country will naturally introduce children to a particular point of view. It is perhaps inevitable that an author's own point of view will guide what is written and what is omitted, even with the sincere intent of being truly objective.

For example, historical accounts – the seemingly straightforward written recounting of something that happened – are of course never actually straightforward. American historian Stephen Ambrose noted in 2002 that "the Japanese presentation of the [Second World] war to its children runs something like this: One day, for no reason we ever understood, the Americans started dropping atomic bombs on us" (Ambrose 2002, p. 112). Ambrose's own view, though also critical of American motives, was substantially different: "[Then-U.S. President] Truman used the bomb not so much to force a Japanese surrender as to show the Russians what we had, and that we were not afraid to use it" (Ambrose 2002, p. 113). In contrast, the Truman administration itself claimed that it was trying to avert the loss of as many as 800,000 American lives in an anticipated Japanese attack (Ambrose 2002). Japanese historian Sadao Asada noted in 2007 that although Japanese textbooks had for many years almost completely neglected to include any sort of historical analysis regarding the bombings, some had recently begun to include brief interpretative remarks in the vein of Ambrose's (2002) views. And historians Laura E. Hein and Mark Selden, writing in 2015, reported that other current secondary school textbooks in Japan simply mentioned that atomic bombs were dropped but not who dropped them or why, instead noting the event much as one would a natural disaster. As a result, as many as 10% of students in Hiroshima and Nagasaki did not know that it was the U.S. who dropped the bombs (Hein & Selden 2015).

The point here is that any techniques aimed at breaking people out of a default confirmatory stance for a single point of view will often go up against years of cultural immersion, sometimes even rooted in information originally conveyed in childhood. The application of psychological research to countering the confirmation bias in extremist thinking, by extension, therefore remains an incredible challenge.

Questions for discussion

1. Consider again Mole and Klein's (2010) and Coltheart's (2013) critiques of how some cognitive neuroscience results have been interpreted. Are their critiques valid or are they too stringent? Is Coltheart's (2013) solution reasonable or not? Why?

2. Explain how a linear test strategy would work in forensic science; for example, in matching a print to a suspect. Will linear reasoning really help overcome the problem of forensic confirmation bias? What are the downsides, if any, of adopting a linear reasoning strategy?

3. Discuss what research can be conducted, and how it can be applied, to help combat ideological extremism when such views threaten others' lives and/or liberties. Does research on thinking and deciding realistically have any substantial role to play in helping to solve this problem?

Suggestions for further reading

Kassin, S. M., Dror, I. E., & Kukucka, J. (2013). The forensic confirmation bias: Problems, perspectives, and proposed solutions. *Journal of Applied Research in Memory and Cognition, 2*(1), 42–52.

Klayman, J., & Ha, Y. W. (1987). Confirmation, disconfirmation, and information in hypothesis testing. *Psychological Review, 94*(2), 211–228.

Mole, C., & Klein, C. (2010). Confirmation, refutation, and the evidence of fMRI. In S. J. Hanson & M. Bunzl (Eds.), *Foundational issues in human brain mapping* (pp. 99–112). Cambridge, MA: MIT Press.

Belief **13**

Learning Goals

By the end of this chapter, you will have:

- Considered various explanatory models for how people come to believe in paranormal phenomena.
- Evaluated several reasoning patterns that lead to the rejection of scientifically supported phenomena.
- Understood the core characteristics of conspiracy theories and how people come to hold and maintain them.
- Considered evidence for the persistence of misinformation after it is corrected, even if one consciously accepts the correction.
- Examined the potential role of top-down executive control in both formulating unusual beliefs and deliberately disbelieving previously accepted phenomena.

Key Terms

Paranormal beliefs	Belief perseverance
Magical contagion effects	Continued influence effect
Evaluative conditioning	Reactance
Conspiracy theories	Backfire effect

In 2005, a professional musician named Chris Butler was delighted to find a house for sale that not only met all of his search criteria but was also priced dramatically below current market rates (Butler 2009). Then his real estate agent called to inform him that the seller had made one key disclosure: It was formerly the childhood home of Jeffrey Dahmer, a convicted cannibalistic serial killer who committed his first murder in its basement in 1978. Even though the home had long since been cleared of the corpse and Dahmer himself had been dead since 1994, the home had proved to be quite difficult to sell. People (i.e., potential buyers) behaved as though there remained some sort of intangible taint upon the house, which – from a purely physical standpoint – was probably as likely as any to be reasonably clean and sound. Reasoning that there was nothing to fear about the house itself per se, Butler managed to overcome his initial, strongly negative reaction to the seller's disclosure and purchase the house, though he later remarked that many of his neighbors absolutely refused to come in for a cup of tea (Butler 2009).

Superstitious, magical, and paranormal beliefs

When faced with scenarios such as this, people often admit explicitly that they cannot think of any *rational* justification for rejecting the "tainted" object, yet at the same time, they feel intuitively that it is something to be actively avoided (Lindeman & Aarnio 2007). In general, such everyday superstitious, magical, and **paranormal beliefs** – which can be defined as beliefs that are scientifically unaccepted – are incredibly common and quite intuitively understandable (Vyse 2000). Ordinary adults hold similar, strong "magical" beliefs about contamination, as systematically documented in a series of groundbreaking studies by Paul Rozin and colleagues. For example, people are reluctant to wear a sweater previously worn by a person they strongly dislike, even if the sweater has been thoroughly washed. Rozin and colleagues argued that such behavior reflects people's belief in an anthropologically documented law of sympathetic magic known as the *law of contagion*, in which an undesirable person coming into contact with an object is perceived as having transmitted some undesirable properties onto that object, which can then be transferred to anyone who touches the object even after it has been cleaned and sterilized (Rozin, Nemeroff, Wane, & Sherrod 1989; Tylor 1871/1974). Persistent beliefs among North American children regarding "cooties," or fictitious, invisible particles transmitted by touching a socially undesirable peer, also adhere to the law of contagion (see also Hirschfeld 2002). In a related phenomenon, people tend to reject an offer to eat fudge in the shape of feces, even though they know it is only candy. This finding has been argued to reflect people's belief in a magical *law of similarity*, in which an object that is perceptually similar to a disgusting object is felt to take on some of the undesirable properties of that disgusting object (Rozin, Millman, & Nemeroff 1986). A fascinating aspect of such **magical contagion effects** is that people hold these preferences – often quite strongly – while simultaneously acknowledging that actually becoming contaminated by these objects would be impossible.

Numerous accounts have been offered to explain how it is that the magical contagion effect comes about. One prominent behaviorist account focuses on **evaluative conditioning** (Walther, Nagengast, & Traselli 2005).

This account suggests that people choose to reject the previously neutral stimulus (e.g., a sweater) because that stimulus has co-occurred with a negatively valenced stimulus (e.g., a person whom one dislikes intensely), even though the sweater has since been thoroughly washed. By this account, the magical contagion effect arises not because people truly believe that a physical contaminant has been transferred to the neutral stimulus per se, but because they have learned to associate the neutral and negatively valenced stimuli merely by virtue of their having co-occurred (Walther 2002).

Another account builds on the notion, which we discussed at length in Chapter 10, that lay people hold core knowledge and naïve beliefs about broad domains (e.g., psychology, biology, physics) that are relatively specific to each of those domains. For example, general knowledge of how people often tend to feel, think, and behave when they are angry at another person is probably applicable to understanding any given interpersonal relationship between humans, but it is presumably irrelevant to understanding the physical world.

In an intriguing proposal, Lindeman and Aarnio (2007) suggested that magical thinking may emerge when people inappropriately overextend their domain knowledge into other domains. For example, take the case of people's apparent belief in the magical law of contagion. Transmission of real invisible contaminants (e.g., bacteria; viruses) can absolutely occur in the biological domain by merely making contact with another person and transferring those contaminants onto one's own body (or even being near them and in the path of a sneeze or cough, as in the case of cold and influenza virus transmission). Belief in this known biological fact becomes irrational when it is extended beyond the biological domain into, for example, the physics or social domains. For example, people dislike others more if they are shown standing next to an overweight person than if they are shown standing next to a person of average weight (Hebl & Mannix 2003). This unreasonable judgment could stem from an overextension of biological mechanisms of contamination to the psychological domain.

In fact, in one surprising study, adults were shown two groups of mugs, one in which the mugs were clustered closely together, and one in which they were placed quite far apart. People tended to pick a mug out of the close-together group if they were told that one mug among the groups had a small gift inside, and they tended to pick their mug out of the far-apart group if they were told one mug among the groups had a (not-visible) defective lid (Mishra, Mishra, & Nayakankuppam 2009). According to Lindeman and Aarnio's (2007) proposal, this apparently irrational behavior could be interpreted as reflecting an overextension of biological mechanisms of contamination to the physical domain (Kim & Kim 2011).

Recent research suggests that there are strong individual differences in the overextension of core knowledge across domains. For example, Lindeman,

Svedholm, Takada, Lönnqvist, and Verkasalo (2011) constructed a *core knowledge confusions scale* that measured people's tendency to agree with five subtypes of overextensions: (1) that natural non-living kinds are alive (e.g., "the moon lives at night"), (2) that force is a living being (e.g., "force senses a human"), (3) that non-living kinds are alive (e.g., "stones sense the cold"), (4) that artifactual kinds are alive (e.g., "a home misses people"), and (5) that mental states are physical objects (e.g., "a mind touches another"). They asked university students in Finland to rate the degree to which they found these statements to be *literally* true versus literally untrue (this wording ensured that the statements were not viewed as being metaphorical). They found that people's belief in such core knowledge confusions varied widely, and generally remained undiminished over the course of an undergraduate education. In addition, the more people endorsed these core knowledge confusions, the more strongly they also held paranormal beliefs (e.g., "astrology is a way to accurately predict the future").

In fact, Lindeman and Aarnio (2007) further suggested that core knowledge confusions may be instrumental in defining how superstitious, magical, and paranormal beliefs are different from other kinds of technically incorrect beliefs (e.g., grapes are not berries; whales are fish). Namely, superstitious, magical, and paranormal beliefs may be fundamentally defined by the tendency to take physical, psychological, and biological properties and inappropriately apply them to a different domain (e.g., taking the physical properties of force and motion and applying them inappropriately to the psychological domain could generate a belief in telekinesis, or the ability to move objects with one's mind). In contrast, believing that grapes are not berries when in fact they are true berries by botanical definition, or that whales are fish when in fact they are mammals, are confusions of knowledge within a single domain (in this case, biology) and would not be classified as superstitious, magical, or paranormal beliefs under this definition.

Where do beliefs in paranormal phenomena come from in the first place? The conventional wisdom is that it is likely learned from cultural scripts passed from person to person. However, one potent hypothesis is that people are generally predisposed to believe in such phenomena, and that in fact, the tendency to believe in the supernatural carries an evolutionary advantage (Bering 2006). It has, of course, been previously argued that there is an evolutionary advantage to being able to detect anti-social behaviors such as cheating (Cosmides 1989). Relatedly, it could be that believing in the supernatural leads people to refrain from dishonest, cheating behaviors (e.g., presumably out of fear of being observed by one or more non-physical beings), increasing their likelihood of surviving long enough to pass on their genetic material (Bering 2006). There is some intriguing evidence for this hypothesis from developmental psychology research; for example, very young infants do not appear to expect humans to follow the same principles of physics as other objects. In one set of studies, Kuhlmeier, Bloom, and Wynn (2004) found that 5-month-old infants looked longer at a display when an inanimate block appeared to violate the principle of continuous motion (i.e., after going behind a pillar, it suddenly reappeared from behind another pillar), but not when a human appeared to do the exact same thing. The implication is that infants may not start out with the tendency to treat humans in the same way as they do other material objects, and may not even expect them to adhere to the laws of physics (Kuhlmeier et al. 2004). This may set the stage for developing the notion that people can have a mental life, and carry out any number of mental phenomena, without accompanying physical brain mechanisms to carry them out (Bloom 2004).

Rejecting science

Smoking increases the risk of lung cancer. Humans evolved by natural selection. Modern vaccines do not cause autism. The earth is undergoing climate change because of human activity. One factor common to all of these statements is that scientists specializing in their corresponding fields of study overwhelmingly agree that they are true, yet many members of the lay public have regarded them with great skepticism (and sometimes even outright rejection). An important question for scientists and science educators – and for any society at large – is what factors influence whether a person will simply reject conclusions that are considered by scientists to be well substantiated by research. The consequences of misinformed rejections of science can be profound, strongly influencing public policy and causing widespread rejection of potentially lifesaving items (e.g., genetically modified foods to provide well-rounded nutrition; vaccines to eradicate deadly diseases; condom use to prevent the spread of HIV; etc.), which can have devastating consequences for public health outcomes (Goertzel 2010).

One striking example comes from the western coast of the U.S., where water agencies asked engineers in 1997 to help solve the problem of continual water shortages in the area. The engineers drafted a plan to clean and purify sewage water and pump it back into the drinking water supply; from a scientific perspective, it was a safe and efficient plan. However, their plan was immediately and flatly rejected by the public, which – according to the frustrated engineers – did not even seem interested in hearing about the science behind the plan (Miller 2012). Haddad, Rozin, Nemeroff, and Slovic (2009) conducted a large-scale study of people's perceptions of water purification and reuse to find a psychological solution to the problem of getting people to accept the engineers' water purification solution. They found that, perhaps not surprisingly, people's perceptions of purified sewage water seemed to follow a very similar pattern to that found in the classic magical contagion effect studies: They were showing an automatic, visceral negative response to a once-contaminated item (i.e., water) that could not be diminished by rational arguments even after the water had been purified and cleaned to levels considered safe by national and local regulatory agencies.

A practical next step was to determine what actions would help ease the public's aversion to the purified water (Haddad et al. 2009). First, Haddad et al. (2009) found that people were more willing to accept purified water if it was first explained to them that literally all drinking water has been pooped in at some point by someone or something. In many areas, after sewage water is cleaned, it is typically released into the groundwater, where it trickles its way back into drinking water supplies; even the "purest" mountain lakes and streams contain, at minimum, the waste products of fish, birds, and other animals (Miller 2012). Second, they found that the idea of directly pumping purified sewage water back into the drinking water supply, though maximally efficient, bothered people because it seemed too quick and unnatural. People were more willing to accept the water if some of it was first released into basins to seep through sand and gravel before eventually trickling into drinking water reserves (Haddad et al. 2009). In Orange County, California, taking this additional step to help people deal with the magical contagion effect eventually led to broad acceptance of the water purification scheme (Miller 2012).

As it turns out, the water purification story is actually quite a success story in that people were eventually brought around to listen to, and accept, the science. This is often not the case, as even when the scientific community researching a topic is in near-complete consensus, the public may still reject their findings. Science education, of course, might be essential in offsetting public rejection of science, starting with the education of current students. Yet a survey of undergraduate students at a large public U.S. university showed that across four years of higher education in which a minimum of three science courses were required, the rate at which students endorsed paranormal beliefs (e.g., about 50% endorsement of the statement "the positions of the planets have an influence on the events of everyday life") changed very little over time (Impey, Buxner, & Antonellis 2012). Eder, Turic, Milasowszky, Van Adzin, and Hergovich (2011) examined the beliefs of secondary students in Austria and found that 50% believed in evolution, 34% endorsed intelligent design, and 28% believed in creationism. Students' belief in paranormal phenomena (e.g., psi, witchcraft, precognition) correlated positively with belief in intelligent design and creationism but not with belief in evolution, suggesting that acceptance of theories not supported by science may reflect one's overall tendency to believe or disbelieve given the presence or absence of scientific support.

This general notion was corroborated by Lewandowsky, Oberauer, and Gignac (2013), who sought to better understand why a subset of lay adults reject the central claim of climate change scientists – that the climate of the world is changing because of carbon dioxide emissions produced by human activity – even when faced with positive evidence. In particular, they asked whether people who reject climate change tend to believe in (1) unregulated free markets and (2) conspiracy theories in general. Their reasoning was as follows. First, historical accounts suggest that those who believe in having a relatively unregulated free market may tend be highly suspicious of scientific findings that have implications for government-imposed regulations. For example, if we believe that climate change is as catastrophic as scientists say, then governments would likely have to interfere with industry to reduce carbon dioxide emissions, or interfere with people's personal freedoms in driving their vehicles. Second, a tendency to endorse conspiracy theories could predict rejection of climate change. If the world's climate change scientists all report research agreeing that climate change is in fact occurring, and one does not believe in climate change, then one needs to come up with another explanation for the scientists' consensus; one such explanation might be the existence of a secret agreement or conspiracy among scientists.

To test these possibilities, Lewandowsky et al. (2013) asked people visiting blogs on climate change to complete an online questionnaire. This questionnaire was designed to measure their beliefs in a free-market ideology (e.g., "an economic system based on free markets unrestrained by government interference automatically works best to meet human needs"), belief in various specific conspiracy theories (e.g., "Princess Diana's death was not an accident but rather an organized assassination by members of the British royal family who disliked her"), and acceptance of climate science findings (e.g., "I believe that burning fossil fuels increases atmospheric temperature to some measurable degree") and other science findings (e.g., "the HIV virus causes AIDS"; "smoking causes lung cancer").

They found that believing in a free-market ideology was an extremely strong predictor of rejecting climate science and rejecting the smoking–lung cancer relationship, but was not a predictor of rejection of the HIV–AIDS causal relationship. Lewandowsky et al. (2013) suggested that this may be because the first two findings have much stronger regulatory implications for industry than does the latter finding. They also found that the tendency to believe conspiracy theories predicted rejection of all the science findings they tested. One possible reason for this finding is that the rejection is based on a general mistrust of authority figures (e.g., they might believe that climate scientists have an agenda, and are fully capable of misreporting or distorting their data), rather than a rejection of any specific aspect of the research itself (Lewandowsky et al. 2013).

Conspiracy theorizing

Given findings such as these, it seems that conspiracy theories are potentially quite powerful and deserve a more focused discussion. **Conspiracy theories** can be defined as attempts to explain significant occurrences (e.g., the devastating earthquake and tsunami off the coast of Japan on March 11, 2011; the life of Paul McCartney of Beatles fame) in terms of plotting among powerful people or organizations who attempt to hide their role (Douglas & Sutton 2008; Sunstein & Vermeule 2009). For example, one conspiracy theory holds that the March 11, 2011 tsunami resulted directly from a deliberate attack on Japan by the U.S. military; another holds that Paul McCartney died in 1966, that his death was covered up, and that an impostor has been living in his place ever since.

It is important to note that truth and falsity need not be part of the definition of conspiracy theories: Conspiracy theories can be false, partially true, or completely true. Leaving out the question of truth versus falsity is especially helpful for conducting research in judgment and decision-making, because we can simply focus solely on understanding the patterns of reasoning that create and sustain conspiracy theories. By definition, conspiracy theories can also be either benign or harmful, although researchers have tended to focus more on the potentially harmful. Some conspiracy theories are relatively harmless; for example, the power-wielding parents of many young children knowingly and secretly perpetrate the false conspiracy theory that a person called Santa Claus delivers presents every Christmas Eve (Sunstein & Vermeule 2009). Yet others have been incredibly harmful, and may even potentially have helped fuel such dramatically harmful outcomes as wars and genocides (Goertzel 2010).

One of the most fascinating characteristics of conspiracy theory reasoning is that once people accept a conspiracy theory, they can be incredibly resistant to accepting any newly presented evidence to the contrary (Clarke 2002). This phenomenon is broadly known as **belief perseverance** (Lieberman & Arndt 2000), and may be particularly powerful in the case of conspiracy theory beliefs. One reason for this is because the core of the conspiracy theory – a belief that the important occurrence can be traced to a secret plot and cover-up by powerful people – can easily explain any contradictory evidence by claiming that the evidence itself is part of the ongoing plot and cover-up. In this sense, people who believe in conspiracy theories are very consistent. In addition, people who take this approach are presuming that events are best explained by assuming that someone *intended* for them to occur (Popper 1959). In keeping with this idea, there have been many classic demonstrations showing that people, particularly in Western countries, have a tendency to assume that a person's behaviors can be traced to internal as opposed to external factors (e.g., Jones & Davis 1965). Finally, people who take this approach are more generally showing a preference for simple, direct causal explanations (as opposed to the more complex causal explanations that involve figuring out how many small, unintentional events perpetrated by different people and entities led up to the major event to be explained; Sunstein & Vermeule 2009).

The conspiracy theory approach to complex events is therefore quite streamlined in that it hinges on a very simple core idea with surprisingly vast explanatory power (Sunstein & Vermeule 2009). However, when people wholly rely on the broad theory that a secret plot and cover-up can explain everything related to an event, they can run into a few problems. Wood, Douglas, and Sutton (2012) recently highlighted one such striking problem in a clever study. Oftentimes, multiple specific conspiracy theories will arise as potential explanations for a single phenomenon, and these theories may blatantly contradict one another. For example, one theory holds that Diana, Princess of Wales, only faked her death on August 31, 1997, and that officials have perpetrated the hoax that she is dead. Another theory claims that the Al-Fayed family's business enemies murdered her, and that officials have perpetrated the hoax that she was killed in an accident. Notice that although these two particular theories are fundamentally incompatible with one another (i.e., Princess Diana can't be both alive and dead at the same time), both are compatible with the core idea of a secret cover-up by official persons.

The question posed by Wood et al. (2012) was whether or not people who believe in one of these specific conspiracy theories tend to also believe in the other. Fascinatingly, they found that university students in Britain who believed that Diana faked her death and is still alive were also significantly likely to simultaneously believe that the Al-Fayeds' business enemies had murdered her. Surprising as these findings are, a follow-up study with a different group of study participants showed a very similar finding. Students in Britain who believed that Osama Bin Laden is still alive and that his purported death is a hoax perpetrated by the U.S. government were also more likely to believe that he was already dead when U.S. military personnel invaded his compound and that his purported death at their hands was a hoax. Again, people endorsed both beliefs despite the undeniable fact that a person cannot simultaneously be alive and dead. Wood et al.'s (2002) findings suggest that believers of conspiracy theories are most strongly influenced by their central belief in a secret cover-up among powerful persons, and are less concerned about the compatibility between the details.

Box 13.1: The Vaccine–Autism Controversy

In 1998, a respected medical journal published a paper suggesting that a vaccine widely administered in childhood could be responsible for an uptick in autism cases. As evidence, the paper described the cases of 12 children that appeared to support this conclusion, with no control condition. Buoyed by a media firestorm, the finding became widely known among lay people in the U.K., the U.S., and other countries that routinely administer the vaccine to small children. However, starting around 2004, the evidence began to be called into question. Most of the paper's authors formally retracted their original interpretation of the data, and the journal's editors formally retracted the entire paper. A multi-part exposé was printed in another respected medical journal. Finally, the U.S. Institute of Medicine conducted a scholarly review of over 200 studies and found that they failed to demonstrate a causal link between vaccines and autism (Nature Publishing Group 2007).

Yet a large proportion of the lay public continued to believe that the link was clearly substantiated by science research. For example, 69% of Americans in a 2011 Harris Interactive/Health Day poll had heard of research showing a link between vaccines and autism, but only 47% had heard that the paper had been retracted. The U.S. Centers for Disease Control and Prevention reported that the percentage of parents who refused or delayed a vaccine on behalf of their children rose from 22% in 2003 to 39% in 2008. Measles cases in the U.K. rose from a low of a few dozen cases in previous years to 1,920 cases in 2012 and 587 cases in the first quarter of 2013 alone (Public Health England 2013). Furthermore, a substantial portion of research resources were shunted to studies testing for a link between vaccines and autism, which necessarily occurred at the expense of other promising avenues of research that would have addressed the prevention and treatment of autism (Institute of Medicine 2004). However, this is certainly neither the first nor the last time that initial information about a medical issue takes on a life of its own in people's minds and beliefs long after it has been retracted. Are there any concrete ways in which reasonable steps could be taken (e.g., by individuals, teachers, researchers, doctors, media, governments) to minimize the impact of a medical study once it has been released for public consumption?

Correcting misinformation

In fact, it has generally been established that once an erroneous idea is planted, it is very difficult to uproot with corrective information, even if people do not show belief perseverance and appear to understand and accept the corrective information (Lewandowsky, Echer, Seifert, Schwartz, & Cook 2012). This phenomenon is known as the **continued influence effect** (Johnson & Seifert 1994). In some of the earliest studies on how people receive corrections to misinformation, people read about an event (e.g., a warehouse fire) and learned a piece of misinformation (e.g., the fire seems to have been caused by oil-based paints and gas cylinders in a closet) that is later retracted (e.g., actually, it turns out that the closet was empty when the fire broke out). With remarkable consistency, this line of work has shown that a retraction never fully erases the effect of the misinformation on people's judgments (Wilkes & Leatherbarrow 1988), regardless of whether people comprehended and accepted the corrective information (Lewandowsky et al. 2012). In some studies, the retraction did nothing at all to reduce the influence of the misinformation on judgments (e.g., Johnson & Seifert 1994).

Even more dramatically, Seifert (2002) ran additional variations of the original "warehouse fire" studies and found that adding a "clarifying" negated statement such as "paint and gas were never on the premises" had a large rebound effect. That is, these clarifying statements made it even more likely that the misinformation would influence people's judgments. Similarly, Gilbert, Krull, and Malone (1990) showed people statements with very explicit negation markers (e.g., *false*: "I am happy") and found that people initially encoded that the person was happy and failed to encode that the information was false when they were interrupted or under high cognitive load. Research in psycholinguistics helps explain further why this would be the case. This work has more generally shown that when people see a negated statement, such as "not guilty," they appear to encode "guilty" as the core portion of the statement and encode the negation marker "not" as an addendum, or tag (Mayo, Schul, & Burnstein 2004). For example, it takes people significantly longer to process the meaning of negated statements ("not guilty") than comparable statements without negation ("innocent"), suggesting that the two types of statements are not encoded identically, despite their equivalent meaning.

Relatedly, hearing a statement repeatedly – even if it is retracted at some point – increases the odds that the statement will be consolidated into memory and also highly available for retrieval, giving the person a feeling of familiarity when hearing the statement yet again (Ecker, Lewandowsky, Swire, & Chang 2011). Schwarz, Sanna, Skurnik, and Yoon (2007) argued that this could be one important reason why "myth versus fact" public information campaigns typically backfire, leading to behavior that is actually more consistent with the myths than with the facts. For example, the World Health Organization posted a 2013 online article listing common myths about vaccinations and then debunking those myths with statements of the known facts (e.g., "Myth 1: Better hygiene and sanitation will make diseases disappear – vaccines are not necessary. FALSE." "Fact 1: The diseases we can vaccinate against will return if we stop vaccination programmes.") People reading such handouts do understand them, and remember immediately afterward which statements are the myths and which are the facts. However, if tested as little as 30 minutes later, people are more likely to misidentify "myths" as "facts" than people who never received a handout in the first place (Schwarz et al. 2007)! They are also subsequently less likely to agree that they intend to get vaccinated than people who never received a handout. Similarly, jurors in court cases are more likely to allow pretrial publicity to affect their judgments about a defendant if they are asked whether they think pretrial publicity will affect their judgments (Freedman, Martin, & Mota 1998). The simplest conclusion is that the more a person is exposed to the undesirable information, the more it appears to influence their thinking.

The tone of a request to disregard earlier information is also important in preventing **reactance**, or people's tendency to experience a strong physiological response when they perceive a threat to their freedom to think and behave as they choose (Brehm & Brehm 1981). Some researchers have shown that this physiological response can intensify people's intent to think or do the opposite of how they have been instructed. For example, when judges ask jurors to disregard evidence that is legally inadmissible in court, jurors tend to cling even more strongly to that prior information than if the judge had not said anything (Lieberman & Arndt 2000). This phenomenon has been widely documented and is known as the **backfire effect** (Cox & Tanford 1989). For example, Cox and Tanford (1989) found that jurors asked to disregard evidence damaging to a defendant (e.g., because it was the product of an illegal police search) tended to prefer harsher punishment for the defendant than did jurors who were not asked to disregard it.

A related question is whether the level of emotionality contained in the misinformation itself influences the strength of the continued influence effect. One plausible hypothesis is that misinformation content that leads people to experience high levels of negative emotion might make people more resistant to corrective information, given past research showing that emotional material can be better remembered (Levine & Pizarro 2004).

A reasonable alternative is that highly negative misinformation may be easier to correct because there is some prior evidence that emotion interferes with the binding of a specific memory to its source (Mather 2007). To test between these possibilities, Ecker, Lewandowsky, and Apai (2011) asked people to read about a hypothetical plane crash and manipulated whether it was associated with a terrorist attack (highly emotional misinformation) or bad weather (less emotional misinformation). In both conditions, the misinformation was then retracted and the "true" cause, a faulty fuel tank, was introduced. The emotionality manipulation significantly affected people's emotions, indicating that the manipulation was successful and that people did notice it. Interestingly, however, the continued influence effect still appeared very reliably, and the emotionality of misinformation did not influence the strength of the continued influence effect at all. Thus, news headlines that create false initial impressions and premature news reports that report erroneous evidence will generally tend to be impervious to correction whether or not the initial report is high in emotionality (Ecker et al. 2011).

Executive control and beliefs

Given findings such as these, a reasonable question is what role top-down executive control plays in combating unsupported beliefs. First, it is important to realize that there might actually be times when controlled, thoughtful processes themselves generate such beliefs. Some have suggested, for example, that claims of alien abduction and experimentation can often be traced back to apparent episodes of sleep paralysis, a non-pathological phenomenon in which people become conscious in the middle of REM sleep but are still experiencing the temporary paralysis characteristic of REM (Holden & French 2002). In addition, hypnopompic hallucinations (various sensory experiences upon wakening) are common in sleep paralysis, and may include electric tingling sensations, visual hallucinations of figures nearby, and buzzing noises (Clancy, McNally, Schacter, Lenzenweger, & Pitman 2002). These experiences are, by some subset of these people, interpreted in terms of a cultural script of alien abduction, commonly known among the lay public in the U.S. and U.K., among other countries (Lynn, Pintar, Stafford, Marmelstein, & Lock 1998). In fact, British lay people who believed they had had extraterrestrial contact were much more likely to have experienced sleep paralysis than a non-believing group of matched controls (French, Santomauro, Hamilton, Fox, & Thalbourne 2008). So, if one experiences episodes of sleep paralysis and hypnopompic hallucinations, and one is very familiar with the alien abduction cultural script, *and* one has never heard of the phenomena of sleep paralysis or hypnopompic hallucinations, then beliefs in alien abduction may arise through controlled processing.

Looking at such cases from the outside, one might still feel that people sometimes make the leap to belief too quickly and easily. One might suppose that it would be best if one approached any new ideas suspiciously, evaluating them thoroughly before accepting them in the first place. However, Gilbert and colleagues suggested that people in general cannot, in fact, first comprehend information and then decide to reject it (Gilbert 1991; Gilbert, Krull, & Malone 1990; Gilbert, Tafarodi, & Malone 1993). Instead, they proposed, in keeping with the ideas of Spinoza (1677/1982), that people automatically accept information in the process of understanding it. That is, we cannot avoid believing information when we first read it, and in order to reject it, we must next evaluate and un-accept it in a deliberate process. In one study, Gilbert et al. (1990) presented people with nonsense statements (e.g., "a monishna is a star") under the guise of studying foreign language learning. After each statement, they saw a blank screen for a few seconds, and then read that the statement was "true" or "false," and an auditory tone interrupted this true-false identification for equal numbers of true and false trials. When they then asked people to then identify a set of statements as either true or false, Gilbert et al. (1990) found that the interruption had no effect on people's ability to correctly identify true statements as true, but that an interruption severely debilitated people's ability to correctly identify false statements as false (i.e., they had a strong tendency to say they were true).

In subsequent work, Gilbert et al. (1993) found that processing false information under time pressure can also prevent people from unaccepting it. In one study, they first showed people mostly neutral statements about a hypothetical peer whom they called "Bob." Then they presented people with a second set of statements about Bob, some of which were true (i.e., previously presented statements) and others of which were false. Some people saw mostly positive statements in this second set, and others saw mostly negative statements. They asked people to either deliberately assess the truth versus falsity of each statement in this second set or simply to speed-read them. The key question was how much people liked or disliked Bob at the end of the study. In keeping with the Spinozan hypothesis, the second set of statements strongly influenced people's liking of Bob, but only if people had speed-read them. If they were allowed to deliberately assess them, they didn't influence people's liking of Bob at all. Similarly, Kelemen and Rosset (2009) showed that when people are under time pressure, they are more likely to accept teleological (purpose-based), scientifically unwarranted explanations for natural phenomena (e.g., "trees produce oxygen so animals can breathe"). Gilbert and colleagues suggested that broadly speaking, people are natural believers who also possess the ability to become skeptics with effort. The potential consequences for person perception are striking: That we should perhaps beware of trusting our first impressions of people if our deliberate disbelieving process was disrupted or prevented (e.g., we were rushed or thinking about something else at the time).

Furthermore, if this is true, then one might expect individual differences in top-down executive control to predict whether or not a person tends to believe in unsupported (e.g., paranormal) phenomena. In fact, correct responses on the Cognitive Reflection Test (CRT, Frederick 2005), which can be interpreted as the capability to override automatic, heuristic-driven responses with more controlled, thoughtful processes, predict less acceptance of paranormal beliefs (Pennycook, Cheyne, Seli, Koehler, & Fugelsang 2012; see Chapter 1). Svedholm and Lindeman (2012) similarly found that individual differences in reflective thought – both with respect to the ability to objectively consider arguments regardless of one's own point of view and in one's willingness to doubt information – predict less acceptance of paranormal beliefs. Especially in light of such apparent individual differences in executive control and skepticism, it is interesting to consider what having Spinozan belief processes would mean for the advisability of free speech (Gilbert et al. 1993). It seems nearly inevitable that some subset of people would believe, and fail to disbelieve, in some of the false beliefs available in the open marketplace of ideas. Yet restricting ideas might make it far less likely that the best ideas would ever make it into the open (Gilbert et al. 1993). Still worse, restricting ideas and limiting public information may even unwittingly create ideal conditions for conspiracy theorizing (Sunstein & Vermeule 2009). Perhaps for these reasons, tension around this issue may always tend to emerge in public discourse.

Conclusions

To summarize, we have considered different ways in which people may form and maintain beliefs about magical contagion, paranormal phenomena unsupported by evidence, and conspiracy theories. Conversely, sometimes people also reject phenomena that are strongly supported by science research. Information once processed is notoriously difficult to remove from consideration in decision-making, even if the person consciously believes and accepts its retraction. Finally, we have discussed the potential role of top-down executive control in fostering both belief and disbelief. In the next chapter, we will consider how our beliefs about ourselves and others unfold within the context of societies.

Questions for discussion

1. Suppose that a university governing board decides to censor a campus student-run newspaper for ideas that run contrary to accepted ideas in science (e.g., rejection of evolutionary theory). Drawing upon evidence from this chapter about the nature and processes underlying belief, discuss whether you believe this is advisable or not, and why.
2. Given the research on correcting misinformation that was discussed in this chapter, what would be the best way of designing a handout to be distributed in schools and workplaces to persuade people to receive a flu vaccine each fall?
3. There is controversy regarding whether or not religions fit the definition of paranormal phenomena (Irwin 2009). Is one an example of the other or are they fundamentally different in some way or ways? Adopting the perspective of someone conducting research in this field, what is your opinion, and why?

Suggestions for further reading

Gilbert, D. T. (1991). How mental systems believe. *American Psychologist, 46*(2), 107–119.

Lewandowsky, S., Echer, U. K. H., Seifert, C., Schwartz, N., & Cook, J. (2012). Misinformation and its correction: Continued influence and successful debiasing. *Psychological Science in the Public Interest, 13*(3), 106–131.

Lindeman, M., & Aarnio, K. (2007). Superstitious, magical, and paranormal beliefs: An integrative model. *Journal of Research in Personality, 41*(4), 731–744.

PART V

Judgment and Decision-Making in Society

Moral Judgment and Cooperation 14

Learning Goals

By the end of this chapter, you will have:

- Evaluated research findings regarding the role of morality in people's concepts of personal identity.
- Compared Kohlberg's (1971) seminal stages of moral development and Gilligan's (1982) counterproposal taking gender into account, and considered research adjudicating between the two.
- Examined differences between rationalist models and dual-process models with respect to how they describe and account for the role of emotion in moral judgments.
- Explained how cognitive neuroscience research and research on responses to moral dilemmas have shaped our current understanding of how judgments are made.
- Considered lay judgments about the relationship between determinism, free will, and moral responsibility.
- Reviewed evidence for how public goods are routinely developed and maintained, even though some rationalist models predict they should not exist.

Key Terms

Kohlberg's stages of moral development	Wag-the-dog illusion
Rationalist view	Wag-the-other-dog's-tail illusion
Pre-conventional level	Somatic marker hypothesis
Conventional level	Trolley dilemma
Post-conventional level	Footbridge dilemma
Social interactionist model	Transfer effects
Social intuitionist model	Causal model theory of transfer effects
	Zero-sum game

Tragedy of the commons	Tit for Tat
Game theory	Public goods
Prisoner's dilemma	Free riding
Nash equilibrium	

When the Romanian-American writer, professor, and social activist Elie Wiesel passed away on July 2, 2016, obituaries describing his major life's work appeared in major news outlets around the world. The descriptions of Wiesel in his obituaries dwelled upon his experiences as a Holocaust survivor, his writings urging people to speak out against evil when they see it, his receipt of the 1986 Nobel Peace Prize, those who critiqued him on moral grounds, and the times he publicly chastised the U.S. government for failing to come to the aid of victims of ongoing mass atrocities around the world (e.g., Homberger 2016).

Wiesel's moral character, in sum, was the central focus of his obituaries. Maybe it stands to reason that his morality would be highlighted, since it was his most famous trait. However, an analysis of nearly all of the obituaries printed in the New York Times from June 2009 to June 2012 showed that descriptions of moral character (i.e., ranging from good to bad) dominated descriptions of interpersonal warmth and sociability (i.e., ranging from warm to cold; Goodwin, Piazza, & Rozin 2014). Perhaps when people die, and we look back upon their lives, we tend to think more about their moral character than about such personality traits as warmth. Or perhaps we generally tend to treat moral character as highly central to a person's identity (Goodwin et al. 2014). Let's suppose that every person develops an individual identity made up of moral (or immoral) character, different personality traits, different abilities, and a range of preferences and desires. Which traits do we feel are most important in defining who a person is? That is, what traits do we think are most important to that person's identity?

As it turns out, a growing body of research suggests that we consider our morality to be an essential component of our personal identities, even more so than our memories. Strohminger and Nichols (2014), for example, asked study participants to consider the hypothetical case of a person who received a partial brain transplant some 40-plus years in the future. Some were told that the person's thoughts and behaviors were unchanged after the transplant (control condition). Others were told that the person's long-term memories were lost, but that the person was the same in all other ways. Still others were told that the person became amoral after the transplant, no longer empathizing with others or able to tell what was morally right versus wrong, but that the person was the same in all other ways. Then, study participants were asked to rate the degree to which the person was still the same person after the brain transplant. The results showed that people who were told that the person had lost morality felt that he had retained his personal identity significantly less than did people judging the other cases, including even the hypothetical person who had lost all of his life memories (Strohminger & Nichols 2014).

Building upon this finding, Strohminger and Nichols (2014) asked another group of people to suppose that they were meeting a long-lost friend after a 40-year absence, and that the friend had changed in a number of different ways. These changes included both positive and negative changes in the friend's morality (e.g., had become racist; generous; more likely to steal; tenderhearted), personality (e.g., had become adventurous; a slow learner; shy; artistic), thinking ability, ability to remember, ability to perceive (e.g., as relates to seeing, hearing, tasting, etc.), and preferences or desires (e.g., enjoys cooking; dislikes exercise). People then rated each of these changes – 56 in total – for how much each change would alter the friend's personal identity (i.e., "true self," Strohminger & Nichols 2014). Strohminger and Nichols (2014) found that the top 14 changes that people, on average, felt contributed most significantly to the "true self," were in fact all 14 of the morality changes that they were shown. (Personality changes were considered the next most important to our identity.) This strikingly clear and surprising finding suggests that we view our morality as central to our personal identities, even more so than our personalities, mental abilities, memories, or our likes or dislikes.

Moral judgment

Kohlberg's stages of moral development

As morality appears to be, at least in theory, of great importance to us, it is not surprising that philosophical arguments about how people *ought* to make moral judgments go back for centuries. On the other hand, descriptive, behavioral theories of how people actually *do* carry out moral judgments can be narrowed down to a smaller and more recent body of work. The traditional descriptive view of moral judgments is a rationalist view, which suggests that people first consciously and deliberately think through a moral problem. Based on this reasoning, we then come up with a moral judgment. This view of how people make moral judgments can be traced to Kohlberg's (1971) seminal approach.

Building upon the developmental theories of Piaget and Inhelder (1969), **Kohlberg's stages of moral development** suggested that children develop the ability to carry out moral reasoning over stages, such that their moral reasoning is limited by their cognitive abilities at each age. To study their moral reasoning, he presented children with moral dilemmas and recorded how they reasoned through them at different ages. In one well-known dilemma, the children were told of a man named Heinz who has to decide whether to steal a drug he cannot afford in order to save his wife's life. The drug maker has already refused to sell Heinz the drug for a down payment of 50%, with the rest to be paid as soon as Heinz can earn the money, even though he is charging Heinz ten times what it cost to make the drug (Kohlberg 1971). Children (and later, adults) were asked to say what they thought it would be right for the person (e.g., Heinz) to do, and why.

Kohlberg (1971) proposed that the data he collected showed the emergence of six stages of moral development, which he classified into three levels. (Note that the basis for classification is the *reason* people give for choosing an answer, rather than the person's answer itself.) **Pre-conventional level** (Stages 1 and 2) moral judgments are based on seeking rewards and avoiding punishment. In Stage 1, a child may decide not to shove her sibling because she knows an authority figure may make her sit in the corner if she does; that is, this moral decision is made to avoid a tangible consequence. In Stage 2, the child realizes one can seek personal advantage by sometimes acting prosocially in the expectation of being treated in the same way. For example, the child might accept two cookies and give one to her sibling, on the understanding that this sharing rule will be followed for the indefinite future and that the child should get a cookie sometime later when her sibling has two.

Conventional level (Stages 3 and 4) moral judgments are driven by social conventions, helping keep society stable by upholding its expectations. In particular, in Stage 3, judgments are based on interpersonal concerns, such as how others would feel (e.g., the child deciding not to shove her sibling because she is trying to be good, and being good involves being caring toward others). In Stage 4, people follow the rules and accept laws, and tend to accept the moral authority of people in charge, so that society will be maintained. **Post-conventional level** (Stages 5 and 6) moral judgments are based on a deeper, more universal understanding of morality (Kohlberg 1971). At the post-conventional level, the child decides not to shove her sibling because it would be morally wrong to cause harm to another and to interfere with another's individual rights. At this level, the child would not shove her sibling even if no one were around to see and she knew there was no way she could possibly get in trouble. People at this stage may also, even in opposition to authority figures, protest against rules or laws that they feel are morally wrong or unfair given deeper principles of justice.

Although Kohlberg claimed that the six stages unfold universally in this temporal order over development (with many people's development culminating at Stages 3 or 4 in adulthood), Gilligan (1982) pointed out that his longitudinal research, though extensive, included only male study participants. She called into question the assumption that a universal standard of moral reasoning was best defined by a sample consisting exclusively of males. It turned out that females, when presented with Kohlberg's moral dilemmas, were most likely to ultimately end up at Stage 3, but that males were most likely to advance to Stage 4. If a person tends to respond to moral dilemmas with a strong social focus – for example, trying to think through how others would feel and being sensitive to interpersonal needs – that person would not be said to achieve a particularly high level of moral reasoning in Kohlberg's theory. Yet it might be said that there is something very morally right about responding to a dilemma in this way, even if one is not necessarily calling upon the rule of law (Gilligan 1982). Gilligan (1982) argued that what is valued as "more advanced" moral reasoning differs by gender, such that men focus more on rights and the law, and women focus more on interpersonal goals. A more recent version of her theory suggests that any given moral dilemma can be approached from two orientations: A care orientation (roughly corresponding to Stage 3) and a justice orientation (Stage 4). Gilligan and Attanucci (1988) reported that both genders reason from both orientations, although women tend to focus more on care and men more on justice.

In a comprehensive follow-up, Jaffee and Hyde (2000) conducted a meta-analysis of 180 studies conducted on this topic, enabling them to determine whether the overall effect of gender emerges across the data from all of these studies taken together. First, they found a weak overall effect size of about $d = -.3$ for the effect of gender on care orientation, such that females adopted the care orientation more than males overall. Interestingly, the *direction* of the gender difference held true across all age groups and all socioeconomic groups, but the *strength* of that difference varied by age and socioeconomic status. For example, children and college students showed a weak gender difference on care orientation, whereas adolescents and young adults showed a moderately strong difference. The strength of the gender difference on care orientation also increased as socioeconomic status increased (Jaffee & Hyde 2000).

There was also a weak overall effect size for the effect of gender on justice orientation ($d = .2$), such that males adopted the justice orientation more than females (Jaffee & Hyde 2000). Age, though not socioeconomic status, affected the strength of gender differences in adopting the justice orientation. For example, adolescents and younger adults showed the gender difference for the justice orientation, but college students did not. In sum, Jaffee and Hyde's (2000) meta-analysis supported Gilligan's (1982) general claims across the board, although to a weaker degree than might have been expected. Of course, regardless of these findings, Gilligan's (1982) arguments regarding whether the care orientation or the justice orientation *ought* to be treated as equivalently ranked developmental stages of moral reasoning remain worthy of serious consideration.

Affect and reasoning in moral judgment

So far, we have been discussing moral judgment only with respect to deliberate reasoning, but it has become clear in recent years that such a model needs to include the role of affect. Moral judgments are often accompanied by affect – that is, a negative or positive feeling – that predicts whether the person judges an action to be immoral or moral (Haidt 2001). One major question in the literature is whether the affect drives the judgment, influences the judgment, or arises only after the judgment is made. Kohlberg's (1971) view was that affect influences judgments, but is not itself inherently moral. Generally, rationalist views of morality suggest that it is our thinking and reasoning that enables us to make moral judgments, and our feelings about it come after the fact. For example, one prominent rationalist model of moral judgment is the **social interactionist model**, which suggests that people first think about whether an action would be unjust toward others, harm others either physically or emotionally, or violate the rights of others (e.g., Turiel 2002). In doing so, we categorize human actions as belonging to one of three possible domains:

- *Personal* domain (e.g., including actions that affect only ourselves, and are therefore no one's business but our own).
- *Moral* domain (e.g., including actions that inherently cause harm to others, and are therefore universally morally wrong).
- *Social* domain (e.g., including actions that don't harm others per se, but violate local societal rules, so that these actions might be wrong in one society but are okay in another).

Turiel's (2002) work showed, for example, that even children know the difference between mere social conventions (e.g., obeying authority figures) and deeper moral principles. For example, 5–6-year-old children were asked to consider a hypothetical case in which some kids were fighting. The children were more willing to accept the command of a child to stop fighting than to accept the command of a teacher to continue fighting. This finding suggests that the children felt that the moral obligation to stop fighting overrode the teacher's command, as fighting can result in harm to others (Turiel 2002).

The idea that we classify actions into these three domains is quite powerful in that it can potentially explain radical differences between different people's moral judgments. Debates about women's right to have a first-trimester abortion, for example, may hinge in large part upon whether one believes that a fetus unable to survive outside the womb is a full-fledged person. If one believes the answer is no (e.g., because one considers the non-viable fetus to be not yet a person, and/or to still be a part of the mother's body), then one might then classify abortion as a *personal* issue. That is, one would see it as affecting the self (i.e., mother) alone, and therefore as being outside the jurisdiction of social convention or moral judgment. If one believes the answer is yes, then one might instead categorize abortion as a *moral* issue (i.e., as it is now viewed as resulting in harm to another person, the fetus). This latter classification would lead one to see first-trimester abortion as morally wrong.

Many such disputes may seem easier to comprehend if we think of them as differences in how one classifies an action into these three categories, rather than as differences in how moral or amoral one is. And as it turns out, factors such as culture and socioeconomic status strongly influence what types of actions one classifies as belonging to the moral domain (Haidt, Koller, & Dias 1993). For example, Haidt et al. (1993) developed descriptions of actions that are offensive but do not cause others harm (e.g., ripping up the flag of one's country because one does not want it anymore and then using it to clean one's toilet). They then presented these actions to people in two Brazilian cities and one U.S. city; in each of these three cities, they included study participants of both low and high socioeconomic status. First, Haidt et al. (1993) found that neither city nor socioeconomic status predicted any differences in how harmless or how offensive people thought the actions were. However, they then asked people to say whether it would be okay if different countries chose whether to allow or disallow such an action. People who said it was okay for countries to differ would essentially be categorizing the action as a social convention; those who said it was not okay would be categorizing it in the moral domain (i.e., saying that there is a universally correct answer about the acceptability of the action). Haidt et al. (1993) found a robust effect of socioeconomic status; people in high socioeconomic status groups were much more likely to classify such actions as social conventions than were people in low socioeconomic status groups. In a considerably weaker, but still detectable, effect, people in the U.S. city were more likely to categorize the action in the social domain than were people in the two Brazilian cities.

In addition to these effects of socioeconomic status and culture, Haidt et al. (1993) noted that people often seemed to have very definite ideas about whether an action was acceptable, but were much less frequently able to produce clear reasons *why* they thought so. In line with such findings, the **social intuitionist model** of Haidt (2001, 2012) disagrees with the idea that reasoning is what *drives* moral judgments. Instead, Haidt (2001, 2012) suggested that we base our moral judgments on our intuition or gut feeling that something is morally wrong or right. Afterwards, we may or may not reason after the fact to come up with ad hoc justifications for the moral judgments that we already made.

Haidt (2001) also suggested that as a consequence, people are prone to two interesting illusions about moral judgments. First, he suggested, we tend to mistakenly *think* that the moral judgments that we make are based on our reasoning, a phenomenon he called the **wag-the-dog illusion**. This illusion leads to a second illusion that may be very important for understanding why people can have a hard time understanding each other's moral judgments. In the **wag-the-other-dog's-tail illusion**, we have the mistaken belief that we can change another person's mind on a moral issue by pointing out why their reasoning is unsound. This is an illusion because if our moral judgments are actually based on our intuitive, emotional responses to a moral situation and not to reasoning, then it won't do any good to try to change the other person's reasoning. Instead, you would probably do much better if you worked on figuring out a way to change their emotional response (Haidt 2012).

Haidt (2001) argued that the social intuitionist model and these illusions can together explain why people on opposite sides of a moral debate often experience each other as being completely unreasonable. Take, for example, debates over whether or not abortion should be made illegal at an earlier point in gestation than it is at present, or whether immigration into one's country should be more restricted than it currently is. The social intuitionist model would suggest that people's moral judgments on these issues are based on their intuitions and that they tend to generate reasons for making that judgment *after* they have already made it. Because of the wag-the-other-dog's-tail-illusion, people who are trying to change the minds of people on the other side will try to do so by making arguments: For example, by arguing that there is no evidence that new immigrants are more likely to generate crime than current citizens or (on the other side) by pointing to news articles reporting a recent crime by an immigrant. Yet people would do better, argued Haidt (2012), to appeal to other people's intuitive or emotional side by using classic interpersonal and persuasive skills such as showing interest in the other person's point of view or

behaving in a pleasant and friendly manner (which will lead them to associate your point of view with more positive feelings). Simply mentioning
or even implying your own point of view may also be effective, as doing so
influences people's impressions of what opinion society at large holds on
the issue (Haidt 2012).

Cognitive neuroscience and dual-process models of moral reasoning

Cognitive neuroscience research has tended to support dual-process models
of moral reasoning, and the trail of evidence goes back quite a long way – at
least to 1848. At the Harvard School of Medicine in Boston, Massachusetts,
flanking an open stairwell in Countway Library, visitors can peruse several
glass-covered cases along the walls containing displays of historical medical
artifacts. These artifacts include human fetal skeletons of varying sizes, old
medical bloodletting paraphernalia, and the bones of former patients who
suffered from genetic anomalies. As part of the Warren Anatomical Museum
collection, these items are rotated in and out of these cases for display.
In contrast, the skull of Phineas Gage – alongside the original tamping iron
that was accidentally blasted through his head in an infamous 1848 rail-
way accident – is on display year-round. Part of the reason why Gage's case
remains so well known is that the doctor who attended him on the day of the
accident published two diary-like reports recapping the events surrounding
the accident and describing some of Phineas Gage's observable traits, behaviors, and physical characteristics (e.g., Harlow 1868).

The fact that there is a hole in the forehead area of Phineas Gage's skull
suggests probable frontal lobe damage, but the more precise likely location of
brain damage remained unknown for some time. Then, Damasio, Grabowski,
Frank, Galaburda, and Damasio (1994) constructed a three-dimensional computer model using data from pictures, x-rays, and measurements they took of
Gage's original skull. They superimposed their three-dimensional skull model
on the Talairach Atlas brain (Talairach & Tournoux 1988), a reference brain
depicting the probable locations of known brain areas. Extrapolating from
the 3-D computerized model of the tamping iron and the hole still remaining in the skull, Damasio et al. (1994) were able to estimate more precisely
which of Phineas Gage's brain areas are most likely to have been damaged.
Specifically, much of the damage very likely occurred in the ventromedial
prefrontal cortex, whereas the dorsolateral prefrontal cortex and motor
cortices (along with all areas outside the frontal lobes) appear to have been
completely untouched, even when accounting for the probable locations of
white matter.

These areas of damage, taken together with Harlow's (1868) reports about Phineas Gage's behaviors after his physical recovery, led Damasio et al. (1994) to form new hypotheses about what brain functions are carried out in the ventromedial prefrontal cortex. As Harlow observed:

> The equilibrium or balance, so to speak, between his intellectual faculties and animal propensities, seems to have been destroyed. He is fitful, irreverent, indulging at times in the grossest profanity (which was not previously his custom), manifesting but little deference for his fellows, impatient of restraint or advice when it conflicts with his desires, at times pertinaciously obstinate, yet capricious and vacillating, devising many plans of future operation, which are no sooner arranged than they are abandoned in turn for others appearing more feasible...his friends and acquaintances said he was "no longer Gage."
>
> (1868, pp. 13–14)

Harlow's (1868) report paints a portrait of a man who, after suffering brain damage, seemed to lack much of his former degree of deliberate, executive control over his own behaviors. Phineas Gage also seemed perfectly capable of forming many different plans, but was unable to decide upon a single course of action and to stick to it. What is especially interesting about this case is that over a century later, something quite like these behavioral traits were observed in a new set of patients with localized damage to the ventromedial prefrontal cortex (also called orbitofrontal cortex) and its connections to areas associated with emotion processing, just like Phineas Gage (Bechara, Damasio, & Damasio 2000; Damasio 1994; Damasio et al. 1994). In particular, these new patients were still functioning normally in many respects; their memories, reasoning abilities, social knowledge, *and* moral reasoning all appeared to be operating as expected. However, although they could discuss future plans and explain how to navigate through social and moral dilemmas, they were now unable to make final *decisions* about daily tasks, social situations, or open-ended moral dilemmas. Furthermore, they seemed to have a diminished experience of emotion in response to previously emotion-inducing stimuli, which Damasio et al. (1994) suggested could be the cause of their inability to make final decisions.

In particular, Bechara et al.'s (2000) **somatic marker hypothesis** is that the diminished experience of emotion makes it hard for such patients to make decisions. Think about what happens when you are faced with making a moral judgment. For example, suppose you know a family whose pet dog was killed in a car accident, and who then cut up, cooked, and ate the dog's body for supper because they thought it might taste good (Haidt et al. 1993). (If this story makes you feel disgusted, you are not alone; as we saw earlier in this chapter, Haidt et al. [1993] purposely designed their stories to be both offensive and harmless.) To recap Haidt's (2001) major point, when you are presented with this case, and when you are asked whether it was right or wrong for the family to eat their dog's corpse, your answer may be strongly influenced by how you *feel* about the case. That is, if this story happens to make you feel disgusted, that feeling may influence, and may even be central to, the moral decision that you make. You might, for instance, feel that it was just not right for them to eat their pet dog. Or perhaps you didn't feel extremely disgusted by this story, in which case you might be more likely to conclude that it was their choice and there isn't anything morally *wrong* per se about eating it. In this same vein, the overall idea of the somatic marker hypothesis is that a person's emotional, bodily (i.e., somatic) experience when faced with a decision – moral or otherwise – has a strong influence on that decision (Bechara et al. 2000). In addition, when one has brain damage that prevents one from having any emotional, gut feeling in response to the story, then one's decision-making ability – including but not limited to moral decision-making – will be affected.

Symptoms very similar to some of those apparently experienced by Phineas Gage (Harlow 1868) and by ventromedial cortex lesion patients (Bechara et al. 2000) have also long been observed in people with psychopathy, which is characterized by a lack of emotion, along with irresponsibility, impulsivity, and an inability to plan for the future (Anderson & Kiehl 2012). Studies have shown that relative to control participants, people with psychopathy tend to have less gray matter in the ventromedial prefrontal cortex (de Oliveira-Souza et al. 2008). People with psychopathy also appear to have reduced gray matter in the basolateral nucleus of the amygdala, which is strongly associated with the experience of emotion, and which is reciprocally connected to the ventromedial cortex (Anderson & Kiehl 2012). These strong similarities between cases of psychopathy, Bechara et al.'s (2000) patients with lesions to the ventromedial cortex, and the historic case of Phineas Gage raise interesting questions about the nature of moral judgment. Namely, those with apparent deficits in emotional experience also tend to show significant problems with decision-making. At the very least, these data are consistent with the hypothesis that basic affect is not only part of decision-making, but potentially even critical to it.

In this vein, Greene, Sommerville, Nystrom, Darley, and Cohen (2001) proposed that affect can drive whether or not people make a utilitarian choice in moral dilemmas. Take, for instance, the classic trolley dilemma: Suppose you are standing near some train tracks when you see that there is a trolley speeding down toward five people who will clearly be killed when struck. You happen to be standing next to a switch that will shift the trolley onto an alternative track. You can also see that if you do throw the switch, one person standing on that alternative track will be killed. The utilitarian choice (i.e., that which will benefit the most people) would be to save the five people at the expense of the one by throwing the switch, and people most often make this choice (Greene et al. 2001).

Now, let's contrast this case with the footbridge dilemma. Suppose instead that you are standing on a footbridge that arches over some train tracks. You see that there is a trolley speeding down toward five people who will clearly be killed when struck. There is a tall, broad person standing next to you on the footbridge; you are too small to stop the trolley, but if you push this person off the footbridge, his larger body will stop the trolley and save the five people. However, it will kill the person you push. Again, the utilitarian choice would be to save more people at the expense of this one person, but people generally say that they will not do so (Greene et al. 2001).

The trolley dilemma and footbridge dilemma are highly similar in structure, yet people tend to make the exact opposite moral judgments for one versus the other. The seemingly rational utilitarian judgment tends to be chosen when it involves flipping a switch and subsequently causing a person's death, but not when it involves pushing a person to his death. Greene et al. (2001) hypothesized that people experience a stronger affective response to pushing a person than to flipping a switch because the former is more personal and the latter more impersonal. Thus, people feel compelled to reject the utilitarian choice in the footbridge dilemma.

To test their hypothesis, they presented people with different dilemmas which were either non-moral (e.g., deciding whether to take a bus versus a train to attend an important meeting), both moral and personal (e.g., the footbridge dilemma), or both moral and impersonal (e.g., the trolley dilemma; Greene et al. 2001). While choosing which action would be most appropriate for each dilemma, study participants underwent fMRI scans. Brain areas previously associated with emotional experience (i.e., posterior cingulate gyrus, medial frontal gyrus, and angular gyrus) showed heightened activity during moral/personal dilemmas relative to moral/impersonal and non-moral dilemmas (Greene et al. 2001). Conversely, some areas associated with working memory (i.e., parietal lobe and right middle frontal gyrus) were more active during moral/impersonal and non-moral dilemmas than during moral/personal dilemmas. These imaging data are consistent with the hypothesis that personal moral dilemmas tend to be accompanied by more emotion processing. By extrapolation, these data offer a potential explanation for what might underlie people's rejection of the utilitarian response in the footbridge dilemma. Greene et al.'s (2001) findings have generally been interpreted as providing evidence for a dual-process account of moral judgment, in which both rational and emotional processes play a major role.

If the dual-process account is true, then we should also be able to observe that experimentally manipulating emotion results in altered moral decision-making. In one striking demonstration of just such an effect, Valdesolo and DeSteno (2006) asked whether inducing people to feel positive emotion just before reading the footbridge dilemma would counteract any negative emotional response. If the positive emotion induction is successful in counteracting the negative emotion response to pushing a person from the footbridge, then we should see an increase in utilitarian responses (i.e., more people will be willing to push one person from the footbridge in order to save five people from being hit by a trolley). In their experiment, positive mood was induced in some participants by showing them a five-minute video segment from the U.S.-based sketch comedy show *Saturday Night Live*. Other participants saw an emotion-neutral clip of the same length. Self-ratings of emotion showed that people in the positive mood condition were indeed feeling more positive than those in the neutral mood condition just after the mood induction. Then, all study participants responded to the trolley and footbridge dilemmas. The researchers found that positive mood significantly increased people's willingness to push a person off the footbridge in the footbridge dilemma, relative to those in the neutral mood condition (Valdesolo & DeSteno 2006). (Utilitarian responses to the trolley dilemma, as expected, were nearly at ceiling in both mood conditions.) This finding suggests that judgments influenced by emotion – such as moral judgments – can be manipulated by one's prior emotions. Furthermore, the effect of emotion on moral judgments does not depend on there being a logical connection between prior emotion and the moral dilemma being considered. That is, people surely knew that a comedy sketch, in terms of content, had nothing to do with the moral reasoning dilemma; yet it had a profound effect upon their judgments.

Additional research has explored the effects of other specific emotions on moral judgments. Schnall, Haidt, Clore, and Jordan (2008), for example, asked whether feelings of disgust might also drive people's judgments in moral dilemmas. They presented people with two types of scenarios for which they were then asked to make moral judgments. In pre-testing, they first established that one type of scenario made people feel disgusted (e.g., asking people whether they thought first cousins should be legally allowed to marry) and that the other type did not (e.g., asking people whether they thought a film studio should have released an ethically contentious movie). People rated their support for each action while exposed to one of three disgust conditions. In one condition, an odor resulting from the spray application of ammonia and hydrogen sulfide (also known as "fart spray") filled the room. In the second condition, the odor was considerably less intense, and in the third condition, no odor was released into the room. Schnall et al. (2008) found that being in a room with fart spray made people less lenient in their moral judgments relative to being in a room with no odor. This finding held true whether the odor was mild or strong, and it also held true for both types of scenarios (i.e., whether disgust-inducing or not).

In follow-up experiments, Schnall et al. (2008) also showed that disgust only influenced moral judgments for people who generally tend to pay attention to their bodily states. They also replicated the effect using a variety of disgust manipulations. For example, they had people write in detail about an incident in their past that made them feel queasy (compared to a control condition in which they were not asked to do so). Again, triggering feelings of disgust made people less morally lenient. Finally, they found that inducing sadness did not have the same effect (and even trended in the opposite direction), suggesting that feelings of disgust in particular, not just any negative emotions, cause people to become less morally lenient (Schnall et al. 2008).

Eskine, Kacinik, and Prinz (2011) further showed that the effect of disgust on moral judgment can be elicited by taste. American undergraduate students who drank Swedish Bitters (a traditional herbal tonic generally judged to have a bitter taste) were significantly less morally lenient in judging scenarios than people who drank fruit punch (judged as sweet) or people who drank water. Eskine et al. (2011) also divided their participants by self-rated political orientation (i.e., liberal; conservative). Generally speaking, U.S. liberalism values equal rights, fair treatment of groups who were historically mistreated, and social responsibility, and is characterized by more lenience in moral judgments (e.g., favors abortion rights; is against the death penalty; Lakoff 2010). Conservatism in the U.S., in contrast, reflects the valuing of self-reliance, respect for higher authority, and individual responsibility, and is associated with less lenience in moral judgments (e.g., is against abortion rights; favors the death penalty; Lakoff 2010). Eskine et al. (2011) found that the effect of experiencing a bitter taste on moral judgments was driven more strongly by conservatives. Liberals' moral judgments ran in the same direction as did the moral judgments of conservatives, but did not reach significance.

Perhaps the most stunning example in this line of research is a study conducted by Danziger, Levav, and Avnaim-Pesso (2011) in Israel. They followed the decisions of eight experienced judges, each independently presiding over two prison parole boards. Every day, each judge considers anywhere between 14 and 35 cases of current prisoners who are seeking to be paroled. The judge hears the details of each case as it comes up and does not yet know any details about the cases to be heard later in the day. Every day, between cases, the judge decides at the spur of the moment when to take a break for a morning snack and when to take a break for lunch. From over 1,000 rulings collected over 10 months, Danziger et al. (2011) were able to calculate the proportion of favorable rulings (i.e., granting parole) for cases in each ordinal position. First, they found that the proportion of favorable rulings for the first case of the day was around 65%. As each subsequent case was heard, the proportion of favorable rulings became lower and lower, hitting zero just before the judges' snack break. After the snack break, the proportion of favorable rulings jumped back to about 65%, getting lower and lower for each subsequent case, hitting a low of about 12% before jumping back to about 65% immediately after the lunch break. Incredibly, these observational results suggest that when judges are hungry and tired, they may be likelier to stick to the status quo (i.e., continuing to keep the person in prison) in making their parole judgments (Danziger et al. 2011). Of course, the judges also took relevant factors into account, most notably whether there was a rehabilitation program available to accept the prisoner if paroled and how many times the prisoner had previously been in prison (i.e., whether he or she was a repeat offender; Danziger et al. 2011). Over and above the effects of these factors, however, these findings suggest that the somatic state of the judge also predicted her or his decisions.

All told, findings such as those by Eskine et al. (2011), Schnall et al. (2008), Valdesolo and DeSteno (2006), and Danziger et al. (2011) seem to suggest that if we want to hand down moral judgments as fairly as possible, we should be mindful about our surroundings and how they might influence us, particularly if we might be especially susceptible to outside cues. The sensation of bitterness of taste, feelings of disgust, and hunger or fatigue, even when irrelevant to the task at hand, could conceivably influence our judgments about morality and punishment.

Transfer effects

The study of moral judgments faces an added complication in that people don't necessarily make the same decision under different conditions. For example, people on the fence about the morality of abortion might be swayed to take a position against it if they are first asked an analogous question about whether it is okay to abort a fetus in the third trimester. If people's clear intuition is that abortion in the third trimester is morally wrong, then they may tend to transfer this intuition to the analogous problem of aborting a fetus in the first trimester. That is, answering the third-trimester question first may make it more likely that they will say abortion in the first trimester is also morally wrong. There is indeed evidence for such **transfer effects** in the literature, although sometimes transfer only occurs from one moral dilemma to another and not in the opposite direction (Wiegmann, Okan, & Nagel 2012). To give one example that has received much attention in recent years, presenting the footbridge dilemma before the trolley dilemma leads people to be more likely to reject the utilitarian response for the trolley dilemma than if only the trolley dilemma is presented (see Wiegmann & Waldmann 2014). That is, people appear to transfer their response from the footbridge dilemma to the trolley dilemma. In contrast, presenting the trolley dilemma first does not change responses on the footbridge dilemma. In other words, the transfer effect only goes in one direction and not the other. Furthermore, Wiegmann et al. (2012) observed that dilemmas that tend to be judged as immoral (e.g., pushing the man in the footbridge dilemma) are the ones that tend to be unaffected by responses to other dilemmas.

One way of making sense of these asymmetrical transfer effects might be to note that the emotional response raised by the footbridge dilemma may carry over to the next (trolley) dilemma, whereas no such emotion is raised by the trolley dilemma when it is encountered first. This explanation seems particularly compelling given Valdesolo and DeSteno's (2006) finding that inducing emotions with a comedy video clip changed responses on the footbridge dilemma, and given Schnall et al.'s (2008) and Eskine et al.'s (2011) arguments for embodied accounts of moral judgment.

Yet alternative accounts can also effectively explain the asymmetry in transfer effects by appealing to reasoning alone. For example, Wiegmann and Waldmann (2014) proposed a **causal model theory of transfer effects** in moral reasoning, such that people transfer the answer they gave to one dilemma to the other dilemma by analogy (as opposed to emotional carry-over). In both the trolley dilemma and the footbridge dilemma, your action saves five people and kills one. However, the causal models describing the trolley scenario versus the footbridge scenario are different. The trolley dilemma illustrates a common-cause structure (see Figure 14.1a) in which your action of flipping the switch (i.e., the cause) simultaneously causes the death of one and the saving of a group of five (i.e., on two separate causal paths). Wiegmann and Waldmann (2014) hypothesized that the common-cause structure allows people to think about the five being saved without necessarily also being forced to think about the one who is being killed. Furthermore, one can envision a possible situation in which the one person is able to spring aside and avoid being hit by the trolley; thus, the negative aspect of the common-cause structure (i.e., killing one person) is inherently *ambiguous*.

The footbridge dilemma, in contrast, illustrates a causal chain structure (see Figure 14.1b) in which your action of pushing the one person causes his

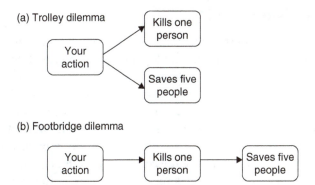

(a) Trolley dilemma

Your action

Kills one person

Saves five people

(b) Footbridge dilemma

Your action → Kills one person → Saves five people

Figure 14.1 Causal structures of the trolley and foot-bridge dilemmas. (a) Trolley dilemma. (b) Footbridge dilemma. (Wiegmann & Waldmann 2014)

death, which in turn causes the group of five to be saved (i.e., everything occurs on the same causal path; Wiegmann & Waldmann 2014). Given the causal chain structure of the footbridge dilemma, killing the person is quite salient to you because you would have kill one in order to save the other five. That is, the negative aspect of the footbridge dilemma (i.e., killing one person) is quite *unambiguous*. The causal model theory proposes that the intuitions people have about an unambiguous moral scenario will transfer to an ambiguous one, but their intuitions about an ambiguous scenario will not transfer to an unambiguous one. In a series of studies, Wiegmann and Wald-mann (2014) showed that the predictions of their theory were supported even when the unambiguous moral scenario was positive in nature. These predictions were also supported with transfer effects between new dilemmas, whose causal structure (i.e., common-cause versus causal chain) were manip-ulated just as in the trolley versus footbridge dilemmas.

Recent work also suggests that people make utilitarian responses much more frequently on both the trolley and footbridge dilemmas if the conse-quences of both action and inaction are made crystal clear (Kusev, van Schaik, Alzahrani, Lonigro, & Purser 2016). That is, if it is explicitly stated in the dilemma what would happen if one chooses *not* to act (i.e., one will be saved and five will be killed), people are more likely to say that they would act to save the five over the one. This framing of the problem may make it clearer to people that not taking action is a real moral decision that has concrete consequences. In addition, stating what would happen if one chooses not to act takes all possible ambiguity out of the moral dilemma. In sum, moral decision-making may be influenced by affect, but can also be explained by the causal structures of moral scenarios. More work is needed to examine whether, and how, affective and cognitive factors interact to drive decisions.

Social decision-making

Now, let's consider another dilemma. If my two siblings and I are each holding one of three doughnuts, and I quickly grab and eat all three doughnuts, I will experience a lot of enjoyment, but my siblings will not. This is an example of what is known as a zero-sum game, in which the possible gains and losses among a set of players equals zero. In this example, I and my two siblings each started with one doughnut; when I gained two, they each lost one (+2 − 1 − 1 = 0). Choosing whether to maximize your own utility (Chapter 8) or to maximize the collective good for a group is the final major issue in moral decision-making we'll consider in this chapter. As in the doughnut example, maximizing one's own utility can sometimes directly clash with maximizing the utility of the group, especially when resources are limited or finite. For example, in the scenario known as the tragedy of the commons, we are asked to imagine a number of cattle farmers who have decided to share a fenced-in piece of land (the "commons") on which they can let their cattle graze in safety (Hardin 1968). If all the individual farmers then try to increase their personal wealth by adding more and more cows, this is good for their personal holdings, but ultimately bad for the group of farmers, as each additional cow will contribute toward overgrazing in the commons. The tragedy, according to Hardin (1968), occurs when each farmer strives endlessly toward gain within a cooperative system that has natural limits, eventually causing so much overgrazing in the commons that it is no longer usable by anyone. Of course, on the flip side, farmers who hold back on purchasing cattle for the good of everyone will end up owning fewer cows than those who chose to prioritize their own gain.

Game theory and the psychology of cooperative decision-making

In many different situations in life, just as in the tragedy of the commons, the consequences of your choices may affect and be affected by other people's choices. If you turn down your first-choice college to go to another college with your best friend from high school, you do so on the assumption that your friend will also choose to enroll in the same college. However, the college choice that your friend makes will greatly influence the consequences of the choice you made, and vice-versa. Game theory is the study of how people's choices interact with one another to affect the utility of the outcomes for each person involved (Ross 2016; von Neumann & Morgenstern 1944/2007). Perhaps the most important contribution of game theory to understanding people's decision-making is that it accounts for how people may often need to consider not only their own preferences but also their *expectations* about other people's preferences and how they will behave.

One of the most common problems studied in game theory is the prisoner's dilemma (Flood 1958; Kuhn 2017; Tucker 1983), a decision scenario which forces people to choose between maximizing personal utility versus group utility in a situation where the other person in the group is also making a choice that affects the utility of your choice. Suppose that two accomplices, whom we'll call Ko and Po, are arrested on suspicion of theft and are held in different cells. First, let's assume that both Ko and Po care a lot about themselves and aren't concerned with the welfare of the other person, and that each dislikes the prospect of jail equally. If they cooperate with one another by both staying silent, then they will both be arraigned for possessing stolen goods, and will each serve 1 year in jail (see Figure 14.2). If one of them cooperates with the other by staying silent, but the other defects by confessing, then the one who confessed will go free, but the one who stayed silent will go to jail for 3 years for theft. If both of them defect, offering confessions, then they'll both be convicted of theft, but the prosecutor will be more lenient, only seeking to keep them each in jail for 2 years. In game theory, the Nash **equilibrium** (Nash 1950) can be thought of as the solution in which any given player cannot achieve a better outcome by a unilateral change of decision. In this particular example, the Nash equilibrium is for both Ko and Po to defect. Put yourself in Ko's shoes, for example. The key to understanding the Nash equilibrium is to assume that you cannot force Po to cooperate with you and stay silent – the only decision you can make is your own. If Po defects by confessing, your best move is to defect as well, because you'd only have

		Po's choice	
		Cooperate	*Defect*
		(stay silent)	(confess)
	Cooperate	Ko: 1 year	Ko: 3 years
	(stay silent)	Po: 1 year	Po: 0 years
Ko's choice	*Defect*	Ko: 0 years	Ko: 2 years
	(confess)	Po: 3 years	Po: 2 years

Figure 14.2 A version of the prisoner's dilemma.

to serve 2 years in jail. If Po cooperates by staying silent, your best move is still to defect by confessing, because then you would serve no jail time. Either way, assuming you can't force Po to cooperate, your best choice is to defect.

Given that the Nash equilibrium for the above version of the prisoner's dilemma is always to defect, this might raise some questions about how cooperation does emerge in societies. First, it turns out that when people are presented with the prisoner's dilemma in behavioral studies, they actually tend to cooperate more than one might have guessed. For example, Khadjavi and Lange (2013) found that prisoners serving time in Germany showed a 55% cooperation rate when playing prisoner's dilemma games (where the potential payoffs were phone call credits). When applying game theory to gain some insight into how cooperative societies evolved, we might also need to consider that people may often have to play competitive games with the same people over and over. For example, today you and your siblings have three doughnuts, but looking ahead to tomorrow, the three of you might have three pieces of pizza then, and so on. It might not make sense for you to grab and eat all the doughnuts today if you consider that your siblings might retaliate tomorrow by eating all the pizza. Knowing that you have some unspecified number of games coming up with these same players in the future, would your strategy change?

In an early competition conducted by Axelrod (1984), professional game theorists submitted programs to play the prisoner's dilemma game repeatedly (i.e., hundreds of times). The idea was to figure out if there was a way in which cooperative societies could have emerged within the structure of the prisoner's dilemma game. Interestingly, the programs that performed the best in this competition all contained *cooperative* elements. The winning program, developed by Anatol Rapoport and entitled **Tit for Tat**, always made the cooperative choice first (Kuhn 2017). After that, it always made the same choice that its opponent program had made on the previous round. Thus, as Axelrod (1984) pointed out, the Tit for Tat program was never the first player to defect, and would cooperate for as long as the other player did so; yet it wasn't a blind or overly naïve cooperator, as it did retaliate against the other player for defecting by doing the same on the next round. It did not pursue long-term revenge, however; once the other player went back to cooperating, it would immediately follow suit, essentially forgiving the other player for previous defections. It did not contain any rules concerned with outscoring its opponent, and thus it won the competition without being directly competitive in nature. Furthermore, in the next iterative prisoner's dilemma competition, Tit for Tat won again, even though all the programmers already knew what it would do and had had time to create a program to beat it (see also Kuhn 2017). Whether or not programs such as Tit for Tat can teach us how cooperative societies evolved is perhaps debatable, but they can certainly be treated as hypotheses as to how people might optimally behave in such situations.

Cooperation toward public goods

Public goods are benefits that are made available to everyone, and which are made possible by the collective contributions (in money or time) of multiple individuals (Parks, Joireman, & Van Lange 2013). For example, public parks and playgrounds, food pantries, and highways are made possible by the contributions of individuals, but everyone can use them. Classic theories of rationality would predict that in a rational world, public goods would never exist, because it makes more sense for individuals to try to benefit from public goods without contributing (i.e., **free riding**; Parks et al. 2013). Such accounts predict that because each individual will see that it makes the most personal sense to free ride, no one will contribute, and ultimately no public goods will be offered. Yet we see public goods emerge in some form in virtually every society (Parks et al. 2013).

How is it that people end up deciding to give toward public goods? One helpful insight is that not everyone does give – unless required (e.g., via taxes). In voluntary giving, there appear to be clear individual differences in the degree to which people think equality, fairness, and reciprocity are highly important (Haidt 2012). Van Lange, Liebrand, and Kuhlman (1990) suggested that this translates to individual differences in what kind of giving behavior is thought to be rational. They argued that those who are "prosocial" tend to believe that cooperative behaviors are rational within a society, and those who are "proself" hold beliefs more in line with the classic rationality view – that non-cooperative behaviors are rational (Van Lange et al. 1990). People who are prosocial tend to choose to cooperate because they have a strong sense of social responsibility and feel that it is important for everyone to gain (De Cremer & Van Lange 2001). In contrast, those who are proself tend to only want to cooperate to the extent that others are cooperating. However, when people who are proself feel strongly committed to a social group, they can be more easily convinced to cooperate (Parks et al. 2013).

Another line of work suggests that cooperative, contributing behavior will only occur when people know that there is a particular goal to be achieved and they have reason to believe that others will also pitch in (Pruitt & Kimmel 1977). That is, people cooperate when they can reasonably expect that a goal will be met if they take part. In addition, Yamagishi (1986) proposed a *structural goal expectation hypothesis*, in which people find it hard to believe that they can easily persuade others to cooperate unless they have a way to pressure them to do so. People are motivated to set up a social system that applies this pressure; for example, a system that would encourage cooperation and punish non-cooperation. Then, people have to choose whether to become part of this social system; this can be seen as a secondary system of cooperation toward the common good (Yamagishi 1986).

In a comprehensive model, Parks et al. (2013) argued that the features of the decision itself (e.g., how it is framed, what the potential payoffs are, and so on) give rise to an initial, self-centered gut preference (e.g., preferring not to cooperate). Then, people may become motivated to reassess their preference with more social good in mind. For example, being in a collectivist culture, having a prosocial value orientation, being someone who tends to trust others, and being better able to think about future consequences can all influence people's ability and motivation to rethink the problem from a more prosocial perspective (Parks et al. 2013). Additional features of the situation can also affect whether people ultimately choose to cooperate toward achieving a collective goal, including the size of the group (e.g., larger groups reduce cooperation, as in the problem of global warming), whether people have reason to fear sanctions if they do not cooperate, and whether people socially identify with the group and feel respected by its leaders (Parks et al. 2013).

Summary

We often wonder whether we have done the right thing, we pass judgment and punishment upon those who have violated our notions of right and wrong, and we assess the degree to which we think someone is morally responsible for an action given various extenuating circumstances. Morality is so important to us that we may even think of it as forming the core, or essence, of our identities. Yet exactly what people think is good moral reasoning differs by gender, age, socioeconomic status, and culture. Our moral judgments are often strongly influenced by our somatic states, yet we hold the illusion that we are rationalists who make moral judgments on the basis of reason rather than feelings. Often it would be in our best personal interest to maximize our own utility, but cooperative behavior, public goods, moral codes, and legal systems still emerge in every society. This curious paradox is worthy of further study.

Questions for discussion

1. From a scientific point of view, what are the pros and cons of using and reusing the same experimental materials across a great many studies on moral judgments? For example, consider the trolley and footbridge dilemmas, the Kohlberg (1971) moral dilemmas, or the Haidt et al. (1993) vignettes.

2. How compelling were the cognitive neuroscience findings in the current chapter? Did they add to your understanding of moral judgment? Formulate your response in the context of our discussion of drawing inferences from cognitive neuroscience research in Chapter 12.

Suggestions for further reading

Haidt, J. (2012). *The righteous mind: Why good people are divided by politics and religion*. New York, NY: Random House.

Lakoff, G. (2010). *Moral politics: How liberals and conservatives think* (2nd ed.). Chicago, IL: University of Chicago Press.

References

Ahn, W., Kalish, C. W., Medin, D. L., & Gelman, S. A. (1995). The role of covariation versus mechanism information in causal attribution. *Cognition, 54*(3), 299–352.

Ahn, W., Novick, L., & Kim, N. S. (2003). Understanding behavior makes it more normal. *Psychonomic Bulletin & Review, 10*(3), 746–752.

Akerlof, K., Maibach, E. W., Fitzgerald, D., Cedeno, A. Y., & Neuman, A. (2013). Do people "personally experience" global warming, and if so how, and does it matter? *Global Environmental Change, 23*(1), 81–91.

Allais, M. (1953). Le comportement de l'homme rationnel devant le risque: Critique des postulats et axiomes de l'école américaine. *Econometrica: Journal of the Econometric Society, 21*(4), 503–546.

Allais, M. (1990). Allais paradox. In J. Eatwell, M. Milgate, & P. Newman (Eds.), *Utility and probability* (pp. 3–9). London, UK: The Macmillan Press Limited.

Ambrose, S. E. (2002). *To America: Personal reflections of a historian.* New York, NY: Simon and Schuster.

American Psychiatric Association. (1994). *Diagnostic and statistical manual of mental disorders* (4th edition). Washington, DC: Author.

American Psychiatric Association. (2013). *Diagnostic and statistical manual of mental disorders* (5th edition). Arlington, VA: American Psychiatric Publishing.

Anderson, N. E., & Kiehl, K. A. (2012). The psychopath magnetized: Insights from brain imaging. *Trends in Cognitive Sciences, 16*(1), 52–60.

Anderson, N. H. (1965). Primacy effects in personality impression formation using a generalized order effect paradigm. *Journal of Personality and Social Psychology, 2*(1), 1–9.

Anderson, N. H., & Barrios, A. A. (1961). Primacy effects in personality impression formation. *The Journal of Abnormal and Social Psychology, 63*(2), 346–350.

Anomaly, J. (2013). Review of *The manipulation of choice: Ethics and libertarian paternalism. The Independent Review, 18*(2), 301–305.

Arkes, H. R. (1981). Impediments to accurate clinical judgment and possible ways to minimize their impact. *Journal of Consulting and Clinical Psychology, 49*(3), 323–330.

Arkes, H. R., & Ayton, P. (1999). The sunk cost and Concorde effects: Are humans less rational than lower animals? *Psychological Bulletin, 125*(5), 591–600.

Arkes, H. R., & Blumer, C. (1985). The psychology of sunk cost. *Organizational Behavior and Human Decision Processes, 35*(1), 124–140.

Arkes, H. R., & Harkness, A. R. (1983). Estimates of contingency between two dichotomous variables. *Journal of Experimental Psychology: General, 112*(1), 117–135.

Asada, S. (2007). *Culture shock and Japanese-American relations: Historical essays.* Columbia, MO: University of Missouri Press.

Asch, S. E. (1946). Forming impressions of personality. *The Journal of Abnormal and Social Psychology, 41*(3), 258–290.

Axelrod, R. (1984). *The evolution of cooperation*. New York, NY: Basic Books.

Bahník, S., & Strack, F. (2016). Overlap of accessible information undermines the anchoring effect. *Judgment and Decision Making, 11*(1), 92–98.

Bar-Hillel, M. (1980). The base-rate fallacy in probability judgments. *Acta Psychologica, 44*, 211–233.

Barberis, N. C. (2013). Thirty years of prospect theory in economics: A review and assessment. *Journal of Economic Perspectives, 27*(1), 173–196.

Baron, J., & Hershey, J. C. (1988). Outcome bias in decision evaluation. *Journal of Personality and Social Psychology, 54*(4), 569–579.

Baron-Cohen, S., Leslie, A. M., & Frith, U. (1985). Does the autistic child have a "theory of mind"? *Cognition, 21*(1), 37–46.

Bayen, U. J., Erdfelder, E., Bearden, N. J., & Lozito, J. P. (2006). The interplay of memory and judgment processes in effects of aging on hindsight bias. *Journal of Experimental Psychology: Learning, Memory, and Cognition, 32*(5), 1003–1018.

Bechara, A., Damasio, H., & Damasio, A. R. (2000). Emotion, decision making and the orbitofrontal cortex. *Cerebral Cortex, 10*(3), 295–307.

Bekker, H. L., Hewison, J., & Thornton, J. G. (2004). Applying decision analysis to facilitate informed decision making about prenatal diagnosis for Down syndrome: A randomised controlled trial. *Prenatal Diagnosis, 24*, 265–275.

Bell, D. E., Raiffa, H., & Tversky, A. (1988). Descriptive, normative, and prescriptive interactions in decision making. In D. E. Bell, H. Raiffa, & A. Tversky (Eds.), *Decision making: Descriptive, normative, and prescriptive interactions* (pp. 9–32). Cambridge, UK: Cambridge University Press.

Bennis, W. M., & Medin, D. L. (2010). Weirdness is in the eye of the beholder. *Behavioral and Brain Sciences, 33*(2–3), 25–26.

Bentham, J. (1789/1907). *An introduction to the principles of morals and legislation*. Oxford, UK: Clarendon Press.

Berens, C., Witteman, C. L. M., & van de Ven, M. O. M. (2015). Is understanding why necessary for treatment choices? *European Journal of Psychological Assessment, 27*(2), 81–87.

Bering, J. M. (2006). The folk psychology of souls. *Behavioral and Brain Sciences, 29*(05), 453–462.

Bernstein, D. M., Atance, C., Loftus, G. R., & Meltzoff, A. N. (2004). We saw it all along: Visual hindsight bias in children and adults. *Psychological Science, 15*(4), 264–267.

Bernstein, D. M, Erdfelder, E., Meltzoff, A. N., Peria, W., & Loftus, G. R. (2011). Hindsight bias from 3 to 95 years of age. *Journal of Experimental Psychology: Learning, Memory, and Cognition, 37*(2), 378–391.

Bernstein, J. (2013). Controlling Medicare with lessons from endowment effect experiments. *California Western Law Review, 49*(2), 169–193.

Birch, S. A. J., & Bernstein, D. M. (2007). What can children tell us about hindsight bias: A fundamental constraint on perspective-taking? *Social Cognition, 25*(1), 98–113.

Birch, S. A. J., & Bloom, P. (2007). The curse of knowledge in reasoning about false beliefs. *Psychological Science, 18*(5), 382–386.

Blackwell, L. S., Trzesniewski, K. H., & Dweck, C. S. (2007). Implicit theories of intelligence predict achievement across an adolescent transition: A longitudinal study and an intervention. *Child Development, 78*(1), 246–263.

Blaisdell, A. P., Sawa, K., Leising, K. J., & Waldmann, M. R. (2006). Causal reasoning in rats. *Science, 311*(5763), 1020–1022.

Blank, H., & Nestler, S. (2006). Perceiving events as both inevitable and unforeseeable in hindsight: The Leipzig candidacy for the Olympics. *British Journal of Social Psychology, 45*(1), 149–160.

Bloom, P. (2004). *Descartes' baby: How the science of child development explains what makes us human.* New York, NY: Basic Books.

Blumenthal-Barby, J. S., & Krieger, H. (2015). Cognitive biases and heuristics in medical decision making: A critical review using a systematic search strategy. *Medical Decision Making, 35*, 539–557.

Bodenhausen, G. V., & Wyer, R. S. (1985). Effects of stereotypes in decision making and information-processing strategies. *Journal of Personality and Social Psychology, 48*(2), 267–282.

Bower, G. H. (1981). Mood and memory. *American Psychologist, 36*(2), 129–148.

Bower, G. H., Black, J. B., & Turner, T. J. (1979). Scripts in memory for text. *Cognitive Psychology, 11*(2), 177–220.

Bransford, J. D., & Johnson, M. K. (1972). Contextual prerequisites for understanding: Some investigations of comprehension and recall. *Journal of Verbal Learning and Verbal Behavior, 11*, 717–726.

Brehm, S. S., & Brehm, J. W. (1981). *Psychological reactance: A theory of freedom and control.* New York, NY: Academic Press.

Briggs, R. (2015, Winter). Normative theories of rational choice: Expected utility. In E. N. Zalta (Ed.), *The Stanford encyclopedia of philosophy.* Retrieved from http://plato.stanford. edu/archives/win2015/entries/rationality-normative-utility.

Brinkman-Stoppelenburg, A., Rietjens, J. A., & van der Heide, A. (2014). The effects of advance care planning on end-of-life care: A systematic review. *Palliative Medicine, 28*(8), 1000–1025.

Bucchianeri, G. W., & Minson, J. A. (2013). A homeowner's dilemma: Anchoring in residential real estate transactions. *Journal of Economic Behavior & Organization, 89*(5), 76–92.

Buehner, M. J. (2012). Understanding the past, predicting the future: Causation, not intentional action, is the root of temporal binding. *Psychological Science, 23*(12), 1490–1497.

Butcher, J. N., Atlis, M. M., & Hahn, J. (2003). The Minnesota Multiphasic Personality Inventory-2 (MMPI-2). In M. J. Hilsenroth, D. L. Segal, & M. Herson (Eds.), *Comprehensive handbook of psychological assessment: Personality assessment* (Vol. 2, pp. 30–38). Hoboken, NJ: John Wiley & Sons, Inc.

Butcher, J. N., Dahlstrom, W. G., Graham, J. R., Tellegen, A. M., & Kreammer, B. (1989). *The Minnesota Multiphasic Personality Inventory-2 (MMPI-2) manual for administration and scoring.* Minneapolis, MN: University of Minnesota Press.

Butler, C. (2009). In serial killer's former home, a search for ghosts. *National Public Radio (U.S.).* Retrieved from www.npr.org/templates/story/story.php?storyId=114303723.

Chapman, G. B. (1996). Temporal discounting and utility for health and money. *Journal of Experimental Psychology: Learning, Memory, and Cognition, 22*(3), 771–791.

Chapman, G. B., & Johnson, E. J. (1994). The limits of anchoring. *Journal of Behavioral Decision Making, 7*(4), 223–242.

Chapman, G. B., & Johnson, E. J. (2002). Incorporating the irrelevant: Anchors in judgments of belief and value. In T. Gilovich, D. Griffin, & D. Kahneman (Eds.), *Heuristics and biases: The psychology of intuitive judgment* (pp. 120–138). Cambridge, UK: Cambridge University Press.

Charman, S. D. (2013). The forensic confirmation bias: A problem of evidence integration, not just evidence evaluation. *Journal of Applied Research in Memory and Cognition, 2*(1), 56–58.

Cheng, P. W., & Novick, L. R. (1990). A probabilistic contrast model of causal induction. *Journal of Personality and Social Psychology, 58*(4), 545–567.

Chernev, A., Böckenholt, U., & Goodman, J. (2015). Choice overload: A conceptual review and meta-analysis. *Journal of Consumer Psychology, 25*(2), 333–358.

Choi, I., & Nisbett, R. E. (2000). Cultural psychology of surprise: Holistic theories and recognition of contradiction. *Journal of Personality and Social Psychology, 79*(6), 890–905.

Chou, H. T. G., & Edge, N. (2012). "They are happier and having better lives than I am": The impact of using Facebook on perceptions of others' lives. *Cyberpsychology, Behavior, and Social Networking, 15*(2), 117–121.

Christensen-Szalanski, J. J. (1984). Discount functions and the measurement of patients' values. Women's decisions during childbirth. *Medical Decision Making, 4*(1), 47–58.

Clancy, S. A., McNally, R. J., Schacter, D. L., Lenzenweger, M. F., & Pitman, R. K. (2002). Memory distortion in people reporting abduction by aliens. *Journal of Abnormal Psychology, 111*(3), 455–461.

Clarke, S. (2002). Conspiracy theories and conspiracy theorizing. *Philosophy of the Social Sciences, 32*(2), 131–150.

Coltheart, M. (2013). How can functional neuroimaging inform cognitive theories? *Perspectives on Psychological Science, 8*(1), 98–103.

Cosmides, L. (1989). The logic of social exchange: Has natural selection shaped how humans reason? Studies with the Wason selection task. *Cognition, 31*(3), 187–276.

Cox, M., & Tanford, S. (1989). Effects of evidence and instructions in civil trials: An experimental investigation of rules of admissibility. *Social Behaviour, 4*(1), 31–55.

Croskerry, P. (2002). Achieving quality in clinical decision making: Cognitive strategies and detection of bias. *Academic Emergency Medicine, 9*(11), 1184–1204.

Damasio, A. (1994). *Descartes' error: Emotion, reason, and the human brain.* New York, NY: G. P. Putnam's Sons.

Damasio, H., Grabowski, T., Frank, R., Galaburda, A. M., & Damasio, A. R. (1994). The return of Phineas Gage: Clues about the brain from the skull of a famous patient. *Science, 264*(5162), 1102–1105.

Danziger, S., Levav, J., & Avnaim-Pesso, L. (2011). Extraneous factors in judicial decisions. *Proceedings of the National Academy of Sciences, 108*(17), 6889–6892.

Darwin, C. (1876). *The autobiography of Charles Darwin: From the life and letters of Charles Darwin.* Retrieved from www.gutenberg.org/files/2010/2010-h/2010-h.htm.

Davies, M., & White, P. A. (1994). Use of the availability heuristic by children. *British Journal of Developmental Psychology, 12*(4), 503–505.

Dawes, R. M. (1994). *House of cards: Psychology and psychotherapy built on myth.* New York, NY: The Free Press.

Dawes, R. M., Faust, D., & Meehl, P. E. (1989). Clinical versus actuarial judgment. *Science, 243*(4899), 1668–1674.

Dawson, N. V., & Arkes, H. R. (1987). Systematic errors in medical decision making. *Journal of General Internal Medicine, 2*(3), 183–187.

De Cremer, D., & Van Lange, P. A. M. (2001). Why prosocials exhibit greater coopera-tion than proselfs: The role of social responsibility and reciprocity. *European Journal of Personality, 15*(S1), S5–S18.

de Kwaadsteniet, L., Hagmayer, Y., Krol, N. P., & Witteman, C. L. (2010). Causal client models in selecting effective interventions: A cognitive mapping study. *Psychological Assessment, 22*(3), 581–592.

De Los Reyes, A., & Marsh, J. K. (2011). Patients' contexts and their effects on clinicians' impressions of conduct disorder symptoms. *Journal of Clinical Child & Adolescent Psychology, 40*(3), 479–485.

de Oliveira-Souza, R., Hare, R. D., Bramati, I. E., Garrido, G. J., Ignácio, F. A., Tovar-Moll, F., & Moll, J. (2008). Psychopathy as a disorder of the moral brain: Fronto-temporo-limbic grey matter reductions demonstrated by voxel-based morphometry. *Neuroimage, 40*(3), 1202–1213.

Dennett, D. (1987). *The intentional stance.* Cambridge, MA: MIT Press.

Ding, D., Maibach, E., Zhao, X., Roser-Renouf, C., & Leserowitz, A. (2011). Support for climate policy and societal action are linked to perceptions about scientific agreement. *Nature Climate Change, 1,* 462–466.

Ditto, P. H., Hawkins, N. A., & Pizarro, D. A. (2005). Imagining the end of life: On the psychol-ogy of advance medical decision making. *Motivation and Emotion, 29*(4), 475–496.

Ditto, P. H., Smucker, W. D., Danks, J. H., Jacobson, J. A., Houts, R. M., Fagerlin, A., ... & Gready, R. M. (2003). Stability of older adults' preferences for life-sustaining medical treatment. *Health Psychology, 22*(6), 605–615.

Dorling, D. (2016). Brexit: The decision of a divided country. *The BMJ, 354,* i3697.

Douglas, K. M., & Sutton, R. M. (2008). The hidden impact of conspiracy theories: Perceived and actual influence of theories surrounding the death of Princess Diana. *The Journal of Social Psychology, 148*(2), 210–222.

Drayton, M. (2009). The Minnesota Multiphasic Personality Inventory-2 (MMPI-2). *Occupational Medicine, 59*(2), 135–136.

Dror, I. E. (2009). How can Francis Bacon help forensic science? The four idols of human biases. *Jurimetrics: The Journal of Law, Science, and Technology, 50*(1), 93–110.

Dror, I. E., & Charlton, D. (2006). Why experts make errors. *Journal of Forensic Identification, 56*(4), 600–616.

Dweck, C. S., Chiu, C. Y., & Hong, Y. Y. (1995). Implicit theories and their role in judgments and reactions: A word from two perspectives. *Psychological Inquiry, 6*(4), 267–285.

Dyer, J. S., Fishburn, P. C., Steuer, R. E., Wallenius, J., & Zionts, S. (1992). Multiple criteria decision making, multiattribute utility theory: The next ten years. *Management Science, 38*(5), 645–654.

Ecker, U. K., Lewandowsky, S., & Apai, J. (2011). Terrorists brought down the plane! – No, actually it was a technical fault: Processing corrections of emotive information. *The Quarterly Journal of Experimental Psychology, 64*(2), 283–310.

Ecker, U. K., Lewandowsky, S., Swire, B., & Chang, D. (2011). Correcting false information in memory: Manipulating the strength of misinformation encoding and its retraction. *Psychonomic Bulletin & Review, 18*(3), 570–578.

Eddy, D. M. (1982). Probabilistic reasoning in clinical medicine: Problems and opportunities. In D. Kahneman, P. Slovic, & A. Tversky (Eds.), *Judgment under uncertainty: Heuristics and biases* (pp. 249–267). Cambridge, UK: Cambridge University Press.

Eder, E., Turic, K., Milasowszky, N., Van Adzin, K., & Hergovich, A. (2011). The relationships between paranormal belief, creationism, intelligent design and evolution at secondary schools in Vienna (Austria). *Science & Education, 20*(5–6), 517–534.

Edwards, W. (1954). The theory of decision making. *Psychological Bulletin, 51*(4), 380–417.

Einhorn, J. H., & Hogarth, R. M. (1978). Confidence in judgment: Persistence of the illusion of validity. *Psychological Review, 85*(5), 395–416.

Einhorn, H. J., & Hogarth, R. M. (1986). Judging probable cause. *Psychological Bulletin, 99*(1), 3–19.

Ellis, H. M. (1970). *The application of decision analysis to the problem of choosing an air pollution control program for New York City* (Unpublished doctoral dissertation). Harvard University, Cambridge, MA.

Elstein, A. S. (1999). Heuristics and biases: Selected errors in clinical reasoning. *Academic Medicine, 74*(7), 791–794.

Emmons, K. M., Linnan, L. A., Shadel, W. G., Marcus, B., & Abrams, D. B. (1999). The Working Healthy Project: A worksite health-promotion trial targeting physical activity, diet, and smoking. *Journal of Occupational and Environmental Medicine, 41*(7), 545–555.

Epley, N., & Gilovich, T. (2001). Putting adjustment back in the anchoring and adjustment heuristic: Differential processing of self-generated and experimenter-provided anchors. *Psychological Science, 12*(5), 391–396.

Erdfelder, E., & Buchner, A. (1998). Decomposing the hindsight bias: A multinomial processing tree model for separating recollection and reconstruction in hindsight. *Journal of Experimental Psychology: Learning, Memory, and Cognition, 24*(2), 387–414.

Ericson, K. M. M., & Fuster, A. (2014). The endowment effect. *Annual Review of Economics, 6*, 555–579.

Eskine, K. J., Kacinik, N. A., & Prinz, J. J. (2011). A bad taste in the mouth: Gustatory disgust influences moral judgment. *Psychological Science, 22*(3), 295–299.

Estrada, C. A., Isen, A. M., & Young, M. J. (1997). Positive affect facilitates integration of information and decreases anchoring in reasoning among physicians. *Organizational Behavior and Human Decision Processes, 72*(1), 117–135.

Evans, J. S. B. (1984). Heuristic and analytic processes in reasoning. *British Journal of Psychology, 75*(4), 451–468.

Evans, J. S. B. (2008). Dual-processing accounts of reasoning, judgment, and social cognition. *Annual Review of Psychology, 59*, 255–278.

Evans, J. S. B., & Stanovich, K. E. (2013). Dual-process theories of higher cognition: Advancing the debate. *Perspectives on Psychological Science, 8*(3), 223–241.

Fan, J., & Levine, R. A. (2007). To amnio or not to amnio: That is the decision for Bayes. *Chance, 20*, 26–32.

Farah, M. J., & Hook, C. J. (2013). The seductive allure of "seductive allure." *Perspectives on Psychological Science, 8*(1), 88–90.

Finucane, M. L., Alhakami, A., Slovic, P., & Johnson, S. M. (2000). The affect heuristic in judgments of risks and benefits. *Journal of Behavioral Decision Making, 13*, 1–17.

Fischhoff, B. (1975). Hindsight ≠ foresight: The effect of outcome knowledge on judgment under uncertainty. *Journal of Experimental Psychology: Human Perception and Performance, 1*(3), 288–299.

Fischhoff, B. (1977). Perceived informativeness of facts. *Journal of Experimental Psychology: Human Perception and Performance, 3*(2), 349–358.

Fischhoff, B., & Beyth, R. (1975). "I knew it would happen:" Remembered probabilities of once-future things. *Organizational Behavior and Human Performance, 13*(1), 1–16.

Fischhoff, B., Slovic, P., Lichtenstein, S., Read, S., & Combs, B. (1978). How safe is safe enough? A psychometric study of attitudes towards technological risks and benefits. *Policy Sciences, 9*, 127–152.

Fishburn, P. C. (1970). *Utility theory for decision making*. New York, NY: John Wiley & Sons, Inc.

Flavin, M., & Yamashita, T. (2002). Owner-occupied housing and the composition of the household portfolio. *The American Economic Review, 92*(1), 345–362.

Flood, M. M. (1958). Some experimental games. *Management Science, 5*(1), 5–26.

Flores, A., Cobos, P. L., López, F. J., Godoy, A., & González-Martín, E. (2014). The influence of causal connections between symptoms on the diagnosis of mental disorders: Evidence from online and offline measures. *Journal of Experimental Psychology: Applied, 20*(3), 175–190.

Foddai, A. C., Grant, I. R., & Dean, M. (2016). Efficacy of instant hand sanitizers against foodborne pathogens compared with hand washing with soap and water in food preparation settings: A systematic review. *Journal of Food Protection, 79*(6), 1040–1054.

Fox, J., & Bailenson, J. N. (2009). Virtual self-modeling: The effects of vicarious reinforcement and identification on exercise behaviors. *Media Psychology, 12*(1), 1–25.

Franklin, B. (1818). *The private correspondence of Benjamin Franklin* (Vol. I, 3rd Ed. (revised), p. 259). London, UK: Henry Colburn.

Frederick, S. (2005). Cognitive reflection and decision making. *The Journal of Economic Perspectives, 19*(4), 25–42.

Freedman, J. L., Martin, C. K., & Mota, V. L. (1998). Pretrial publicity: Effects of admonition and expressing pretrial opinions. *Legal and Criminological Psychology, 3*(2), 255–270.

French, C. C., Santomauro, J., Hamilton, V., Fox, R., & Thalbourne, M. A. (2008). Psychological aspects of the alien contact experience. *Cortex, 44*(10), 1387–1395.

Fugelsang, J. A., & Thompson, V. A. (2003). A dual-process model of belief and evidence interactions in causal reasoning. *Memory & Cognition, 31*(5), 800–815.

Furedi, A. (1999). The public health implications of the 1995 'pill scare.' *Human Reproduction Update, 5*, 621–626.

Furnham, A., & Boo, H. C. (2011). A literature review of the anchoring effect. *The Journal of Socio-Economics, 40*(1), 35–42.

Galotti, K. M. (1995). A longitudinal study of real-life decision making: Choosing a college. *Applied Cognitive Psychology, 9*(6), 459–484.

Galotti, K. M. (2007). Decision structuring in important real-life choices. *Psychological Science, 18*(4), 320–325.

Garb, H. N. (1998). *Studying the clinician*. Washington, DC: American Psychological Association.

Garg, A. X., Adhikari, N. K., McDonald, H., Rosas-Arellano, M. P., Devereaux, P. J., Beyene, J., ... & Haynes, R. B. (2005). Effects of computerized clinical decision support systems on practitioner performance and patient outcomes: A systematic review. *JAMA, 293*(10), 1223–1238.

Gawande, A. (2014). *Being mortal: Medicine and what matters in the end.* New York, NY: Metropolitan Books.

Geisel, T. S. (1960/1988). *Green eggs and ham.* New York, NY: Random House, Inc.

George, J. F., Duffy, K., & Ahuja, M. (2000). Countering the anchoring and adjustment bias with decision support systems. *Decision Support Systems, 29*(2), 195–206.

Ghosh, V. E., Moscovitch, M., Colella, B. M., & Gilboa, A. (2014). Schema representation in patients with ventromedial PFC lesions. *The Journal of Neuroscience, 34*(36), 12057–12070.

Gigerenzer, G. (1996). On narrow norms and vague heuristics: A reply to Kahneman and Tversky. *Psychological Review, 103*(3), 592–596.

Gigerenzer, G. (2004). Dread risk, September 11, and fatal traffic accidents. *Psychological Science, 15,* 286–287.

Gigerenzer, G. (2007). *Gut feelings: The intelligence of the unconscious.* New York, NY: Penguin Group (USA), Inc.

Gigerenzer, G., Gaissmaier, W., Kurz-Milcke, E., Schwartz, L. M., & Woloshin, S. (2008). Helping doctors and patients make sense of health statistics. *Psychological Science in the Public Interest, 8,* 53–96.

Gigerenzer, G., & Goldstein, D. G. (1999). Betting on one good reason: The take the best heuristic. In G. Gigerenzer, P. M. Todd, & the ABC Research Group (Eds.), *Simple heuristics that make us smart* (pp. 75–95). Oxford, UK: Oxford University Press.

Gigerenzer, G., & Gray, J. A. M. (2011). *Better doctors, better patients, better decisions: Envisioning health care 2020.* Cambridge, MA: MIT Press.

Gigerenzer, G., Hertwig, R., Van Den Broek, E., Fasolo, B., & Katsikopoulos, K. V. (2005). "A 30% chance of rain tomorrow": How does the public understand probabilistic weather forecasts? *Risk Analysis, 25*(3), 623–629.

Gigerenzer, G., & Regier, T. (1996). How do we tell an association from a rule? Comment on Sloman (1996). *Psychological Bulletin, 119*(1), 23–26.

Gigerenzer, G., Todd, P. M., & The ABC Research Group (1999). *Simple heuristics that make us smart.* Oxford, UK: Oxford University Press.

Gilbert, D. T. (1991). How mental systems believe. *American Psychologist, 46*(2), 107–119.

Gilbert, D. T., Driver-Linn, E., & Wilson, T. D. (2002). The trouble with Vronsky: Impact bias in the forecasting of future affective states. In L. F. Barrett & P. Salovey (Eds.), *The wisdom in feeling: Psychological processes in emotional intelligence* (pp. 114–143). New York, NY: Guilford Press.

Gilbert, D. T., Krull, D. S., & Malone, P. S. (1990). Unbelieving the unbelievable: Some problems in the rejection of false information. *Journal of Personality and Social Psychology, 59*(4), 601–613.

Gilbert, D. T., & Malone, P. S. (1995). The correspondence bias. *Psychological Bulletin, 117*(1), 21–38.

Gilbert, D. T., Tafarodi, R. W., & Malone, P. S. (1993). You can't not believe everything you read. *Journal of Personality and Social Psychology, 65*(2), 221–233.

Gilligan, C. (1982). *In a different voice*. Cambridge, MA: Harvard University Press.

Gilligan, C., & Attanucci, J. (1988). Two moral orientations: Gender differences and similarities. *Merrill-Palmer Quarterly, 34*(3), 223–237.

Goedert, K. M., Ellefson, M. R., & Rehder, B. (2014). Differences in the weighting and choice of evidence for plausible versus implausible causes. *Journal of Experimental Psychology: Learning, Memory, and Cognition, 40*(3), 683–702.

Goertzel, T. (2010). Conspiracy theories in science. *EMBO reports, 11*(7), 493–499.

Goodwin, G. P., Piazza, J., & Rozin, P. (2014). Moral character predominates in person perception and evaluation. *Journal of Personality and Social Psychology, 106*(1), 148–168.

Gopnik, A. (2000). Explanation as orgasm and the drive for causal knowledge: The function, evolution, and phenomenology of the theory formation system. In F. C. Keil & R. A. Wilson (Eds.), *Explanation and cognition* (pp. 299–323). Cambridge, MA: The MIT Press.

Gorini, A., & Pravettoni, G. (2011). An overview on cognitive aspects implicated in medical decisions. *European Journal of Internal Medicine, 22*(6), 547–553.

Green, L., Fry, A. F., & Myerson, J. (1994). Discounting of delayed rewards: A life-span comparison. *Psychological Science, 5*(1), 33–36.

Green, L., Myerson, J., & McFadden, E. (1997). Rate of temporal discounting decreases with amount of reward. *Memory & Cognition, 25*(5), 715–723.

Greene, J. D., Sommerville, R. B., Nystrom, L. E., Darley, J. M., & Cohen, J. D. (2001). An fMRI investigation of emotional engagement in moral judgment. *Science, 293*(5537), 2105–2108.

Greene, R. L. (1984). Incidental learning of event frequency. *Memory & Cognition, 12*(1), 90–95.

Grove, W. M., Zald, D. H., Lebow, B. S., Snitz, B. E., & Nelson, C. (2000). Clinical versus mechanical prediction: A meta-analysis. *Psychological Assessment, 12*(1), 19–30.

Haddad, B. M., Rozin, P., Nemeroff, C., and Slovic, P. (2009). *The psychology of water reclamation and reuse*. Alexandria, VA: The WateReuse Foundation.

Haidt, J. (2001). The emotional dog and its rational tail: A social intuitionist approach to moral judgment. *Psychological Review, 108*(4), 814–834.

Haidt, J. (2012). *The righteous mind: Why good people are divided by politics and religion*. New York, NY: Random House.

Haidt, J., Koller, S. H., & Dias, M. G. (1993). Affect, culture, and morality, or is it wrong to eat your dog? *Journal of Personality and Social Psychology, 65*(4), 613–628.

Handler, D. (2000). *A series of unfortunate events #3: The wide window*. New York, NY: HarperCollins.

Hansen, K., Gerbasi, M., Todorov, A., Kruse, E., & Pronin, E. (2014). People claim objectivity after knowingly using biased strategies. *Personality and Social Psychology Bulletin, 40*(6), 691–699.

Hardin, G. (1968). The tragedy of the commons. *Science, 162*(3859), 1243–1248.

Harless, D. W., & Camerer, C. F. (1994). The predictive utility of generalized expected utility theories. *Econometrica: Journal of the Econometric Society, 62*(6), 1251–1289.

Harlow, J. M. (1868). Recovery from the passage of an iron bar through the head. *Publications of the Massachusetts Medical Society, 2*(3), 327–346.

Harris, P., & Middleton, W. (1994). The illusion of control and optimism about health: On being less at risk but no more in control than others. *British Journal of Social Psychology, 33*(4), 369–386.

Harris, A. J. L., & Speekenbrink, M. (2016). Semantic cross-scale numerical anchoring. *Judgment and Decision Making, 11*(6), 572–581.

Haselgrove, M. (2016). Overcoming associative learning. *Journal of Comparative Psychology, 130*(3), 226–240.

Hastie, R. (1994). *Inside the juror: The psychology of juror decision making*. Cambridge, UK: Cambridge University Press.

Hastie, R. (2015). Causal thinking in judgments. In G. Keren & G. Wu (Eds.), *The Wiley Blackwell handbook of judgment and decision making* (Vol. 1, pp. 590–628). Chichester, UK: John Wiley & Sons, Ltd.

Hastie, R., & Pennington, N. (2000). Explanation-based decision making. In T. Connolly, H. R. Arkes, & K. R. Hammond (Eds.), *Judgment and decision making: An interdisciplinary reader* (2nd Ed., pp. 212–228). Cambridge, UK: Cambridge University Press.

Hastie, R., Schroeder, C., & Weber, R. (1990). Creating complex social conjunction categories from simple categories. *Bulletin of the Psychonomic Society, 28*(3), 242–247.

Hathaway, S. R., & McKinley, J. C. (1940). A multiphasic personality schedule (Minnesota): I. Construction of the schedule. *The Journal of Psychology, 10*(2), 249–254.

Hawkins, S. A., & Hastie, R. (1990). Hindsight: Biased judgments of past events after the outcomes are known. *Psychological Bulletin, 107*(3), 311–327.

Heath, C., & Tversky, A. (1991). Preference and belief: Ambiguity and competence in choice under uncertainty. *Journal of Risk and Uncertainty, 4*(1), 5–28.

Hebl, M. R., & Mannix, L. M. (2003). The weight of obesity in evaluating others: A mere proximity effect. *Personality and Social Psychology Bulletin, 29*(1), 28–38.

Heider, F. (1958/2015). *The psychology of interpersonal relations*. Mansfield Center, CT: Martino Publishing.

Hein, L. E., & Selden, M. (2015). *Living with the bomb: American and Japanese cultural conflicts in the nuclear age*. New York, NY: M. E. Sharpe, Inc.

Heine, S. J., & Lehman, D. R. (1996). Hindsight bias: A cross-cultural analysis. *The Japanese Journal of Experimental Social Psychology, 35*(3), 317–323.

Hempel, C. G. (1945). Studies in the logic of confirmation (I.). *Mind, 54*(113), 1–26.

Henrich, J., Heine, S. J., & Norenzayan, A. (2010). The weirdest people in the world? *Behavioral and Brain Sciences, 33*(2–3), 1–75.

Hershfield, H. E., Goldstein, D. G., Sharpe, W. F., Fox, J., Yeykelis, L., Carstensen, L. L., & Bailenson, J. N. (2011). Increasing saving behavior through age-progressed renderings of the future self. *Journal of Marketing Research, 48*(SPL), S23–S37.

Hertwig, R., & Gigerenzer, G. (1999). The "conjunction fallacy" revisited: How intelligent inferences look like reasoning errors. *Journal of Behavioral Decision Making, 12*, 275–305.

Heron, M. (2016). Deaths: Leading causes for 2013. *National Vital Statistics Reports, 65*(2), 1–95.

Hilton, D. (2007). Causal explanation: From social perception to knowledge-based attribution. In A. W. Kruglanski & E. T. Higgins (Eds.), *Social psychology: Handbook of basic principles* (2nd Ed., pp. 232–253). New York, NY: The Guilford Press.

Hirschfeld, L. A. (2002). Why don't anthropologists like children? *American Anthropologist, 104*(2), 611–627.

Hoffrage, U., & Gigerenzer, G. (1998). Using natural frequencies to improve diagnostic inferences. *Academic Medicine, 73*, 538–540.

Hoffrage, U., Hertwig, R., & Gigerenzer, G. (2000). Hindsight bias: A by-product of knowledge updating? *Journal of Experimental Psychology: Learning, Memory and Cognition, 26*(3), 566–581.

Hogarth, R. M., & Einhorn, H. J. (1992). Order effects in belief updating: The belief-adjustment model. *Cognitive Psychology, 24*(1), 1–55.

Holden, K. J., & French, C. C. (2002). Alien abduction experiences: Some clues from neuropsychology and neuropsychiatry. *Cognitive Neuropsychiatry, 7*(3), 163–178.

Hölzl, E., & Kirchler, E. (2005). Causal attribution and hindsight bias for economic developments. *Journal of Applied Psychology, 90*(1), 267–174.

Homant, R. J., & Kennedy, D. B. (1998). Psychological aspects of crime scene profiling: Validity research. *Criminal Justice and Behavior, 25*(3), 319–343.

Homberger, E. (2016, July 3). Elie Wiesel obituary. *The Guardian.*

Horswill, M. S., & McKenna, F. P. (1999). The effect of perceived control on risk taking. *Journal of Applied Social Psychology, 29*(2), 377–391.

Hume, D. (1739/2000). *A treatise of human nature.* Oxford, UK: Oxford University Press.

Hunt, D. L., Haynes, R. B., Hanna, S. E., & Smith, K. (1998). Effects of computer-based clinical decision support systems on physician performance and patient outcomes: A systematic review. *JAMA: The Journal of the American Medical Association, 280*(15), 1339–1346.

Impey, C., Buxner, S., & Antonellis, J. (2012). Non-scientific beliefs among undergraduate students. *Astronomy Education Review, 11*(1), 1–12.

Institute of Medicine (U.S.). (2004). *Immunization safety review: Vaccines and autism.* Washington, DC: The National Academies Press.

Irwin, H. J. (2009). *The psychology of paranormal belief: A researcher's handbook.* Hatfield, UK: University of Hertfordshire Press.

Ishikawa, T., & Ueda, K. (1984). The bonus payment system and Japanese personal savings. In M. Aoki (Ed.), *The economic analysis of the Japanese firm* (pp. 133–192). New York, NY: Elsevier Science Ltd.

Iyengar, S. S., & Lepper, M. R. (2000). When choice is demotivating: Can one desire too much of a good thing? *Journal of Personality and Social Psychology, 79*(6), 995–1006.

Jaffee, S., & Hyde, J. S. (2000). Gender differences in moral orientation: A meta-analysis. *Psychological Bulletin, 126*(5), 703–726.

Johnson, E. J., & Goldstein, D. G. (2004). Defaults and donation decisions. *Transplantation, 78*(12), 1713–1716.

Johnson, H. M., & Seifert, C. M. (1994). Sources of the continued influence effect: When misinformation in memory affects later inferences. *Journal of Experimental Psychology: Learning, Memory, and Cognition, 20*(6), 1420–1436.

Jones, E. E., & Davis, K. E. (1965). From acts to dispositions: The attribution process in person perception. *Advances in Experimental Social Psychology, 2*, 219–266.

Kahneman, D. (2003). A perspective on judgment and choice: Mapping bounded rationality. *American Psychologist, 58*(9), 697–720.

Kahneman, D. (2011). *Thinking, fast and slow*. London, UK: Macmillan.

Kahneman, D., & Frederick, S. (2002). Representativeness revisited: Attribute substitution in intuitive judgment. In T. Gilovich, D. Griffin, & D. Kahneman (Eds.), *Heuristics and biases: The psychology of intuitive judgment* (pp. 49–81). Cambridge, UK: Cambridge University Press.

Kahneman, D., Fredrickson, B. L., Schreiber, C. A., & Redelmeier, D. A. (1993). When more pain is preferred to less: Adding a better end. *Psychological Science, 4*(6), 401–405.

Kahneman, D., Knetsch, J. L., & Thaler, R. H. (1990). Experimental tests of the endowment effect and the Coase theorem. *Journal of Political Economy, 98*(6), 1325–1348.

Kahneman, D., & Snell, J. (1992). Predicting a changing taste: Do people know what they will like? *Journal of Behavioral Decision Making, 5*(3), 187–200.

Kahneman, D., & Tversky, A. (1972). Subjective probability: A judgment of representativeness. *Cognitive Psychology, 3*(3), 430–454.

Kahneman, D., & Tversky, A. (1973). On the psychology of prediction. *Psychological Review, 80*(4), 237–251.

Kahneman, D., & Tversky, A. (1979). Prospect theory: An analysis of decision under risk. *Econometrica: Journal of the Econometric Society, 47*(2), 263–291.

Kahneman, D., & Tversky, A. (1982). The simulation heuristic. In D. Kahneman, P. Slovic, & A. Tversky (Eds.), *Judgment under uncertainty: Heuristics and biases* (pp. 201–208). New York, NY: Cambridge University Press.

Kaplan, M. F., & Kemmerick, G. D. (1974). Juror judgment as information integration: Combining evidential and nonevidential information. *Journal of Personality and Social Psychology, 30*(4), 493–499.

Karmarkar, U. R., Shiv, B., & Knutson, B. (2015). Cost conscious? The neural and behavioral impact of price primacy on decision making. *Journal of Marketing Research, 52*(4), 467–481.

Kassin, S. M., Dror, I. E., & Kukucka, J. (2013). The forensic confirmation bias: Problems, perspectives, and proposed solutions. *Journal of Applied Research in Memory and Cognition, 2*(1), 42–52.

Katsikopoulos, K. V., & Gigerenzer, G. (2008). One-reason decision-making: Modeling violations of expected utility theory. *Journal of Risk and Uncertainty, 37*(1), 35–56.

Kawamoto, K., Houlihan, C. A., Balas, E. A., & Lobach, D. F. (2005). Improving clinical practice using clinical decision support systems: A systematic review of trials to identify features critical to success. *BMJ: British Medical Journal, 330*(7494), 765–768.

Keeney, R. L. (2008). Personal decisions are the leading cause of death. *Operations Research, 56*(6), 1335–1347.

Keeney, R. L., & Raiffa, H. (1993). *Decisions with multiple objectives: Preferences and value tradeoffs*. New York, NY: Cambridge University Press.

Keil, F. C. (1989). *Concepts, kinds, and conceptual development*. Cambridge, MA: MIT Press.

Keil, F. C. (1995). The growth of causal understandings of natural kinds: Modes of construal and the emergence of biological thought. In D. Sperber, D. Premack, & A. J. Premack (Eds.), *Causal cognition* (pp. 234–262). New York, NY: Oxford University Press.

Keil, F. C. (2006). Explanation and understanding. *Annual Review of Psychology, 57*, 227–254.

Kelemen, D., & Rosset, E. (2009). The human function compunction: Teleological explanation in adults. *Cognition, 111*(1), 138–143.

Kelley, H. H. (1973). The processes of causal attribution. *American Psychologist, 28*(2), 107–128.

Keren, G. (2013). A tale of two systems: A scientific advance or a theoretical stone soup? Commentary on Evans & Stanovich (2013). *Perspectives on Psychological Science, 8*(3), 257–262.

Keren, G., & Schul, Y. (2009). Two is not always better than one: A critical evaluation of two-system theories. *Perspectives on Psychological Science, 4*(6), 533–550.

Khadjavi, M., & Lange, A. (2013). Prisoners and their dilemma. *Journal of Economic Behavior & Organization, 92*, 163–175.

Khemlani, S. S., Barbey, A. K., & Johnson-Laird, P. N. (2014). Causal reasoning with mental models. *Frontiers in Human Neuroscience, 8*, 849.

Kim, L. R., & Kim, N. S. (2011). A proximity effect in adults' contamination intuitions. *Judgment and Decision Making, 6*(3), 222–229.

Kim, N. S., & Ahn, W. (2002a). The influence of naive causal theories on lay concepts of mental illness. *American Journal of Psychology, 115*(1), 33–66.

Kim, N. S., & Ahn, W. K. (2002b). Clinical psychologists' theory-based representations of mental disorders predict their diagnostic reasoning and memory. *Journal of Experimental Psychology: General, 131*(4), 451–476.

Klayman, J., & Ha, Y. W. (1987). Confirmation, disconfirmation, and information in hypothesis testing. *Psychological Review, 94*(2), 211–228.

Knight, F. H. (1921). *Risk, uncertainty, and profit.* Library of Economics and Liberty. Retrieved from www.econlib.org/library/Knight/knRUP.html.

Knutson, B., Rick, S., Wimmer, G. E., Prelec, D., & Loewenstein, G. (2007). Neural predictors of purchases. *Neuron, 53*(1), 147–156.

Kocsis, R. N., Cooksey, R. W., & Irwin, H. J. (2002). Psychological profiling of sexual murders: An empirical model. *International Journal of Offender Therapy and Comparative Criminology, 46*(5), 532–554.

Kohlberg. L. (1971). From is to ought: How to commit the naturalistic fallacy and get away with it in the study of moral development. In T. Mischel (Ed.), *Cognitive development and epistemology* (pp. 151–235). New York, NY: Academic Press.

Koriat, A., Lichtenstein, S., & Fischhoff, B. (1980). Reasons for confidence. *Journal of Experimental Psychology: Human Learning and Memory, 6*(2), 107–118.

Kostopoulou, O., Russo, J. E., Keenan, G., Delaney, B. C., & Douiri, A. (2012). Information distortion in physicians' diagnostic judgments. *Medical Decision Making, 32*(6), 831–839.

Kőszegi, B., & Rabin, M. (2006). A model of reference-dependent preferences. *The Quarterly Journal of Economics, 121*(4), 1133–1165.

Kruglanski, A. W., & Gigerenzer, G. (2011). Intuitive and deliberate judgments are based on common principles. *Psychological Review, 118*(1), 97–109.

Kuhlmeier, V. A., Bloom, P., & Wynn, K. (2004). Do 5-month-old infants see humans as material objects? *Cognition, 94*(1), 95–103.

Kuhn, S. (2017). Prisoner's dilemma. In E. N. Zalta (Ed.), *The Stanford encyclopedia of philosophy* (Spring 2017 Edition). Retrieved from https://plato.stanford.edu/archives/spr2017/entries/prisoner-dilemma.

Kunda, Z., Miller, D. T., & Claire, T. (1990). Combining social concepts: The role of causal reasoning. *Cognitive Science, 14*(4), 551–577.

Kunreuther, H., Meyer, R., Zeckhauser, R., Slovic, P., Schwartz, B., Schade, C., ... & Hogarth, R. (2002). High stakes decision making: Normative, descriptive, and prescriptive considerations. *Marketing Letters, 13*, 259–268.

Kunreuther, H., Onculer, A., & Slovic, P. (1998). Time insensitivity for protective investments. *Journal of Risk and Uncertainty, 16*, 279–299.

Kusev, P., van Schaik, P., Alzahrani, S., Lonigro, S., & Purser, H. (2016). Judging the morality of utilitarian actions: How poor utilitarian accessibility makes judges irrational. *Psychonomic Bulletin & Review, 23*(6), 1961–1967.

Lakoff, G. (2010). *Moral politics: How liberals and conservatives think* (2nd Ed.). Chicago, IL: University of Chicago Press.

Langer, E. J. (1975). The illusion of control. *Journal of Personality and Social Psychology, 32*(2), 311–328.

Lee, L., Lee, M. P., Bertini, M., Zauberman, G., & Ariely, D. (2015). Money, time, and the stability of consumer preferences. *Journal of Marketing Research, 52*(2), 184–199.

Leslie, A. M. (1987). Pretense and representation: The origins of "theory of mind." *Psychological Review, 94*(4), 412–426.

Levine, L. J., & Pizarro, D. A. (2004). Emotion and memory research: A grumpy overview. *Social Cognition, 22*(5), 530–554.

Lewandowsky, S., Echer, U. K. H., Seifert, C., Schwartz, N., & Cook, J. (2012). Misinformation and its correction: Continued influence and successful debiasing. *Psychological Science in the Public Interest, 13*(3), 106–131.

Lewandowsky, S., Oberauer, K., & Gignac, G. E. (2013). NASA faked the moon landing – therefore, climate science is a hoax: An anatomy of the motivated rejection of science. *Psychological Science, 24*(5), 622–633.

Lewis, M. (2004). *Moneyball: The art of winning an unfair game.* New York, NY: W. W. Norton & Company.

Lieberman, J. D., & Arndt, J. (2000). Understanding the limits of limiting instructions: Social psychological explanations for the failures of instructions to disregard pretrial publicity and other inadmissible evidence. *Psychology, Public Policy, and Law, 6*(3), 677–711.

Lilienfeld, S. O., Ammirati, R., & Landfield, K. (2009). Giving debiasing away: Can psychological research on correcting cognitive errors promote human welfare? *Perspectives on Psychological Science, 4*(4), 390–398.

Lim, D., Ha, M., & Song, I. (2014). Trends in the leading causes of death in Korea, 1983–2012. *Journal of Korean Medical Science, 29*(12), 1597–1603.

Lindeman, M., & Aarnio, K. (2007). Superstitious, magical, and paranormal beliefs: An integrative model. *Journal of Research in Personality, 41*(4), 731–744.

Lindeman, M., Svedholm, A. M., Takada, M., Lönnqvist, J. E., & Verkasalo, M. (2011). Core knowledge confusions among university students. *Science & Education, 20*(5–6), 439–451.

Lipe, M. G. (1990). A lens model analysis of covariation research. *Journal of Behavioral Decision Making, 3*(1), 47–59.

List, J. A. (2004). Neoclassical theory versus prospect theory: Evidence from the marketplace. *Econometrica, 72*(2), 615–625.

Lo, B., Quill, T., & Tulsky, J. (1999). Discussing palliative care with patients. *Annals of Internal Medicine, 130*(9), 744–749.

Loewenstein, G. (2005). Projection bias in medical decision making. *Medical Decision Making, 25*(1), 96–104.

Lopes, L. (1985). Averaging rules and adjustment processes in Bayesian inference. *Bulletin of the Psychonomic Society,* (6), 509–512.

Lopes, L. L., & Oden, G. C. (1991). The rationality of intelligence. In E. Eells & T. Maruszewski (Eds.), *Rationality and reasoning* (pp. 225–249). Amsterdam: Rodopi.

López-Rousseau, A. (2005). Avoiding the death risk of avoiding a dread risk. *Psychological Science, 16,* 426–428.

Lynn, S. J., Pintar, J., Stafford, J., Marmelstein, L., & Lock, T. (1998). Rendering the implausible plausible: Narrative construction, suggestion, and memory. In J. de Rivera & T. R. Sarbin (Eds.), *Believed-in imaginings: The narrative construction of reality* (pp. 123–143). Washington, DC: American Psychological Association.

Mackie, J. L. (1965). Causes and conditions. *American Philosophical Quarterly, 2*(4), 245–264.

Mackie, J. L. (1974). *The cement of the universe: A study of causation.* Oxford, UK: Clarendon Press.

MacLeod, C., & Campbell, L. (1992). Memory accessibility and probability judgments: An experimental evaluation of the availability heuristic. *Journal of Personality and Social Psychology, 63*(6), 890–902.

Maley, J. E., Hunt, M., & Parr, W. (2000). Set-size and frequency-of-occurrence judgments in young and older adults: The role of the availability heuristic. *The Quarterly Journal of Experimental Psychology: Section A, 53*(1), 247–269.

Mamede, S., van Gog, T., van den Berge, K., Rikers, R. M., van Saase, J. L., van Guldener, C., & Schmidt, H. G. (2010). Effect of availability bias and reflective reasoning on diagnostic accuracy among internal medicine residents. *JAMA, 304*(11), 1198–1203.

Mandel, D. R., & Lehman, D. R. (1998). Integration of contingency information in judgments of cause, covariation, and probability. *Journal of Experimental Psychology: General, 127*(3), 269–285.

Mark, M. M., & Mellor, S. (1991). Effect of self-relevance of an event on hindsight bias: The foreseeability of a layoff. *Journal of Applied Psychology, 76*(4), 569–577.

Markowitz, H. (1952). The utility of wealth. *Journal of Political Economy, 60*(2), 151–158.

Mather, M. (2007). Emotional arousal and memory binding: An object-based framework. *Perspectives on Psychological Science, 2*(1), 33–52.

Matute, H., Yarritu, I., & Vadillo, M. A. (2011). Illusions of causality at the heart of pseudoscience. *British Journal of Psychology, 102*(3), 392–405.

Mayo, R., Schul, Y., & Burnstein, E. (2004). "I am not guilty" vs. "I am innocent": Successful negation may depend on the schema used for its encoding. *Journal of Experimental Social Psychology, 40*(4), 433–449.

Medvec, V. H., Madey, S. F., & Gilovich, T. (1995). When less is more: Counterfactual thinking and satisfaction among Olympic medalists. *Journal of Personality and Social Psychology, 69*(4), 603–610.

Meehl, P. E. (1954/1996). *Clinical versus statistical prediction: A theoretical analysis and a review of the evidence.* Northvale, NJ: Jason Aronson, Inc.

Meehl, P. E. (1973). Why I do not attend case conferences. In *Psychodiagnosis: Selected papers* (pp. 225–302). Minneapolis, MN: University of Minnesota Press.

Meehl, P. E. (1986). Causes and effects of my disturbing little book. *Journal of Personality Assessment, 50*(3), 370–375.

Mendel, R., Traut-Mattausch, E., Jonas, E., Leucht, S., Kane, J. M., Maino, K., ... & Hamann, J. (2011). Confirmation bias: Why psychiatrists stick to wrong preliminary diagnoses. *Psychological Medicine, 41*(12), 2651–2659.

Michael, R. B., Newman, E. J., Vuorre, M., Cumming, G., & Garry, M. (2013). On the (non) persuasive power of a brain image. *Psychonomic Bulletin & Review, 20*(4), 720–725.

Michotte, A. (1946/1963). *The perception of causality.* Oxford, UK: Basic Books.

Mill, J. S. (1861/1998). *Utilitarianism.* New York, NY: Oxford University Press.

Miller, D. T., & Ross, M. (1975). Self-serving biases in the attribution of causality: Fact or fiction. *Psychological Bulletin, 82*(2), 213–225.

Miller, G. (2012, August 10). Getting minds out of the sewer: How human psychology gets in the way of sensible solutions to recycling wastewater. *Science, 337*, 679–680.

Miron-Shatz, T., Hanoch, Y., Graef, D., & Sagi, M. (2009). Presentation format affects comprehension and risk assessment: The case of prenatal screening. *Journal of Health Communication, 14*, 439–450.

Mishra, A., Mishra, H., & Nayakankuppam, D. (2009). The group-contagion effect: The influence of spatial groupings on perceived contagion and preferences. *Psychological Science, 20*(7), 867–870.

Mole, C., & Klein, C. (2010). Confirmation, refutation, and the evidence of fMRI. In S. J. Hanson & M. Bunzl (Eds.), *Foundational issues in human brain mapping* (pp. 99–112). Cambridge, MA: MIT Press.

Monahan, J., & Steadman, H. J. (1996). Violent storms and violent people: How meteorology can inform risk communication in mental health law. *American Psychologist, 51*(9), 931–938.

Mussweiler, T., & Englich, B. (2005). Subliminal anchoring: Judgmental consequences and underlying mechanisms. *Organizational Behavior and Human Decision Processes, 98*(2), 133–143.

Myers, D. G. (2001, December). Do we fear the right things? *American Psychological Society Observer, 14*(10), 3.

Narayanamurti, V., & Odumosu, T. (2016). *Cycles of invention and discovery: Rethinking the endless frontier.* Cambridge, MA: Harvard University Press.

Nash, J. F. (1950). Equilibrium points in n-person games. *Proceedings of the National Academy of Sciences, 36*(1), 48–49.

Nature Publishing Group. (2007). Editorial: Silencing debate over autism. *Nature Neuroscience, 10*(5), 531.

Navarro-Martinez, D., Salisbury, L. C., Lemon, K. N., Stewart, N., Matthews, W. J., & Harris, A. J. L. (2011). Minimum required payment and supplemental information disclosure effects on consumer debt repayment decisions. *Journal of Marketing Research, 48*(SPL), S60–S77.

Nestler, S., Blank, H., & von Collani, G. (2008). Hindsight bias doesn't always come easy: Causal models, cognitive effort, and creeping determinism. *Journal of Experimental Psychology: Learning, Memory, and Cognition, 34*(5), 1043–1054.

Nickerson, R. S. (1998). Confirmation bias: A ubiquitous phenomenon in many guises. *Review of General Psychology, 2*(2), 175–220.

Nisbett, R. E., & Wilson, T. D. (1977). Telling more than we can know: Verbal reports on mental processes. *Psychological Review, 84*(3), 231–259.

Norman, G. R., & Eva, K. W. (2010). Diagnostic error and clinical reasoning. *Medical Education, 44*(1), 94–100.

Northcraft, G. B., & Neale, M. A. (1987). Experts, amateurs, and real estate: An anchoring-and-adjustment perspective on property pricing decisions. *Organizational Behavior and Human Decision Processes, 39*(1), 84–97.

Office of the Inspector General [OIG]. (2006). *A review of the FBI's handling of the Brandon Mayfield case.* Office of the Inspector General, Oversight & Review Division, U.S. Department of Justice.

Office of the Inspector General [OIG]. (2011). *A review of the FBI's progress in responding to the recommendations in the Office of the Inspector General Report on the fingerprint misidentification in the Brandon Mayfield case.* Office of the Inspector General, Oversight & Review Division, U.S. Department of Justice.

Ofir, C., & Mazursky, D. (1997). Does a surprising outcome reinforce or reverse the hindsight bias? *Organizational Behavior and Human Decision Process, 69*(1), 51–57.

Oppenheimer, D. M., LeBoeuf, R. A., & Brewer, N. T. (2008). Anchors aweigh: A demonstration of cross-modality anchoring and magnitude priming. *Cognition, 106*(1), 13–26.

Oskamp, S. (1965). Overconfidence in case-study judgments. *Journal of Consulting Psychology, 29*(3), 261–265.

Osman, M. (2004). An evaluation of dual-process theories of reasoning. *Psychonomic Bulletin & Review, 11*(6), 988–1010.

Parfit, D. (1971). Personal identity. *The Philosophical Review, 80*(1), 3–27.

Parks, C. D., Joireman, J., & Van Lange, P. A. (2013). Cooperation, trust, and antagonism: How public goods are promoted. *Psychological Science in the Public Interest, 14*(3), 119–165.

Pearce, J. M. S. (2008). The doctrine of signatures. *European Neurology, 60*(1), 51–52.

Pennington, N., & Hastie, R. (1986). Evidence evaluation in complex decision making. *Journal of Personality and Social Psychology, 51*(2), 242–258.

Pennington, N., & Hastie, R. (1988). Explanation-based decision making: Effects of memory structure on judgment. *Journal of Experimental Psychology: Learning, Memory, and Cognition, 14*(3), 521–533.

Pennington, N., & Hastie, R. (1992). Explaining the evidence: Tests of the Story Model for juror decision making. *Journal of Personality and Social Psychology, 62*(2), 189–206.

Pennycook, G., Cheyne, J. A., Seli, P., Koehler, D. J., & Fugelsang, J. A. (2012). Analytic cognitive style predicts religious and paranormal belief. *Cognition, 123*(3), 335–346.

Perner, J., Leekam, S. R., & Wimmer, H. (1987). Three-year-olds' difficulty with false belief: The case for a conceptual deficit. *British Journal of Developmental Psychology, 5*(2), 125–137.

Peters, E., & Slovic, P. (2000). The springs of action: Affective and analytical information processing in choice. *Personality and Social Psychology Bulletin, 26*, 1465–1475.

Pezzo, M. V. (2003). Surprise, defence or making sense: What removes hindsight bias? *Memory, 11*(4/5), 421–441.

Pezzo, M. V. (2011). Hindsight bias: A primer for motivational researchers. *Social and Personality Psychology Compass, 5*(9), 655–678.

Pezzo, M. V., & Pezzo, S. P. (2007). Making sense of failure: A motivated model of hindsight bias. *Social Cognition, 25*(1), 147–164.

Piaget, J., & Inhelder, B. (1969). *The psychology of the child* (2nd Ed.; H. Weaver, Trans.). New York, NY: Basic Books.

Pohl, R. F. (2004). *Cognitive illusions: A handbook of fallacies and biases in thinking, judgement, and memory.* Hove, UK: Psychology Press.

Pohl, R. F. (2007). Ways to assess hindsight bias. *Social Cognition, 25*(1), 14–31.

Pohl, R. F., Bayen, U. J., & Martin, C. (2010). A multiprocess account of hindsight bias in children. *Developmental Psychology, 46*(5), 1268–1282.

Pohl, R. F., Bender, M., & Lachmann, G. (2002). Hindsight bias around the world. *Experimental Psychology, 49*(4), 270–282.

Pohl, R. F., Eisenhauer, M., & Hardt, O. (2003). SARA: A cognitive process model to simulate the anchoring effect and hindsight bias. *Memory, 11*(4/5), 337–356.

Popper, K. R. (1959). Prediction and prophecy in the social sciences. In P. Gardiner (Ed.), *Theories of history* (pp. 276–285). New York, NY: The Free Press.

Popper, K. (1959/1968). *The logic of scientific discovery.* New York, NY: Harper & Row.

Prager, F., Asay, G. R. B., Lee, B., & von Winterfeldt, D. (2011). Exploring reductions in London Underground passenger journeys following the July 2005 bombings. *Risk Analysis, 31,* 773–786.

Pronin, E., Lin, D. Y., & Ross, L. (2002). The bias blind spot: Perceptions of bias in self versus others. *Personality and Social Psychology Bulletin, 28*(3), 369–381.

Pruitt, D. G., & Kimmel, M. J. (1977). Twenty years of experimental gaming: Critique, synthesis, and suggestions for the future. *Annual Review of Psychology, 28*(1), 363–392.

Public Health England. (2013). *Measles cases in England: January to March 2013.* Retrieved from www.hpa.org.uk/webc/HPAwebFile/HPAweb_C/1317138802384.

Pulay, A. J., Stinson, F. S., Dawson, D. A., Goldstein, R. B., Chou, S. P., Huang, B., ... & Grant, B. F. (2009). Prevalence, correlates, disability, and comorbidity of DSM-IV schizotypal personality disorder: Results from the wave 2 national epidemiologic survey on alcohol and related conditions. *Primary Care Companion to the Journal of Clinical Psychiatry, 11*(2), 53–67.

Quattrone, G. A., Lawrence, C. P., Finkel, S. E., & Andrus, D. C. (1984). *Explorations in anchoring: The effects of prior range, anchor extremity, and suggestive hints* (Unpublished manuscript). Stanford University, Stanford, CA.

Ramesh, R., & Zionts, S. (2013). Multiple criteria decision making. In S. I. Gass & M. C. Fu (Eds.), *Encyclopedia of operations research and management science* (pp. 1007–1013). New York, NY: Springer US.

Reason, J. (1995). Understanding adverse events: Human factors. *Quality in Health Care, 4*(2), 80–89.

Redelmeier, D. A., & Kahneman, D. (1996). Patients' memories of painful medical treatments: Real-time and retrospective evaluations of two minimally invasive procedures. *Pain, 66*(1), 3–8.

Reitsma-van Rooijen, M., & Daamen, D. D. L. (2006). Subliminal anchoring: The effects of subliminally presented numbers on probability estimates. *Journal of Experimental Social Psychology, 42*(3), 380–387.

Rescorla, R. A., & Wagner, A. R. (1972). A theory of Pavlovian conditioning: Variations in the effectiveness of reinforcement and non-reinforcement. In A. H. Black & W. F. Prokasy (Eds.), *Classical conditioning II: Current research and theory* (pp. 64–99). New York, NY: Appleton-Century-Crofts.

Reyna, V. F., Lloyd, F. J., & Whalen, P. (2001). Genetic testing and medical decision making. *Archives of Internal Medicine, 161,* 2406–2408.

Reyna, V. F., Nelson, W. L., Han, P. K., & Dieckmann, N. F. (2009). How numeracy influences risk comprehension and medical decision making. *Psychological Bulletin, 135,* 943–973.

Richards, D. D., & Siegler, R. S. (1986). Children's understandings of the attributes of life. *Journal of Experimental Child Psychology, 42*(1), 1–22.

Rid, A., & Wendler, D. (2014). Use of a Patient Preference Predictor to help make medical decisions for incapacitated patients. *Journal of Medicine and Philosophy, 39*(2), 104–129.

Roberto, C. A., Swinburn, B., Hawkes, C., Huang, T. T., Costa, S. A., Ashe, M., ... & Brownell, K. D. (2015). Patchy progress on obesity prevention: Emerging examples, entrenched barriers, and new thinking. *The Lancet, 385*(9985), 2400–2409.

Roese, N. J., & Vohs, K. D. (2012). Hindsight bias. *Perspectives on Psychological Science, 7*(5), 411–426.

Ross, D. (2016). Game theory. In E. N. Zalta (Ed.), *The Stanford encyclopedia of philosophy* (Winter 2016 Edition). Retrieved from https://plato.stanford.edu/archives/win2016/entries/game-theory.

Rothman, A. J., Martino, S. C., Bedell, B. T., Detweiler, J. B., & Salovey, P. (1999). The systematic influence of gain- and loss-framed messages on interest in and use of different types of health behavior. *Personality and Social Psychology Bulletin, 25*(11), 1355–1369.

Rothman, A. J., & Salovey, P. (1997). Shaping perceptions to motivate healthy behavior: The role of message framing. *Psychological Bulletin, 121*(1), 3–19.

Royzman, E. B., Cassidy, K. W., & Baron, J. (2003). "I know, you know": Epistemic egocentrism in children and adults. *Review of General Psychology, 7*(1), 38–65.

Rozin, P., Millman, L., & Nemeroff, C. (1986). Operation of the laws of sympathetic magic in disgust and other domains. *Journal of Personality and Social Psychology, 50*(4), 703–712.

Rozin, P., Nemeroff, C., Wane, M., & Sherrod, A. (1989). Operation of the sympathetic magical law of contagion in interpersonal attitudes among Americans. *Bulletin of the Psychonomic Society, 27,* 367–370.

Samuelson, W., & Zeckhauser, R. (1988). Status quo bias in decision making. *Journal of Risk and Uncertainty, 1,* 7–59.

Schacter, D. L., Guerin, S. A., & St. Jacques, P. L. (2011). Memory distortion: An adaptive perspective. *Trends in Cognitive Sciences, 15*(10), 467–474.

Schank, R. C., & Abelson, R. P. (1977). *Scripts, plans, goals, and understanding: An inquiry into human knowledge structures.* New York, NY: Psychology Press.

Scheibehenne, B., Greifeneder, R., & Todd, P. M. (2010). Can there ever be too many options? A meta-analytic review of choice overload. *Journal of Consumer Research, 37*(3), 409–425.

Schnall, S., Haidt, J., Clore, G. L., & Jordan, A. H. (2008). Disgust as embodied moral judgment. *Personality and Social Psychology Bulletin, 34*(8), 1096–1109.

Schwartz, B., Ben-Haim, Y., & Dacso, C. (2010). What makes a good decision? Robust satisficing as a normative standard of rational decision making. *Journal for the Theory of Social Behaviour, 41*(2), 209–227.

Schwartz, B., & Ward, A. (2004). Doing better but feeling worse: The paradox of choice. In P. A. Linley & S. Joseph (Eds.), *Positive psychology in practice* (pp. 86–104). Hoboken, NJ: Wiley and Sons.

Schwartz, B., Ward, A., Monterosso, J., Lyubomirsky, S., White, K., & Lehman, D. R. (2002). Maximizing versus satisficing: Happiness is a matter of choice. *Journal of Personality and Social Psychology, 83*(5), 1178–1197.

Schwarz, N., Bless, H., Strack, F., Klumpp, G., Rittenauer-Schatka, H., & Simons, A. (1991). Ease of retrieval as information: Another look at the availability heuristic. *Journal of Personality and Social Psychology, 61*(2), 195–202.

Schwarz, N., Sanna, L. J., Skurnik, I., & Yoon, C. (2007). Metacognitive experiences and the intricacies of setting people straight: Implications for debiasing and public information campaigns. *Advances in Experimental Social Psychology, 39*, 127–161.

Scott, I. A., Mitchell, G. K., Reymond, E. J., & Daly, M. P. (2013). Difficult but necessary conversations: The case for advance care planning. *The Medical Journal of Australia, 199*(10), 662–666.

Sedlmeier, P. (1997). BasicBayes: A tutor system for simple Bayesian inference. *Behavior Research Methods, Instruments, and Computers, 27*, 327–336.

Sedlmeier, P., Hertwig, R., & Gigerenzer, G. (1998). Are judgments of the positional frequencies of letters systematically biased due to availability? *Journal of Experimental Psychology: Learning, Memory, and Cognition, 24*(3), 754–770.

Seifert, C. M. (2002). The continued influence of misinformation in memory: What makes a correction effective? *Psychology of Learning and Motivation, 41*, 265–292.

Shafir, E. (1993). Choosing versus rejecting: Why some options are both better and worse than others. *Memory & Cognition, 21*(4), 546–556.

Shefrin, H. M., & Thaler, R. H. (1988). The behavioral life-cycle hypothesis. *Economic Inquiry, 26*(4), 609–643.

Shiffrin, R. M., & Schneider, W. (1977). Controlled and automatic human information processing: II. Perceptual learning, automatic attending and a general theory. *Psychological Review, 84*(2), 127–190.

Siegrist, M., Cousin, M.-E., & Keller, C. (2008). Risk communication, prenatal screening, and prenatal diagnosis: The illusion of informed decision-making. *Journal of Risk Research, 11*, 87–97.

Simon, H. A. (1955). A behavioral model of rational choice. *The Quarterly Journal of Economics, 69*(1), 99–118.

Simon, H. A. (1956). Rational choice and the structure of the environment. *Psychological Review, 63*(2), 129–138.

Simon, H. A. (1959). Theories of decision-making in economics and behavioral science. *The American Economic Review, 49*(3), 253–283.

Simon, H. A. (1972). Theories of bounded rationality. *Decision and Organization, 1*(1), 161–176.

Sivak, M., and Flannagan, M. (2003). Flying and driving after the September 11 attacks. *American Scientist, 91*(1), 6–8.

Slevin, M. L., Stubbs, L., Plant, H. J., Wilson, P., Gregory, W. M., Armes, P. J., & Downer, S. M. (1990). Attitudes to chemotherapy: Comparing views of patients with cancer with those of doctors, nurses, and general public. *BMJ, 300*(6737), 1458–1460.

Sloman, S. (2005). *Causal models: How people think about the world and its alternatives.* Oxford, UK: Oxford University Press.

Sloman, S. A. (1996). The empirical case for two systems of reasoning. *Psychological Bulletin, 119*(1), 3–22.

Slovic, P. (1987). Perception of risk. *Science, 236*, 280–285.

Slovic, P., Finucane, M. L., Peters, E., & MacGregor, D. G. (2007). The affect heuristic. *European Journal of Operational Research, 177*(3), 1333–1352.

Slovic, P., Fischhoff, B., & Lichtenstein, S. (1982). Why study risk perception? *Risk Analysis, 2*, 83–93.

Smith, R. S. W. (2011). The chasm between evidence and practice: Extent, causes, and remedies. In G. Gigerenzer & J. A. M. Gray (Eds.), *Better doctors, better patients, better decisions: Envisioning healthcare in 2020* (pp. 265–280). Cambridge, MA: MIT Press.

Snyder, M. R. (1974). Self-monitoring of expressive behavior. *Journal of Personality and Social Psychology, 30*(4), 526–537.

Soman, D. (2001). The mental accounting of sunk time costs: Why time is not like money. *Journal of Behavioral Decision Making, 14*(3), 169–185.

Spaanjaars, N. L., Groenier, M., van de Ven, M. O., & Witteman, C. L. (2015). Experience and diagnostic anchors in referral letters. *European Journal of Psychological Assessment, 31*(4), 280–286.

Spellman, B. A. (1997). Crediting causality. *Journal of Experimental Psychology: General, 126*(4), 323–348.

Spellman, B. A., & Kincannon, A. (2001). The relation between counterfactual ("but for") and causal reasoning: Experimental findings and implications for jurors' decisions. *Law and Contemporary Problems, 64*(4), 241–264.

Spellman, B. A., & Mandel, D. R. (1999). When possibility informs reality: Counterfactual thinking as a cue to causality. *Current Directions in Psychological Science, 8*(4), 120–123.

Spengler, P. M., Strohmer, D. C., Dixon, D. N., & Shivy, V. A. (1995). A scientist-practitioner model of psychological assessment: Implications for training, practice, and research. *Counseling Psychologist, 23*(3), 506–534.

Spinoza, B. (1677/1982). *The ethics and selected letters* (S. Shirley, Trans.). Indianapolis, IN: Hackett Publishing Co., Inc.

Stanovich, K. E., & West, R. F. (2000). Individual differences in reasoning: Implications for the rationality debate? *Behavioral and Brain Sciences, 23*(5), 701–717.

Stanovich, K. E., & West, R. F. (2008). On the relative independence of thinking biases and cognitive ability. *Journal of Personality and Social Psychology, 94*(4), 672–695.

Starr, C. (1969). Social benefit versus technological risk: What is our society willing to pay for safety? *Science, 165*, 1232–1238.

Statistisches Bundesamt (2017). *Causes of death.* Retrieved from www.destatis.de/EN/FactsFigures/SocietyState/Health/CausesDeath/CausesDeath.html.

Stavy, R., & Wax, N. (1989). Children's conceptions of plants as living things. *Human Development, 32*(2), 88–94.

Stewart, N. (2009). The cost of anchoring on credit-card minimum repayments. *Psychological Science, 20*(1), 39–41.

Stewart, R. H. (1965). Effect of continuous responding on the order effect in personality impression formation. *Journal of Personality and Social Psychology, 1*(2), 161–165.

Stewart, T. R., Roebber, P. J., & Bosart, L. F. (1997). The importance of the task in analyzing expert judgment. *Organizational Behavior and Human Decision Processes, 69*(3), 205–219.

Strack, F., & Mussweiler, T. (1997). Explaining the enigmatic anchoring effect: Mechanisms of selective accessibility. *Journal of Personality and Social Psychology, 73*(3), 437–446.

Strohminger, N., & Nichols, S. (2014). The essential moral self. *Cognition, 131*(1), 159–171.

Sunstein, C. R. (2014). Nudging: A very short guide. *Journal of Consumer Policy, 37*(4), 583–588.

Sunstein, C. R. (2015). Nudges do not undermine human agency. *Journal of Consumer Policy, 38*(3), 207–210.

Sunstein, C. R., & Vermeule, A. (2009). Conspiracy theories: Causes and cures. *Journal of Political Philosophy, 17*(2), 202–227.

Svedholm, A. M., & Lindeman, M. (2012). The separate roles of the reflective mind and involuntary inhibitory control in gatekeeping paranormal beliefs and the underlying intuitive confusions. *British Journal of Psychology, 104*(3), 303–319.

Talairach, J., & Tournoux, P. (1988). *Co-planar stereotaxic atlas of the human brain.* New York, NY: Thieme.

Taylor, A. H., Hunt, G. R., Medina, F. S., & Gray, R. D. (2009). Do New Caledonian crows solve physical problems through causal reasoning? *Proceedings of the Royal Society of London B: Biological Sciences, 276*(1655), 247–254.

Thaler, R. (1980). Toward a positive theory of consumer choice. *Journal of Economic Behavior & Organization, 1*(1), 39–60.

Thaler, R. H. (1999). Mental accounting matters. *Journal of Behavioral Decision Making, 12*(3), 183–206.

Thaler, R. H., & Sunstein, C. R. (2008). *Nudge: Improving decisions about health, wealth, and happiness.* New Haven, CT: Yale University Press.

Tom, S. M., Fox, C. R., Trepel, C., & Poldrack, R. A. (2007). The neural basis of loss aversion in decision-making under risk. *Science, 315*(5811), 515–518.

Toplak, M. E., West, R. F., & Stanovich, K. E. (2014). Assessing miserly information processing: An expansion of the Cognitive Reflection Test. *Thinking & Reasoning, 20*(2), 147–168.

Tse, D., Takeuchi, T., Kakeyama, M., Kajii, Y., Okuno, H., Tohyama, C., ... & Morris, R. G. (2011). Schema-dependent gene activation and memory encoding in neocortex. *Science, 333*(6044), 891–895.

Tucker, A. W. (1983). The mathematics of Tucker: A sampler. *The Two-Year College Mathematics Journal, 14*(3), 228–232.

Tulving, E., & Pearlstone, Z. (1966). Availability versus accessibility of information in memory for words. *Journal of Verbal Learning and Verbal Behavior, 5*, 381–391.

Turiel, E. (2002). *The culture of morality: Social development, context, and conflict.* Cambridge, UK: Cambridge University Press.

Tversky, A., & Kahneman, D. (1971). The belief in the law of small numbers. *Psychological Bulletin, 76*, 105–110.

Tversky, A., & Kahneman, D. (1973). Availability: A heuristic for judging frequency and probability. *Cognitive Psychology, 5*(2), 207–232.

Tversky, A., & Kahneman, D. (1974). Judgment under uncertainty: Heuristics and biases. *Science, 185*(4157), 1124–1131.

Tversky, A., & Kahneman, D. (1980). Causal schemas in judgments under uncertainty. In M. Fishbein (Ed.), *Progress in social psychology* (pp. 49–72). New York, NY: Psychology Press.

Tversky, A., & Kahneman, D. (1981). The framing of decisions and the psychology of choice. *Science, 211*(4481), 453–458.

Tversky, A., & Kahneman, D. (1983). Extensional versus intuitive reasoning: The conjunction fallacy in probability judgment. *Psychological Review, 90*(4), 293–315.

Tversky, A., & Kahneman, D. (1986). Rational choice and the framing of decisions. *Journal of Business, 59*(4), S251–S278.

Tversky, A., & Kahneman, D. (1992). Advances in prospect theory: Cumulative representation of uncertainty. *Journal of Risk and Uncertainty, 5*(4), 297–323.

Tykosinski, O. E. (2001). I never had a chance: Using hindsight tactics to mitigate disappointments. *Personality and Social Psychology Bulletin, 27*(3), 376–282.

Tylor, E. B. (1871/1974). *Primitive culture: Research into the development of mythology, philosophy, religion, art, and custom.* New York, NY: Gordon Press.

U.S. Social Security Administration. (2015). *Popularity of a name.* Retrieved from www.ssa.gov/oact/babynames/#&ht=2.

U.K. Vital Statistics Outputs Branch. (2015). *Mortality statistics: Deaths registered in England and Wales (Series DR), 2014.* Retrieved from www.ons.gov.uk/ons/rel/vsob1/mortality-statistics--deaths-registered-in-england-and-wales--series-dr-/2014/index.html.

Valdesolo, P., & DeSteno, D. (2006). Manipulations of emotional context shape moral judgment. *Psychological Science, 17*(6), 476–477.

Van Lange, P. A. M., Liebrand, W. B. G., & Kuhlman, D. M. (1990). Causal attribution of choice behavior in three N-person prisoner's dilemmas. *Journal of Experimental Social Psychology, 26*(1), 34–48.

Varey, C. A., Mellers, B. A., & Birnbaum, M. H. (1990). Judgments of proportions. *Journal of Experimental Psychology: Human Perception and Performance, 16*(3), 613–625.

Velasquez, M., & Hester, P. T. (2013). An analysis of multi-criteria decision making methods. *International Journal of Operations Research, 10*(2), 56–66.

von Neumann, J., & Morgenstern, O. (1944/2007). *Theory of games and economic behavior.* Princeton, NJ: Princeton University Press.

Vyse, S. A. (2000). *Believing in magic: The psychology of superstition.* Oxford, UK: Oxford University Press.

Waldmann, M. R., & Holyoak, K. J. (1992). Predictive and diagnostic learning within causal models: Asymmetries in cue competition. *Journal of Experimental Psychology: General, 121*(2), 222–236.

Wallenius, J., Dyer, J. S., Fishburn, P. C., Steuer, R. E., Zionts, S., & Deb, K. (2008). Multiple criteria decision making, multiattribute utility theory: Recent accomplishments and what lies ahead. *Management Science, 54*(7), 1336–1349.

Walster, E. (1967). "Second guessing" important events. *Human Relations, 20*(3), 239–249.

Walther, E. (2002). Guilty by mere association: Evaluative conditioning and the spreading attitude effect. *Journal of Personality and Social Psychology, 82*(6), 919–934.

Walther, E., Nagengast, B. & Traselli, C. (2005). Evaluative conditioning in social psychology: Facts and speculations. *Cognition & Emotion, 19*(2), 175–196.

Wason, P. C. (1960). On the failure to eliminate hypotheses in a conceptual task. *Quarterly Journal of Experimental Psychology, 12*(3), 129–140.

Wasserman, D., Lempert, R. O., & Hastie, R. (1991). Hindsight and causality. *Personality and Social Psychology Bulletin, 17*(1), 30–35.

Weber, E. U. (2006). Experience-based and description-based perceptions of long-term risk: Why global warming does not scare us (yet). *Climatic Change, 77*(1–2), 103–120.

Webley, P., & Plaisier, Z. (1998). Mental accounting in childhood. *Citizenship, Social and Economics Education, 3*(2), 55–64.

Wegwarth, O., & Gigerenzer, G. (2011). Statistical illiteracy in doctors. In G. Gigerenzer & J. A. M. Gray (Eds.), *Better doctors, better patients, better decisions: Envisioning healthcare in 2020* (pp. 137–151). Cambridge, MA: MIT Press.

Weine, E. R., Kim, N. S., & Lincoln, A. K. (2016). Understanding lay assessments of alcohol use disorder: Need for treatment and associated stigma. *Alcohol and Alcoholism, 51*(1), 98–105.

Weinstein, N. D. (1980). Unrealistic optimism about future life events. *Journal of Personality and Social Psychology, 39*(5), 806–820.

Weisberg, D. S., Keil, F. C., Goodstein, J., Rawson, E., & Gray, J. R. (2008). The seductive allure of neuroscience explanations. *Journal of Cognitive Neuroscience, 20*(3), 470–477.

Weisberg, D. S., Taylor, J. C., & Hopkins, E. J. (2015). Deconstructing the seductive allure of neuroscience explanations. *Judgment and Decision Making, 10*(5), 429–441.

Wellman, H. M., & Gelman, S. A. (1992). Cognitive development: Foundational theories of core domains. *Annual Review of Psychology, 43*(1), 337–375.

Westen, D., & Weinberger, J. (2004). When clinical description becomes statistical prediction. *American Psychologist, 59*(7), 595–613.

Wheeler, B., & Hunt, A. (2016, June 24). *The UK's EU referendum: All you need to know.* BBC News. Retrieved from www.bbc.com/news/uk-politics-32810887/.

White, M. D. (2013). *The manipulation of choice: Ethics and libertarian paternalism.* Basingstoke, UK: Palgrave Macmillan.

Whyte, G., & Sebenius, J. K. (1997). The effect of multiple anchors on anchoring in individual and group judgment. *Organizational Behavior and Human Decision Processes, 69*(1), 74–85.

Wiegmann, A., Okan, Y., & Nagel, J. (2012). Order effects in moral judgment. *Philosophical Psychology, 25*(6), 813–836.

Wiegmann, A., & Waldmann, M. R. (2014). Transfer effects between moral dilemmas: A causal model theory. *Cognition, 131*(1), 28–43.

Wilkes, A. L., & Leatherbarrow, M. (1988). Editing episodic memory following the identification of error. *The Quarterly Journal of Experimental Psychology, 40*(2), 361–387.

Williams, M. (2015). *Behind the name.* Retrieved from www.behindthename.com.

Wilson, T. D., & Gilbert, D. T. (2003). Affective forecasting. *Advances in experimental social psychology* (Vol. 35, pp. 345–411). San Diego, CA: Academic Press.

Wilson, T. D., & Gilbert, D. T. (2005). Affective forecasting: Knowing what to want. *Current Directions in Psychological Science, 14*(3), 131–134.

Wilson, T. D., Gilbert, D. T., & Centerbar, D. B. (2003). Making sense: The causes of emotional evanescence. In I. Brocas & J. D. Carrillo (Eds.), *The psychology of economic decisions* (Vol. 1, pp. 209–233). Oxford, UK: Oxford University Press.

Wilson, T. D., Houston, C., Etling, K. M., & Brekke, N. (1996). A new look at anchoring effects: Basic anchoring and its antecedents. *Journal of Experimental Psychology: General, 125*(4), 387–402.

Wolfe, J. M. (2016). Rethinking the basic-applied dichotomy. *Cognitive Research: Principles and Implications, 1*(1), 1–2.

Wolff, P. (2007). Representing causation. *Journal of Experimental Psychology: General, 136*(1), 82–111.

Wolff, P., & Barbey, A. K. (2015). Causal reasoning with forces. *Frontiers in Human Neuroscience, 9*(1), 1–21.

Wood, M. J., Douglas, K. M., & Sutton, R. M. (2012). Dead and alive: Beliefs in contradictory conspiracy theories. *Social Psychological and Personality Science, 3*(6), 767–773.

Yamagishi, T. (1986). The provision of a sanctioning system as a public good. *Journal of Personality and Social Psychology, 51*(1), 110–116.

Yeager, D. S., & Dweck, C. S. (2012). Mindsets that promote resilience: When students believe that personal characteristics can be developed. *Educational Psychologist, 47*(4), 302–314.

Yopchick, J. E. (2012). *Causal explanations and judgments about children's potentially problematic behaviors* (Unpublished doctoral dissertation). Northeastern University, Boston, MA.

Yopchick, J. E., & Kim, N. S. (2012). Hindsight bias and causal reasoning: A minimalist approach. *Cognitive Processing, 13*(1), 63–72.

Zenko, M. (2012). America is a safe place. *Council on Foreign Relations*. Retrieved from http://blogs.cfr.org/zenko/2012/02/24/america-is-a-safe-place/.

Index